· IRISH ·
BATTLES
A Military History
of IRELAND

G. A. Hayes-McCoy

Appletree Press

Published and printed by
The Appletree Press Ltd
7 James Street South
Belfast BT2 8DL
First published in paperback 1990

British Library Cataloguing in Publication Data
Hayes – McCoy, G. A. (Gerard Anthony)
Irish battles: a military history of Ireland.
1. Ireland. Battle, History
I. Title
941.5

ISBN 0-86281-250-X

9 8 7 6 5 4 3 2 1

Picture Acknowledgements

National Gallery of Ireland, 7, 15, 16, 18, 19;
National Museum of Ireland, 1, 2; National
Library of Ireland, 5, 9, 10, 17, 20;
The Board of Trinity College Dublin, 6,
8, 12, 13, 14.

Cover illustration: Picture map of the battle of
Kinsale, 1601 (The Board of Trinity College
Dublin).

Contents

Introduction

'Gentle when stroked', says the slogan of the United States 69th Regiment—the regiment which has for so long gloried in the name of the Fighting Irish—'Gentle when stroked; fierce when provoked'. The aphorism was suggested by the qualities of the Irish wolfhound, and it was accepted as a summary of the Irish national character at least as early as 1780, when the Volunteers of that time made a propagandist use of it. It is probably apposite. History gives evidence of the combative characteristics of the Irish; yet it might equally well be argued that, left to themselves, the Irish were never given to militarism. The facts remain, however, that Irish history is full of battles and that Irishmen have always been attracted by military service, so much so indeed that the type and figure of the historic Irishman might well be a man in uniform. Theobald Wolfe Tone, the father of Irish republicanism, would certainly have liked to think of the Irish as soldiers, and we remember Dean Swift's statement that 'most sorts of diversion in men, children and other animals are in imitation of fighting'—and that Swift was an Irishman.

One can list more than 200 military engagements, great and small, although for the most part minor affairs, which took place in Ireland from medieval times to 1798. If the sites of these engagements are plotted on a map an interesting pattern emerges. One finds that most of the fighting took place within a belt fifty or so miles wide extending around the coast of the island. No major battle was fought more than thirty miles inland, and indeed the whole area of the midlands, extending southward from Fermanagh to Tipperary and westward from Kildare to the Shannon, is almost devoid of battle sites. Most of the battles were fought in Leinster, in east Ulster and in south Munster, although the plains of Connacht, the entry from Ulster to Connacht in the neighbourhood of Sligo, and east Donegal were also the scenes of warfare. It is not difficult to explain this geographical distribution, although, as with all the affairs of men, it did not proceed from a single cause. Wars are the clash of systems and battles are the result of hostile movements. In Ireland as elsewhere, battles were fought in places where progress along lines of communication was interrupted by natural obstacles. Warfare, once begun, was conditioned by the terrain. But the physical aspect of Ireland had as much to do with the causes as with the course of her wars.

Ireland is flat in the centre and mountainous to the north and south, with further mountains rising along the greater part of the west coast and a long chain stretching parallel with the east coast south of Dublin. Drainage is effected largely by rivers flowing south. Access to the interior in the days when bog and forest made progress difficult was afforded by the river valleys. This was most notably so in regard to the southern half of the island, where the valleys of the rivers Lee, Blackwater, Suir-Nore-Barrow and Slaney provide passages through the mountains into the low limestone country which lies behind them. But the main entry into the heart of Ireland—the gateway to the island as a whole—has always been the flat stretch of fifty or so miles of eastern coastline lying between the granite masses of the Mourne and Wicklow mountains, the area which is watered by the rivers Boyne and Liffey and which, from the time of the incursions of the Norsemen, has had Dublin as its chief town. Here the central plain reaches to the Irish Sea. Since, in historic times, outside influences have been exerted on Ireland largely through England, and since influence is exerted along lines of communication, it has been of the greatest significance that the passages leading towards Ireland from the centre of English power—that is, the south of England—reach the Irish Sea at points directly opposite the best entries to the Irish interior.

The Cheshire plain, the gap between the English Pennines and the Cambrian mountains, faces the north Leinster entry to the Irish central plain. This always was, and still is, the best route from London to Ireland. With the development of Anglo-Irish relations after the twelfth century, the position of the already well established urban centre of Dublin, the port of the entry, was assured. Dublin became the Irish capital, and control of Dublin meant the ultimate control of the whole island of Ireland. The second passage leading through England towards Ireland is that which reaches the Irish Sea at the Severn and the Bristol Channel. Again, this faces a series of convenient entries to Ireland, the mouths of the river valleys of the south-east and south coasts.

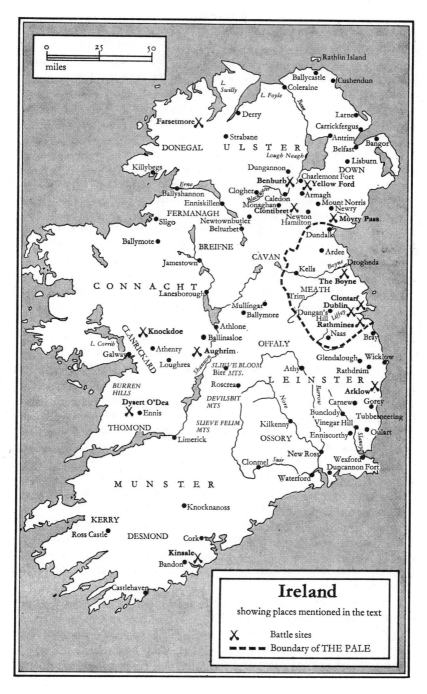

miles

Rathlin Island

Ballycastle
Cushendun
Coleraine
Larne
Derry
Carrickfergus
Antrim
Bangor
Strabane
Belfast
Lisburn
Farsetmore ✗
DONEGAL
U L S T E R
Lough Neagh
DOWN
Killybegs
Dungannon
Charlemont Fort
Benburb ✗
Yellow Ford ✗
Erne
Clogher
Armagh
Ballyshannon
Caledon
Mount Norris
Enniskillen
Monaghan
Newry
FERMANAGH
Clontibret ✗
Newtownbutler
Newton
Moyry Pass ✗
Sligo
Belturbet
Hamilton
Ballymote
Dundalk
BREIFNE
Ardee
CAVAN
Jamestown
Kells
Drogheda
Boyne
C O N N A C H T
The Boyne ✗
Lanesborough
MEATH
Trim
Clontarf
Mullingar
Dublin
Dungan's
Ballymore
Hill
Knockdoe ✗
Athlone
Rathmines ✗
Ballinasloe
Naas
Bray
L. Corrib
OFFALY
Galway
Aughrim ✗
Athenry
Glendalough
Wicklow
Loughrea
SLIEVE BLOOM
Athy
Rathdrum
MTS.
Birr
L E I N S T E R
BURREN
Roscrea
Arklow ✗
HILLS
DEVILSBIT
Carnew
Gorey
Dysert O'Dea ✗
MTS
Bunclody
Tubberneering
Ennis
SLIEVE FELIM
Vinegar Hill
THOMOND
MTS
Kilkenny
Enniscorthy
Oulart
Limerick
OSSORY
New Ross
Clonmel
Wexford
M U N S T E R
Waterford
Duncannon Fort
Knocknanoss
KERRY
Ross Castle
DESMOND
Cork
Kinsale ✗
Bandon
Castlehaven

Ireland

showing places mentioned in the text

✗ Battle sites
- - - Boundary of THE PALE

The early battles fought by the Irish against Norsemen and Normans were the consequences of invasion. Clontarf, the struggle for Dublin in 1171 and the many contests between the Norman knights and archers and the local Gaelic rulers, of which Dysert O'Dea, fought in 1318, is one example, were brought on by native resistance to the incursions of outsiders who were bent on exploitation or conquest. These outsiders were frequently assisted by disgruntled or ambitious native rulers. The Norsemen at Clontarf, for example, were attempting to strengthen their hold on Dublin and its hinterland, but they were also intervening in a local struggle between the kingdom of Leinster and Brian Boru, the ruler who had made himself High King of Ireland. The battle was fought at Clontarf, outside Dublin, because Dublin was a Norse town. Possession of the Norse towns of Wexford, Waterford, and—above all—of Dublin was the first objective of the twelfth-century Norman invaders. These towns provided ports through which communications with England could be kept up, bases for further aggressive activities, and points of entry to the interior.

Irish warfare from the twelfth to the sixteenth century was thus for the main part a series of struggles between the invaders and their descendants on the one hand—backed increasingly by the growing power of England—and the Gaelic Irish lords on the other. Rory O'Connor, the High King at the time of the Norman invasion, had recognised the king of England as his overlord; but neither Rory nor the English king nor any of their immediate successors exercised a centralised control. Although English law and the feudal system were introduced by the invaders, their introduction did not mean an overthrow of the Gaelic institutions. The two systems, old and new, continued to function side by side. Power in Ireland in the thirteenth century was exercised by individuals, Gaelic and Norman, who had established themselves as local lords, and whose efforts were directed towards the maintenance or extension of their lordships. There was no concerted plan either of conquest or of resistance, nor were such plans possible.

Within a century of the invasion, the Normans had consolidated themselves in Leinster and Meath and had overrun great parts of Munster and Connacht. They had also established an outlying settlement in east Ulster. In general, they had seized the good land of the central plain and the southern river valleys. and they had taken over control of the Norse towns. The Irish, who lived in a loosely organised series of kingdoms and lordships, and who had never sought to set up urban communities of their own, had tolerated the Norse towns. They had done this, it seems, not simply because they were unable to eliminate them; they appreciated their function as trading centres. Nor did the settlement of the Normans and their administrative control of great parts of the country mean a clearance of the original inhabitants. The population of Ireland was not great and there was much unoccupied, or sparsely occupied, land. The workers, the lower order of the Irish social pyramid, remained in the areas under Norman rule, and in many places throughout the 'conquered' provinces Gaelic institutions were maintained and the rule of the Gaelic dynastic families was uninterrupted. This was so in poorer and less accessible places, in the Leinster mountain chain and in the boggy part of the south midlands, west of Kildare.

In these circumstances, the main military contests of the first century and more following the invasion occurred on the periphery of the Norman penetration. The battles of the late twelfth century—the engagements at Cashel, Thurles and Downpatrick —were fought on the frontier of areas which were the first to be overrun. The battlefields of the thirteenth century were still more remote from Leinster and the midlands—Kenmare, where the MacCarthys successfully resisted further Norman progress into Kerry, Caol Uisge on the river Erne and the Rosses near Sligo, where the O'Donnells of Tir Conaill fought it out with the Normans of Connacht, and again Down, where the rising power of the O'Neills was checked by the sturdy Norman settlers of east Ulster.

If matters had progressed differently the sequel to this tale of Norman invasion, consolidation and advance would almost certainly have been an advance of the frontier. The resistance put up by the MacCarthys in south-west Munster, the O'Briens in Thomond, the O'Donnells and O'Neills in Ulster and other Gaelic lords elsewhere would eventually have been overcome, although the Anglo-Normans would have been changed in the process. What happened in Scotland might have happened in Ireland. Indeed the Irish development of modern times might have been anticipated, and a nation of mixed blood might have emerged centuries before it did. But the frontier which lay between the Norman and Gaelic worlds did not advance. It receded. Gaelic

Ireland was not submerged. The Norman conquest of Ireland was not completed.

The reasons for this were complex. The Normans were not, as time went on, sufficiently reinforced from England, where the development of a powerful state under a strong monarchy was slow and was subject to many interruptions. Their original impetus was lost. They became to a considerable extent Gaelicised, although not sufficiently Gaelicised to throw off their English allegiance. The Gaelic part of Ireland, on the other hand, experienced a development which increased its power of resistance to institutional change. These modifications, the weakening of the descendants of the invaders and the strengthening of the original inhabitants, were powerfully affected by a fresh military intervention which took place at the beginning of the fourteenth century. This was the Scottish invasion of Ireland led by Edward Bruce, the brother of the Scots king who was at that moment successfully resisting an English attempt to overrun his own country. The Bruce invasion was successful in what seems to have been its primary purpose, for it weakened the English colony in Ireland from which the English invaders of Scotland had drawn much support. It had the effect too of militarising the Gaelic Irish lordships, and it brought about the first extended campaigns in Irish history. It was much more than an incident, a series of raids that was part of Scottish and English rather than Irish history and that did not, in the long run, greatly affect the course of affairs in Ireland; while the Bruce invasion did not upset the balance of power, it strengthened the capacity of resistance of the Gaelic world and by doing so postponed the completion of the conquest; it ensured the ultimate flowering of an Irish nationality that would, in the distant future, demand separate statehood.

The seat of the Bruce warfare of 1315–18 was the territory of the Anglo-Norman colony. Defeating the force of the east Ulster settlement near Antrim, Bruce marched southward as far as Ardee. Opposed there by a combined army made up of the forces of the English lordship and the Irish of Connacht, he fell back to the mouth of the river Bann near Coleraine, but later faced his opponents at Connor north of Lough Neagh, compelled their withdrawal and again marched southward to Kells. Here he defeated another Anglo-Norman force. Bruce spent the winter of 1315–16 in the midlands. He took Carrickfergus castle in 1316 and, joined by his brother, King Robert, marched in the following year to Dublin. But the Bruces considered Dublin too strong to attack; they turned away, and, burning and destroying in the settled areas which lay in their way, continued their march almost to Limerick. They retired thence to Ulster, and Robert returned to Scotland. In 1318 Edward Bruce was defeated and killed at Faughart, near Dundalk, where he had been crowned king of Ireland two years previously.

Such marching and fighting had not been seen before in Ireland. Two further battles of these years—Athenry, where the Anglo-Normans of Connacht under Bermingham, who was to be the victor of Faughart, defeated the last hope of his royal house, Felim O'Connor, and Dysert O'Dea, of which we shall have much to say later—heightened the militarism of a period that was to witness a notable decline in the fortunes of the English lordship.

The two centuries which followed saw much bickering, much local strife and much destruction, but they saw no great battles. The English lordship contracted to the area around Dublin known as the English Pale. Outside of this, the towns, the number of which had been increased by the foundation of Galway, Carrick-fergus and a few minor places, continued to develop as English institutions, and the rulership of the remainder of the island was in the hands of many lords, Anglo-Irish and Gaelic. The most powerful of the former were the Fitzgerald Earls of Kildare and Desmond and the Butlers of Ormond, who exercised an almost independent control of the belt of original Norman penetration extending from the east of the central plain to Cork—the best land in Ireland—and the Burkes, who were still more independent and more Gaelicised, and who had made their own of the plains of Connacht. The most powerful of the latter were the lords of the periphery, those who had done most to withstand the Norman penetration, the O'Neills and O'Donnells in Ulster, the O'Briens in the present Co. Clare and the MacCarthys in west Munster. Power was very limited. The English lordship was on the defensive, and no lord, Anglo-Irish or Gaelic, could dominate the others. Still, the strongest force was Anglo-Irish rather than Gaelic. The greatest man in Ireland at the beginning of the sixteenth century was the Earl of Kildare, whose strength and limitation were disclosed in the greatest battle fought since the time of the Bruces, Knockdoe, which he won in 1504. Again, Knockdoe was peripheral. It was fought in Co. Galway, far from the centre of influence, and its result was no more than marginally decisive.

The later battles assumed increasingly a wider significance, but again they were, as far as Ireland was concerned, mostly defensive. The conquest of Ireland was completed in the sixteenth century by the most powerful succession of English monarchs that had yet appeared, the Tudors, the shapers of the modern destinies of England. Rulers in an age which saw the birth of European power politics, the Tudors were constrained to complete the conquest of Ireland largely by their fear of the consequences of a possible intervention in Ireland of their continental enemies. The completion of the conquest meant the elimination of the local lordships, and, as far as Gaelic Ireland was concerned, the destruction of the native institutional system. This was fiercely resisted. It brought on, in the last decade of the sixteenth century, a war which was prolonged and widespread, a war in which, since it involved the movement and maintenance of large forces, and since the Irish, being without towns, were resilient, the nature of the terrain was a factor of the utmost significance.

The war which Hugh O'Neill and his supporters waged against Queen Elizabeth I was primarily a struggle for the defence of Ulster, or, to view it from the English side, a long deferred penetration into that part of Ireland which had so far, and for so many reasons, escaped effective English attention. Its major engagements were, all save the last decisive one, fought in two areas, the approaches to the O'Neill and O'Donnell lordships from the south-east and south-west. This added to the already notable total of battles which were fought at either extremity of the northern province. While they fought in these areas the Ulstermen held the tactical initiative and brilliantly combined the new methods of the age of gunpowder and pikes with a utilisation of terrain that was traditional in the Irish wars; they were almost uniformly successful. When they came outside their province and, by marching to Kinsale in Co. Cork to co-operate with their newly arrived allies the Spaniards, accepted the hazards of a different kind of warfare, they were defeated. In this last struggle of the old Gaelic Ireland, terrain was vital; unfortunately for Hugh O'Neill, who had for so long made the difficult countryside of Ulster fight for him, the ground suited the English at the moment of decision.

James I, who ascended to the throne in 1603, was the first

king of a united Ireland, an Ireland which had been brought under unified control after centuries of compromise and conflict. He initiated a new period, one which proved to be a period of transition. When the seventeenth century, the century of the Stuart kings, opened, the land of Ireland, in which lay the wealth of the country, was still very largely owned by long established proprietors, Gaelic and Anglo-Irish. When the century closed, the estates held by the descendants of these proprietors constituted much less than twenty per cent of the whole. Three confiscations, those of the Ulster from which Hugh O'Neill had fled in 1607, of Oliver Cromwell and of William III, had completely altered the structure of property holding and the basis of power. The new proprietors, who formed a new ascendancy under the altered government produced by the English revolution of 1641–89, were, outside Ulster, the victors and the beneficiaries of two wars. James I's plantation of Ulster introduced a Protestant Anglo-Scottish element into the Irish population and led ultimately to the partitioning of Ireland into the territories of Northern Ireland and the Republic.

The two seventeenth-century wars were, to speak of their immediate causes, the results of the English struggle which, as the American revolutionaries of a hundred years later were to recall, 'cost one king his head, another his throne'. The Irish Catholics who fought, as they claimed, for Charles I in 1641 and the years following, tried to secure an Irish solution of problems many of which were matters of contention in England and Scotland as well, and the same element struggled again in 1689–91 to replace James II, a king whom the English had rejected.

The altered, but still unsettled, state of Ireland was clearly shown in these seventeenth-century wars. They were no longer struggles of the frontier. Uneasily, but yet inevitably and irrevocably, the old Gaelic and Anglo-Irish elements were coalescing; they were driven together in defence of their common Catholicism. The wars were now country-wide contests fought for causes that were—at least in 1641–52—complex and confused, but that stirred men throughout the four provinces. The whole island was, in Charles I's time as in that of James II, the theatre of war. The importance of possession of Dublin was clearly marked. The victors in 1652 as in 1691 were those who possessed it; the really significant battles were those which were fought for its possession. Thus the victory of Owen Roe O'Neill at Benburb in Co. Tyrone in 1646 was as indecisive as that of Hugh O'Neill at the Yellow Ford in Co. Armagh in 1598. Both battles were peripheral, and although what happened on the periphery could prolong, it could not decide a contest. Dungan's Hill and Rathmines might, if their results had been different, have tipped the balance against the supporters of the English Parliament—although it is inconceivable that the Parliamentarians, having won in England, would accept less than victory in Ireland. The supporters of James II lost Dublin when they were defeated at the Boyne, and if they were to win their war they would have to take Dublin again. Similarly, if Hugh O'Neill and the Spaniards had won at Kinsale they would still have had to take Dublin before O'Neill could have made a reality of what Sir Robert Cecil, Queen Elizabeth's minister, had called Utopia—a Catholic Ireland ruled by Irishmen.

In these wars of a wider scope the river Shannon assumes a new military significance. In Ireland as elsewhere in the wars of the past, the rivers were the real obstacles, and in Ireland particularly the bogs, rather than the mountains, were the fastnesses. The bogs, because of the climate and the terrain, were everywhere. But the river Shannon, as was seen in the campaigns of 1690 and 1691, was the major barrier. The battles of the war of the Catholic Confederation were fought in Munster, Leinster and Ulster and the Shannon had little place in the military movements of that time, but the fact that the army which had been defeated at the Boyne in 1690 could retire behind the Shannon, and could deny a passage of that river to King William's forces, postponed the Jacobite defeat.

As the centuries advanced too the Irish wars assumed increasingly an international complexion. The English fought at Kinsale in 1601 as much to repel a Spanish invasion as to put down an Irish revolt. The Catholic Confederates, although they gained little by it, were represented at the Catholic courts of Europe. There were French troops at the Boyne, a French general commanded—and lost his life—at Aughrim, and the whole contest between Kings William and James was a phase of a great European struggle to uphold and to overthrow the ascendancy of France. In the last of the Irish military struggles before the twentieth century—the rebellion of 1798—the government was more fearful of a French invasion than it was of a popular uprising, and a greater concentration of troops was brought about by the landing of a French force in Co. Mayo than by the revolt of the people in Co. Wexford.

If most of the earlier battles were fought far away from Dublin in places nearer to the south, the west and the northern coasts, later centuries redressed the balance. The engagements of the later period were very many of them fought in the approaches to Dublin, and, save for the fighting in Antrim and Down and the battles with the French in Connacht and Longford, the rebellion of 1798 was almost altogether a Leinster affair.

Sea power was an important factor, even though it has not been a widely noticed one, in the Irish wars. The Irish were not interested in the sea, a curious deficiency in an island people. The maritime exploits of the dwellers on the west coast, particularly the O'Malleys and O'Flahertys, are notable only because they are unusual; they show up the lack of interest of the rest. The English, on the other hand, were amphibious. They used their prowess at sea with great effect in the war against Hugh O'Neill, and from the sixteenth century forward they never failed to guard the coasts of Ireland against invasion. Since Norman times, they ferried warlike supplies across the Irish Sea, and when the theatre of war lay on the east coast of Ireland, as it did in Cromwell's time and again in 1690, the use of English shipping for reinforcement and supply facilitated the movements of the English armies. Cromwell never operated in Ireland far away from the sea.

Thus, a general survey of the Irish wars provides an explanation of the territorial distribution of the battlefields. It also explains the pattern of this distribution. The history of Ireland is one of assimilation and resistance, the assimilation of outside elements into the population and the resistance of outside control. This control was exercised from Dublin, and when resistance showed itself in organised military effort Dublin became naturally and increasingly the prime military objective. P. H. Pearse, the leader of the 1916 rising, was an organiser of revolution rather than a soldier, but his attention and that of his comrades was directed almost exclusively to Dublin. Irish resistance had, by 1916, come back to the scene of the original penetration.

Clontarf, 1014

The battle of Clontarf, fought outside Dublin on Good Friday, 23 April 1014, was the greatest battle of the early period of Irish history. Its lustre has not, over the intervening centuries, been dimmed; rather has its fame increased, so that it has come to be remembered as an event of a golden age, a mighty feat of arms of which Ireland was capable 'ere her faithless sons betrayed her'.

Clontarf was a victory for the native side; Hastings, fought for the defence of England half a century later, was—on the same analysis—a defeat. Yet the Irish battle was not followed, as the victory of William the Conqueror was, by an era of nation-building. It was followed by a century and more of disorder culminating in the successful invasion of Ireland by the victors of Hastings, the Normans. Since Clontarf ended in the tumbling of the Norsemen into the sea, and since Ireland experienced no more Viking raids after 1014, we regard it as the repulse of an invasion; but it was that only in a minor degree. Primarily it was a great and unsuccessful battle fought for the unity of Ireland. It is not, perhaps, surprising that we have chosen to remember the one aspect of it and to forget the other. We forget that an army of Leinster Irishmen fought beside the Norsemen on the losing side.

If Brian Boru—Brian of the Tributes—High King of Ireland, had been a younger man when he won the battle of Clontarf, and if he had lived to exploit his victory, his hand would, almost certainly, have descended heavily on the kingdom of Leinster. The Leinstermen had never willingly recognised a High King. By their action in opposing Brian at Clontarf they sought to destroy the unity of Ireland which he had envisaged ten years previously when, at a solemn moment in the church at Armagh, he declared himself Emperor of the Gael.

If Brian had been able to justify assumption of that title and to make good that unity, then Clontarf would have been a victory indeed. But he whose personality colours his age and whose name has come resounding down the centuries was an old man at the climax of his career and was killed at the moment of his success.

He began as the leader of the small state of Dál Chais at the mouth of the river Shannon. His neighbours were the Norse invaders, the descendants of the Vikings, who had founded the town of Limerick. By the end of the tenth century he had subdued these isolated Norsemen and had won for himself, first, the kingship of Munster and then, by defeating the Leinstermen and the Norse inhabitants of Dublin, the overlordship of the southern half of Ireland. The Dublin Norse were the founders of what was to become the capital of Ireland, and they ruled at this time over a considerable part of the seacoast stretching from the mouth of the river Boyne to Arklow.

In 1002 Brian Boru overawed the only other ruler who could rival him in power or in prospects, Malachy, King of Meath and holder of the High Kingship. Brian became High King. Malachy and the north and west of Ireland seem to have acquiesced in this assumption of a title of paramountcy which conferred on its holder as much authority as he could enforce. Leinster, in the persons of Maelmora, who was its king, and Gormflath, who was Maelmora's sister, did not acquiesce. The name of Gormflath, who, according to the Norsemen, was 'the fairest of all women' but who 'did all things ill over which she had any power', comes down to us in the drama of history as the evil genius of what followed.

Some of the romantic accounts of the battle that were written soon after it was fought make a great deal of the personalities concerned. According to their writers, the conflict of Clontarf was a matter of the passions of a few people—the passions of Kings Brian and Malachy; of Murchad, who was Brian's son; of the Leinster pair, Maelmora and Gormflath; and of Sitric, the Norse-Irish King of Dublin, whose mother was the much-married Gormflath and whose father was the Norseman Olaf Cuaran.

The story is complicated by the fact that the relationships of these people were involved. Gormflath, who incited her brother Maelmora to challenge Brian, was—most amazingly—the discarded wife of both Brian and Malachy. In view of this entanglement of the dramatis personae, Clontarf was a domestic squabble of the first order. But there were much wider issues.

Leinster was a misfit in Brian's new kingdom. The Leinstermen must be coerced into submission to him; otherwise they might destroy him. They were, in their desire for independence, prepared to break up the unity which he had built. The Dublin Norse, who were a rich and powerful body, had not yet been absorbed into the Irish system. They too were a dangerous element, an alien element in a country of explosive minor states. Until Malachy, King of Meath, had pushed them back some years before this, they had threatened to dominate the midlands. Outside Ireland the Norse peoples were still on the move. There were still Vikings on the seas. Svend, King of Denmark, had just then established his dominion over a great part of England. Half a century later Harold Hardrada of Norway, bent on plunder or conquest, was killed while leading a new invasion of England. The rise of a Norse kingdom of Ireland on the ruins of Brian's empire of the Gael was not an impossibility.

The story of Gormflath's jealousy that makes up the greater part of what the chroniclers have to tell us of Clontarf may be an intimate disclosure of real court intrigue; but there were greater forces moving in the background. There were motives other than personal ones for the strife.

The war began in 1013, with Brian and Malachy, the reigning High King and the previous one, on one side and Maelmora and Sitric, the brother of Gormflath and her son, on the other. According to the romantic literature, Gormflath chided Maelmora for his lack of spirit in paying tribute to Brian. Stung by her words, Maelmora was easily led to quarrel with Brian's son Murchad. There were angry passages, and Maelmora left Brian's court, vowing vengeance for the insults which he had received. He roused the Leinstermen and the Norsemen of Dublin against Brian, who collected his forces and marched against them. Dublin was besieged.

The first was a drawn round. Brian gave up the siege at Christmas and went home to his territory of Dál Chais. Both sides, however, made ready to renew the fight. When they took the field again in spring both had been reinforced. Sitric's Dublinmen had with them Sigurd from the Orkneys, Brodar from the Isle of Man, and their followers, a small but formidable gathering of the famous fighting material that had already overrun the Western Isles and that was to contribute so much, in the commingling of blood, to the Highland Scottish race. The Norse account of these happenings, the Saga of Burnt Njal, bears out the Irish ones in the extraordinary role attributed to Gormflath.

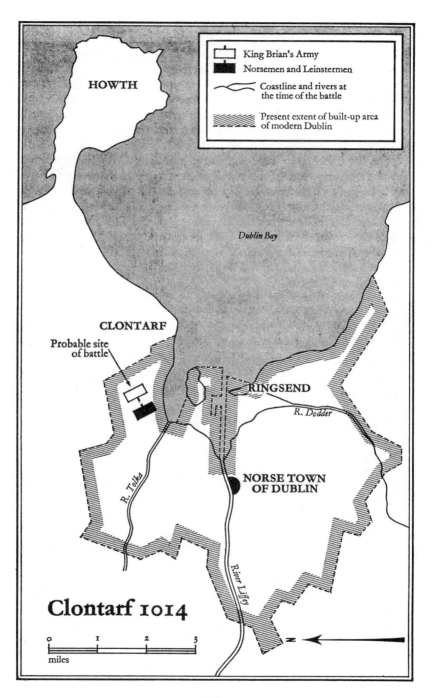

King Brian's Army

Norsemen and Leinstermen

Coastline and rivers at
the time of the battle

Present extent of built-up area
of modern Dublin

HOWTH

Dublin Bay

CLONTARF

Probable site
of battle

RINGSEND

R. Dodder

R. Tolka

NORSE TOWN
OF DUBLIN

Clontarf 1014

0   1   2   3
miles

River Liffey

According to the Saga, Sitric promised his mother's hand, together with the rule of the Norse Kingdom of Dublin, to *both* Sigurd and Brodar. Maelmora's contribution to the Dublin force was the full hosting of the men of North Leinster. South Leinster, adopting the attitude of the greater part of Ireland, held aloof. The authority of the North Leinster rulers was seldom effective there.

On the other side were the warriors of the Dál Chais, assisted by the fighting men of the remaining parts of Munster and of the two Galway districts of Uí Máine and Uí Fiachrach Aidne, areas that stretched from the Shannon to the headwaters of Galway Bay and lay adjacent to the homeland of the Dál Chais. These, since Brian was over seventy years of age and too old to lead them, were commanded by Brian's son Murchad. Malachy's army of Meathmen was also in the field, but, as we shall see, was not engaged at Clontarf.

The Irish forces present at the battle were, as is apparent, drawn only from a limited part of the country. None hailed from the northern half of the island. It is clear, however, that by contemporary standards the opposing armies were big ones. We have no parade states to guide us. The Irish literary genius of the past ran neither to statistics nor to simple narrative; the writers were too busy weaving high drama from the loves and hates of Gormflath, or too active in pursuing endless genealogies to improbable beginnings, to have either the energy or the ability left to make plain statements of fact; and so there are no contemporary pronouncements of strength. It has been reckoned that at the battle of Hastings, where the Normans won Britain in 1066, Harold's army may have been as low as 4,000 and Duke William's no bigger than 5,000. Since Clontarf was certainly not a bigger battle than Hastings, we may perhaps conclude that the total strength of both sides added together did not exceed 5,000 men. Even at that, the battle would have stood out as a great one of its age, a clash of the most powerful forces yet seen in Ireland.

Where and how these armies fought are alike—thanks to the poor descriptive powers of the chroniclers—obscure. We know that the fight was in the district of Clontarf, at present represented by the Dublin suburb of that name; but we know nothing more. When the last man who could have pointed out the battlefield to his son died without doing so, it was forgotten. Now when we speak of Clontarf we can speak only in generalities.

Sitric's overseas allies joined him in Dublin on Palm Sunday, 1014, or a little before that. The Leinster army came up about the same time. Their opponents, Malachy's and Murchad's men, soon appeared. Murchad's force, which was accompanied by Brian Boru, was less a detachment that had been sent off to raid Leinster behind Maelmora's back.

The Dublin area was enemy territory for both Munstermen and Meathmen, and they fell to plundering the rich district between the town and Howth on the north side of the river Liffey. To prevent further depredations, and judging it to be a favourable moment to show fight, Maelmora and his Norse allies marched against their enemies on the morning of Good Friday. They came out from the little town, crossed the Liffey and its tributary the Tolka, and entered the district of Clontarf. That the Norsemen and Leinstermen went this far, and that the battle took place east of the Tolka seem almost certain.

Somewhere beyond the reclaimed area of the present north side docks—where the Belfast trains run north-eastward out of Amiens Street station, cross the Howth Road, and gather speed above the tops of the houses—on flat ground within sight of Dublin, Brian's army under Murchad met their advancing enemies—Brian's army alone. Malachy's Meathmen, although they had co-operated with their Munster allies up to this, now stood aloof.

Why? What sudden insult had been offered Malachy? Or perhaps he had, during all those years since he stood aside and saw Brian made High King in his place, dissembled a fierc hatred of his rival. Was this his revenge? Or, since in the end th Munstermen won without his aid, are we to believe that they did not need it now, and that they preferred to fight alone? We shall never know. This is a matter of personalities that the chroniclers have not explained.

The battle was a bloody struggle of men who fought on foot. From what we know of the warfare of the time we can visualise it as a clash of two lines of closely packed forces with the best men, the champions and leaders, in front and the meaner folk scrambling and pushing behind. There was then no science of war; there was no ability to manœuvre, nor appreciation that more than blows was necessary for victory. Opponents were slung out in tightly packed lines of battle, their shields held close, one to the other, in long 'shield walls' from the slight shelter of which men hacked and stabbed at their enemies to the limit of their strength and courage.

According to the Irish account of Clontarf and the events of the time which has been translated under the title *The War of the Gaedhil with the Gaill*, Brian's army was in a 'battle phalanx, compact, huge, disciplined', and the men stood so close together in the lines on either side as they faced one another that a four-horsed chariot could be driven on their heads from one flank to the other. The Norse Saga of Burnt Njal says that both armies were drawn up in battle array. Both records mention banners. It is claimed that the Irish had three score and ten of them, of many colours; the Saga says that the Norse banners were borne before their 'mid battle', or centre. These banners may or may not have been flags. It is possible that they were, like Harold's standard as shown in the Bayeux Tapestry, actual figures of dragons, birds or other creatures.

Although the details are scanty, the evidence suggests a tripartite arrangement of forces that was common to both armies, an arrangement of centre, or main battle, and two wings; that is, the universal method of drawing up fighting forces that was in use down the centuries. The Norse chronicler, who omits the Leinstermen from his scheme, says that Sigurd led the 'mid battle', Brodar one wing and Sitric the other. Opposite these were Brian's grandson Turlough in the centre and two Norse allies of the Irish, Wolf the Quarrelsome and Ospak, one on either wing. The Irish accounts speak of three lines, one behind the other, on either side. On their side the Dál Chais were in front, the remainder of the Munstermen behind them, and the Connachtmen in a third formation, presumably behind that again. Brian's Norse allies, mentioned also by the Irish, were, according to this description, formed on a wing. The Irish say that their enemies placed Mael-mora's overseas allies in front, the Dublinmen behind them, and the Leinstermen in a third line.

Once begun, the fighting was continued from high tide to high tide, through the day. It was a conflict that was 'wounding, noisy, bloody, crimsoned, terrible, fierce, quarrelsome'—the chroniclers, rising to the occasion, pile on the expletives. Hour by hour the warriors clashed and drew off to draw breath, to rest their arms, to rearrange their front—clashed and drew off, and then fell on again, swaying and stumbling.

The wings, says the Saga, fell on one another, 'and there was a very hard fight'. Individuals were outstanding. Brodar 'went through the host of the foe and felled all the foremost that stood there', until he met Wolf, who struck him down three times and send him flying into the near-by wood of Tomar. Turlough, Brian's grandson, brought on a struggle around Sigurd's standard. He killed the standard-bearer, and when another man took up the banner 'there was again a hard fight'. He too was killed, 'and so on one after the other all who stood near him'. Sigurd called upon Thorstein, son of Hall of the Side, to bear the banner, but when he was about to take it Asmund the White cried, 'Don't bear the banner, for all they who bear it get their death!' Then Sigurd called on Hrafn the Red, but his answer was 'Bear thine own devil thyself!' Soon Sigurd, his banner under his cloak, was pierced through with a spear and killed.

Much of this may be no more than the romance of the story-tellers and saga-men, the fictitious element intruded on the basic record of facts; but the predominance of individual champions over the rest, which was part of the warfare of the age, must be factual. The Norsemen, because of their superior armour and weapons, and because fighting was second nature to them, may in this way have had an advantage, man for man, over all but the best of their Irish opponents. They were well equipped. They wore byrnies, or mail shirts of interlinked iron rings, and carried circular shields, and their weapons were axes, swords, spears and bows. The short-hafted, wide-bladed axes, the weapons of the Viking galleys, could be grasped with both hands to add weight to their blows; they must have been as terrible in a mêlée on land as they were on shipboard in a sea fight. And the Norse were renowned swordsmen, with a mystic regard for their straight, broad-bladed, often beautifully ornamented swords.

The armoury of 'the terrible, nimble wolf-hounds of victorious Banba' was little different from that of their foes. The Irish too had swords and spears and carried shields with metal bosses. Their leaders wore crested helmets; some even bore the enemy's weapons, the 'Lochlann axes'. They do not seem to have had armour; the only garments of theirs which are mentioned are cloth ones. Neither side was well equipped with missile weapons. Although both had bows, neither the Norse nor the Irish were renowned archers. The Irish missile, then and later, was the casting spear, javelin, or dart. At Clontarf, says *The War of the Gaedhil with the Gaill*, they had 'darts with variegated silken strings, thick set with bright, dazzling, shining nails, to be violently cast at the heroes of valour and bravery'. The string was the thong which was retained by the thrower to ensure retrieval of his missile; such throwing weapons were used by the Irish for centuries.

Whatever advantage their armour and their tradition of fighting gave them, however, the Norsemen were outfought. As the day wore on 'the fight broke out throughout all the host'; every man was engaged. By evening the 'shield wall' in front of what was left of Sitric's men collapsed. Rout followed. The Norse and the Leinstermen, with their backs to the Tolka and the sea, were borne further backward by the pressure of the victors. 'They retreated to the sea like a herd of cows in heat, from sun, and from gadflies, and from insects, and they were pursued closely, rapidly and lightly; and the foreigners were drowned in great numbers in the sea'. The chroniclers supply the details; most of which, we must suspect, are imaginary.

And in the midst of this victory Brian died. Before the battle a 'shieldburg' had been 'thrown round him', that is, he was left under guard behind his line. After the rout had commenced, and when most of the guard had gone off to join in the pursuit—the occasion of plunder—Brodar, the sea-rover, who had lurked through the later part of the day in the wood to which he had earlier fled, came forth. He saw 'that there were few men by the shieldburg', and, breaking through these, he forced his way to Brian and 'hewed at the king'.

Although Clontarf was clouded by the death of Brian, Emperor of the Gael, and although it was followed by an era of strife that seems like the aftermath of a defeat, it was still—as a combat —a mighty victory, and was remembered as such throughout the Gaelic and the Norse world. To have overcome 'men of such hardihood that nothing can withstand them', men on whose mail shirts 'no steel would bite', was a proud achievement.

The literature of Clontarf is extensive, but not all valuable. There are two sub-contemporary accounts, those in—(1) *The War of the Gaedhil with the Gaill* (edited by J. H. Todd and published in the Rolls Series), and (2) Njáls Saga (edited in various editions by G. W. Dasent as *The Story of Burnt Njal*; the passages relating to the battle were edited and published by Dr Colm O Lochlainn in 1933 under the title *The Story of King Brian's Battle*). The most detailed and reliable of the modern accounts of the battle is Rev. Professor John Ryan's 'The Battle of Clontarf' in the *Journal of the Royal Society of Antiquaries of Ireland*, LXVIII (1938), pp. 1 ff. This contains in its footnotes an extensive bibliography.

See also, among many popular descriptions, Mrs Stopford Green's paper on Clontarf in *Irish History Studies*, 2nd series (1927), pp. 63 ff. Mrs Green, in common with many earlier writers (including W. St J. Joyce in his *Ireland's Battles and Battlefields*, published in 1892, p. 8), places the battlefield in the district between the mouths of the Liffey and Tolka—i.e. from Drumcondra southwards. For an estimate of the Vikings as fighters see H. Nickerson, 'Warfare in the Roman Empire, the Dark and Middle Ages' in *Warfare*, published by Harrap in 1924, pp. 284 f; for an enquiry regarding the time of high tide on the day of the battle see *Proceedings of the Royal Irish Academy*, VII (1857–61), pp. 495 ff; for correspondence regarding a mound said to mark the site of the battlefield see *The Irish Independent*, Dublin for 2–12 January 1907.

Dublin, 1171

When the American historian William Hickling Prescott concluded his classic account of the conquest of Mexico he reflected that the accomplishment by 'a mere handful of indigent adventurers' of the vast enterprise which he had chronicled must seem to his readers 'too startling for the probabilities demanded by fiction'. He realised that the Spanish *conquistadores* had done something almost too good to be true. Bernal Díaz, who was one of the conquerors and who was conscious of the magnitude of the achievement, asked what other soldiers in the world could have done as much.

The victory gained by the Norman invaders of Ireland over the forces of the High King outside Dublin in 1171 was scarcely less extraordinary. They too were a handful against thousands, a handful of indigent adventurers who made possible the eventual conquest of a kingdom.

The Norman invasion was over two years old by the time of that battle. The struggles of the Irish kings, which were the immediate cause of it, were far older. Brian Boru, who perished at the moment of victory at Clontarf, had taken the High Kingship by force. After him Malachy, whom Brian had displaced, reigned until 1022. After Malachy there was a succession of inferior Brians, the 'kings with opposition', none of whom was powerful enough to rule what his ambition bade him covet. By the middle of the twelfth century these kings of Connacht and Munster and Meath and Leinster and Breifne and Ossory, the would-be High Kings and their supporters and rivals, had, by their marches and their wars, most effectually upset Ireland. They had, in the expressive phrase, already made Ireland 'a trembling sod'. Their number was increased at that time by the entry to the stage of the northern King of Cinel Owen, who was, however, no more fitted than the rest to rule the lot.

In time, and if the remainder of Europe—and, in particular, England—had been like Ireland, no doubt one of these royal houses would have asserted its permanent rule over the others; but time is not endless, nor do the speedy wait upon the slow.

Among the struggling ones was Dermot MacMurrogh, King of Leinster. Dermot had fought to retain local power and, perhaps with wider hopes, had supported the claim of Murtogh, King of Cinel Owen, to the High Kingship. When Murtogh was eclipsed and killed in 1166 Dermot suffered by his downfall. Soon Rory O'Connor of Connacht, the last of the High Kings, together with Dermot's particular enemy Tiernan O'Rourke, King of Breifne and others, threatened Leinster. Added to the wider causes of the enmity which these men showed to Dermot was a personal one that is best remembered.

Years before, Dermot had stolen O'Rourke's wife. Now, alarmed at the growing strength of his opponents and conscious that O'Rourke's chances of revenge were increasing, Dermot broke the rules of the grim game of royal rivalry that they had all been playing for so long. Up to this they had shown violence in plenty. Temporarily successful competitors in the struggle for power had, apparently as a matter of course, blinded and maimed their opponents, thus putting them out of the race for kingship. Few holds had been barred. But the results of this strife had been, at least since the time of the Norse incursions, domestic matters. At this point all things were changed.

In August 1166, Dermot MacMurrogh left Ireland and sought the aid of the Norman King Henry II of England. He asked Henry, who probably had designs of his own on Ireland, to assist him in the recovery of his kingdom of Leinster. Thus for the second time in a century and a half a Leinster ruler showed himself willing to ally himself with foreigners against the High King. First Maelmora, who lost at Clontarf, had done it; now Dermot proposed to do it again.

The result was the Norman invasion, which began with the arrival of Robert FitzStephen, Maurice de Prendergast and their followers in Bannow Bay, Co. Wexford, in May 1169. These forerunners of the English forces of seven centuries consisted of forty knights, sixty other horsemen and some 500 archers. They had chosen what was militarily a good place of entry to Ireland, although they probably did so not so much with that in mind as for the reasons that it lay opposite south Wales, whence they came, and that it was close to Dermot's former seat of power. Eastward of Bannow lay the river Slaney, the valley of which provided a pathway into the interior. Westward lay the estuary of the three great rivers, Suir, Nore and Barrow, the valleys of which offered still greater facilities of penetration into the heart of the country.

Since the Norsemen, the intruders of an earlier age, commanded these two entries from their settlements at Wexford and Waterford, and furthermore held the harbours so necessary for communications with Wales, the first clash of the Norman invaders was with them. Joined by Dermot MacMurrogh, they took Wexford. They then penetrated twice into Ossory—the present Co. Kilkenny—the allegiance of which Dermot claimed, and raided North Leinster. With such assistance Dermot soon re-established himself in his kingdom.

At this stage the High King Rory led a hostile force as far as Ferns, which was the centre of Dermot's power; but Dermot was now willing to temporise and the High King—according to the accepted practice—was satisfied to take hostages for Dermot's good behaviour. There was no fighting. Such compromise was, in the twilight of the existence of their office, typical of the High Kings. It argues a higher regard for negotiation than those who call the Irish a warlike race would perhaps allow. Unfortunately, it also provides an explanation for the failure of the Kings to overcome their 'opposition'.

The more realistic Normans were soon to use more brutal, but more effective, methods than these to gain their ends. Fitz-Stephen was now reinforced by the arrival in Wexford of Maurice, the first of the great FitzGerald family destined later to play so notable a part in Irish history. He brought ten knights, thirty other horsemen and a hundred archers. Accompanied by his powerful auxiliaries, Dermot MacMurrogh again descended in the following year on a Norse settlement over which he claimed suzerainty and which commanded an entry from the sea. He marched to Dublin, overawed the town and secured its submission.

In 1170 also Richard FitzGilbert, known as Strongbow, arrived and the invasion assumed, with a new leader, a new aspect; its motive was no longer assistance of Dermot, but conquest. Strongbow, together with his supporter Raymond le Gros who preceded him, brought 210 knights and over a thousand archers and other footmen. His first action—following the earlier pattern—was the assault and capture of a Norse town, this time

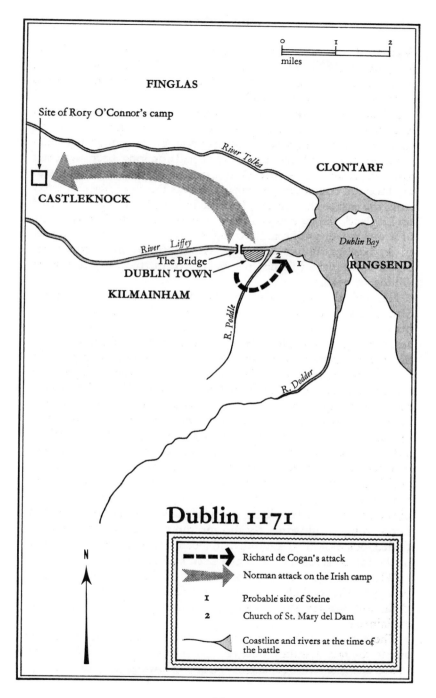

FINGLAS

Site of Rory O'Connor's camp

River Tolka

CLONTARF

CASTLEKNOCK

River Liffey

The Bridge
DUBLIN TOWN

KILMAINHAM

R. Poddle

Dublin Bay

RINGSEND

2

I

R. Dodder

Dublin 1171

N

➡	Richard de Cogan's attack
➡	Norman attack on the Irish camp
I	Probable site of Steine
2	Church of St. Mary del Dam
	Coastline and rivers at the time of the battle

miles
0   1   2

Waterford. His second was similar. Leaving a garrison in Waterford, and depending for the moment on the security of Wexford, he marched at once on Dublin, no doubt using one of the southern river valleys for his approach.

It has been pointed out by Orpen, the first of the modern historians of the Norman invasion, that, before this, each of the claimants of the High Kingship had sought, as though his claim required it, the submission of what had for long been the chief town in Ireland. This precedent apart, possession of Dublin was vital for the conquering Normans. It was the chief place of entry from the east to the central plain and indeed, for any power based on England, the gateway to the whole island. As such, possession of it was worth a fight, and Strongbow showed that he was aware of it; besides, unlike the High Kings, to whom towns were prizes to be won but not places to live in, the Normans were willing to possess it.

Haskulf, the Norse King of Dublin, was prepared to resist Strongbow, and the High King, Rory O'Connor, brought up his own forces and those of Breifne (or Leitrim-Cavan), Meath and Oriel (or Monaghan-Armagh) to help the Dublinmen. But Strongbow moved swiftly and cleverly. Descending unexpectedly by a mountain track from Glendalough, he arrived in September 1170 under the walls. Protracted negotiations followed but were rudely interrupted by the Normans, who suddenly assaulted the town and seized it. Haskulf and many of the townsmen fled overseas. Rory and the Irish forces withdrew; the Irish annalists indicate that Rory and his allies believed themselves to have been deserted by the Dublin Norsemen. Dermot, improving on his position, raided the territory of his personal enemy O'rourke. However, Dermot's race was run. He by whom, in the language of the annalists, 'a trembling sod was made of all Ireland', died in Ferns in May following. By the autumn the question of the continued possession of Dublin had been decided and the pattern of the future rule of Ireland had been laid down.

What was the secret of the success of these Normans in the two years that had elapsed since their first coming and how can their still greater success in the battle of Dublin in 1171 be explained?

The victory of the Normans was due to their military ability, and to the fact that they were better equipped than the Irish were; it was also the consequence of the Irish slowness in action and of

the Irish political circumstances, which made effective opposition
to the intruders almost impossible. But primarily it was a matter
of military superiority.

The Normans were the descendants of a warlike race that, in
the century of transition from Vikings to feudal rulers in northern
France and the further century of conquest and struggle in England and Wales, had grown increasingly formidable. In France
they became horsemen. In the eleventh century the age of the
cavalry soldier had begun; the Normans entered into the spirit
and adopted the practice of the age. When they crossed to Ireland
they brought their horses with them, as their ancestors had
brought horses across the Channel to fight the battle of Hastings.
In battle their best men fought mounted and wore byrnies or
hauberks of mail—long skirted coats of iron rings, or of quilted
fabric, or leather reinforced with metal studs. They had hoods
or coifs of mail, over which they wore conical iron helmets; some
wore leggings or chausses of mail. Their shields were kite-shaped,
a form adapted for mounted use and giving complete cover to the
left side of a rider. Their weapons were a lance, a long, straight-
bladed sword, and sometimes a club or mace. Such arms, such
armour, the heavy horses which they rode and the skill and daring
of the riders gave the Normans great power as shock troops. The
Irish had no such warriors as these Norman knights. Like the
Spanish horsemen in Mexico, the knights dominated the battlefield.

Nor were these the Normans' only fighters. They had also
good archers, skilled bowmen from the Welsh marches, the forerunners of the famous longbowmen of England who, two centuries
later, won the battles of Crécy and Agincourt. The Normans were
archers before their arrival in England, and they had improved
their archery by contact with the native bowmen of Wales. In
Ireland their archers gave them a fire-power which their opponents
lacked. The Irish made little use of the bow in battle.

These two qualities, the weight of mailed horsemen in a charge
and the missile strength of bowmen, formed the basis of the Norman tactics. They sought consistently to exploit their advantage
of material. Always they attacked, always they sought to fight in
the open, where they could use their horses; to be outnumbered
meant nothing to them. When the Waterfordmen closed in on
Raymond le Gros in 1170 he sallied out to meet them; de Courcy
came out to meet MacDonlevy at Down in 1177; Strongbow and

de Cogan, as we shall see, came out to meet the Norsemen and the Irish at Dublin. Each of these was heavily outnumbered, but each was victorious.

The Normans were swift in their movements, as they showed at Bannow Bay, at Wexford, at Dublin, and in Down. They were able to attack fortifications—and here their archery served them; but they avoided fighting behind walls. They had an eye for strategy, and so they made certain of possession of the towns. They had an eye for terrain: they were cautious on the forest paths, they avoided the bogs, and, in 1170, they chose the best way into Dublin behind the High King's back. They were infinitely crafty. They feigned retreats, they planted ambushes, they delivered flank attacks, they attacked at night.

In contrast, the Irish were poorly equipped, dilatory, and too prone to the defensive. A few of their leaders may have had armour, but in general they had none. In general too they were infantry. They fought on foot with spears, javelins, battle axes, and swords; the only item of their missile armoury that their opponents found worthy of mention was the antediluvian hand stone. The attack of mailed horse could, on firm ground, overrun them and against a combination of horse and archers—of shock and fire-power—they were helpless. They behaved always as though they had plenty of time. When Strongbow seized Dublin in 1170 the High King went home: he would come back next year. Fortifications, then as for centuries afterwards, daunted them.

At the date of the Dublin fighting there were not, it appears, more than 2,500 Normans in Ireland, that is, perhaps 250 knights, 500 other horsemen, and 1,750 infantry, including archers. Some of these had remained to hold Wexford and Waterford, so that the Norman strength at Dublin cannot in the early part of the year have greatly exceeded 2,000, or perhaps 200 knights, 400 other horsemen, and 1,500 or so archers and other infantry.

The knights were not the chivalric figures of romantic fiction and of later admiration who 'swung their swords in wrong cause or in right'. They were fighting men whose service was the result of a system of landholding, the feudal system. Land was given in that age by kings and great lords to lesser lords, who held it on condition of providing knights, or fully armed, trained and mounted men, for service in the wars. These were the knights of the invasion: tough professionals, well equipped and, above all, well horsed. Such heavily armed horsemen were the tanks of the occasion; like the tanks of 1940, they were irresistible when they attacked on ground that suited them an enemy deficient in striking power. They were the élite troops. The other mounted men were less heavily armed and of a poorer quality. The foot included spearmen and men fighting with sword and shield, but were mostly archers, whose role was second in importance only to that of the knights. Unsupported by archers, horsemen could not face archers. Although the Irish made no great use of the bow in battle, and so gave the knights an easy victory over them, the Norman-Welsh archers nevertheless played a vital part in Strongbow's struggle against numerical odds.

In 1171 two forces arrived outside Dublin to contest its possession with the Normans, who were within. One was led by the Norse king of Dublin, Haskulf. Haskulf had gone overseas in the previous year to enlist support, and he now had with him, together with his own men drawn from the town and the surrounding Norse area, men also from the Scottish islands and the Isle of Man. The other force was the army of Rory O'Connor, the High King, and his adherents. Whether these two bodies were outside Dublin at the same time, whether they co-operated with one another, in opposition to the invaders, and which was first engaged with the Normans are alike matters of obscurity. The contemporary evidence seems, however, to indicate that Haskulf came up first and that he attacked the Normans and was defeated before the efforts made by the Irish had greatly affected the position.

We are told that Haskulf arrived about Whitsun, which in 1171 was in the middle of May. The Dublin of that time was a small fortified settlement on the south bank of the Liffey, the centre of which was the high ground later crowned by Dublin Castle. The town extended northward to the Liffey, westward to the site of the bridge, which was probably marked by the later Bridge Street, southward to where the river Poddle flowed below the Castle hill, and eastward to the point near the present Parliament Street where the Poddle—long since covered over and running invisibly beneath the modern city—discharges into the Liffey. Haskulf and his companions, who included a renowned warrior known as John the Wode, or Mad, came ashore below the town at the place called the Steine. This was an open space on the south bank of the Liffey in the area where Trinity College now stands, and it derived its name from a pillar stone which had been erected there, probably by the Norsemen.

We have no way of saying when Haskulf's force fell foul of the Normans, but hostilities seem to have continued between them for some time before the day when the first phase of the battle of Dublin was decided.

On this occasion, as usual, we find the Normans outside the fortifications and fighting in the open against the combined force of the Dublinmen and their allies, which exceeded the Normans in numbers. The struggle took place in the vicinity of the present Dame Street, between the Steine and the east gate of the town, the gate of St Mary del dam—the mill dam at the mouth of the Poddle. Miles de Cogan, who led the Normans, was worsted, and fell back fighting to the gate. Even in this extremity, however, the aggressive Normans were unwilling to seek shelter and to fight on the defensive.

While he continued the struggle at the east gate, de Cogan sent his brother Richard secretly and hurriedly through the west gate, on the other side of the town. Richard had thirty knights. Riding hard, he fetched a circuit around what is now the centre of the south side of the city of Dublin and came down heavily and noisily on Haskulf's rear, threatening his line of retreat to his camp and his shipping and completely surprising him.

The rear of the Norse force turned to face Richard. Miles sallied over the Poddle; can we doubt that—ever audacious—he flung his last man at the red, iron-rimmed shields, locked now in a hasty shield-wall? Haskulf was caught. The archers shot gaps in his packed warriors; the heavy horsemen rode over them. John the Wode died fighting, his terrible axe that had chopped limbs at a stroke unavailing to save him. And around him died Dublinmen and Islanders. Dispirited and suddenly weary, what was left of them fled. Haskulf, taken, was later put to death.

This was the end of the first phase of the fight for Dublin; the later phases culminated in a scene of rout that was far more extraordinary.

During the summer Rory O'Connor, the High King, blockaded the town with large forces. He had brought up his own Connachtmen and lay encamped with them at Castleknock. With him were Tiernan O'Rourke of Breifne and Meath, O'Melaghlin, also of Meath, and O'Carroll of Oriel, each with his following. Rory was aided also by MacDonlevy, King of Ulidia—that is, the present

Antrim and Down—who was encamped at Clontarf, and by Murtogh, nephew of Dermot MacMurrogh, by O'Toole, and by other Leinster rulers, who were at Dalkey. The presence of Donell O'Brien, King of Thomond, seems doubtful; he is said to have been encamped at Kilmainham. Even without O'Brien, Strongbow's opponents were very numerous. Contemporaries place the force commanded by Rory alone at 30,000. This must be much exaggerated; but Rory and his allies represented the best of the Irish fighters, and they were well placed, north and south of the Liffey, to enforce the blockade.

There seems to have been no possibility of an Irish assault. Attacking fortifications was not an Irish specialty. Rory and his allies did not take part in Haskulf's fight, and may not have come up—or may not all have come up—when it occurred. The remnants of Haskulf's force may have co-operated with them afterwards. The impression given by the meagre accounts which we have of the events of the summer is of a two months' blockade or siege during which little, if any, serious fighting occurred.

Rory's seeming inactivity was not, however, without effect. In Dublin supplies ran short. Blockaded by land and sea and experiencing, as well, the momentary displeasure of King Henry II, which prevented the despatch of supplies from England, the Normans had to tighten their belts. Laurence O'Toole, the Archbishop, who was in Dublin but apparently in touch with affairs outside, is said to have done his best to encourage their Norse and Irish opponents to intensify the blockade. In September Strongbow offered to negotiate with the High King. But Rory overestimated his own strength and tried to gain too much. He proposed peace on the condition that Strongbow and his intruders might retain Dublin, Wexford and Waterford, but no more—they could have neither Leinster, which Dermot MacMurrogh had purported to give them, nor any other part of Ireland which they might covet.

It was contrary to every inclination of the Normans to accept a condition such as this, which would coop them up behind walls. They reacted in the spirit of the enterprise to which they were committed, aggressively. 'What are we waiting for?' cried Maurice FitzGerald. 'Do we expect help from our own people? No! This is how we stand: we are Englishmen to the Irish and Irishmen to the English!' They were abandoned by King Henry to fend for themselves, and if they wanted better terms than Rory offered they must fight for them.

The Normans sallied suddenly from Dublin at one o'clock on a September afternoon and attacked the High King. They went out in three divisions, the ubiquitous formation that became right, left and centre in action. Raymond le Gros led with twenty knights; Miles de Cogan followed with thirty; Strongbow and Maurice FitzGerald led the third division—the main body, or centre—of forty knights. Each had other troops as well, horsemen and archers. Probably all were mounted; some of the archers—who of course fought on foot—may have been carried on the cruppers of the horsemen. As well as these Normans, we are told that those of the Leinster Irish who had remained faithful to them, and some of the citizens, went out with them; but Strongbow's force cannot have numbered much more than 2,000 in all. Some men must have been left behind to hold the town, and the fight with Haskulf and service during the summer had taken their toll of Strongbow's original strength. There is a suggestion that some of the Normans had returned to England from Dublin during the summer.

The column crossed the Liffey bridge and moved north towards Finglas. Soon they turned to the left; whether they were beyond the Tolka or still south of it when they turned we do not know. Moving rapidly in the Tolka valley behind the present Phoenix Park, they came down heavily and unexpectedly on Rory's camp at Castleknock. It was their favourite tactic, and its result, as intended, was surprise. Time and place alike favoured them: the idle hour of early afternoon and the flank and rear of the investment. The Irish must have been totally unprepared.

In this situation numbers meant little. Raymond, Miles, Gerald and Alexander, the sons of Maurice FitzGerald—they vied with one another in the impetuosity of their attack. The details of the struggle are completely lost to us. How the Irish reacted we do not know, but we are told that there was great confusion, and there seems little doubt that the Irish casualties were very large. The High King was caught in his bath. The indignity of his situation seems heightened by every schoolboy's knowing of it; but he escaped.

The slaughter of the fugitives continued until evening, by which time the Irish were routed. Here as elsewhere in these early years of the invasion the knight and the archer, fighting on their own ground, were invincible; when they could effect surprise they were invincible against any odds. The Normans came back to Dublin in the darkness of the autumn evening, laden with food and the spoils of battle and covered with glory.

The other Irish armies which lay around Dublin disintegrated and the siege was soon raised. A shadowy and abortive attempt to engaged the Normans, led by Tiernan O'Rourke and mentioned by the Irish annalists, may have been made about this time. In it O'Rourke's son was killed and his men discomfited. On the other hand, O'Rourke's defeat may have preceded Rory's. Much is obscure. There is no doubt about the Norman victory, however; it was complete.

Most of our information about the Dublin fighting, and indeed about the Norman invasion as a whole, is derived from a work written shortly after, *Expugnatio Hibernica*, by Gerald de Barry, or Giraldus Cambrensis. The Latin text of this work was edited by J. F. Dimock and published in the Rolls Series, London in 1867. An English translation by Thomas Forester appears in *The Historical Works of Giraldus Cambrensis*, edited by T. Wright and published in 1881. Another work of Gerald's, *The Topography of Ireland* (translated by J. J. O'Meara in *The First Version of the Topography of Ireland by Giraldus Cambrensis*, 1951), may also be read with profit. The Irish annalists (Annals of Tigernach, Ulster, and the Four Masters—all published) give very brief accounts. The romantic Anglo-French poem or *chanson de geste* which G. H. Orpen (who edited it in 1892) called 'The Song of Dermot and the Earl' is a later composition which describes events of the invasion—including the battle of Dublin—and which is based on possibly contemporary material. (See J. F. O'Doherty, 'Historical Criticism of the Song of Dermot and the Earl' in *Irish Historical Studies*, I, pp. 4 ff, whose view must be preferred to Orpen's regarding the relative dates of Haskulf's attack on Dublin and Rory O'Connor's rout.)

Modern descriptions (all very brief) of the fighting appear in G. H. Orpen, *Ireland under the Normans* (1911), I, pp. 221 ff; E. Curtis, *A History of Mediaeval Ireland*, pp. 47 ff; C. Oman, *A History of the Art of War in the Middle Ages* (2nd edn, 1924), I, pp. 402 ff. For the armour and arms of the Normans, see C. Blair, *European Armour* (1958), pp. 23 ff; R. E. Oakeshott, *The Archaeology of Weapons* (1960), pp. 174 ff; and, for contemporary illustrations of the Normans, E. Maclagan, *The Bayeux Tapestry* (1945). See a representation from the Bayeux Tapestry, Plate 2. For information on the political state of Ireland in the years preceding the Norman invasion see J. Ryan, S.J., *Toirdelbach O Conchubair, 1088–1156* (National University of Ireland, O'Donnell Lecture, 1966), where this statement is made: 'The country was in a state of near anarchy. Everywhere men were on the march; everywhere armies were locked in deadly combat; everywhere the result was the same—the wheel of fortune turned and another point was reached in military and political futility.'

Dysert O'Dea, 1318

Sir Charles Oman, the military historian, believed that the Irish did not change their methods of fighting between the time of the Norman invasion and that of the new conquest of Queen Elizabeth I, 400 years later. They used, he said, the same arms and the same 'primitive tactics' in the sixteenth century as they had used in the twelfth. While their enemies progressed they stood still. Other writers have agreed with him.

There were undoubtedly many things that did not change, or that changed slowly, in medieval Ireland. Many aspects of warfare remained the same over long periods. The progress of the Normans through the woods of Ossory in 1169 was delayed by MacGillapatrick, who cut trenches across the forest paths and threw up ramparts behind the trenches. He erected stockades of wattles on top of the ramparts, manned them with his fighting men, and fought the advancing Normans from behind these formidable defences. Dermot MacMurrogh prepared the same kind of earthworks in his fastness near Ferns in Wexford when the High King advanced against him in the same year. In order to keep attackers to the paths and to prevent infiltration into the woods, which might outflank him, Dermot 'plashed' the margins of the pathways in the approaches to his barriers; he made, that is, impenetrable hedgerows of the undergrowth on either side by interweaving cut branches amid the growing shrubs and saplings.

There must be hundreds of references in late sixteenth-century documents to show that, in Ulster, in Munster, in the midlands, in the wooded foothills of the Leinster mountains—wherever the Irish fought—they still did these things at that date. Trenches, stockades and plashed woods were commonplaces—for aggressors ugly commonplaces—of Queen Elizabeth's Irish wars. That much was the same.

Through all these centuries from the twelfth to the sixteenth the Irish terrain did not change. There were at the end, as there had been at the beginning, deep woods, great areas of bog, much rough ground, many mountains. Roads, tracks or paths thus remained few, narrow and difficult. Progress away from these roads was an uncertain matter not ordinarily attempted by travellers; it could seldom have been attempted by marching armies. The result was the abiding danger of the 'pass'. Passes were narrow ways through woods, defiles between hills, causeways over bogs; places, that is, where ambush was always a possibility. Because tracks were constricted at such places march formation had to be changed to negotiate them, which usually meant that the moving column became more vulnerable. Earthworks and plashing strengthened the defences and further increased the dangers of the pass. In Tudor as in Norman times there were marching armies and hostile forces to dispute their progress. It would be inconceivable that, in the intervening period, the 'primitive tactics' of the prepared ambush should have been given up. Indeed there was nothing primitive about them; they were still suggested in Elizabeth's time by an unchanged terrain.

But the methods of early times, and those only, did not, in fact, continue in use for centuries. There was progress. What seems to have led historians to think otherwise is the fact that basic methods of fighting, which favoured defence rather than aggression and which took advantage of terrain, were not given up; they were, rather, developed. It is possible to be misled too by the wealth of contemporary descriptions of sixteenth-century fighting in contrast to the paucity of earlier records. It is easier, when similarities are encountered at intervals of centuries, to suppose a complete absence of change than to search among unpromising material for evidence of growth and development.

The warfare of the early part of the fourteenth century, the period of the Bruce invasion of Ireland and of the waning of the power of the descendants of the Normans, saw the use by the Irish of methods that were quite different from those that had earned them defeat in Strongbow's time. After that there was a notable addition to the personnel of the fighters and notable developments in arms and in tactics, culminating in the extraordinary sixteenth-century changes that produced the great armies of Hugh O'Neill, Earl of Tyrone and of Hugh O'Donnell.

The battle of Dysert O'Dea, fought in Co. Clare on 10 May 1318 between Richard de Clare and the O'Briens, O'Deas and

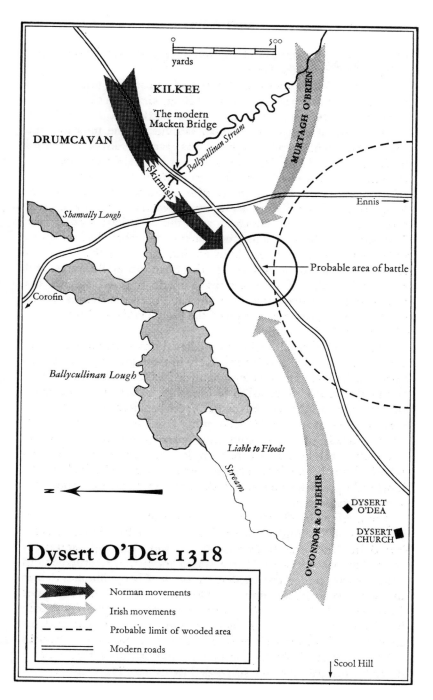

KILKEE

DRUMCAVAN

The modern
Macken Bridge

Ballycullinan Stream

MURTAGH O'BRIEN

Skirmish

Ennis →

Shanvally Lough

Corofin

Probable area of battle

Ballycullinan Lough

Liable to Floods

Stream

N ←

DYSERT
O'DEA

O'CONNOR & O'HEHIR

DYSERT
CHURCH

Dysert O'Dea 1318

	Norman movements
	Irish movements
– – – –	Probable limit of wooded area
═══	Modern roads

↓ Scool Hill

others, vividly illustrates the improved methods and the improved military quality of the Irish.

Dysert O'Dea lies between Ennis and Corofin, in territory that was, in medieval times, part of the O'Brien kingdom of Thomond. Forty-two years before the date of the battle Thomas de Clare, head of one of the great Norman families of the invasion and fourth in descent from Strongbow, was given a grant of Thomond by King Edward I of England. This was not the first intrusion of the Normans, who had secured themselves in the old Norse town of Limerick at the end of the twelfth century, into the country lying north of the Shannon estuary. They had for long assisted one O'Brien against another, and the O'Briens against the Macnamaras, the O'Quins and others, and they had received earlier land grants and had built castles, including the first of at least four successive ones beside the Shannon at Bunratty. But de Clare's grant, if he could have made it good against the inhabitants, was sweeping. It might have been the foundation of a dominion as powerful as that of the FitzGeralds in Desmond or the de Burghs in Clanrickard.

Every Gaelic Irish lordship in medieval times, and down to the extinction of organised Gaelic society in the reign of James I, was unstable. The system of rule, whatever its theoretical merits, was in practice brittle. Succession to kingship, or lordship, depended on selection, not, as in the Norman feudal society, on primogeniture. The result was that Gaelic ruling families were periodically, on the death of lords, split into warring factions; on these occasions weak human nature trampled on the rules and the ones who had not been selected fought against those who had. Every king had opposition; every lordship, at one time or another, was shattered from within.

The factions in Thomond in the thirteenth century were those of Brian and Turlough O'Brien. Turlough sought aid in Connacht, but Brian, and after Brian's death his son Donough, sought it from Thomas de Clare. There was a momentary settlement in 1281, when, under the mediation of de Clare, Thomond was divided between Turlough and Donough; but three years later Turlough killed Donough and made a bid for the whole. Before his death in 1306 he was effective King of Thomond and his followers—showing their resentment of the presence of intruders —had burnt the Norman Quin Castle and had done their best to destroy Bunratty. He was succeeded by his son Donough.

Thomas de Clare died in 1287. Following his royal grant, he had driven a wedge into Thomond; it remained for his heir Richard, who succeeded his brother Gilbert in 1308, to attempt to strike the wedge home.

A new generation had now arisen to inherit the old quarrels. This time the de Clares backed Dermot, grandson of Brian O'Brien, and, further to confuse the issue, the Norman de Burghs of Connacht entered the lists as allies of King Donough. Donough was killed in 1311, and Dermot and the de Clares emerged for the moment victorious. But Dermot died in 1313. Another Donough of the faction of Brian carried on the struggle against the faction of Turlough, now led by Murtough O'Brien. In 1317 the two factions fought a great battle at Corcomroe Abbey in the Burren hills, overlooking Galway Bay. Murtough prevailed. Within a year he was to pursue his advantage, and, by defeating them at Dysert O'Dea, was to scatter the Normans and drive them out of Clare.

This was the local scene. These happenings had, however, a wider significance. In May 1315 Edward Bruce, brother of Robert, King of Scotland, landed with a powerful army at Larne, Co. Antrim, and began an invasion that was to upset Ireland for the next three years and to leave its mark on the country for generations. The purpose of the Bruces was, as has been made clearer by recent research, almost certainly defensive: they were carrying the Scottish war of defence against Edward II into Ireland. Viewed thus, their chief motives were to lift the English pressure on Scotland by compelling Edward to attend to the defence of Ireland and, by the spoliation of the Irish countryside, to prohibit the continued use of Ireland as a source of supplies for England's Scottish wars. No doubt there were other motives as well. The Scots had friends among the Gaelic lords and the Anglo-Irish. As the recent victors of Bannockburn, they may have wished to share their success by helping them; later on Edward Bruce accepted the crown of Ireland from Donal O'Neill, King of Tyrone, and others who coupled traditions of the old High Kingship with resentment of English sovereignty. But the ruthlessness with which the Scots destroyed the English areas through which they marched—a ruthlessness such as Wallace showed in England after his victory at Stirling in 1297—disclosed their real intent; and it had its reward, for the English did not again use Ireland against Scotland.

Whatever the reasons for the Bruce invasion may have been, it had two very clear results. Like all wars, it spread an element of militarism beyond its seat of operations; and it served to play up the Irish in Ireland and to play down the English.

Edward Bruce's army was probably the greatest yet seen in Ireland; it was certainly the finest, since it was a veteran force, fresh from a major victory. Until 1318 it was invincible. The Scots overcame or overawed Richard de Burgh, the Red Earl of Ulster, at Connor in Antrim in 1315. Moving south, they defeated Roger Mortimer at Kells in Meath. In the following year they scattered another Anglo-Norman force near Athy in Kildare. In 1317 they threatened Dublin, and then, shying away, marched to Limerick and back. They had, by the time of their final retreat to Ulster, moved through a great part of the Ireland of the Norman settlement, and everywhere they went they had destroyed crops, burnt houses and lived on the country. They left famine behind them. As the annalists say: 'Theft, famine and destruction of men occurred throughout Ireland for the space of three years and a half, and people used actually to eat one another throughout Ireland.'

On the periphery of this warfare and destruction other struggles took place. The O'Donnells raided Sligo. The O'Moores, O'Tooles, O'Byrnes and O'Hanlons became restive in Leinster and south Ulster. Felim O'Connor, King of Connacht, turned against the de Burghs and, in the biggest battle yet fought in Connacht, was defeated by William de Burgh and Richard de Bermingham at Athenry in August 1316.

Ireland grew accustomed to warfare, not local warfare on a small scale, but the warfare of big battles, hardened fighters, good weapons and new techniques. The Scots were fine soldiers. They were at this time beginning a long career as stubborn infantrymen that was to earn for their country no little military fame. Bannockburn was a foot battle. So for the Scots were Flodden in 1513 and Pinkie in 1547; and the best soldiers of the armies of the Covenant in the seventeenth century were infantry. Ireland, like Scotland, was a poor country where foot soldiers were easier to raise and support than horse. The example of Bruce's army cannot have been lost on his Irish supporters and imitators; as we shall see later, the galloglas, the fighters of Scottish origin who transformed Irish warfare in the centuries after the time of the Bruces, were footmen too. And the two big Gaelic battles of the Bruce period, Athenry and Dysert O'Dea, were, like all Gaelic battles, foot fights.

The practice of the time showed that the age of the dominance of the mounted knight, the great paladin of the Norman invasion, was passing away. He was not succeeded in Ireland, as he was elsewhere, either by archers or spearmen. Big native armies which could show large bodies of infantry did not appear in Ireland until fighting ceased in the sixteenth century to be the exclusive preserve of the upper classes. But a decline in his own warlike qualities and an improvement in those of the individuals who opposed him, together with an improvement in their equipment, dimmed the knight's lustre. The heavy horsemen of the de Clares at the beginning of the fourteenth century, still wearing mail armour—or perhaps some with the rudiments of the plate armour that was to supersede it—and still carrying lance and sword, no longer dominated the battlefield. They no longer showed the aggressive spirit of Raymond le Gros and Miles de Cogan. The archers who went with them were no longer the bowmen of the Welsh marches.

Moreover, and of more significance, the Irish had stolen some of their thunder. More than a century's association, fraternisation and struggle had led to an interchange in which the Irish, militarily, were the gainers. The Normans appear to have adopted the lighter Irish horses—or, more likely, the qualities of the native breed predominated; thus as shock troops the Normans lost weight. In earlier times the Irish were notably deficient in armour. Now they had come to adopt or to copy the armour of the intruders. It is recorded that the victors at the battle of Athenry gave up some of the armour which they had captured from the vanquished—that is, from the Irish—to pay for the erection of the wall of the town of Athenry: 'for every Englishman that won a double harness gave half of his booty to help to build the walls of the same town.' This means that armour was, if not plentiful, certainly not unknown among the Irish at that time. The leaders of the Clare O'Briens at the time of the battle of Dysert O'Dea are described as wearing shirts or hauberks of mail over padded aketons, together with mail coifs or hoods and conical iron helmets. The aketon or garment padded with cotton, here worn as was usual under the mail, was a protection in itself, and, being cheaper than mail, was no doubt worn independently by warriors of lesser substance. Leather armour was also in use at the time, and may have been used by the Irish. Such equipment was new to the Irish armoury.

Much that was new in the way of suggestion, if not of material, must have come too in very recent years from the Scots and the feudal forces that opposed them. Felim O'Connor, who was defeated and killed at Athenry, had been present with his forces at the battle of Connor. Many of the Thomond O'Briens fought at Athenry. Many of them too were in contact with the Scots near Limerick at Easter, 1317. There were plenty of opportunities for the spread of ideas, and ideas have never been slow to spread during war.

There were all these reasons for the battle of Dysert O'Dea's being a new type of contest. It is perhaps the least known, but it is certainly not the least interesting of Irish battles.

In 1318, the year after his victory over his rivals at Corcomroe, Murtough O'Brien faced Richard de Clare in a contest that was to decide which of them would control Thomond. Richard marched against Murtough, who had been raiding his cattle. He came up from the Bunratty area, the centre of his lordship, to Quin. Unfortunately, it is not possible to say what force either Richard or Murtough O'Brien had, or how the forces were composed. De Clare had his knights, who cannot have been numerous, and whatever strength the tenants on his lands in Thomond could muster—bowmen and spearmen on foot, and light horsemen; since they were frontiersmen they must have been good fighters. He had also some of the O'Briens, of the faction of Brian O'Brien, Murtough's rivals. The Irish on both sides must almost all have been footmen. There might perhaps have been a thousand, all told, in either host.

De Clare moved westward from Ruan, which is north of Quin and north of Ennis, on the morning of 10 May. He entered the O'Deas' country. Although he knew that there was a hostile force under Conor O'Dea somewhere in front of him, he was confident enough of his ability to deal with it to divide his men. They marched in three companies, spread out north and south so that they might plunder the country. One body moved to the right towards Tully, another to the left towards Magowna. De Clare himself advanced in the centre with the main force towards Dysert, where O'Dea's chief house was, bent on its destruction.

Near Lough Ballycullinan, north-east of Dysert, de Clare's

advance came on a party of Conor O'Dea's men—the Irish account describes it as 'a well ordered detachment of horse and foot'—driving a herd of cattle across a stream. The Normans pressed on by Dromcavan, hoping to seize such promising spoil. At first the Irish seemed full of fight. They faced round and began skirmishing, assailing the Normans with the usual showers of darts, slingstones and handstones. Soon, however, they began to retire slowly, hurrying off their cattle behind them. In this way pursuers and pursued reached a place where a second stream was fordable, probably in marshy land near the present Macken bridge. Here the Irish made a more stubborn stand.

The O'Deas counted on the assistance of two other forces, one under O'Connor of Corcomroe and Loughlin O'Hehir, which was close by, and the other Murtough O'Briens main force, which had been chasing some rival O'Briens and was further off. Conor O'Dea hoped to delay de Clare sufficiently to give time for these to come up to help him. He also hoped to lead de Clare into an ambush. The skirmishers were only a small part of his strength. His main body was concealed on the margin of a wood a little further back, somewhere south of the lake.

The Normans won the ford and crossed over. The Irish fell back. The head of the Norman column reached the wood and out streamed the ambushers, splitting at once into two parties. One party reinforced the skirmishers and attacked de Clare in front; the other rushed towards the ford and fell upon the tail of the column, which was still crossing and was badly placed to defend itself.

So far the contest had followed the familiar, time-honoured pattern of Irish warfare, the pattern of which Barbour, Bruce's chronicler, thought when he made the Irishmen say:

> For our maner is, of this land,
> Till follow and ficht, and ficht fleand,
> And nocht till stand in plane melle
> Quhill the ta part discumfit be.

The O'Deas were using their knowledge of the terrain to practise a stratagem and to lure the Normans into danger. They were willing to 'ficht fleand'—to make a running fight—but would they stand 'in plane melle', that is, in open combat?

They soon showed that they would. Presently the character of the fighting changed. O'Dea scored one immediate advantage.

Richard de Clare, fighting with a small party in advance of his column, was killed; 'the O'Deas killed both himself and every man that he had with him'. Otherwise the ambush was scarcely successful. The rear of the Norman column was not held up for very long and the Irish, pressed now by the full Norman force acting together, soon found themselves in difficulties. They retired into the wood, were pursued, were surrounded, and were closely beset by the 'battle-hedge' of the Normans.

Both sides were reinforced as the fight progressed. Numbers of men from the other two companies of the Normans arrived, their plundering interrupted, and joined in. So, on the Irish side, did O'Connor's and O'Hehir's forces; they came up swiftly over Scool Hill, west of Dysert, descended to the battlefield and attacked the Normans.

Conor O'Dea's men cut their way through their attackers to join these reinforcements outside the wood. The united force formed in the strongest position they could find and the battle became a mêlée. The Irish were engulfed in a surging, hacking mass as the Normans redoubled their efforts to overrun them, now that the fight could be waged away from the shelter of the trees. 'Both parties,' says the Irish chronicler, 'the Gall and the Gael, mowed down and mishandled each other, so that of either set many gentlemen and fine warriors were destroyed.'

How long this continued we do not know. The struggle was severe, the casualties heavy. O'Dea and his allies were outnumbered, and as their ranks thinned they must have drawn closer together, gathering into a hard knot of combat on the little ridge or hill, or wherever it was that they made their stand. They were driven 'to form themselves into a fast, impenetrable phalanx that their enemies should not break through them'. Individual fighters stood out from the mass, and here the new armour of the Irish must have served them well. O'Connor of Corcomroe and young de Clare sought one another out and de Clare perished. Father and son had now been removed from the scene.

If the fight had gone on in this way it is possible, despite the death of the de Clares, that the Normans might in the end have tightened their 'battle hedge', and shot down and cut down enough Irishmen to overcome their resistance. But the full force of the Irish was not yet engaged. The O'Deas and O'Connors and O'Hehirs had, by their determination, made ultimate victory possible; but they had not yet achieved it. Murtough O'Brien and his men still remained outside the combat. It was their intervention that was decisive.

King Murtough came by Spancel Hill from north-east Clare, and as he crossed the river Fergus and approached the battlefield he must have seen the plundered countryside in flames before him. We are told that his men rushed forward so impetuously to join in the fray that they arrived in disorder, and that they were at first mistaken by the Irish for further reinforcements of their foes. That this could have happened is, incidentally, further evidence that by this date there was little difference in appearance between the warriors of the two nations; earlier, when one was armoured and the other not, they must have been quite distinct.

The weight of the newcomers tipped the balance. The Normans, still fighting with the utmost ferocity, were pounded between the O'Briens and the O'Deas and completely overthrown; 'so dour the hand-to-hand work was, that neither noble nor commander of them left the ground, but the far greater part fell where they stood'.

As far as the de Clare power in Thomond was concerned, the result was decisive. The Normans lost everything, even Bunratty Castle, which was their strongest hold. Murtough pursued the survivors to Bunratty and found the castle and the English settlement there in flames; Richard's widow had set alight what would burn and had fled by boat to Limerick. The de Clares never came back. The victorious O'Briens preserved that part of the old Thomond which lay north of the Shannon for the Gaelic order until the sixteenth century. When at that time they took the opposite side to O'Neill and O'Donnell, who were the last defenders of that order, they did so of their own free will. Like the Campbells in Scotland, they elected to go a different way from their neighbours. The present Bunratty Castle, built in the fifteenth century, is an Irish, not an Anglo-Norman structure.

The Irish of Thomond did at Dysert O'Dea what the Irish of Connacht, facing the longer established and tougher houses of de Burgh and de Bermingham, failed to do at Athenry. It was the greatest Gaelic victory of a period which, because of the sufferings of the Anglo-Norman colony from the Scots, was full of promise for Gaelic Ireland. And it was a new kind of battle for the Irish. The delaying action at the stream and the ambush in the wood, which marked its opening phases, were well-tried tactics; but the stubborn stand of heavily armed Gaelic warriors willing to accept casualties and determined to fight it out was something new. It was seen for the first time in the Irish wars at Athenry, where it was a stand made in vain, and for the second at Dysert O'Dea, where it brought victory. These were standing fights—occasions of a 'plain mêlée'; they were not hit and miss affairs of the bogs and forests that some writers have regarded as typical of medieval Irish warfare.

The only early account of the battle of Dysert O'Dea which enters into any detail is that in *Caithréim Thoirdhealbhaigh* (*The Triumphs of Turlough*), written in the third quarter of the fourteenth century by one of the MacGraths, the hereditary historians of Thomond. The *Caithréim* has been translated by Standish H. O'Grady and was published by the Irish Texts Society in 1929. (The translation is in Vol. II and the account of the battle on pp. 119 ff). See also E. Curtis, 'The Wars of Turlough' in *The Irish Review*, 1913—January, pp. 577 ff, February, pp. 644 ff, March, pp. 34 ff, and T. J. Westropp, 'On the external evidences bearing on the historic character of the "Wars of Torlough" by John, son of Rory MacGrath' in *Transactions of the Royal Irish Academy*, XXXIII, C, pp. 133 ff.

There are modern accounts of the battle and an identification of the battlefield in Westropp's paper just mentioned (pp. 155 f), and in another work by the same author, 'The Normans in Thomond' in *Journal of the Royal Society of Antiquaries of Ireland*, XXI (1890–91), pp. 284 ff, 381 ff, 462 ff. (The account of the battle is on pp. 469 ff and there is a map of the battlefield facing p. 470.)

For the background of Thomond history see, as well as West- ropp's second paper, G. H. Orpen, *Ireland Under the Normans*, IV, pp. 53 ff. For the Bruce invasion see O. Armstrong, *Edward Bruce's Invasion of Ireland* (1923), which contains a map showing the Bruce marches; J. F. Lydon, 'The Bruce Invasion of Ireland' in *Historical Studies*, IV (1963), pp. 111 ff. which develops the thesis that 'Robert Bruce was carrying his war against England into this country', and 'The Bruces in Ireland' in *Ulster Journal of Archaeology*, first series, V, pp. 1 ff, 128 ff. The quotation from Barbour is in W. W. Skeat's edition of *The Bruce* (1894), II, p. 118.

For the period in general see E. Curtis, *A History of Mediaeval Ireland*, pp. 222 ff.

The quotation regarding the building of the wall of Athenry, which indicates that some of the Irish who fought in that battle wore armour, is from the Annals of Ireland in British Museum Additional MS 4789, fol. 158. (quoted in *Ulster Journal of Archaeology*, first series, V, p. 132).

Knockdoe, 1504

In the two centuries that elapsed between the date of the battle of Dysert O'Dea, fought in 1318, and that of the battle of Knockdoe the Irish military scene was transformed. A type of warrior new to the Irish wars was introduced. This was the gallowglass, or, to give him his proper Irish name, *gall óglach*, that is, foreign warrior.

The coming and gradual spreading throughout Ireland of these galloglas* followed a militarisation of the country that, if it had taken place earlier, would have been a considerable obstacle to the Norman advance. Contrary to the general belief, the older Ireland was not warlike; the Irish annals certainly record frequent hostings and raids, and there was much violence in public affairs, but there were few battles, and there was no warrior class. There were no housecarles in Gaelic as there were in Anglo-Saxon society, no kings' bodyguards; and there was no fyrd, or national militia. Neither was there knight service, as there was in feudalism, the military obligations of which could be discharged by hiring knights, and which thus ensured the support within the community of landless professional warriors.

Military service in the older Ireland was the duty of the landed freemen, or the upper classes in the separate kingdoms or lordships. In the discharge of this duty these men assembled for limited periods when called upon by the king or lord, accompanied him on his hostings, or military expeditions, and fought, if necessary, to support his claims or to defend their homeland. When the occasion of service had passed they went home. They may, whether the moment was propitious or not, have gone home on the expiry of a prearranged period, and this may be the explanation of such withdrawals as Rory O'Connor's from Dublin in 1170; even the service of the feudal host, which was, unlike the Gaelic rising-out, the product of a warlike society, was subject

---

* It seems time that the unwieldy double plural gallowglasses was dropped. The Irish plural is *gall óglaigh*. The plural form used most frequently by sixteenth-century English writers was galloglas.

to time limits. At any rate, Gaelic Ireland knew no permanent military service.

In the period following the Bruce invasion warfare became a much more usual feature of Irish society than it was before. War has always suggested war. Gaelic Ireland, in eventual reaction to Norman aggression, was becoming militarised before the Bruces' time; the campaigns of the Scots and the related struggles which the Scots and their Irish supporters provoked or inspired set off a further train of explosions.

In these altered circumstances, the lords soon found the need of better and more permanent forces than the existing system could be depended on to provide. They needed professional fighters, and they procured them as rulers before then and since then have procured them, by hiring them from outside. As it happened, their supply was at hand.

Mercenaries for the Irish wars came from Scotland, whence they could readily cross to the northern Irish coast. The western Highlands and the Scottish isles, narrow, mountainous and remote, were poorer areas than Ireland, but they held a relatively large population. Lying open to the sea, they had been invaded and partly settled by the Vikings, whose descendants had mingled with the earlier Gaelic inhabitants to produce a mixed race. This people was loosely organised under the rule of the Lords of the Isles, who, as time advanced, were overcome by their rivals, the kings of Scotland. The pressure of a Scots kingdom slowly growing in power was first felt in the west early in the fourteenth century. After that it was all but continuous. Although the hope of maintaining an independent Lordship of the Isles survived for 200 years more, the late medieval period in the Hebrides, the South Isles and the mainland facing them saw the break up of local institutions, the failure of violent efforts to oppose the Scots state, and the consequent scattering of fighting men.

This was the background of the galloglas, the supply of whom, as such circumstances provided, was equal to the demand. They were mercenary soldiers introduced into Ireland from the Scottish Isles and West Highlands to provide forces that could not be raised among the population of the Irish lordships. The Irish called them foreign warriors because of the Norse strain in their ancestry, just as they called the inhabitants of the territories whence they came Gall-Gael, or foreign Gaels, and the Scottish Isles as a whole Insi-Gall, or the islands of the foreigners. But their origin was as much Gaelic as Norse. Their language was Gaelic, and their new surroundings in Ireland can have been little different from the old ones which they left behind them in the Highlands and Isles.

The first mention of galloglas occurs in the Irish annals under the date of 1290, but there is evidence to show that such Scots warriors had been coming to Ireland for half a century and more before that. This mercenary trade was greatly encouraged by the Bruce invasion, and it continued to flourish after the Bruces and their army had gone.

The galloglas, or at least the leaders of them, belonged to a limited number of Norse-Scottish families among the members of which mercenary service became hereditary—the MacDonalds, MacSwineys, MacSheehys, MacDowells, MacRorys, MacCabes and others. They served first, as would be expected, in Ulster, where they assisted the O'Donnells and O'Neills in their wars. By the middle of the fourteenth century they had spread to Connacht, where the O'Connors, and later the Mayo and Clan-rickard Burkes and the O'Kellys, employed them; by the fifteenth century the MacSwineys were serving the O'Briens in Thomond, the MacSheehys and another branch of the MacSwineys were in Desmond, there were more MacSwineys in Ormond, and the MacDonalds had got as far as Leinster, where they were settled as galloglas in government employment (it had come to that) in Tynekille in Co. Leix.

There are many sixteenth-century descriptions of these gallo-glas. We know that they were strong and skilful fighters, and that they wore, for the most part, shirts of mail over quilted or padded jacks or aketons, and that they had skulls, bascinets or helmets of iron or steel. Some had hoods or tippets of mail to protect their necks and shoulders. Their characteristic arm was the axe or sparth, and it is said to have been in their hands a deadly weapon. According to the descriptions, it was most frequently—perhaps uniformly—a pole axe; one writer says: 'Their weapons are one foot in length [he was thinking of the measurement of the heads of the axes alone], resembling double bladed hatchets, almost sharper than razors, fixed on shafts of more than ordinary length, with which when they strike they inflict a dreadful wound.' Another calls the galloglas the 'lustiest men' of the Irish, and says that they were 'armed chiefly with staves, headed somewhat like unto battle axes'. Still another says

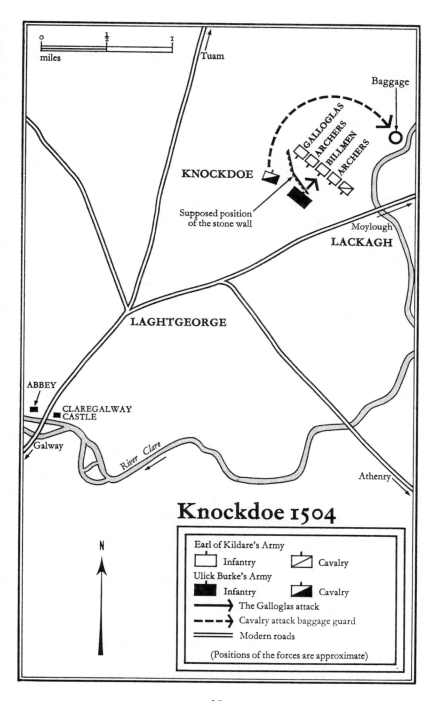

miles

Tuam

Baggage

GALLOGLAS

ARCHERS

BILLMEN

ARCHERS

KNOCKDOE

Supposed position
of the stone wall

Moylough

LACKAGH

LAGHTGEORGE

ABBEY

CLAREGALWAY
CASTLE

Galway

River Clare

Athenry

Knockdoe 1504

N

Earl of Kildare's Army
☐ Infantry   ▱ Cavalry
Ulick Burke's Army
■ Infantry   ◨ Cavalry
→ The Galloglas attack
--→ Cavalry attack baggage guard
═══ Modern roads

(Positions of the forces are approximate)

that 'they bear sparths in their hands instead of staves'. Each galloglach was ordinarily accompanied in action by two boys, one of whom carried his armour, the other his provisions. 'For the most part,' we are told, 'their boys bear for them three darts apiece, which darts they throw ere they come to the hand stripe', or to hand-to-hand fighting. Darts and javelins, and not arrows, were the traditional Irish missile weapons; we see from this that they were combined with the armoury of the galloglas to lend missile force to the shock strength of the newcomers. Irish darts, at the end of the sixteenth century at any rate, were 'much less and lighter' than English javelins. The Irish could at that time handle them nimbly and throw them steadily, although the range of their casts may not have equalled that of some Central Africans of the last century, whose aim was accurate for a distance of fifty yards. The Irish, says Dimmock, could 'cast with wonderful facility and nearness'; their darts could not pierce armour, but they could bring down horses and wound and sometimes kill unarmoured men. Like the javelins which the Mexicans used so widely against Cortez' Spaniards, the Irish weapons could wound extensively rather than fatally.

Eighty of these redoubtable mercenaries, or, with their auxiliaries, 240 fighters in all, were reckoned in each battle or battalion of galloglas. Their armour was, in the age of the development of the plate armour that succeeded mail, antiquated, but it was none the less effective. Their weapons, derivatives—as was remarked even in the sixteenth century—of the Norse axes of their Viking ancestors, must have been as good as the bills that were carried by the contemporary English footmen, and that were then, with bows, the national English weapons. The broad socketed iron axeheads were readily made by the Irish smiths. The addition of these heavily equipped warriors to the armoured men of the kind whom the O'Briens brought into action at Dysert O'Dea, the O'Connors at Athenry and other Gaelic leaders elsewhere stiffened the native forces. The galloglas, fierce professional foot fighters, counter-balanced the successors of the invincible Norman knights. By the fifteenth century, when they had spread through the island into those places the rulers of which were warlike enough to employ them, they had revolutionised Irish military affairs. They settled on the land in many areas, and this without losing their fighting character. Indeed— so profound was the conservatism of the Gaelic world—they changed very little in their spread from generation to generation across Ireland; it was as though the Irish in bringing them in, and they themselves in coming in, had exhausted the possibilities of innovation. The galloglas received recruits from the population which they served, but they remained to the end predominantly of Scots origin, and they retained to the end the arms and equipment of their beginnings. They were the 'castle of bones' referred to by an Anglo-Irishman in the fourteenth century. Better, said this man, a castle of bones than a castle of stones; better a battalion of galloglas in the moving warfare of the fields than a fixed position of defence behind walls.

The greatest battle fought by these professional axemen was Knockdoe. The protagonists in this contest were Gerald Fitz-Gerald, the Great Earl of Kildare, on the one side and his son-in-law, Ulick de Burgh, or Burke, of Clanrickard on the other. The Earl had with him a force from Dublin and the English Pale, including his own Kildare retainers, and he was assisted by the Mayo Burkes, the O'Donnells, some of the O'Neills, the Mac-Mahons, Magennises, O'Reillys, O'Connors, MacDermots and others, both Gaelic and Anglo-Irish, drawn from the northern half of Ireland—the Leath Chuinn of ancient designation. Ulick Burke was supported by his neighbours, O'Brien of Thomond, the Macnamaras, O'Kennedys, O'Carroll of Ely and other Munster warriors—men, that is, from either side of the lower Shannon basin, and all from Leath Mogha, or the southern half. These forces may have totalled 10,000 or more, with the balance in favour of Kildare.

The battle was fought on 19 August 1504 on a hill appropriately named Knockdoe, or the hill of axes, eight miles north-east of Galway town; a low hill that stands prominently above the flat and pleasant countryside through which the river Clare winds towards Lough Corrib.

Poynings' Parliament, held in 1494, as well as stamping Ireland as an inferior state, as it did in the eyes of later patriots, provided that no Irish subject should make war or peace without the special icence of the king's representative. There were to be no more aristocratic faction fights such as had paralleled on the Irish side of the water the wars of the roses on the English; no more Irish hostings, which were a specialty of the Irish situation. War cries like the FitzGeralds' *Crom abu* and the Butlers' *Butler abu—abu* being simply 'above'—were interdicted. If a man, in lawful battle, had to cry up some name, then let him call on 'St George, or the name of his sovereign lord, the King of England for the time being'; henceforth no battles could be lawful but the king's battles.

Since Gerald FitzGerald represented the king, Knockdoe was not openly a faction fight; but the veneer of legality was thin. It was not fought, said a seventeenth-century writer, 'by warrant from the King, or upon his charge, but only upon a private quarrel of the Earl of Kildare: so loosely were the martial affairs of Ireland carried during the reign of King Henry the Seventh'.

Gerald was, said the Irish, 'a knight famous in deeds of arms, royal and just in word and judgement'. He was a descendant of the Maurice FitzGerald of Strongbow's invasion, the head of the great house of Kildare, and the strongest man in Ireland. The king of England, governing Ireland with increasing forcefulness but insufficient funds, found him indispensable. If the Earl was not permitted to rule Ireland, he could prevent anyone else from ruling it; the only alternative to his flamboyant and dangerous independence in administration was government by an English-born Deputy, with an English retinue, and that was impossible because it cost too much.

Kildare clearly loved power and sought throughout his career to exercise it: the power of his house, which was founded on his great estates; on the support of the officers of the Pale, whom he kept in office; on the armed force of the Pale, which he organised; on the assistance of many Gaelic lords, which he steadfastly cultivated; but, above all, power founded on the king. The Earl succeeded in holding on to his office even when Henry VII, the first of the Tudors, overthrew and killed his earlier patron, Richard III, at the battle of Bosworth in 1485. The office of king's Deputy was dear to Kildare and he was well content to enjoy the fruits of it; he made no bid to win the kingship of Ireland for himself. He was present when the pretender, Lambert Simnel, was crowned king of England in Dublin, and apparently would have been willing to make good Simnel's claim if he could, but he never sought to place a crown of Ireland on his own head. We, from our far off vantage point, can look back and see that the reality of kingship, which Kildare possessed, could not have been left indefinitely to his house. What he looked forward to we do not know; perhaps even an Anglo-Irishman might believe with the Gaelic lords that things could go on as they were for ever.

Kildare was called to order after the Simnel interlude, when Sir

Richard Edgecombe came to Ireland in 1488 to limit his power. He was deprived of his Deputyship in 1492. Two years later Sir Edward Poynings' famous Parliament attainted him of treason and overturned his system of government. He was imprisoned in the Tower in 1495. As when Parnell was gaoled in Kilmainham four centuries later, violence replaced him. There was none who could keep the peace in his absence from Ireland and from power, so that we may well believe the story of King Henry's change of purpose and of his outcry—'He is meet to rule all Ireland, seeing all Ireland cannot rule him!' In 1496 Henry restored the Earl to office, and on the eve of the battle of Knockdoe he was as strong for the moment as he had been before.

The Earl had many friends among the Anglo-Irish and Gaelic lords, and some enemies. Knockdoe saw their collision. It saw too the explosion of feuds that had agitated the west of Ireland for generations.

The de Burgh, or Burke, family, the greatest Anglo-Norman house in Connacht, had been for long divided in two branches, that of MacWilliam of Clanrickard, with territory in Galway, and the branch of MacWilliam of Mayo. Like many Irish lords who were neighbours, the two MacWilliams were intermittently hostile, the one towards the other. In 1503, on the death of the leader of the Mayo branch, Ulick Burke, lord of Clanrickard, attacked his neighbours, the O'Kellys, who were in alliance with the Mayo Burkes. In the following year Ulick demolished three O'Kelly castles. Melaghlin O'Kelly appealed to the Great Earl for help against him. Although his own daughter Eustacia was Ulick Burke's wife, the Earl proved sympathetic. Had Burke perhaps—as was suggested—been maltreating the daughter, or did the king's service demand that the father-in-law's feelings be suppressed? Was the Earl putting the law in motion against those who had broken the king's peace by levying war? We do not know. At any rate, the Earl resolved to chastise Ulick, Ulick determined to make a fight of it, and both sides mobilised.

The O'Briens of Thomond were old allies of the Clanrickards, and Ulick's mother was an O'Brien. Turlough O'Brien, their leader, was, said the Great Earl, 'a mortal enemy to all Englishmen', and was, as well as that, the 'most maliciously disposed' person he had ever heard of. Turlough supported Ulick with the full power of his lordship. So did the Macnamaras, from the area that lies between the present Shannon airport and Limerick;

Ulick's first wife was a Macnamara. Ulick's other allies, the O'Carrolls of Ely and O'Kennedys of Ormond—who lived across the Shannon from Clanrickard—carried with them the ends of an earlier feud in which they, with the O'Briens and Ulick, had supported Sir James Butler, the Great Earl's enemy. All of these were old companions in arms.

Ulick Burke's ambition and the Great Earl's power made Knockdoe a battle the like of which, say the Irish annalists, was not fought 'in latter times'. At some time in the early part of 1504, probably early in the summer, Ulick seized the town of Galway. Galway was founded in the thirteenth century by Ulick's ancestors, who remained its overlords and patrons for 200 years. Since 1464, however, the townsmen were empowered by royal charter to forbid entry to all save the king's representatives. Ulick, who no doubt wanted to revive the prerogative claims of his house, was therefore an intruder by force. This and the demolition of his neighbours' castles show his independence and his determination to strengthen himself for the tussle with the Great Earl.

How seriously Gerald FitzGerald regarded the war in the west may be judged from the forces which he brought against Clanrickard. He had wide personal associations with the Ulster lords and had helped to arrange their affairs for many years. They now stood by him. The O'Neills, who were represented in his host by the tanist or successor designate of their lordship, were—like Ulick Burke—his relations by marriage. His sister Eleanor, who died in 1497, was the wife of Conn Mór O'Neill. Conn was killed by Henry O'Neill, his brother, in 1493 and the succession in Tyrone was thereafter in dispute between Henry and his family and another brother whose name was Donal. The Great Earl backed Conn Mór's sons, who eventually triumphed over the factions of their uncles, one of them, Conn Bacach, being made O'Neill in 1519 and Earl of Tyrone in 1542. The other great Ulster lord, O'Donnell, who came to the hosting in person, was the foster father of the Great Earl's son. The O'Donnells were old allies not only of the principals in the dispute, the O'Kellys and MacWilliams of Mayo, but of another Connacht lord, O'Connor Roe, who accordingly joined them. Others from Ulster who were present with their forces were Magennis from Down, MacMahon from Monaghan, O'Hanlon from Armagh, and O'Reilly from Cavan. MacDermot from Roscommon, O'Farrell from Longford, and O'Connor from Offaly—to name for each the modern county where his lands lay—were present too.

It was a remarkable hosting. It was, as far as we know, the most varied, if not the greatest, muster of the Irish Gaelic lords and their forces that ever took place, a rally comparable for Ireland with those of Bannockburn and Flodden and of the '15 and the '45 for Scotland. It was a tribute to the greatness of the Earl of Kildare, and proof positive of his power.

With all these elements was combined another. Poynings' Parliament had authorised the king's Deputy to 'go with the King's power against those who will not submit to justice'. The Great Earl accordingly had with him the Anglo-Irish forces of the king. These were a small professional body of about forty spearmen and eighty archers, forming the standing force of the Irish Lordship; the muster of the four counties of the Pale; two urban forces, one raised by the city of Dublin, the other by Drogheda; and his own retainers, including his mercenaries, from the Kildare lordship. No figures are given for the strength of any of these bodies. Even that quoted for the first is uncertain. The Great Earl was allowed forty spears and eighty archers in 1480, but there seems to be no evidence to show whether this strength was maintained in subsequent years. He asked the king in 1498 to send him 300 English archers and 60 gunners, 'to be waged at the charge of me and others of my friends in this country'; there is no indication that he received them. Whatever bodyguard of this kind the Earl had as the king's Deputy was a small one, consisting of spearmen and archers, most—if not all—of whom may have been Englishmen, the only Englishmen on the field at Knockdoe. The spearmen were the degenerate sixteenth-century form of the medieval knights, demi-lances, or horsemen less heavily armed and armoured than their predecessors; the triumph of the English longbowmen had led to the eclipse of cavalry by a combination of billmen and bowmen. Although the Deputy's archers are described as mounted men, they used their horses on the march only; their fighting was done on foot.

The muster of the Pale was led by the Anglo-Irish magnates, by Sir Robert Preston, Viscount Gormanstown, the Lords Barnewall of Trimlestown, Fleming of Slane, St Lawrence of Howth, the Plunketts of Dunsany and Killeen, and others, including 'the Great Darcy' of Platen, on whose lofty shoulders Lambert Simnel, the 'organ-maker's son', was carried after his coronation in Christchurch in 1487. Many of the Palesmen were related to the Great Earl. Some years before this, under the leadership of the FitzGeralds of Kildare, they had organised a force of 63 spears and 160 mounted archers, drawn from Counties Dublin, Kildare, Meath and Louth and held in permanent readiness to assemble for the defence of the Pale. This was the Guild of St George, which in 1473 became the Fraternity of Arms and was paid for out of public funds, and which has been called a FitzGerald standing army. The Fraternity was abolished by the crown in 1475, but was restored under the captaincy of the Great Earl in 1480. Whether it still existed in 1504 is uncertain, but there is no doubt that a body like it, supplemented by the billmen that a general muster would produce, formed the basis of the Pale force at Knockdoe. The Palesmen were ordered fifty years after Knockdoe to provide 'a convenient and warlike ensign with a red cross of St George therein' to be carried before the mustered men of each of the Dublin baronies. In all probability similar flags proclaimed the English origin and allegiance of the Palesmen who accompanied the Earl. The two town contingents, of Dublin —which was led by the Mayor, John Blake—and Drogheda, were no doubt also made up of the contemporary infantry types of billmen and bowmen. In Dublin in 1493 a municipal grant was made to arm the citizens with bows and arrows.

The Great Earl's own force of retainers and the muster of his tenants from Kildare were added to these. They included the mercenaries whom we have already met, and whom we shall meet again, the galloglas. Early in his career Gerald FitzGerald employed twenty-four galloglas who had come to him from Connacht; he kept them permanently quartered in Kildare. Later he increased their number to 120. The MacMahons of Oriel had to support 160 more galloglas for him. Undoubtedly all of these, and possibly more, were with him now.

The occasion produced one novelty, a significant one, in view of future developments. Knockdoe was the first Irish battle in which firearms were used. Guns had been known in Ireland for a long time before that. The first reference to a gun in an Irish context appears to be as early as the middle of the fourteenth century, when it is recorded that one was sent from England to Dublin; but the first specific mention of the discharge of a gun in the Irish wars does not occur until 1487 when one was used by an O'Donnell to shoot an O'Rourke at Castlecar in Co. Leitrim. The

Great Earl, who met his death from a gun shot in 1513, was a keen artillerist. He used the king's guns to demolish the castles of the king's—and his own—enemies from 1488 forward, when he battered Balrath Castle in Westmeath. He dragged them to Dungannon in 1498 and used them against the Connacht castles of Athleague, Tulsk, Roscommon and Castlerea in 1499. The Knockdoe firearms were not, however, cannon. It is most unlikely that the Earl brought cannon with him in 1504. If he did, there is no reference to their use in the battle. A handgun, which was the original type of hand firearm, is, as we shall see, mentioned at Knockdoe; from what we know of the Earl's use of handguns, we may infer that some of his men bore them there, and thus introduced them to the Irish battlefields. They may have been German guns. A force of 2,000 German mercenaries sent to Dublin by the Duchess of Burgundy to aid Lambert Simnel in 1487 seems to have been the first one in Ireland to carry any considerable number of firearms. They went to their defeat at the battle of Stoke in Nottinghamshire, but two years later—had he coveted them when he saw them with the Germans?—six handguns were sent from Germany as a present to the Great Earl. They were 'a great rarity' in Dublin as his sentries bore them outside his house of Thomas Court. They may well have been borne later to Knockdoe.

The Palesmen marched westward about the beginning of August in a year in which, as we might note, Francesco d'Almeida went with fewer men to make the Portuguese the masters of the Indian Ocean. It appears that their allies from Ulster, north Connacht and the north midlands had joined them before they left O'Kelly's country and entered Clanrickard. According to the chronicle of the St Lawrence family of Howth, which is the only reasonably full account of the expedition that we have, they held a council of war.

The Baron of Delvin was for deeds rather than words. He was not one who 'could utter his stomach' with 'a glorious tale'; but he promised to be the first to cast a spear at the enemy when it came to action. His promise is interesting. In 1498 the Irish Parliament had ordered the Anglo-Irish to use English weapons, that is, swords, bows, arrows, crossbows, bills and guns, and to carry bucklers and pavises, or archers' shields. The Palesmen, said the enactment, had 'taken to casting darts and spears' in imitation of the Irish, and this despite the fact that 'they had not the profound way and feat of it', as they found to their cost when they pitted themselves against those who had. They should stick to their own weapons. The Baron of Delvin had not, apparently, heeded the advice. Lord Gormanstown was cautious; he believed 'a hasty man never lacked woe', and that they might 'put the whole realm in hazard' if they were beaten. The Lords of Killeen and Trimlestown agreed, saying that they were outnumbered six to one. (The reverse seems more likely.) But St Lawrence of Howth, says his chronicler, believed that they were committed to action. They should prepare to fight, he said, and should put their 'battles in perfect order this night, that every man shall know tomorrow his charge'. The Irish also were combative.

So was the Great Earl. In view of what we know of his leanings towards the Gaelic system, and of what we have said of the mercenaries, his action at this time is significant. He called the captain of his galloglas, saying that 'he and his shall begin this game for it is less force of their lusties than it is of our young men' —or, that the captain's lusty warriors would require to expend less force in overcoming their opponents than would the young men of the Pale. And the captain acted his part. 'I am glad', said he. 'You can do me no more honour, by God's blood!' and he grasped his axe and began to flourish it. Fighting was his trade.

They moved further westward and encamped on the evening of 18 August. Either then or on the day before that, while the council was being held, 200 of the enemy's horse came in sight. The Earl's son, Garret Óg, then a youth of seventeen fresh from the London where he was later to be executed, wanted to attack them. They restrained his ardour. Early on the morning of the 19th they drew up in battle array on Knockdoe.

Presumably they faced westward, towards Galway and towards Lough Corrib, behind which, shadowy in the morning light, were the mountains of Connemara. Our information is scanty. We cannot be sure which army was drawn up first. Probably the Earl's was, since he seems to have had time to arrange his forces as he wished. He kept the Palesmen and the Irish separate, drawing up the former in the usual English manner, that is, the manner best suited to the use of the English weapons which they carried. He placed the billmen in the centre, to form his main battle, under the command of St Lawrence of Howth; and on either wing he placed archers, one wing under Gormanstown, the other under Killeen. This was the usual formation in the infantry battles of the time, the function of the billmen being to 'fix' the enemy's attack while the bowmen, as was hoped, shot it to pieces.

Extending across the Earl's front and for some distance to his right was 'a little wall of two foot height' made by the people of the place 'for safeguard of their corn'. To us this is an interesting addition to the evidence of the use of field boundaries in an age and place in which so many writers have claimed there were none. It is of interest also to know that, even then, Knockdoe was a place where corn was grown; it is so still and it is remembered that in the last century there were seventeen ricks of corn in the haggard of the 'big house' the ruin of which crowns the hilltop. To the Great Earl, however, the wall was a topographical feature to be turned to his advantage. Although it gave some little cover to his main battle, it interfered with the free use of his horse. In order to avoid it, he placed all his cavalry, under Delvin, over on his left, beyond the bowmen. He stationed 'the galloglas and the Irish in another quarter'. Where? Presumably on his right wing, to form a flank there as the cavalry did on the other side. It seems unlikely, in view of his intention of letting them 'begin the game', that his own galloglas were in this part of the field— even though the Scottish Gael would have regarded it as the place of honour. His main battle was first engaged, and his galloglas, with their sanguine captain, may have stood there with the billmen. The Howth chronicler makes St Lawrence declare that the galloglas 'shall not be mixed among us'; but this seems to be an interpolation of a later age when the Earl's debt to his Gaelic allies was forgotten and Knockdoe had come to be looked upon as a battle in which, as Holinshed puts it, 'in effect all the Irish rebels of Ireland were gathered against the English pale'.

The Earl's son, Garret Óg, commanded the reserve, which also acted as a baggage guard, and which was posted somewhere behind the main battle. The total force present on the Earl's side can scarcely have been less than 6,000; we have no contemporary figures to help us and can arrive at this arbitrary statement of strength only by allowing something for each of the many contingents involved.

Ulick Burke's deployment was simpler. He may have come on to the field later than the Earl; doubtless he kept between his enemies and Galway, so that his men looked into the rising sun—unless it was a wet August and a grey morning. He drew up his footmen in one great battle facing the Earl's centre, and he placed his horse on his left, facing the two-foot wall. Almost certainly, despite the Howth chronicler's claim, his was the weaker of the two armies; perhaps he had 4,000 men. As with the Earl, he led what was predominantly an infantry force. Knockdoe was a foot fight.

On either side there were galloglas, the armoured veterans whose advent had changed the character of the Irish wars. This was their specialty: a fixed battle, indeed the greatest that they were ever to see. On the Great Earl's side there were the Kildare galloglas, who were MacDonalds, and all the mercenaries that his Gaelic allies had sent or brought. For service such as this, at an unwonted distance from their homes, it is almost certain that their warriors were mostly galloglas—the O'Donnells' MacSwineys; the O'Neills' MacDonalds; the other lords' waged men of other Hebridean families. And there must also have been in the Earl's force the galloglas of O'Connor Roe, who were MacDonalds, and of MacWilliam Burke of Mayo, who were MacDonalds too and MacSwineys as well. On Ulick Burke's side there were the galloglas of the MacSwineys of Clanrickard, and—with the O'Briens—of the MacSwineys of Thomond. It was characteristic of the mercenary service that different branches of the MacSwiney family fought impartially on either side. The O'Briens, who five years previously had captured 'sixteen score' of what the annalists call *lúireacha* or mail shirts from the Butlers of Ormond, must have been able to muster many men in armour.

Ulick Burke attacked. The chronicle says that his men had spent the night 'drinking and playing at cards', playing to decide 'who should have this prisoner and that prisoner'. If they had done so it had not sapped their energy. They showed themselves full of fight when their galloglas moved forward. On the other side the Earl's men, or some of them, may have heard his oration: 'here is against us great numbers of people without weapons and without wisdom or good order. They march to battle as drunken as swine to a trough. . . . Remember—all that we have doth rest upon this day's issue, and also the honour of our prince. And remember how we are in a country unknown to the most number of us, and far from our towns and castles.' The record suggests subsequent amplification, or, it may be, invention. Yet the Earl may have expressed such sentiments; after all, Ian Hamilton in a more material age inspired the troops who were about to attack at Elandslaagte in 1899 with a prediction of what 'the little newsboys in the streets of London' would cry out about them on the following morning.

The Earl's men stood waiting, or perhaps we may believe the story which tells of the Baron of Delvin's making good his promise to strike the first blow. He was with the horse, we remember, on the left wing. It is said that Delvin, 'a little before the joining of the battle', spurred forward—like Sir Henry de Boune at Bannockburn—and cast his spear into the forces of the enemy, killing one of the Burkes. This may be a dramatisation of an abortive attack by Delvin's cavalry. Whatever part Delvin played, if any, the onset of Ulick's galloglas was not stayed.

As their attack gathered impetus, the galloglas vented three great shouts that might, with the sight of their terrible axes, have daunted less resolute opponents. But the bowmen on the wings of the Earl's battle were not daunted. They shook out their sheaves of arrows, and as rapidly as they could pick them up, fit them, and draw their bowstrings they let fly a shower of death that thinned the ranks of the galloglas and broke the force of their attack. Still, many reached the billmen, and in the surge of an attack resisted the fight was joined.

MacSwiney, captain of the Clanrickard galloglas (individuals, as always, attract the chronicler's attention), cried out for the Great Darcy, the only opponent worthy of his notice. Darcy stood forth and they fought. MacSwiney struck him to his knees with a mighty blow on his helmet. Nangle of Navan, another Palesman, took Darcy's place and 'gave MacSwiney such payment that he was satisfied ever after'.

'They fought terrible and bold a while', bill and spear and sword against axe and javelin and knife. The bills and axes, long-shafted and needing to be swung, with long, cutting blades needing a wide sweep, were clumsy weapons in a mêlée; the bills perhaps, particularly in the hands of men who were not professionals, the clumsier. The whole strength of footmen on either side seems soon to have become engaged. The Irish annalists, laconic, formally poetical, inexperienced in the ways of war, have done their best for us: 'heard afar from these bands were the battling of the battle-heroes and feats of the champions and rush of the royal-heirs, and thunder of the troops and bruit of the bands imperilled; the courage and impetuosity of the youths and of the striplings and the enthusiasm of the brave men in their falling, and the prevailing of the nobles over the lowly.' All accounts speak of a dour struggle, lasting for hours; a collision of two forces ready to give blow for blow until one was beaten. There is no indication of manœuvre, no evidence of what the Earl's Gaelic allies did, little about the use of the horsemen on either side. But the meagre accounts bear out to the letter what the sixteenth-century writer Richard Stanihurst says of the galloglas, whom he calls 'men of great stature, of more than ordinary strength of limb, powerful swordsmen, but at the same time altogether sanguinary and by no means inclined to give quarter'; Stanihurst continues: 'In every sharp and severe engagement, should they come to close fighting, they either soon kill or are killed'.

Some time during the day at Knockdoe the tide turned. Ulick's men, who had been stopped, and then held by the Earl, were born back. Their casualties mounted, until, as the annalists say—expressing it all in their few words—in 'the place wherein were nine battalions of galloglas in compact array of battle, there escaped not alive of them but one thin battalion alone'. Nine battles, or battalions, reckoning two auxiliaries to each galloglach, would have made up over 2,000 men.

Whether all who were engaged fought with the same determination as the mercenaries we do not know. There is only one reference to the use of a gun—to its use, not to the firing of it. When a Clanrickard horseman came riding among the victors and called out to know who had the Earl and the lords of the Pale prisoners, we are told that a Dublin soldier 'struck him with a gun with both his hands and so beat out his brains'. If there were other handguns carried, and we may be sure there were at least a few, they can have had little effect on the issue. Gunpowder was still weak. But guns would in due course oust bows and bills and axes, and it adds to the interest of Knockdoe that it is the first Irish battle in an account of which a gun is mentioned.

The horseman's unexpected query may be explained by the activities of Ulick's cavalry. Perhaps they fetched a circuit to clear the end of the wall, or perhaps they were unwilling to encounter the Earl's Gaelic allies, whom we suppose to have been on the wing opposite them; at any rate they rode round their enemies' position and, having done so, fell on the baggage. That is their sole recorded contribution to events. Garret Óg, who had been left with the reserve to guard the baggage, had abandoned his post to follow the victory, and Ulick's horse had easy pickings. Possibly the bemused horseman, entering the fight from the rear, thought that the victory over what was left of the baggage guard was part of a general one.

The remains of Ulick's force almost certainly retired towards Galway, or to the south. The traditional account of the fighting, part of the folklore of the area, speaks of last stands at various crossing places of the river Clare, which flows southward and then westward around the foot of the hill; it may preserve a memory of the scattering of a composite force, each element of which might try to retire towards its own home, but the main retreat appears to have been in the direction of the victors' subsequent advance. The vanquished 'gathered again, and said they would give to the Earl another field', but in fact they were routed. They must have suffered heavy casualties. The Palesmen, exulting later on, put their enemy's losses as high as 9,000, which certainly was much greater than their total force. Even Sir James Ware's seventeenth-century estimate of 2,000 may be exaggerated; yet suffer the Galwaymen and their allies did. 'It was impossible', said the annalists, 'to put an estimate on the slain horsemen, or on the footmen there, so that the field became uneven from those heaps of slaughter, with the multitude of spears and of swords, and of battle-shields, and of corpses cross-thrown, confused, and of slain youths stretched stark-dead, and of gillies beardless, loathsome, unsightly'. The language is stylised, but so, if it comes to that, is death on a battlefield.

The Great Earl too lost 'many multitudes'. He encamped on the field to rest his forces and to rally those scattered in the pursuit. On the day following he marched to Galway. Entering the town in triumph, he bestowed thirty tuns of wine on his men.

In a sense the battle had been fought for Galway. The town of the carousal of the victors was the first fruit of victory, and Athenry, where they went next, was the second. The preservation of these places from the control of a forceful local lord may well explain the king's approval of what had been done. That he did approve seems certain; he made Gerald FitzGerald a Knight of the Garter in the following year. What the Galwegians thought of the events leading up to Knockdoe and of its issue is not, perhaps, so clear. They had been strengthening their defences, and they continued to do so. They saw in Gerald a lord stronger than Ulick, and, moreover, the king's representative. They probably welcomed him with enthusiasm. Ulick Burke vanished temporarily, leaving two sons and a daughter in the Earl's hands, that is, in their grandfather's hands, if they were Eustacia Fitz-Gerald's children.

The storm subsided. The Great Earl had had his way. Much later, when his house was in ruins and there was no great Irishman with a foot in both camps to hold both peoples together, the issue at Knockdoe was modified to match national antagonism. It became a victory of the Palesmen over the rest. It was said that the Earl, on being asked on the field where a particular band of Gaelic warriors should serve, said, 'Marry, let them stand by and give us the gaze'. And it was said that Viscount Gormanstown wanted, after the victory, to improve on the occasion by killing 'all the Irishmen that we have with us'. These seem later sentiments, the sentiments of an age in which a battle like Knockdoe, which settled little, was old-fashioned and in which war was waged to the death—the death of Gaelic Ireland.

The account of the battle which appears in the manuscript known as the Book of Howth, and which has been so frequently referred to in the foregoing, is published in the *Calendar of the Carew Manuscripts*, V, pp. 181 ff. The original manuscript, written about 1544 and later, is in the Lambeth Palace Library, London. Other accounts are in the *Annals of Ulster*, III, p. 469, the *Annals of the Four Masters*, V, p. 1277, and Sir J. Ware, *The Antiquities and History of Ireland* (1705 edn)—Annals of Ireland, Henry VII, p. 47. For the Great Earl see D. Bryan, *Gerald Fitzgerald, the Great Earl of Kildare* and for Poynings' Parliament A. Conway, *Henry VII's relations with Scotland and Ireland, 1485–98*. I have given the history of the galloglas in my *Scots Mercenary Forces in Ireland* (1937) and an account of their weapons in 'The Gallóglach Axe', published in the *Journal of the Galway Archaeological and Historical Society*, XVII (1937), pp. 101 ff. Further information about the Kildare galloglas is given in the *Journal of the Royal Society of Antiquaries of Ireland*, new series, II, pp. 274 and in the *Ulster Journal of Archaeology*, first series, II. The 'castle of bones' reference is in Sir J. Davies, *A Discovery of the true cause why Ireland was never brought under obedience of the crown of England* (1787), p. 148. For early Irish firearms see my paper 'The Early History of Guns in Ireland' in the Galway Society's *Journal* already referred to, XVIII (1938), pp. 43 ff, and for a good account of firearms in general W. Y. Carman, *A History of Firearms* (1955). This last book may also be consulted with profit regarding types of firearms used in later Irish battles. Similarly, T. Ropp, *War in the modern world* (1959) will be found readable and useful for a general survey of developments in warfare from the fifteenth century forward. His bibliography, contained in his footnotes, is invaluable. For the sixteenth-century changes in European warfare following the decline of feudalism, see F. Gilbert's essay on Machiavelli in E. M. Earle, *Makers of Modern Strategy* (1944).

The reference to the Great Earl's saying of the Irish 'let them . . . give us the gaze' is in R. Holinshed, *Chronicles of England, Scotland and Ireland* (1807–08), VI, p. 277. Perhaps we should not take the annalists literally when they speak of nine battalions of galloglas. The numeral may indicate a great, rather than an exact, number; compare the reference in the Annals of Loch Cé under date 1559–60 (II, p. 377) to a defeat of the Earls of Thomond and Clanrickard: 'all the constables of Tuadh-Mumha were slain there. Nine standards of the descendants of Domhnall-na-madhmann [he was a MacSweeney who flourished in Co. Galway at the beginning of the fifteenth century] were lost there'.

The capture of armour from the Butlers by the O'Briens in 1499 is recorded in the *Annals of Ulster*. There are good sixteenth- and early seventeenth-century representations of the dart, the characteristic Irish weapon, in D. B. Quinn, *The Elizabethans and the Irish* (1966), Plates 7 and 9, and see also pp. 23, 99. For a hitherto unpublished picture of a man carrying two darts see Plate 9.

Farsetmore, 1567

When Shane O'Neill, who was known and is remembered as the Proud, visited Queen Elizabeth I in London in 1562 we are told that 'the courtiers, noting his haughtiness and barbarity, devised his style thus: O'Neill the great, cousin to St Patrick, friend to the Queen of England, enemy to all the world besides'. They thought him a figure of fun, dressed in his outlandish Irish mantle and trews, speaking the Irish tongue, and leading his grim galloglas whom they 'followed with as much wonderment as if they had come from China or America', into the splendid presence of their sovereign; but they were also a little afraid of him. They were afraid because O'Neill's strength, which rested on the sovereignty of peoples and places remote and unknown to them, might be greater than it appeared, and because he himself was so obviously not afraid of them. They saw that he was in mien and manner as great as he was in fame.

Before Shane went to London the Earl of Sussex, the Irish Lord Lieutenant, had tried to have him assassinated, thus showing how dangerous England believed him to be. When that attempt and the invasion of Tyrone, which Sussex also tried, had both failed, every effort was made at the Queen's express wish to bring Shane into the royal presence. As time went by it became clearer that it was in the interest of both parties that he should go. Each was an autocrat and each was ambitious. They shared the hope that at close quarters the greater or the more subtle would overawe or outwit the less, and they were both optimists. The Queen desired O'Neill's submission because he stood in the way of her sovereignty in Ireland; O'Neill wanted the Queen's backing against his rivals at home because they stood in the way of his sovereignty in Ulster.

There was a possibility of manœuvre, but fundamentally their interests conflicted, and in the long run it was the Queen's interest that won. England was wealthier and more powerful than Ireland, and her wealth and power were more fully organised. In the face of her consequent superiority, and while material considerations ruled, no obstacle to English supremacy within these islands could be permanent. The rule of Ulster by a survivor of the Gaelic world of the past—like the rule of the Isles by Lords independent of the kings of Scotland, and like the rule of Scotland as an independent kingdom—must give place to the ultimate rule of Great Britain and Ireland by the successors of the Queen. But when this cousin of St Patrick came home his defeat was not quite so apparent. He had promised much, as became a subject, but he seemed to have lost nothing as an independent lord. For one thing—and it was no small thing to the parsimonious Queen— he got away with the huge sum of £2,500 that had been lent to him to pay the expenses of his journey. Shane held that it had been 'given him to buy his peace', and he never returned it. 'Nothing', said a later statement, 'had ever the Queen for it again, saving his head'. She got his head following his defeat at Farsetmore, a battle fought on 8 May 1567, and a defeat inflicted on Shane O'Neill not by the forces of the Queen, but by his Ulster rivals the O'Donnells.

Shane, the leader of the powerful O'Neill house and the claimant of the hegemony of Ulster, was, as he said himself, 'the true and legitimate son and heir' of Conn Bacach O'Neill, first Earl of Tyrone, who was the son of Conn Mór. His facetiously alleged relationship to the national apostle was a tribute to his Irishness, but his relationship to the Earls of Kildare was a fact. Speaking of the other Irish lords, Shane said: 'I am in blood and power better than the best of them, and will give place to none but my cousin of Kildare, for that he is of mine house'. The Great Earl's daughter was either Shane's mother or his stepmother, and the Great Earl's sister was Conn Mór's wife, that is, she was Shane's grandmother. It was thus in the spirit of his Geraldine forbears as well as the consciousness of the glories of his own house—and with much too of the aggressiveness of one whose inheritance is in jeopardy—that Shane cried: 'My ancestors were kings of Ulster and Ulster is mine and shall be mine'.

These were fighting words, all the more so because they expressed a determination rather than stated a fact. There were obstacles to Shane's overlordship. Even his leadership of the O'Neills was disputed. Matthew, who was another son of Conn Bacach's, but—men believed—an illegitimate one, was recommended by Conn and was preferred to Shane by the English for succession to the Earldom. After Matthew's death in the struggle for lordship with Shane, Matthew's eldest son Brian inherited his father's claim and the Queen's support. Brian also was killed. Brian's brother Hugh remained. Hugh, later to become the second Earl of Tyrone and an even greater O'Neill than Shane, was carried off to England, where, during the rest of Shane's life, he remained. His existence was a permanent threat to Shane; he was a rival unassailable, one who might be indoctrinated at leisure and returned by the Queen to Ulster as required.

And Shane had other enemies. These included the O'Reillys of Cavan, the Maguires of Fermanagh, the O'Donnells of Donegal, and the Antrim Scots. 'He yoked and spoiled at pleasure', said his enemies, the lords of Ulster, 'and by his cruelty and power did against their wills subdue them and force them to yield to his insatiable and detestable tyranny', but these lords, whose territories lay around the borders of Tyrone, rejected Shane's yoke and struggled against him.

The Antrim Scots, who were a branch of the MacDonalds of the Western Highlands and Isles, were different from the rest. They were the Queen's enemies as well as Shane's. They had found a foothold in the Glens of Antrim following the marriage about 1400 of Eoghan, brother of the Lord of the Isles, to the Scoto-Norman heiress of this beautiful and secluded land that seems so much a part of sea-cleft Scotland. Later marriages with ladies of the O'Donnells, the O'Neills and other Irish families strengthened them. The same reasons that had caused the influx of the original galloglas from Scotland urged further MacDonalds and their followers—MacNeills, MacAllisters, MacKays, Magees and others—across the narrow sea, and by the sixteenth century their numbers, and with them their pretensions, had greatly grown. They had begun to press westward towards the Bann. Their strength, said Sir Henry Bagenal, who was a neighbour of theirs living in Newry, and who wrote in 1586, was uncertain, 'for that they are supplied as need requireth from Scotland, with what numbers they list to call, by making of fires upon certain steep rocks hanging over the sea'. They had a foot in Scotland and a foot in Ireland.

The Queen regarded them as intruders. 'We take it for certain', she said, 'that the best way were, if time and other opportunities might serve us, to suffer no Scot to have any habitation or abode in Ireland.' But opportunity did not serve. The Queen was not

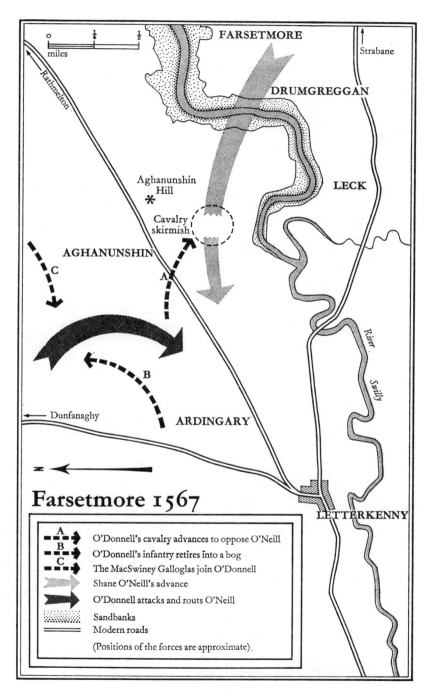

miles

FARSETMORE

↑ Strabane

Rathmelton

DRUMGREGGAN

LECK

Aghanunshin
Hill
*

Cavalry
skirmish

AGHANUNSHIN

C

A

B

← Dunfanaghy

ARDINGARY

River Swilly

N ←

Farsetmore 1567

LETTERKENNY

A ➤	O'Donnell's cavalry advances to oppose O'Neill
B ➤	O'Donnell's infantry retires into a bog
C ➤	The MacSwiney Galloglas join O'Donnell
➤	Shane O'Neill's advance
➤	O'Donnell attacks and routs O'Neill
	Sandbanks
	Modern roads

(Positions of the forces are approximate).

strong enough to oppose at the same time both the Scots and Shane O'Neill. She permitted English raids on Antrim in 1551, 1556 and 1557. Then she blew cold instead of hot. By 1559 when Shane had become dangerous she had ceased to treat the Scots as 'foreign enemies' and she no longer spurned them when they sought to 'reconcile themselves' to her 'grace and favour'. She temporised. When Shane grew hostile again after his return from London she continued her policy of frosty friendship and the Scots tried to stand neutral; but they found that they could not do so. They were as much in Shane's way as the English were. This time it was Shane who attacked them; he claimed, possibly following a promise made while he was in London, that he was acting 'in the Queen's service against the Scots, who are her Majesty's enemies and the usurpers of her territory'. In reality, in this triangular war, it was each for himself, or herself—Shane, the Scots and the Queen.

And the Queen's Scottish problem was more than an Antrim one. By this time the galloglas, who were the original Scots immigrants, were beginning to lose something of their monopoly as mercenaries. Forces of purely native origin were now being hired and supported by the lords. These may have been an imitation of the galloglas; at least they were an answer to the same call for manpower that had brought in the galloglas. Since they were billeted on the peoples of the lordships, mercenaries in general, including galloglas, were properly called *buannadha*, or billeted men, a term anglicised as bonnaghts. This name was, however, usually applied in the sixteenth century to the native mercenaries, and we have come to regard it as exclusive to them; hence the reference in the song to what the poet regards as two distinct types of warrior, the 'Bonnaght and gallowglass' who, we are told, thronged from each mountain pass. These native mercenaries swelled the ranks of the opponents of the Queen. So did a fresh wave of freelance fighters from Scotland who were called simply 'Scots'. Just as the earlier wars had summoned the original galloglas from their Highland and Island homes, the gathering momentum of sixteenth-century strife in Ireland called in these 'new Scots'. They came principally to Ulster, although many served in Connacht as well. They made seasonal excursions from their homeland, crossing to the Ulster shore in their galleys, fighting for reward, and returning to Scotland when their time of service had expired.

There were thus, by Shane O'Neill's time, three distinct types of mercenaries employed by the Irish, of whom the Scots were one; and these Scots were, many of them, of the same families as the Scots of Antrim. The annalists, speaking of a hosting of 1562, tell us that it included 'three hundred Albanachs [Scots] and gallowglasses'—here were the two types: the original Scots mercenaries and the new sixteenth-century ones. When, in 1561, they specify that another host was made up of 'gallowglasses, mercenaries and Albanachs' they mention all three types, including the native bonnaghts. The Queen's hostility to the Antrim Scots was part of a larger hostility to Highland and Island Scots in general who, in the time of the unity of the old Gaelic world, crossed the sea to co-operate with the Irish. If Shane crushed the Scots she would grudge him the victory; but she would rejoice in their defeat.

Shane commenced operations against the Scots in the autumn of 1564, when he built a fort at the mouth of the Bann and raided the MacDonald territory to the east of that river. In the following May he attacked them in force. Summoned from Cantire by the warning fires, James MacDonald of Dunyveg, leader of the Clan Donald of the South Isles, joined his brother Sorley Buidhe of Antrim in opposition to Shane; but the MacDonalds' efforts to save themselves were vain. Their enemies fell on them near Ballycastle early on the morning of 2 May and cut them to pieces. Shane's count of the Scots dead reached 700. Said he, 'God, best and greatest, of his mere grace, and for the welfare of her Majesty the Queen, gave us the victory against them.' James MacDonald was mortally wounded and Sorley Buidhe captured. Shane had not, as he later claimed, 'killed and banished all the Scots out of the North', but he had dealt them a heavy blow. As for the Queen, she could not resist the temptation to turn the new situation to her advantage. She ordered that Alexander Óg MacDonald, a surviving brother of the dead James and the imprisoned Sorley, who had offered to serve against Shane, should be treated with 'good words and reasonable entertainment'. His thirst for vengeance on O'Neill made him, as the sequel showed, an ally worth having.

All this was the background of the battle of Farsetmore and of the downfall of Shane. He had two more years to live, following his victory over the Scots, and they were his years of greatness, a greatness that flowed from his forceful personality and his military strength. We are told of him, most significantly, that 'he armeth and weaponeth all the peasants of his country', and that he was the first Irishman to do so, or, as another observer puts it, that he 'furnished all the peasants and husbandmen of his country with armour and weapons, and trained them up in the knowledge of the wars'.

There was a clear distinction in the Irish communities of the sixteenth and earlier centuries between those people who were described as free and those who were unfree. The unfree people were the tillers of the soil in the lord's demesne and the demesnes of his sub-chieftains, and all those workers and poor folk who had no title to any part of the community's land, in other words, the 'peasants and husbandmen', the 'churls', and the 'poor earth tillers' who are so often mentioned by contemporaries. Like the unfree portion of the urban population of the time, they no doubt accounted for the greater part of the whole. They were, by tradition, prohibited from carrying arms. Only the freemen assembled at hostings and formed the rising out; and that this was so also in Gaelic Scotland is suggested by the statement that the workers in the fields were not permitted to leave the Isles on warlike expeditions lest the crops might be uncared for in the absence of the fighting men, who might 'bide forth ane whole year, as oft-times it happens when any of their particular islands has to do with Ireland or neighbours'. This was the custom from which Shane O'Neill departed. In his efforts to increase the numbers of his forces beyond what the rising out of his freemen and the assembly of all available mercenaries could supply, he made soldiers of a class not hitherto called to the wars. He militarised 'the ploughman that never bare weapon'.

Shane's strength when he overthrew the Scots was about 2,000 men. He had, in preparation for the campaign, employed as mercenaries 'gunners, galloglas and all other men of war that he conveniently can get', and had asked 'to have licence for the Queen's galloglas to serve him', although that request was refused. With so many lords bidding against each other for their services, and since the state was an employer as well, mercenaries were not always easy to get; hence Shane's militarisation of his own people. He was, said Sir George Carew, 'a prudent, wise captain, and a good giver of an onset or charge upon his enemies during the time of his reign, and was given from fourteen years of age till the day of his death always in the wars. . . . He had great policy in the wars that he was practised with, no man more in his time.' Although some said that 'he was the last that would give the charge upon his foes, and the first that would flee', Carew believed that 'he could well procure his men to do well, for he had many good men according to the wars of his country'.

Shane, like other Irishmen of his time and later, suited his methods of fighting to his enemies. His victory near Ballycastle—or the battle of Glenshesk, as it has come to be called—and his defeat at Farsetmore were engagements in the open, each decided by blows; but when Shane fought the forces of the Queen rather than those of his neighbours he was more cautious. When Lord Lieutenant Sussex and the English marched in pursuit of him through the woods between Dungannon and Lough Neagh 'from eight of the clock in the morning till seven afternoon O'Neill never gave over to skirmish with them. All that while the woods so rang with the shot that it was strange to hear, and also the noise of the Scots [mercenaries] that O'Neill had, crying all that day till a little afore night.' He used here the tactics of the ambush, tactics that were at least as old as the Norman invasion and that were given a new lease of life by the introduction of firearms. We shall hear more of them, for they were employed with ever increasing success in the Ulster battles during the later part of the century. The point is that Shane and his Gaelic contemporaries waged pitched battles among themselves but used a different kind of warfare, a warfare in which they made the countryside fight for them, when their opponents were the better armed and formally trained professionals of the Queen. They were aggressive and vigorous enough when they knew what was opposed to them, but they were cautious when caution was required. If the art of war is, as the great Moltke says, the practical adaptation of the means at hand towards the attainment of the object in view, that is, the defeat of the enemy, the sixteenth-century Irish were no mean exponents of it.

Shane's best troops were still the galloglas, although the Scots, when he could get them, were good material too. His antagonism to the Antrim Scots, although it interfered to some extent with his supply of Scots mercenaries, did not preclude it. Not all the mercenaries from Scotland were MacDonalds, or friends of the MacDonalds.

The Irish annalists' account of Shane's invasion of O'Donnell's country in 1557 introduces us to a camp of the Tyronemen in which there were troops of many different kinds, drawn from different places. So mixed were they and so recently had they come together that two of O'Donnell's spies could mingle with them without fear of detection, moving freely among the tents and booths and from fire to fire, and even taking a share of the rations of meal and butter. Since there were renegade O'Donnells in the camp, who might recognise their own, the spies selected for the mission were not Donegalmen but a Maguire from Fermanagh and a MacAilin, who was probably a Campbell from Argyll. These two penetrated to a great central fire which blazed at the entrance of O'Neill's tent, and close to which flamed a giant torch 'thicker than a man's body'. Here stood the guard of 'sixty grim and redoubtable galloglas, with sharp, keen axes, terrible and ready for action, and sixty stern and terrific Scots, with massive broad and heavy-striking swords in their hands, ready to strike and parry'. These were some of the 'six hundred armed men' by whom, said the English, Shane was continually guarded; it was as though he was 'the Great Turk' and these were 'his Janissaries'. He was credited at the height of his power with the ability to bring huge forces into the field. One account says that he had a thousand horse and 4,000 foot; another gives him 'of Scots and Irish seven thousand men that wear weapon'.

Mention of Shane O'Neill's gunners reminds us that the use of guns, in Ireland as elsewhere—and in remote Ulster as in the more accessible parts of Ireland—increased as the sixteenth century progressed. The O'Donnells used the guns of a French ship to batter the castles of their enemies in 1516. Later on they got guns from Scotland. Calvagh O'Donnell in particular had the use in 1555 of a Scottish weapon called the 'gonna cam', or crooked gun, which may have been merely an arquebus or hand-gun with a curved stock. This was sent to him by the Earl of Argyll pursuant to a 'contract and mutual bond' made between them in that year, an agreement that has the form of a treaty entered into by independent powers, although Calvagh, for his part, and as the document records, was at that time 'deprived of the Lordship of Tirconnell'. The Earl undertook to lend Calvagh 'a gun for breaking walls'—which would have been something heavier than an arquebus—and to supply him with mercenaries, in return for which O'Donnell was to pay 400 Scots marks a year to Argyll as 'a token of submission and service, and as a perpetual tribute for ever'. The O'Donnells had used guns against their enemies in Connacht in 1527 and 1536, and the king's artillery was used against them by the Earl of Kildare, that is, the Great Earl's son, in 1524. One of the charges made against this Earl in 1537 was that he gave the king's guns, powder and shot 'to wild Irishmen, being the King's mortal enemies'. We know that the Irish got further supplies from the towns. A Galway by-law of 1517, for example, which prohibited the sale of guns or ammunition to them, indicates that, even at that early date, there was such a trade.

Early cannon which were thus employed in Ireland were, as far as we know, ordinarily used against castles, and not in the field. The use of field guns in Ireland in the sixteenth century was very rare. Hand firearms were, as time went on, slowly improved. A new type called an arquebus or hagbut, which was the first matchlock, was brought in at the beginning of the century to supersede the original handgun, and Shane's gunners, who helped as we are told to ambush Sussex near Armagh in 1563, were arquebusiers. Although these new weapons were still scarce in Shane's time and the great mass of his men still carried axes, spears, swords, javelins and bows as their forerunners of earlier times had done, the Queen's army had no monopoly of firearms. Heard first at Knockdoe, guns crackled and roared in ever increasing numbers on later Irish battlefields. 'As for gunners', said an Englishman of the Irish in 1543, 'there be no better in no land than they be, for the number [of guns] they have, which be more than I would wish they had.'

After his defeat of the Scots Shane behaved with increasing confidence in himself as, in the language of Sidney, a 'monstrous monarchal tyrant of all Ulster'. He tried to win support in Edinburgh, where his clipping of the wings of the Highlanders might not necessarily be regarded as a hostile act; he was later accused of entertaining the notion of marrying Mary, Queen of Scots. He wrote to Charles IX of France to ask for 5,000 or 6,000 troops to help him to expel the English from Ireland, and he wrote to the Cardinal of Lorraine to request his support on religious grounds for this petition to the king. But in all that he did, no matter how far he might look outside Ireland, his real anxiety was to strengthen himself at home. For him the only realities were Ulster realities; he was the last of the Provincial Kings.

In 1566 the new viceroy, Sir Henry Sidney, strengthened Shane's enemy O'Donnell and by doing so weakened Shane. The

Queen was by then determined that 'such a cankrid dangerous rebel' as Shane must be 'utterly extirped'. The small effect that 'her gentle, favourable and merciful dealing with him hath wrought in his cankered and traitorous stomach' had years before this been noted. Now it seemed more apparent than ever. The Queen reinforced Sidney with 300 arquebusiers from the Scottish Border post of Berwick and 700 men newly levied in the West country, and she authorised him to raise 200 horse and 200 foot in Ireland to add to his existing force. Thus strengthened, Sidney was ordered to back O'Donnell, defend the Pale, and do what he could to prevent Shane from employing more Scots and galloglas. He was to take the field at harvest time, when he could do most damage in Tyrone.

Sidney's plan of operations was ambitious. The English reinforcements, coming from Northumberland and Bristol, were to meet at the Isle of Man, where Edward Randolph, Lieutenant of the Ordnance, was to take command of the whole force. They were to go on by sea to Lough Foyle, where they were to land and entrench themselves. Meanwhile Sidney was to bring up the Queen's Irish forces, including the rising out of the Pale, and was to march through Tyrone and join hands with Randolph. Between them they would reinstate Calvagh O'Donnell, who was at enmity with Shane and well disposed towards the Queen, and also Maguire, whom Shane had ejected from Fermanagh; and if they could bring Shane to action they were to engage him.

Sidney and Randolph joined hands in September 1566. Sidney's force consisted of 200 horse and 1,200 archers and arquebusiers from the Pale together with 100 horse, 300 galloglas and 92 'gonners' from Desmond. Thereafter O'Donnell was left in control of what is now Donegal, Randolph remained in garrison in Derry, and Sidney marched back in triumph through Connacht. It appeared that what was the first of several combined operations against Tyrone had been successfully completed. But Shane, although his power was restricted by these movements, remained largely intact. While Sidney was in Ulster Shane had kept out of his way. His forests hid him. He would neither treat nor fight; nor could Sidney, for all the strength that he showed, force him to do either.

When Sidney had gone Shane attacked the Derry garrison; although Randolph was killed the troops held out without much difficulty. In the spring of 1567, however, disaster overtook them, disaster of a kind that became increasingly common as the use of firearms spread. Their powder blew up, killing many and causing the withdrawal of those who survived. That was in April. In May Shane, relieved for the moment of anxiety regarding the English, struck at his remaining Ulster enemy. His campaign against Derry had weakened him, and it was said that 'the rebel lost the most of his best footmen, as well galloglas as shot' in the fight in which Randolph was killed, and that 'many of his Scots for that day's work left his service'; but he showed his old arrogance and his old vigour.

The O'Donnells had been goading him, not indeed without provocation on his part. They were led in Shane's time first by the elderly Manus, next by Calvagh, who was Manus's son and Shane's father-in-law, and then, on Calvagh's death in October 1566, by Calvagh's brother Hugh. Shane claimed to be their overlord. Theirs was, said Sidney, 'as great a country as his'; but it was a country 'on which he totally tyrannized', holding as he did that 'there should be but one king in Ulster for the future'. When he had invaded their territory in 1557 the O'Donnells had surprised his camp and ignominiously routed him; but he soon turned the tables on them. In 1559 he captured Calvagh and his Scottish wife, Catherine MacLean. He might thereafter, as the annalists say, 'have been called with propriety the provincial King of Ulster, were it not for the opposition of the English to him'. When Calvagh was ransomed and conditionally released in 1561 he naturally turned to the English for support, and they as naturally indulged his expectations of it.

Calvagh must have hated his son-in-law. Before his release Mary, who was Calvagh's daughter and Shane's wife, had 'died of horror, loathing, grief, and deep anguish in consequence of the severity of the imprisonment inflicted on her father in her presence', and in consequence too, no doubt, of Shane's unnatural conduct in cohabiting with Catherine, his wife's stepmother, 'so that she bore children unto him'. When old Manus O'Donnell, whose uncertain existence during his declining years was a sad reminder of the eclipse of his house, died in 1563, Calvagh tried without success to shake off O'Neill's yoke. Three years later, as we have seen, Sidney restored him in control of his lordship. Within a month he was dead. His brother Hugh succeeded him, and, so little had he been intimidated by Shane's aggression, immediately raided Tyrone. In the spring of 1567 he repeated his attack and 'totally ravaged the whole neighbourhood' of Strabane. Again we remind ourselves that this Hugh, the new O'Donnell, was Shane's sister's son.

Shane retaliated. Mustering what must have been a large army, he marched westward, intending still another invasion and another chastisement of Tirconnell. He came to the southern shore of the estuary of the river Swilly. Hugh O'Donnell was at Ardingary near Letterkenny, on the other side of the river, where he held a fort with a small body of his men. He knew that O'Neill was advancing against him, and he had sent out messengers to summon his forces to defend their homeland. Either his men were slow in assembling, however, or Shane was too quick for them. None of the defenders had arrived when, at daybreak on 8 May, the Tyrone men were seen advancing in squadrons of horse and battalions of foot towards Farsetmore, or Fearsad Suilighe, the great ford of the Swilly which lay below Ardingary. The river is tidal for some distance above this place, but, this being the hour of low water, O'Neill's army, which soon reached the ford, passed over the sandbank which there constricts the flow of water without difficulty. It was an historic place. Here, where the river forms the boundary of the parishes of Leck and Aghanunshin, the Tirconnell men had defeated the Tyrone men in 1098. Here too, in 1392, peace had been made between the rival lordships, their two armies standing ready for another eventuality on the opposite banks.

O'Donnell was strong enough neither to contest the crossing nor to defend his position at Ardingary, but he was determined not to allow O'Neill to advance into his lordship without a fight. He drew out his little force, and, taking the footmen himself, made off as quickly as possible across flat ground to a position amid bogs where he was, for the moment, secure from attack. He sent his horsemen under the command of his son, who also was named Hugh, towards the ford, with orders to do what they could to delay O'Neill's progress. He wanted to gain time for his expected host to assemble.

Young Hugh had as stout a heart as his father's. He attacked the vanguard of O'Neill's cavalry. In the tussle which followed many notables fell on either side, but O'Neill's superior numbers told. Feeling himself borne back, but noting too that his father had by now reached his objective in the bog, young Hugh retired and the little Tirconnell force stood reunited. They awaited the arrival of their supports.

The first to come up to help them was Murrough MacSwiney, the leader of one of the three septs of the galloglas of Clan Swiney that served the O'Donnells, that is, the sept of na dTuath. He was followed by the sons of MacSwiney Fanad, leading the galloglas of their sept, which was the senior one, and later by Maolmuire MacSwiney Baghaineach, leader of the third sept. The Irish annalists, who are partial to O'Donnell rather than O'Neill, and so would magnify his victories, claim that these galloglas, together with the body which they joined, made up no more than 400 men, and that this was O'Donnell's full force. This is unlikely, in view of what followed. Other warriors, not mentioned by the annalists, may have joined as well. Even if there was a greater numerical reinforcement than is recorded, however, the implication of the entry in the annals is that the defence of Tirconnell was undertaken almost entirely by the mercenaries, which suggests that, at this time, the O'Donnells and their followers were not a warlike people. Manus O'Donnell, the father of the elder Hugh, was, we are told, the first to billet bonnaghts on church land within Tirconnell. This is evidence of an attempt on the O'Donnells' part to build up a military force, but Shane would have seen to it that theirs was not a militarised lordship like Tyrone.

Yet the O'Donnells were a spirited people, and their blood was up. Shane had, for the past ten years, treated them abominably, and they were resolved to die rather than remain longer subject to him. Greatly outnumbered as he was, Hugh O'Donnell prepared to attack.

O'Neill had pitched his camp to the north of the estuary, evidently at Ardingary. As was the practice then, when there were no towns to take, no accumulations of wealth to seize, no means of grappling with the elusive force of an enemy, he would enforce his will on Tirconnell by entrenching himself within it and dragooning it. A few weeks' systematic raiding had reduced it before, and should reduce it again.

Hugh, his men arranged in a formation unspecified, descended on O'Neill. We are told that O'Neill had warning of his approach, and that he drew out his force to meet him. Of O'Neill's men it was said: 'Fierce and desperate were the grim and terrible looks that each cast at the other from their starlike eyes; they raised the battle cry aloud, and their united shouting, when rushing together, was sufficient to strike with dismay and turn to flight the feeble and the unwarlike'. So speak some of the reporters whom Professor Cyril Falls, sighing for description where description is lacking and speaking for every modern historian, calls 'the infuriating annalists'; and yet so often it is such near-poetry or nothing at all. Once again, as with so many Irish battles, all detail is lost. We know that on one side was 'a venomous phalanx', on the other men with 'starlike eyes'. We are left to imagine the rest.

The infantry part of the battle must have been like Knockdoe. Farsetmore was not a surprise, and so there must have been a line of battle on Shane's side as well as a column of attack on Hugh's. Weapons were still sparthes or galloglas axes, spears, swords, javelins—which the English considered 'more noisome [that is, annoying] than deadly'—and bows. There were undoubtedly many more gunners present than at Knockdoe, gunners armed with the arquebus. Helmets were worn and targets, or round shields, were carried. Such armour as there was was old-fashioned. The jack or coat of canvas or leather into which were stitched small plates of iron was, we know, worn at that time in the Pale, and no doubt some of the warriors at Farsetmore had jacks; but the medieval mail shirt must have predominated.

The horsemen in the Irish battles appear to have fought separately from the foot. Horse fought horse, and this was as much evidence of the class distinction so noticeable in the proud, aristocratic Gaelic world as a matter of tactics. A picture map of a battle fought near Ballyshannon in 1593 shows O'Donnell's cavalry drawn up in a long column to the left of his footmen. We remember that Clanrickard's cavalry at Knockdoe was also on the left, and we note that John Derrick's picture of 1581 'which showeth the fatal end aright of rebels to our Queen' places them similarly. The horsemen were 'armed in mail with pesantses and skulls', that is, they wore mail shirts and had iron helmets and pizaines, which were collars, or perhaps tippets, of mail. As 'light scourers', or skirmishers, said a writer of 1543, there were 'no properer horsemen in Christian ground, nor more hardy, nor yet that can better endure hardness'; but they were essentially light horse: their mounts were small and 'they were more ready', said Lord Deputy Perrot, 'to turn upon the hand, to shake and some-times to charge with their spears above hand, than to come close to the charge, or strong to endure the shock when they were charged.' As another Elizabethan writer, John Dimmock, puts it, 'They ride on pads without stirrups. In joining battle they do not bear the lance under arm, and so put it to the rest, but, taking it by the middle, bear it above the arm and so encounter'. Their chief weapons were lances, the so-called horsemen's staves (one writer calls them half pikes) and they held them, as Dimmock and others remark, overarm like javelins, not couched at the hip as the English did. They used spurs but no stirrups, and they had pillions, or as Dimmock calls them pads, secured by surcingles and straps around the breasts and hindquarters of their horses rather than real saddles; so that they were but lightly seated on the animals and could not stand the shock of charging or being charged.

Such were the warriors of Farsetmore, where Shane suffered, as Sidney says, 'the slaughter of many of his principal horsemen'. Once joined in battle the two forces fought it out, blow for blow. 'They proceeded', say the annalists, 'to strike, mangle, slaughter, and cut down one another for a long time, so that men were soon laid low, heroes wounded, youths slain, and robust heroes mangled in the slaughter.' They must have fought for some hours. In the end O'Neill's men drew back. Worsted and pursued by O'Donnell, they made sullenly for the estuary; but the tide had now risen, the sand was covered, and to recross was not the simple matter it had been to come over. The fugitives were 'driven for safeguard of their lives to take the great water of Lough Swilly, where the most of them, man or horse, were drowned'. A sandbank in the estuary is still called the Marcaghs' (or horsemen's) bed and is shown as a place which became the grave of many horsemen who fell there. They may have been some of the dead of this battle.

The misfortune in the estuary completed the rout of Shane O'Neill. The annalists give 1,300 as their estimate of his loss in killed and drowned, and they mention the claim of other reporters that his total casualties were as great as 3,000. The English estimate is more conservative. Sidney told the Queen that 613 men were 'found dead'. Two grandsons of Shane's fell. So did MacDonald, the leader of his galloglas, with many of his axemen, and Dubhaltach O'Donnelly, Shane's foster-brother, and 'the person most faithful and dear to him in existence'. Great numbers of the O'Donnellys fell, and of the O'Hagans and the O'Quinns and other Tyrone septs. The Tirconnell men had the spoils of victory—horses, arms, armour; everything that was in O'Neill's camp.

Shane escaped. He went upstream to a ford near Scarriffhollis, some two miles west of Letterkenny, where, on another sad day for the O'Neills, Coote broke the remains of the Catholic army of Ulster in 1651. He crossed there, guided by a party of the O'Gallaghers who were renegades from the Tirconnell camp, and made his way back to Tyrone.

The annalists say that after Farsetmore Shane's 'reason and senses' became deranged. His actions certainly suggest it. He sent to Scotland to ask the MacDonalds of Cantire to come to help him, and Alexander Óg, whom we have met, and who was, we remember, the brother of the James whom Shane had mortally wounded at Glenshesk, and who had since died, and of Sorley Buidhe, who was still Shane's prisoner, came over. Alexander had already been negotiating with the English to serve as a mercenary against Shane, and Sidney could later claim that it was he who had fetched him to Ireland. That Shane, routed and almost helpless, should put himself in Alexander's power seems madness. Hill, the historian of the MacDonalds of Antrim, suggests that it was Sorley Buidhe who, dissembling motives of family vengeance and perhaps promising mediation, suggested this desperate remedy, and so led Shane into a trap. Perhaps it was. Up to this Shane, if forthright in utterance, had shown himself not devoid of caution. He may have had more reason to trust the MacDonalds than appears.

At any rate he went to Alexander to Cushendun in Co. Antrim. The Scots at first welcomed him and the fifty horsemen who were with him, and they 'fell to quaffing'; but the air where such men as these met was too heavily charged with passion to be long breathed in peace. They quarrelled and fought. Alexander's men fell upon Shane with their 'slaughter swords'—the *Schlachtschwerter* or original claymores, the great two-hander swords of the Highlanders—and 'mangled him cruelly'. They wrapped his lifeless body in 'an old Irish shirt' and tumbled it into a pit. Later his haughty head was 'pickled in a pipkin' and sent to Dublin, where it was stuck up on a spike over the gateway of the Castle. A reward of a thousand marks had been offered for that head; whether it was ever paid and, if it was, who received it are things unknown.

Many claimed credit for Shane's death. Sidney did. Turlough

Luineach O'Neill, Shane's successor, did. Piers, the Constable of Carrickfergus, did. The Queen gave 'thanks to Almighty God by whom we hold and rule all that we enjoy, for his goodness and favour shown in the punishment and extinguishing of such a rebellion so long continued'. Sir John Davies, the Irish Attorney General of thirty-nine years later, was in no doubt of where the credit did not lie. He said that Sidney 'did much distress, but not fully defeat' Shane O'Neill, and that Shane 'was afterwards slain upon a mere accident by the Scots, and not by the Queen's army'.

The only account of the battle of Farsetmore—a brief and unsatisfactory one—is in the *Annals of the Four Masters*, V, pp. 1611 ff. For some local topographical information see W. J. Doherty, *Inis-Owen and Tirconnell*, I, p. 136. There is no biography of Shane O'Neill, but there is a readable fictional account of him, based on some research, in *The Great O'Neill*, by E. Boyd Barrett, published in Boston in 1939. The most penetrating study of his character appears in Professor James Hogan's 'Shane O'Neill comes to the Court of Elizabeth' in *Essays and Studies presented to Professor Tadhg Ua Donnchadha* (ed. S. Pender, 1947), pp. 154 ff.

Quotations from contemporary accounts of Shane which appear in the above are drawn from E. Campion, *History of Ireland* (*circa* 1571); W. Camden, *Hibernia* (with *Annals*, 1610); J. Hooker, in R. Hollinshed, *Chronicles of England, Scotland and Ireland*; Sir George Carew, printed in the *Calendar of the Carew Manuscripts*, V, p. 205; Sir Henry Sidney's remarks in the same *Calendar*, II (1575–88), p. 341, in his *Memoir* in the *Ulster Journal of Archaeology*, first series, and in his letters in A. Collins, *Letters and Memorials of State* (1746); and the Proclamation of 1561 against Shane, printed in the *Ulster Journal* referred to, V, pp. 260 ff.

For the Queen's remarks on Shane see T. ÓLaidhin, *Sidney State Papers, 1565–70* (1962). For the English operations against him see Cyril Falls, *Elizabeth's Irish Wars* (1950), pp. 86 ff. The map of the Ballyshannon battle which I have mentioned is in the British Museum (Cotton, Augustus I, ii, 38), and Derrick's picture is in his *Image of Irelande* (see below). For the military forces in the Gaelic lordships see my 'Gaelic society in Ireland in the late sixteenth century' in *Historical Studies IV* (1963), pp. 45 ff, and 'The Army of Ulster, 1593–1601' in *The Irish Sword*, I, pp. 105 ff. The reference to the fact that Manus O'Donnell 'first began to impose bonnaghts and the like against the churchmen's wills' is in *Irish Patent Rolls of James I* (Facsimile of the Irish Record Commission's Calendar published by the Irish Manuscripts Commission, 1966), p. 383. For the MacDonalds see G. Hill, *The Macdonnells of Antrim* (1873). The distinctive method of riding and of handling the lance practised by Irish sixteenth-century horsemen are shown pictorially in J. Derrick, *Image of Ireland* (1581, reprinted—edited by Small—1883. See Plate 10 herewith and see plates 24 and 28 of H. F. McClintock, *Old Irish and Highland Dress*) and by the cartographer Richard Bartlett (see my *Ulster and other Irish maps, c. 1600*, plate V, facing p. 10). Compare a sculptured equestrian figure at Glenarm Castle, Co. Antrim (Plate 4 herewith) which may possibly have come from Glenarm Friary, and see D. B. Quinn, *The Elizabethans and the Irish* (1966), pp. 98, 169—in which book may also be seen (p. 133) the statement that the ploughmen were ordinarily unarmed.

A tiny picture of 'Oneal kild by the wild Scots' appears on John Speed's map of 'The Invasions of England and Ireland with al their Civill Wars since the Conquest', which was drawn about 1600. It is reproduced in Plate 8. This seems to be the earliest representation (it is far too small to call it a portrait) of Shane. The text of the agreement between O'Donnell and the Earl of Argyll (1555, renewed in 1560) is published in *Scottish Gaelic Studies*, VII, pt. 1, pp. 94 ff (edited, with translation, by John Mackechnie) and (English version) in *Highland Papers* (Scottish History Society), IV, pp. 212 ff, edited by J. R. N. Macphail. This document appears, among papers that have survived from the sixteenth century, to be unique, but there must have been many such formal deeds drawn up in the Irish language. Alas for the losses! How much clearer would be our picture of the old Gaelic world if we had more such documents.

Clontibret, 1595

On 9 September 1883—to leap for a moment over time and space
—Hicks Pasha, who was Commander-in-Chief for the Khedive
of Egypt in the Sudan, marched out of Omdurman with 10,000
men. He marched by the Nile for twelve days and then struck
westwards towards Kordofan. He was under orders to seek and
to destroy the rebel forces of the religious leader known as the
Mahdi. Twelve more days went by, and then he sent back his last
despatch. Thereafter the desert—and the Mahdi—swallowed him.

So far as is known, Hicks, always moving forward, had fought
off the attacks of his enemies for three days; then on the fourth,
which was his last day, his tired, thirsty, frustrated men had walked
into a major ambush. Poor material from the start, worn out by
their days on end of marching and fighting, they were already the
victims of the worst ordeal perhaps that troops can suffer; now
they were rushed, overwhelmed and massacred. None came back;
with them, we may recall, perished at least one Irishman, Edmund,
the newspaper correspondent—and Fenian—son of the famous
Gaelic scholar John O'Donovan.

The human form has not changed, and neither have the limits
of human endurance. Whether he carried the nineteenth-century
rifle or the sixteenth-century caliver, a soldier could stand a
certain amount from an enemy who attacked him on the march—
an enemy who hit him and drew off, lured him on and hit him
again, disappeared only to spring up in his face, closed only to
retire, and retired only to close once more at the weariest, most
waterless, most ammunitionless moment—a soldier, even a good
soldier, could stand a certain amount of that treatment, but no
more. The breaking point came for the Elizabethan conscript as
for the Egyptian fellah. In the sixteenth century as in the nineteenth, and in Ireland as in the Sudan, attack on the march, where
the terrain favoured the attacker and baffled the unfortunate foot-
slogger in the column, was as deadly a tactic as at any time in the
history of war. It was as deadly as it was to be to Elphinstone's

men, who failed to struggle back from Kabul in 1842. It was the tactic of all others that enabled Hugh O'Neill, Earl of Tyrone, and his Ulster allies to build up the most notable series of victories ever gained by the Irish over the English. Attack on the march was the tactic pursued by O'Neill against Marshal Sir Henry Bagenal at and near Clontibret in Co. Monaghan on 27 May 1595.

It is a far cry from Kordofan to Monaghan; yet, just as the Sudan massacre was the start of fifteen years of independent rule for the Mahdi and his successor, so did Clontibret stand at the head of O'Neill's battles and mark the beginning for Tyrone of a period of freedom from outside interference. Clontibret was not a massacre. It was not even an open defeat of the Queen's army, for Bagenal, although he was badly mauled, carried through the operation that he had undertaken; he brought his force—or part of it—into Monaghan and out again, and from Monaghan to Newry. But O'Neill won a great moral victory. He had discovered, at the beginning of his active participation in warfare with the Queen, the way to handle his opponents. He gained prestige; his men gained confidence. Given a wider terrain and the inclination on O'Neill's part to go to extremes, Bagenal might have suffered Hicks's fate. The English administration, amazed at the result of the day's fighting, was frightened of what might happen next.

Clontibret reminds us of Hicks's defeat for another reason. Each was held in its time to be a mystery, the Sudan massacre because there was no survivor to tell of its last mad moments and it was impossible to say with certainty what had happened, the Irish battle because it was a galling reverse for the Queen and must therefore be written off as inexplicable. And the mystery of Clontibret has been deepened by Irish historians, who have fallen more than once into error in writing about it.

Hugh O'Neill, second Earl of Tyrone, who in Shane O'Neill's time was a protégé of the English, became the leader of his people and the ruler of the Gaelic lordship of Tyrone on the retirement of Turlough Luineach in 1593. Hugh was at home in both worlds, English and Gaelic. As a politician he was subtle, as a soldier outstanding, and as an organiser a genius; he was far-seeing, courageous, and resolute. He was as arrogant as his age and place, but he had a capacity for patience unusual even in an Irishman, and he possessed another quality that was certainly a rare one amid the factions and the treacheries of Ulster: he could inspire great loyalty. He was the greatest of the Great O'Neills

1 & 2. Viking weapons from the period of the battle of Clontarf, 1014.

Top: 3. Mounted Norman warriors and archers from the period of the battle of Dublin, 1171 (from the Bayeux tapestry).

Above: 4. A shield-wall of armoured axeman of the same period (Bayeux tapestry).

5. A mounted Irish warrior, period of the battle of Dysert O'Dea, 1318.

6. Manuscript drawing of mediaeval knights, period of the battle of Dysert O'Dea, 1318.

7. Detail of mounted lancers and foot soldiers, period of the battle of Knockdoe, 1504, from a painting of the Florentine school.

8. An Irish horseman of the sixteenth century. As was the usual practice of the period, he is riding without stirrups and carries his lance, or horseman's staff, in an overhand fashion.

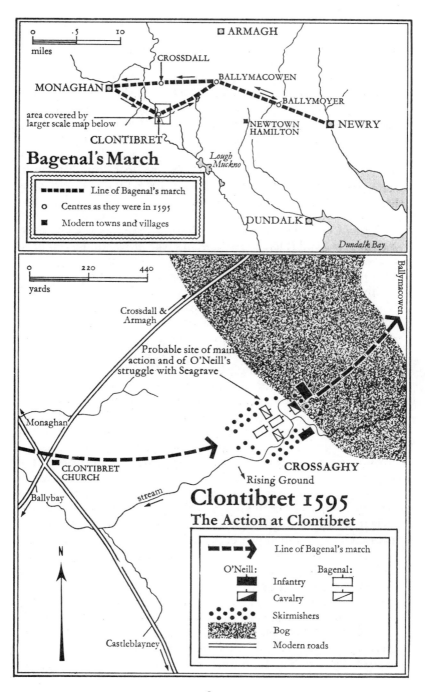

Bagenal's March

- - - - - - Line of Bagenal's march
○ Centres as they were in 1595
■ Modern towns and villages

Clontibret 1595
The Action at Clontibret

O'Neill: Bagenal:

Infantry
Cavalry
Skirmishers
Bog
Modern roads
Line of Bagenal's march

and must rank with Brian Boru and O'Connell and Parnell—and who should we add to these?—as one of the Irish immortals.

In his younger days Hugh seemed a man of promise to the English. If he had supported the Queen—as we see in retrospect—the extension of English authority to Ulster might not have involved plantation; and Ireland might not now be partitioned. Much turned on his attitude and his actions. After deliberation he backed the Gaelic world against the Queen's world, Ulster against London, the past against the future. He lost. But his choice disturbed Ireland for three centuries. It forced the Queen to carry through a military conquest, and when that conquest had been completed it left, instead of a dead past to be forgotten, a living memory to be cherished and to claim increasingly the allegiance of Irishmen, and it left too an abiding fear of reaction to embitter the victors. In this way Hugh O'Neill, by his action in opposing the Queen, denied to her successors the fruits of her victory.

His motives for rebellion were complex. He was not a Wolfe Tone crusading to break the connection with England. He went to war because he saw no other alternative to eventual acceptance of English rule—English rule rather than English suzerainty: the kind of rule that the Connacht lords had accepted in 1585 and that would bring English law and English landholding and the English church into Ulster. His indoctrination in England had not conditioned him to accept that. Like Shane he regarded himself as a king in Ulster, a king with power over sub-kings, and he wanted to maintain his position. Furthermore, he mistrusted the new type of Tudor English administrator; there was, unfortunately for English hopes, a growing list of instances of administrative treachery which put the Gaelic lords on their guard against the servants of the Queen. O'Neill fought because he had come to believe after much delay and much deliberation that it was fight or lose all. The English had not so greatly impressed him with their power that he believed it impossible to gain by using force against them. Some of his allies were in the field before him, others joined in as the fight went on. Their motives were like his in that none of them wanted the old Gaelic order to be changed; but none had his experience, nor could any of them have calculated, as he must have done, the risks.

The Ulster war, which commenced in 1593 when Maguire of Fermanagh raided the newly shired area of Monaghan, was thus a war of defence. The Ulstermen defended their old order against the new one; but they struggled too to make possible a slow development and to prevent a drastic change, for the old order was not stagnant. Theirs was a war often waged in the world's history: the losing contest of the slow mover with the quick.

Yet O'Neill's one hope of success, since he was the slow one and since he could not win by force, lay in prolonging the fight. Thus only could he perfect his military arrangements, and, as he hoped, rouse all Ireland to make common cause with him. Thus only might the English machine be worn down and the Queen, her patience and her resources perhaps exhausted, be compelled to abandon her policy of conquest. A dragging war might outlive her. Better terms might be got from James of Scotland, her probable successor. Spanish help, coming at last, might tip the balance.

O'Neill's defence of Ulster meant keeping English troops out of it. Ever since 1551, when a garrison was first placed in Armagh, the English had believed maintenance of military posts on or near the Ulster border to be the best means of keeping open so many doors into Tyrone. Shane in his time had reacted violently against this practical application of a policy designed to subjugate the north. He had at first refused to go to London to submit to the Queen unless the force which the Earl of Sussex had stationed in Armagh cathedral in 1561 was removed—'and I have more to say on this subject, if it were necessary; but I say this only, that, until you take away your said soldiers from Armagh, I will not go anywhere else, but will, to the best of my ability, by God's favour, defend myself against your unjust war'; but the Queen was equally insistent that that garrison should remain. In the end, the Earl of Kildare persuaded Shane to let her have her way, but in his last fling five years later Shane burnt the roof of the cathedral and pulled down part of the walls to prevent its further use as an English fortress.

Hugh inherited Shane's intransigence. In the interval between the death of the one and the rise of the other the English had crept forward. The Armagh garrison had been moved north to the river Blackwater, which was bridged close to the present Blackwatertown in 1575 or a little earlier. Here, to protect the wooden bridge, and as a frontier post on the highway between Dublin and Tyrone, the Earl of Essex built two works in 1575, an earth fort on the Armagh side and a stone tower on the north bank. Hugh O'Neill's first overt act of war against the Queen was an attack on this post, made in February 1595. He captured the place, destroyed it, and destroyed the bridge. Thereafter, although there were momentary cessations of hostilities during periods of truce or negotiations, the united Ulster which was the product of O'Neill's leadership organised itself ceaselessly for war, and from 1599 until the Queen's death it was open war to a finish, with no respite allowed on either side.

For the first few years it was the Queen's posts in the wilderness, and, more particularly, the forces sent periodically to relieve them, that drew fire. The English had to expose themselves to attack at a disadvantage in their effort to relieve Enniskillen in 1594, when they were routed at the Ford of the Biscuits. Enniskillen was eventually lost. With the loss of the Blackwater fort in 1595 Armagh, which was still occupied, and Monaghan alone remained. Each year brought its problem for the Queen, and the problem of the campaigning season of 1595 was the relief of Monaghan. The ruined Franciscan abbey there had been occupied by the English since 1589, and it had suffered attack from the MacMahons, the lords of the area, in 1593. Now that the Irish raids were, with O'Neill's backing, gaining strength, it was again beset, and its communications with Newry, which was the northern outpost of the English Pale, were cut off. By May the necessity of organised relief was apparent.

The whole marching army of the Queen in Ireland had usually to be employed to convey supplies and reinforcements into these northern posts in the face of a country at war. O'Neill and his adherents were quick to profit by the consequences. To draw their opponents on to ground best suited to their own methods of warfare they had merely to blockade a post and await results. The Queen's isolated garrisons in Ulster thus became, from the Irish point of view, baits to lure her army to destruction. By placing small forces in what was for them the wilderness, where they were bound to get into difficulties, and by sending large forces to relieve them she played into O'Neill's hands. Coerced by circumstances of her own creation, she had to give up the advantages of her experience, her greater wealth, her secure bases, and her superior organisation and to resign herself to fight the war in the Irish way; she had to abandon her men to the ordeal of attack on the march. The relief of Monaghan was the occasion of the march in the course of which the battle of Clontibret was fought.

The English increased the strength of their army in Ireland as this war, which was the greatest yet fought in the island, progressed. An infantry reinforcement of 2,000 men to be drawn from the Queen's army then campaigning in Brittany and a thousand more who were to be raised in England, so many in each of several specified shires, was authorised in 1594. The number of arrivals was, however, somewhat smaller. In April 1595 when the Brittany men came and were paraded in Dublin their strength was less than 1,400. The levies from England no doubt fell short of the proposed effective total in the same way. These newcomers were added as separate companies to the small army of 'old soldiers' which was already maintained in Ireland. The latter, most of whom had seen at least one campaign, were the remains of companies levied on the English shires in earlier years, padded out by Irishmen to bring them up to strength.

The nominal strength of the infantry company in Ireland at this time was a hundred men. Larger companies were employed on the Continent, and when the Brittany men were reorganised in twelve companies after their arrival in Ireland it was found that there were not enough company captains to go round. This was to be a matter of some significance at Clontibret.

Two new infantry weapons had been introduced since Shane O'Neill's time, the musket and pike. More than half the infantry now had firearms and were known collectively as 'shot', These firearms were of two types, the caliver and the musket. The caliver, or military form of arquebus, weighed about twelve pounds, fired twenty or thirty balls each weighing an ounce or an ounce and a half for an expenditure of a pound of gunpowder, had an effective range of less than a hundred yards, and bore a name derived from the French attempt to standardise the calibre of service weapons. The musket was originally a special arm of Spanish origin. Longer than the caliver, it weighed some twenty pounds and was fired from a rest. It had an effective range of about 150 yards and fired from eight to ten balls, each weighing two ounces, to a pound of powder. The average English foot company had four times as many calivers as muskets; but muskets increased in numbers, and grew lighter and more manageable, as time went on. They eventually supplanted calivers.

Crude, cumbersome, and uncertain; slow firing, and wasteful of powder and slow match; the firearms of the sixteenth century nevertheless revolutionised warfare—in Ulster as elsewhere.

The pike, the weapon of less than half the infantry, was also new. It was a long spear with a stout shaft, usually of ash. Its novelty lay in its great length of twelve feet and upwards, and in the drill which, first used by the Swiss, had been evolved for its use in close formation. A revolutionary weapon in itself, the pike has been overshadowed by firearms; but its development in the late fifteenth and in the sixteenth century, when it spread from northern Italy to Switzerland and Germany and from these countries all over Europe, had much to do with the modern rise to prominence of the infantry. Pikes were carried by the strongest men in the company and were held horizontally at shoulder height and with their points depressed for attack in line, or with the butts of their shafts grounded and the points raised to form the characteristic infantry hedgehog—the forerunner of the nineteenth-century square—to resist cavalry or to hold off enemy pikemen. As well as firearms and pikes, halberds and swords were carried; the latter, in combination with targets or round shields, were used for close fighting. The traditional English weapons which were still in use at the beginning of Queen Elizabeth's reign, bills and bows, soon disappeared; bows were no longer used by English troops in O'Neill's time.

Marshal Bagenal's force, which consisted of nineteen companies of foot and six troops of horse and which amounted to some 1,750 men, marched from Dundalk towards the end of May 1595. Bagenal reached Newry on the 24th and marched out again on the road to Monaghan on the day following. His was a full campaigning column, up to available strength, of the best material that could be mustered from the Queen's army. His purpose was not aggression, or even reconnaissance in force. It was simply to escort a convoy of supplies into Monaghan, relieve the garrison there, and bring his column back safely to the Pale.

Bagenal laboured under several disabilities. He had not sufficient senior company officers, and no field officers to lead the infantry; save for Sir Edward York, who commanded the horse, he had no officers of intermediate rank between the company captains and his own staff, which latter consisted merely of himself, his Sergeant-Major and his Quartermaster, both of whom 'managed' rather than led the men. There were only three Brittany captains, Sir Thomas Maria Wingfield and Captains Wilmot and Brett; the remaining Brittany companies were led by subalterns. Although the Brittany companies and the recruit companies marched separately, there is no mention of either category having been regimented. Regiment and colonel—the officer who commanded it—were new words, not always applied with precision, at the end of the sixteenth century, but it is noticeable that no officer of Bagenal's force was called a colonel. Furthermore—although this was a common defect at the time—the recruits were untrained and untried. Much worse, there was a shortage of ammunition.

A contemporary writer reports a conversation which he says took place between one of the Brittany captains and the Lord Deputy, Sir William Russell, before the march began. The captain, believing that the supply of ammunition allotted to the troops was not sufficient, remonstrated with the Deputy, and the latter answered: 'Captain, you are deceived; you are not now in France or the Low Countries, for you shall not be put here to fight as there.' 'Why then, my Lord', asked the captain cogently, 'go we with such forces into the field?' And Russell answered: 'To give countenance to the service you have in hand for the victualling of this fort.' The march, if this was so, was to be a showing of the flag; and Russell, who had marched to Fermanagh and Cavan and back in the previous year without meeting opposition—although under far different conditions—might well have thought the Marshal strong enough to overawe O'Neill by the appearance of his force. Perhaps Hicks, with his memories of victory in India and Abyssinia, thought similarly of the Mahdi in 1883.

The Queen's army marched into a trap. The road from Newry to Monaghan led westward to Ballymoyer, or the Eight-mile Church, near the present Newtown Hamilton, Co. Armagh. Even then there were roads or tracks. Except in very favourable circumstances, in open country and with guides, troops on the march had to keep to these defined ways; beyond them lay bogs, thickets, forests, and the rough and treacherous ground of an undrained and overgrown countryside. Progress along the accepted routes was difficult enough; outside them—at any rate for an army—it would have been almost impossible. Bagenal encamped at Ballymoyer, where the way lay over the Owenduff stream.

At this stage Hugh O'Neill made his first appearance. He rode up with a troop of horse to reconnoitre the camp. The English beat the alarm and Sir Edward York went out with his horsemen to face the Irish. O'Neill drew off and crossed a river, perhaps the

Owenduff. York came up and they held a parley, O'Neill on one side of the water, Sir Edward on the other. According to a contemporary report, O'Neill said that by ten o'clock next morning 'it should be seen whether the Queen or they should be masters of the field and owners of Ulster'. Shane couldn't have done better.

On the 26th the march was resumed. It was apparently without incident until the column came to Crossdall, four miles from Monaghan. Here O'Neill again appeared, this time with a considerable force, and began an attack on the weakest part of the column, the vanguard, where the raw companies were. Bagenal was marching in the usual three divisions of vanguard, battle and rearward. He himself marched with the rear, possibly because he expected it to be the danger point; he had made no appointment of officers to command the other two sections. Consequently, when the attack began the company captains in the van were undecided what to do. The column was halted, the captains conferred among themselves, and one of them, Captain Richard Cuney, seems to have been chosen to act in command. Cuney, who led one of two Staffordshire companies which were present, a company in which musketeers predominated, drew out a skirmishing force of 150 or so shot and pikes and ordered it forward. The Irish meanwhile closed in in large numbers and pressed on boldly with seven or eight companies of foot detached from their main force. As they came up, they were seen to have 300 shot clad, as the Lord Deputy later reported, in red coats 'like English soldiers'.

This was the first surprise of many for Bagenal's men. While he was still loyal to the Queen, O'Neill had been given six English captains to train six companies of Tyrone men for action, as was intended, against the Queen's enemies in Ulster. These were the so-called 'Butter captains', named from an important item in the dietary of the Irish soldiers. It was said that, by constantly changing the men who served under these captains, O'Neill had secured instruction for many more than the contemplated 600. No doubt the Irish redcoats at Crossdall were some of the Butter captains' men. Some horsemen, relics likewise of the time of O'Neill's loyalty to the Queen, were to appear later.

The column, it seems, did not remain halted for long. Bagenal, who must have closed up before he stopped the rear, did not come forward. He was a brave and a determined man, but no great soldier. Incidentally, to keep up the tradition of the relationship of the opponents which is such a curious feature of Irish battles, he was O'Neill's brother-in-law. Captain Cuney and the vanguard appear to have been the only part of the English force engaged at Crossdall. Their skirmishers were soon driven in; but the Irish did not offer to come any closer. While some of them kept up their fire on the van, others were observed pushing forward in the direction of Monaghan to occupy a wood beside the pathway. Cuney, anxious to keep the way open, sent on a sergeant and a party of shot to forestall this move. The sergeant got to the woodside first. It was a broken, stony place, and a good defensive position. The sergeant held on to it, beating the Irish back. Cuney followed him up, but with what force is uncertain.

Presently Bagenal sent Captain Wilmot to bid Cuney retire. Cuney said that 'he could better make good that place than come off without more aid', and Bagenal changed his mind and ordered the march to be continued. The whole column now moved on and joined Cuney. At this O'Neill suddenly called off the fight and drew back his men. Such abrupt disengagement had been an Irish tactic from time immemorial. O'Neill had, in a very special way, made it his own and would develop it until his retirements were to the English as unpredictable, and almost as terrifying, as his attacks. No doubt failure to possess the vantage point of the wood was on this occasion the deciding factor. He could afford to await a better opportunity.

Bagenal reached Monaghan without further molestation, a force of the garrison marching out to meet him, and the MacMahons and Maguires, who were blockading the place, retiring before him. He admitted having had twelve men killed and thirty, including three lieutenants, wounded. And he had burnt a great deal of his precious powder.

On the day following, which was 27 May, the English left a fresh company in garrison and began their return march. This was the day of the battle. Crossdall had been but a foretaste of what was now to come.

They were late in starting. It was about ten o'clock when they marched out in three sections forming one column, van, main battle, and rear. This time they had made a better distribution of responsible officers. Bagenal had moved up to the vanguard, and he had placed Sir John Chichester, who was the Sergeant-Major, and Brett, a Brittany officer, in the battle. Cuney, who had proven his mettle on the previous day, and Wingfield, the remaining Brittany captain, were in the rear. There was now no convoy to incommode the column, and so they marched the better. And they practised what they must have thought was shrewdness. They took a different route. They avoided the dangers of the pass at Crossdall, and instead of moving eastward moved south-east by the path towards Muckno Lake and the Twelve-mile church, in the direction, that is, of the present Castleblayney.

But O'Neill was not so easily shaken off. All the advantages that might be derived from the terrain were still his. The frequent wooded areas of MacMahon's country of that age, the little hills that limited the view, the boggy and broken ground, the streams, the terrain that was made up, in the words of Sir James Perrot, of 'thick, but especially short and scrubby, woods and thickets, deep and dangerous bogs, steep and craggy hills and mountains, uneven and waterish plashes, straight and narrow passages'—all this made it easy for O'Neill's skirmishers to work up close to the column. Such country provided points of vantage for sudden attack and created obstacles to the kind of orderly advance that was necessary if the marching troops were to remain always ready to fight at the shortest notice and with the best effect. Such country was full of 'passes', or places where moving forces were at a disadvantage in respect of a waiting enemy. To deploy a marching force from the ordinary route formation of a column of fives to the fighting formation of a line made up of pike squares suitably flanked by 'sleeves' or 'wings' of shot took time. It was an evolution much more difficult to complete if the change had to be made at short notice in a pass. The moment of change was the moment of danger; and the Irish, increasingly as they came to assess the strength and weakness of the English, made it also the moment of attack. Ulster was full of places where, as Thomas Gainsford says, 'a few muskets well placed will stagger a pretty army', and the inhabitants of Ulster knew these places and knew how to use them.

O'Neill awaited the intruders into Ulster, and he had been reinforced. Maguire and MacMahon were now with him. He had received timely warning of the alteration in route, and once again he lay across Bagenal's path. In a moment of panic later on Lord Deputy Russell claimed that the Irish forces in the field that day were 15,000 strong. Bagenal reported them immediately after the fight as less than 6,000. It is doubtful if they were even 4,000, and there certainly were not, as some said, 2,000 men among them who had firearms.

Late in the forenoon, when he was about three miles out from Monaghan, Bagenal saw the Irish in the distance. Soon the column entered what an Irish writer calls 'an open and level plain, but somewhat heavy with moisture'. Later they reached Clontibret, near the border of the present counties Monaghan and Armagh, where they should turn eastward to skirt the rising ground to the south of them and head for Newry. Close to this place O'Neill, 'having for his advantage a bog on every side', began the day's attack. He sent in his shot as skirmishers and they opened fire from both sides along the whole length of the column. But they soon concentrated on the rear. Cuney was unlucky. He had been in the van when it was attacked on the day before; now he and his green soldiers were once more in the thick of the battle.

Once engaged—it was afternoon then—O'Neill never altogether relaxed his efforts for seven, or as Sir Edward York said, eight, hours. During that time Bagenal must have covered upwards of fourteen miles. It was a running fight for most of the day.

We are not told when the column first halted, but it must have been early. Their fighting formation, when they assumed it, was in two pike battles, each flanked with shot. The skirmishers' fusillade soon gave place to closer work, when the Irish charged 'them in flank as they marched'. No matter how anxious they were to push on, they must have halted and deployed for that. When the attacks came to be made mostly on the rear, the whole column must have been held up until they were beaten back; for the rear must have stood, and the battle and van would have to stand too.

O'Neill, said the English, showed himself 'a very skilful commander'. He had made soldiers of the Ulstermen, and he used his horse and foot in formation according to the best practice of the time. One helped the other. The horse worked forward by troops, each troop protected from the English fire and the English cavalry by a formation of shot. In this way they came up 'within half caliver shot of the main stand of our pikes', that is, the English main battle, commanded by Chichester. This was the manœuvre which, in the great wars of the age, would have been completed by the horsemen firing into the pikemen and then rushing, sword in hand, into whatever openings their fire had made. But the horseman's pistol of the Continent had barely been introduced to the Irish wars, and almost certainly O'Neill's troopers did not carry it. They must have cast their javelins instead.

When Bagenal, struggling for elbow room, sent his own cavalry against these attackers, Sir Edward York, although he drew out his whole force, could advance no more than forty paces from the main battle. At that distance he was stopped by double his number. Facing him were O'Neill's horse, in front and on the flanks of whom stood always the musketeers and calivermen, and—the old with the new—the Scottish mercenary archers.

Of these worthy opponents the English said in amazement: 'It is evident now in all men's opinions—contrary to the former universal opinion—that the rebel if he have double our numbers will fight with us upon any ground of himself [that is, unsupported], much more if he shall have any foreign force to assist him.' This was praise: two Irishmen were as good as one Englishman. Sir Edward York said 'that in no place wheresoever he had served in all his life he never saw more readier or perfecter shot' than the Irish. They and the Irish horse, seconding each other, hung like terriers to the column; they pressed all arms of the English together and never gave them a chance to spread out and shake them off.

It was at Clontibret that the heaviest fighting, and the most dramatic incident of the day, occurred. Here, where the path ran through a bog and beneath a hill—apparently Crossaghy Hill, half a mile east of Clontibret church—O'Neill made a determined effort to overrun his foes. This time, unlike Crossdall, he was quicker than they were, and had occupied the pass before they reached it. He held them and pounded them for three hours. Twice he threw them back from a stream which they sought to cross. Their ammunition ran low and their pikemen, 'for lack of shot to save them', began to waver. It seemed to O'Neill, said the English, that 'with the next volley of his shot brought up close unto them who had no shot to answer them again that a breech should have been made in both battles to have given an entry to all his horse to their utter overthrow'.

At this moment the rebel Earl in person was seen and recognised on the other side of the stream. He sat his horse in full view, 'surveying the battle thence and giving his orders', and behind him were the troops of Tyrone cavalry which, like the red-coated infantry of the previous day, had once formed part of the Queen's force in Ulster.

Bagenal's situation was desperate, and it required a desperate remedy. Seagrave, a Palesman who served with the English horse, spurred forward across the water. Forty troopers rode with him. Some were shot down in the ford, but Seagrave went on. He reached O'Neill. Each had a lance, or horseman's staff, and each splintered his weapon on the corselet of the other. Seagrave seized the Earl and they fell together to the ground. O'Neill was in deadly peril; how much of the future of Ireland would have been different if he had died there? But the son of O'Cahan, who was one of his subsidiary lords, saved him. Young O'Cahan cut off Seagrave's arm and O'Neill despatched Seagrave with his dagger.

Eventually the column forced its way through. The Irish, said Lieutenant Perkins, who was present, had stopped 'all straights and passages', and much time elapsed 'before we could wind ourselves through one of them, being driven to exceeding many stands'. But they pushed on. Whether there were, after this, long intervals when they had freedom from attack we do not know. The fighting was not continuous; if it had been the column could not have covered the distance which it did.

Bagenal says that O'Neill approached him 'with horse and foot as he found occasions, being ever strengthened with battalions for his better retreat, placed in the skirts of their fastness'. This indicates that the Irish attacked as the ground suited them and as the state of the alternately advancing and halting column favoured them. Their 'fastness' was the particular vantage point, bog or hilly or broken ground, from which the attacks were launched. O'Neill took on Bagenal's main battle himself and his brother Cormac attacked the vanguard. Maguire led the Irish horse.

So the fight went as the long day wore on. The weather, whether it was hot or windy, dry or wet, is unrecorded. The temper of the English must have worsened as the hours went by and the Irish stuck like burrs to their flanks. Casualties mounted. Duke, who had already suffered defeat at the Ford of the Biscuits, was hit. Cuney, struggling along in the rear, was wounded, as was his ensign. So were Lieutenants Sandys and Lloyd; many of the rank and file fell. Ammunition ran shorter still. Captain Merriman, an officer of one of the old companies, had to resort to the final expedient of sending out 'a sleeve [that is, a detached formation] of pikes for lack of munition to charge upon Tyrone's shot'.

By late afternoon things had grown almost hopeless. The men, encumbered with the wounded and as watchful as they were able, were tired out. They said later that they marched continuously in battle formation 'with all the colours flying and sound of drum and continually upon our guard', which is perhaps too heroic a picture of the reality. The Brittany men and the men of the old companies behaved well; but the recruits—who can blame them? —showed that they were 'new come to the wars'. Dogged always by an enemy who seemed to know every tussock and every boghole, whose captains and soldiers showed a newly acquired skill, whose shot behaved with 'readiness and perfection' and were 'as good as the world hath', who ranged the column at will, always seeking a weak place, the weary troops dragged on, hoping for what relief they knew not. 'For still, as the forces marched on, the rebels with loose wings of shot played on them and came on often with a countenance of much resolution'; even though they were 'most commonly beaten back, and many times would retire themselves when they had discharged their vollies of shot', they never withdrew.

Dusk found the column still moving. They did not reach the Eight-mile church but halted at Ballymacowen, where, picking the best position that offered 'on the side of a morish ground' (seventeenth-century writers frequently speak of 'bogs and moor-ish grounds', that is, moors, and of course readers of Robert Louis Stevenson will remember how much he liked the word), they sat down in order of battle. That was to be their encampment for the night, if they could hold it. They shared their powder and found that they had a third of a pound left for each piece, sufficient for three or four rounds for a musket and perhaps ten for a caliver. Bagenal's and Chichester's pewter dishes were melted to make bullets, and a frantic appeal was conveyed to Newry by Felim O'Hanlon, an old servitor of the Bagenals, for ammunition.

But their trial was over. The Irish encamped near them, probably as tired as they were, but in far different spirits. They did not offer to attack, and the English had, as Bagenal says, 'some ease'. Lietenant Perkins says that O'Neill also had used all his ammunition, having burnt fourteen barrels of powder, that is, 1,400 pounds, to Bagenal's ten, and that he sent off that evening to his castle, and the capital of his lordship, at Dungannon for more.

Early on the following morning relief in the shape of 200 men and some ammunition came from Newry. Both forces, Bagenal's and O'Neill's, marched; but the attacks of the previous days were not renewed, the Irish drawing off southward to block the Moyry pass between Newry and Dundalk. That evening Bagenal's men entered Newry 'wearied and hungry'. Their loss on the previous day was, according to Bagenal, 31 killed and 109 officers and men wounded. The Irish claimed to have accounted for 700, and the English admitted later that there were 'more hurt men in the late service than was convenient to declare'.

When the English encamped for the night after their march from Clontibret they were at the end of their tether. Another such day must have brought them—if O'Neill had pressed it—to Hicks's fate. They were saved by proximity to Newry and by the empty ammunition bags of the Irish.

The immediate effect of the battle was to reduce not only the survivors, who had 'had their hands full and were glad to be rid of the match', but the Dublin administration to a state bordering on panic. Bagenal informed Russell from Newry that he was short of food and powder, but that he dared not march to Dundalk for fear of O'Neill who lay midway in the Moyry pass. One of his officers, speaking of the men, said that 'if they had all the munition in Ireland they would not have undertaken to come to Drogheda'. Powder was sent promptly by sea to Newry and, with it, orders that the foot should return to Dublin in the ships and that the horse should remain in Newry. It was the final humiliation, a confession that the Queen's army dared not show its face in the field. Elizabeth, who mourned 'the loss and death of so many good soldiers in relieving Monaghan', spoke bitterly of the dishonour that she had been made to suffer.

She was spared the worst. At the beginning of June the Irish left the pass and moved westward. Tirconnell had been raided by sea from Connacht, and Sir Richard Bingham, the President of Connacht, was attacking Donegal. The Ulstermen marched to its relief; besides, O'Neill may well have felt—for he disliked pushing things to extremes—that the Monaghan occasion was sufficiently served by the rough hustling out of Ulster of Bagenal's parade. By 6 June Bagenal, having received the ammunition and sent off his wounded to Dublin by sea, was in Drogheda. For the English an unsavoury affair was over. For the Irish the years of success had begun. They had hit upon the formula of victory: a defensive strategy and the tactics of controlled attacks on marching columns; each time the Monaghan expedition was repeated the Queen courted disaster.

The best modern account of Clontibret, which contains much information about topography and which prints all the relevant contemporary accounts, appears in an article by Very Rev. L. Marron in *The Clogher Record,* I, No. 4, pp. 1 ff. Fr Marron also prints the muster lists of Bagenal's force before the battle in *The Irish Sword,* II, pp. 368 ff. The best contemporary accounts are in the reports of Bagenal and his officers who survived the march. These are contained in the state papers in the Public Record Office, London, and are very inadequately summarised in the *Calendar of State Papers, Ireland, 1592-96,* pp. 320 ff. See also the *Calendar of the Carew Manuscripts,* III, pp. 109 f. See further Sir James Perrott, *The Chronicle of Ireland,* pp. 93 ff; and, for sub-contemporary Irish accounts, see the *Annals of the Four Masters* under the year 1595 (and see the note by the editor, J. O'Donovan, whose son was killed in Hicks's disaster, VI, p. 1970) and Philip O'Sullivan (in M. J. Byrne, *Ireland under Elizabeth,* p. 87). Consult R. Bagwell, *Ireland under the Tudors, III,* for the background. Sean O'Faolain *The Great O'Neill* (1942) is a colourful and readable life of Hugh O'Neill in which his motives for revolt are imaginatively discussed.

The battle of Clontibret has been confused with a totally distinct engagement fought between O'Neill and Sir John Norris at Mullaghbrack, north of Newry, on 5 September of the same year. Norris was not at Clontibret on 27 May; a mistake of O'Donovan's perpetuated by Bagwell has led to the belief that he was. Fr Paul Walsh (*Irish Book Lover, XXI,* pp. 103 ff) was the first to correct this error.

Note that the reference to English red coats is among the earliest mentions of what later became universally known as the characteristic English—and British—military attire. Gainsford's reference to the Ulster terrain is in *The Glory of England,* p. 144. The early history of pikes may be followed in H. Seitz, 'Some traits of the international expansion of edged weapons during the XVI century' in *Armi Antiche* (Turin, 1956).

The Yellow Ford, 1598

Ulster had produced valiant warriors before Hugh O'Neill's time, but never in the earlier wars of her reign had Irish companies of red-coated musketeers and calivermen been seen in action against the Queen. Their appearance at Clontibret indicated that the struggle of O'Neill and his adherents was to be a new kind of struggle, and was to be fought with fresh determination and a new resource; O'Neill's ambition was to confront the English with soldiers who were in training and equipment as good as themselves.

The armies of this last stand of Gaelic Ireland were made up of the rising out or traditional force of the Ulster lordships, together with some galloglas, some bodies of Scots mercenaries, and—most notably—great numbers of the so-called bonnaghts. These last, who were native Irish mercenaries, were not a new class of warrior, but O'Neill's use of them was revolutionary; they had never been employed in such numbers or under such conditions before.

The galloglas were largely a spent force by the end of the sixteenth century; Thomas Gainsford, writing in 1618, could say that 'the name of galloglass is in a manner extinct'. Their numbers were, however, still considerable in Hugh O'Neill's time, and they had until recently played with effect their traditional role of dependable professionals. They were not entirely a closed body, for although their leaders and most of their men were still of Scottish ancestry, some Irishmen were admitted to their ranks. But their real place was in a narrower kind of warfare, the warfare of earlier times. They were incapable of rapid expansion to meet the unprecedented call for manpower of the great struggle that had now begun. Although some of them, like O'Neill's own galloglas, the MacDonald septs of the Blackwater valley, had become 'shot and pikemen' by 1595, the galloglas on the whole had not done much to adapt themselves to the changed conditions of fighting which followed the extension of the use of firearms.

O'Neill could not look to the galloglas for much support in this war, even though it was a war waged in defence of the institutional system whereby they lived. Nor, as it happened, could he hope for much from the Scots. He tried hard, with promises of pay and plunder, to attract mercenaries from the Highlands and Isles, and bands of MacDonalds, MacLeans and Campbells did, from time to time, serve him and his allies; but things were changing in Scotland too. The power of the Campbells of Argyll was growing and they were setting the other clans against one another. The disturbed conditions which they found in Scotland increased the difficulties of O'Neill's recruiters, who had also to contend with the efforts of Queen Elizabeth's agents in Scotland to stop the mercenary trade at its source. King James VI, although he slyly encouraged O'Neill, would never help him; to do so might endanger his chance of succession to the English throne. Furthermore, English naval power was thrown into the scale, and the Queen's pinnaces patrolled the narrow seas and chased the Highland galleys with vigour and not without effect. All this meant, by the end of the century, a distinct falling off in the numbers of mercenaries who crossed to Ulster.

O'Neill, O'Donnell and the rest of the lords could not have fought as they did if they were dependent only on the kinds of fighting men whom their ancestors had used. But they were not so dependent. Denied the assistance that they required from the ranks of the galloglas and the Scots mercenaries, bodies that were the one old-fashioned and the other erratic in its comings and goings, they had to make up their numbers elsewhere. They did so by raising large forces of bonnaghts in their own territories, forces that were, in effect, the Irish counterpart of the national militias which, in the same age, superseded the *condottieri* and the *landsknechts* and the Swiss and the other mercenaries all over Europe. And the material for these forces came from the churls or peasants, the unfree class in the Gaelic communities which Shane O'Neill was the first to call to arms.

The distinction between the traditional rising out of the aristocracy and freemen and these bonnaghts is made clear in contemporary references. O'Neill, speaking of the days of his loyalty to the Queen, said that he had not spared his country in defence of her interest, 'either in charging it with hired men', who were the bonnaghts, or 'taking their rising out unto this service', that is, the muster of those over whom he exercised lordship. It was said in 1598 that if the English did not attack the north at that time O'Neill would leave its defence to the 'natural people of Ulster, who are not chargeable unto him, but such as yield him revenue', that is, the landed men, who made up the rising out, and that he would carry the war into Leinster and Munster with his 'mercenaries', or bonnaghts. And it was the same with O'Donnell, who, receiving news of a sudden rising against him in Sligo in 1596, 'did not wait to muster an army, except his soldiers and mercenaries', but marched there at once.

These new Ulster armies were raised by proclamation made in the churches and places of public assembly throughout the north. Each year in February or March recruits were called for to serve for the campaigning season, the rates of pay and other terms of service being announced in formal fashion by the recruiting agents. The bonnaghts were formed in companies of nominal hundreds, just as the English troops were. They marched and attacked to the sound of the drum and the bagpipes, and they carried colours.

In 1594 O'Neill and his allies had enrolled and billeted in Ulster some 2,000 bonnaghts. Later this number was doubled and trebled. They were trained to some extent by outsiders, by the Butter captains, and later by Spanish officers and by Irishmen who had served in the Spanish army in the Low Countries. English amazement at their efficiency grew as the war went on. They were, they said in 1595, better trained than Shane O'Neill's men had been; a year later they were 'other enemies, and not those that in times past were wont never to attempt Her Majesty's forces in the plain field, but in some passes or straits'; they had been 'infinitely belaboured with training in all parts of Ulster' for the past three years, and were now 'most ready, well disciplined and as good marksmen as France, Flanders, or Spain can show'. 'In discipline and weapons', said the English, the Irish soldier was 'little inferior, in body and courage equal, if not superior, to us'. The men of military age within O'Neill's confederacy were, by 1598, 'all soldiers'; there was no longer a distinction between the aristocratic fighting classes and those who had formerly been prohibited by their low birth from bearing arms. Churls, horseboys and the servile orders, as well as those ordinarily forming part of the rising out and classed as *ceatharnaigh* or kern—the nonprofessional, part-time warriors in contradistinction to the galloglas—were all trained to the use of weapons. 'These northern

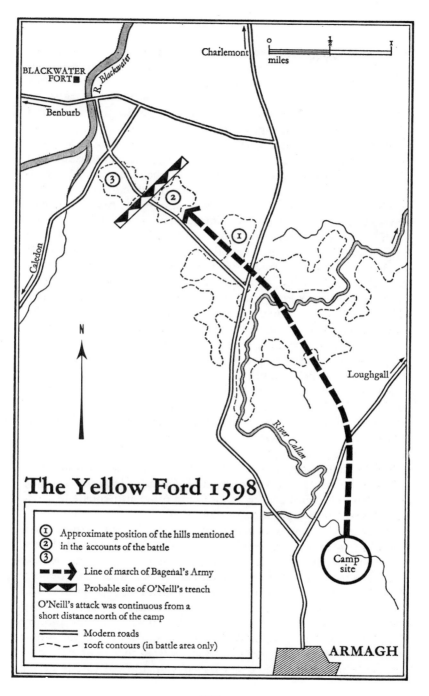

Charlemont

BLACKWATER
FORT

R. Blackwater

Benburb

Caledon

N

③

②

①

Loughgall

River Callan

The Yellow Ford 1598

① Approximate position of the hills mentioned
② in the accounts of the battle
③

➤ Line of march of Bagenal's Army

Probable site of O'Neill's trench

O'Neill's attack was continuous from a
short distance north of the camp

Modern roads

100ft contours (in battle area only)

Camp
site

ARMAGH

½   I

miles

miscreants within these few years knew not what the due order of fighting was', said a report of 1599, 'and now it is a professed art amongst the cowherds of Ulster.' Furthermore, these forces could gather 'their utmost strength from the remotest parts' in less than three days, whereas it would take the English more than three weeks to mobilise against them.

The weapons of the Irish were as up-to-date as they could make them. Their 'shot' had matchlock calivers and muskets like the English. In 1595 they were said to have 4,000 such men, together with a thousand pikemen and a thousand horse. English statements of O'Neill's numbers were largely the result of guess-work, but the proportions are interesting. The number of men with firearms in a detached force of O'Neill's in 1594 is equally impressive—400, against 180 pikemen, 200 horse, and (further evidence of the militarisation of Tyrone) 'two hundred churls with darts and skeins', or daggers. Of the 400 some, we are told, 'were furnished as kern with pieces', that is, no doubt, they had the lighter calivers. It was said in 1596 that the Irish, having plenty of muskets, fowling pieces, calivers, swords, helmets, powder and shot, had converted most of their kern into musketeers and their galloglas into pikemen. The reporter of this information expressed the hope that their supplies of munitions might be cut off, and that they might once more be forced to fight 'with stones, casting spears and galloglas axes as they had been accustomed'; but their supplies, which came from Spain, from Scotland, from Danzig, from the Irish towns, even from England, were not cut off, or even seriously interrupted. They got much warlike material from Spain, culminating in deliveries of a thousand arquebuses, a thousand pikes, $7\frac{1}{2}$ tons of powder, five tons of lead and a supply of match in December 1599, a thousand more arquebuses in 1600, and a further cargo at the beginning of 1601.

Although it was a penal offence to do so, the Anglo-Irish merchants—as was reported in 1599—bought swords, helmets, firearms, powder and lead in England and elsewhere and, bribing the searchers in the ports, smuggled them into the country. Supplies from England came from Manchester, Liverpool and Birmingham, whence they were sent concealed in hogsheads and dryfats, or casks respectively for the transport of liquids and dry merchandise. The merchants in the Irish ports—or, as the writer Barnaby Rich put it, 'every peddling fellow that kept a shop'— sold this contraband of war to men who disposed of it to the

Ulstermen according to a regular system of barter. A sword, a helmet, a caliver or a musket fetched each six cows; a pound of powder fetched one.

Nor were the Ulstermen without means to pay for what they wanted. It was said that 'ill inhabited as it was, with no industry and most part wasted' O'Neill could raise £80,000 a year in Ulster. He was paying 2s 6d a pound for powder in Glasgow in 1597 and getting as much of it as he wanted. He was said to have bought £2,000 worth there from a merchant named Alexander Stewart. He employed an agent named Harcles in England who, as was said, had in 1595–7 provided 'all the lead for the north of Ireland'.

Pikes were readily made at home, although some were, as we have seen, sent from Spain. O'Neill, who kept the Spanish pikes for his best forces, 'armed the very shepherds of his country with a kind of pike'. Three hundred Ulster bonnaghts serving in the midlands in 1600 were 'the best furnished men for the war, and the best apparelled that we have seen in the kingdom'; they were well trained men, drawn up in order 'as close as they might, every one trailing his pike and holding the cheek of the same in his left hand ready to push'—that is, ready to lunge forward on the word of command. Even the O'Byrnes of Wicklow, far distant from O'Neill's country but following his example of intransigence, had, we are told, 'set all the axemen to make pikes, and the smiths to make heads for them'.

The Irish writer Peter Lombard, speaking of O'Neill's foresight, has told of the preparations which he made before he entered the war. He imported lead, collected powder and experimented with its manufacture, and did what he could to familiarise his people with firearms. He gave presents of guns to those who showed aptitude in their use and encouraged shooting competitions. One could scarcely believe, said Lombard, how well 'all here, even the farmers, ploughmen, swineherds, shepherds, and very boys have learned to use this weapon'. The result was acknowledged by Lord Deputy Mountjoy, who said in 1602 that Irish fighting men, 'so far from being naked people, as before times, were generally better armed than we, knew better the use of their weapons than our men, and even exceeded us in that discipline which was fittest for the advantage of the natural strength of the country, for that they, being very many, and expert shot, and excelling in footmanship all other nations, did by that means make better use of those strengths [that is, their own wild terrain], both for offence and defence, than could have been made of any squadrons of pikes or artificial fortifications of towns'.

With such men Hugh O'Neill and his allies soon improved on the military advantage which they had gained at Clontibret. What the English felt of that battle is suggested by the conduct of a company of Cheshiremen who had been there and who were ordered to Connacht shortly afterwards. Of this company, originally a hundred strong, only sixteen men got to their destination. The rest of these survivors of Clontibret, having had enough of that kind of soldiering, had deserted on the march.

O'Neill was proclaimed a traitor in June 1595. Later in the summer Armagh cathedral was again garrisoned, and O'Neill, determined not to give the English an objective against which they might strike, broke down his castle of Dungannon and distributed its contents among the crannoges, or fortresses built on artificial islands in the Tyrone lakes, which thereafter became his storehouses and places of retreat.

This year was one of almost uniform success for the Irish. In June and July Lord Deputy Russell and Sir John Norris, with a large force, got as far as the Blackwater, but thought better of trying to cross. Norris, who was the new commander in Ulster, was 'a great leader, and famous in the wars of the Low Countries and France'; it might be added that he was also the slaughterer of the Scots in Rathlin island in 1575, and the leader of the land forces, and one of a minority of the survivors, of the abortive expedition to Portugal of 1589. In August and September Norris and Bagenal twice brought supplies to Armagh. They had to use the whole field force for these operations and were attacked and roughly handled nine miles north of Newry on their way back from the second expedition. When the campaigning season closed the English had no more to show for their efforts in south-east Ulster, the main seat of the war, than the substitution of a garrison at Armagh for one in advance of it on the Blackwater. And they had done no better in south-west Ulster and Connacht, where they had to give up hope of a forward post at the Erne, accept the loss of Sligo, and try to save what they could from O'Donnell's raids.

From the end of 1595 to the summer of 1597 hostilities virtually ceased in south-east Ulster. Lord Deputy Russell was glad to prolong what was at first intended to be a brief truce because he was 'very unable to make head against' O'Neill.

Thomas Lord Burgh replaced Russell in May 1597. He was a restless person and a keen fighter, and the short period of his administration saw the fiercest contest that had so far been waged in Ulster. Believing, despite the evidence to the contrary, that O'Neill could never face 'Her Majesty's ensigns', and that if he 'be well pressed, all is got', Burgh assembled forces for an advance to Dungannon and beyond. He proposed to bring down O'Neill, O'Donnell and the rest by the tactics of converging columns and appointed Sir Conyers Clifford, Governor of Connacht, to co-operate with him by crossing the Erne at Bally-shannon and pushing towards Lifford. Like Sidney and Randolph in 1566, the two were to unite in the Foyle valley; then they were to march to Derry, where they were to receive supplies by sea. After that they were to harry the country west of the Bann.

It was a paper programme, part of the pattern of unreality that made up many of the plans of Burgh, who, we are told, had 'a flat-bottomed vessel, capable of transporting 150 men at a time' made in Dublin for his intended passage of the Blackwater. There is no indication of how it was proposed to bring this vessel, or materials to make one like it, on the scene, and although, years later, Lord Deputy Mountjoy used a raft made of planks and barrels on the Blackwater he had to fight several campaigns against O'Neill before he could do so.

But Burgh was a hustler. He marched to schedule and at speed. On 12 July he was beyond Newry with about 3,500 men. Covering the intervening space in the following day, he passed through Armagh, dropped his baggage and a third of his force there, and reached the Blackwater at two o'clock on the next morning. He had O'Neill's half-brother, who had surrendered, with him, and this man, speaking Irish, tried to allay the suspicions of O'Neill's scouts, who challenged the English as they moved up in the star-light. Although the scouts, seeing the column go on 'with haste and fury', shot off their pieces to raise the alarm, Burgh got to the river unopposed.

Immediately opposite the English on the north bank was an earthwork which O'Neill had built and in which he had placed a ward of some forty men with four arquebuses-en-croc, or wall guns. These light guns appear to be the only pieces of artillery—of the many which they eventually possessed—recorded as being in Irish hands on the scene of an action in this war. They fired none of them. Either their hearts failed them, or ammunition was lacking, or, as the English supposed, 'they wanted skill in discharging of ordnance'.

Burgh rushed the crossing at the ford, which lay a little below the first bend downstream from the present Blackwatertown bridge, and which was full of 'great pebble stones, slippery and having some pits'. The ford, we are told, was dead ground as far as the fire of the earthwork was concerned. The attackers, a thousand strong, drove out the ward and carried the place. But they got no further. O'Neill, as daylight showed, was far from being intimidated. His whole force still blocked the way, and continued to do so for the eight weeks during which the English remained at the river. After heavy skirmishing Burgh changed his mind about advancing and about the converging columns. Caution supervened. It was remembered that 'raiding journeys' in Ulster had already cost the Queen £300,000 and that there was nothing to show for the expenditure. News of Clifford's failure to take O'Donnell's castle of Ballyshannon and of his ignominious retreat to Connacht, which came in August, decided the matter.

Burgh commenced building a new Blackwater fort—to replace that destroyed by O'Neill in 1595—on the Tyrone or northern bank of the river, close to or partly on the site of the captured earthwork, a fort that would be 'an eyesore in the heart of Tyrone's country'. It soon became an object of as great tenderness to him 'as my first begotten child'. He gave up Armagh for it. He no longer spoke of the invasion of Ulster, no longer denied the utility of garrisons to reduce O'Neill. Blackwater fort became for him the key to victory.

But perhaps there was another reason for all this, a greater urgency of defence than appeared, for Burgh struggled with a wrestler stronger than O'Neill. He was sick to death when he reached Armagh in October in a headlong rush to bring supplies to the fort. He got to the Blackwater but could move no further. They carried him to Newry, where he died of the Irish ague, that is, typhus, on the 13th.

Burgh was wrong. His fort was not the key to an English victory. In the following year its existence provoked the battle of the Yellow Ford, which was an English defeat.

Blackwater fort was an earthwork of the roughest construction, a mere earthen parapet and ditch protecting an enclosure or terreplein of square or oblong ground plan. There were no flankers to protect the corners. It was garrisoned by 150 men under the command of Captain Thomas Williams, a gallant veteran who had 'served most of the princes of Christendom for these three and twenty years, and never was out of entertainment but two years'. Williams had mounted two robinets or light field guns on their carriages opposite embrasures cut in the parapet, and he had also two arquebuses-en-croc—two of those captured from O'Neill? His defences were soon tested. About Michaelmas, shortly before Burgh's death, the Irish assaulted the fort. Using thirty scaling ladders, they made three attempts to rush the walls, but were beaten back with some losses, including Morgan Kavanagh, an Irishman returned from the Spanish service, who held a command of O'Neill's bonnaghts and who was killed there. 'The defendants battered and overturned them with black bills'—the traditional, but now obsolescent, English weapons—and Williams himself fired a robinet 'laden with bullets' in their faces. After this repulse the Irish attacked no more. The English said later that 'the Earl could not get them any more to give the onset upon the fort' and that they were 'very cowards if they see they have not some retreat to run away' to. But they lay close up to the walls and blockaded the place. Williams found it hard even to get drinking water from the nearby river, and he had to fight for wood for his fires. Sleeping on the bare earth with no covering save their scanty clothing, living on a diminishing supply of beef and biscuit, and cursing the duty that deprived them of their army beer, his men were in difficulties by November.

After Burgh's death the civil administration fell to Lords Justices Loftus and Gardiner and the command of the forces to the Earl of Ormond. O'Neill saw an opportunity of gaining time by negotiating with the new appointees, and a truce was made and eventually continued until the following summer.

During this period the whole future seemed to depend upon the fate of Blackwater fort. The English, in particular, were compromised by its existence. It was so weak that the garrison could barely defend it; to use it for aggressive action against O'Neill was impossible. What then was the point of maintaining it? But to withdraw would be to lose face. Williams could not hold out indefinitely against a hostile O'Neill unless the Queen was prepared to assemble a whole army from time to time to send him supplies. Therefore O'Neill's was the whip hand. He could, and did, compel the continuance of a truce advantageous to himself by exploiting the English reluctance to mount a full—and an expensive—offensive; and he knew that if it came to blows the Queen's troops must present themselves to be struck where he held the tactical advantage. The Earl of Ormond, and many others, believed that it would have been better if 'the scurvy fort of Blackwater' had never been built. 'There was choice of fitter places', Ormond said, 'if it were but Armagh, where the soldiers might lie dry overhead, and her majesty's victuals be better bestowed.'

At Christmas Williams had a month's supply of beef and biscuit, twelve barrels of powder, and lead proportionable. He lacked match, salt, entrenching tools and money to buy the food which the truce had made available. He could cut firewood, but only in a specified place; O'Neill made sure that his forest defences, his wild undergrowth and his plashed ways, did not go up in smoke. Early in the new year Williams got food and tools and some reinforcements from Dublin, and at the end of January he had six months' supplies. But the rain washed down his walls. His men toiled continually to prop up a 'rampier daily falling down', and 'what they repair in one day, twice as much falleth the next day'. And O'Neill's strength grew. Of the Irish the 'worser sort were led with hope of spoil, the more powerful with desire of liberty and dominion, the fearful and weak with dread to be made a prey'.

What should be done? In June, when the truce ended, the Irish Council wanted to give up the fort. They feared that, if they tried to relieve it, the relieving force might 'receive such disaster as we shall be sorry for'. Then they had second thoughts. O'Neill was bestirring himself and was threatening the Pale. In July 1,500 men landed in Dublin, and although they were new levies and were 'such as for the most part had not seen the faces of an enemy in the field', they were available for service. At the beginning of August, partly because these troops were now at hand, partly because they feared the Queen's disapproval of withdrawal, but mostly because a leader had meanwhile offered himself—one who had no doubt at all of what should be done, and was prepared to do it; one who in the end died in the attempt to do it—the Council veered again, changed their minds, and wanted to hold on. The leader was Sir Henry Bagenal of Newry, the Marshal, 'a man better experienced in the knowledge of that country than in the command of an army, for he was never trained in any foreign service'. Bagenal was, we remember, O'Neill's brother-in-law and personal enemy, and was as well, as he and everybody else remembered, the one who had been made to run the gauntlet at Clontibret. He asked for the command of a relieving force to go to the Blackwater. Ormond, the Lieutenant-General and supreme commander of the army, concurred, and he was given it. It was decided to reinforce a position that, as the sequel showed, should have been written off; it was not the last time in the history of war that such a thing was done, or that the consequences of an error in judgment were suffered.

Bagenal had a force of almost 4,000 foot and 300 horse, a large army by the standards of the time and place. The foot were in forty companies and were of three different types. There were, first, the companies of the standing army of the kingdom, the 'old companies', made up of men who had served under Burgh and in other campaigns. The total effective strength of these old companies at the time was over 5,000; since most of them were on garrison duty throughout the country, however, only some 900 men were available for field service and were with Bagenal. Three hundred of these were from the force of the Presidency of Connacht. Perhaps half were native Irishmen; Burgh particularly had introduced large numbers of Irish into the ranks to swell his forces, and the Irish Council said in June 1598 that three-quarters of the Queen's troops then in Ireland were Irish. Also in the old companies was the remainder of the Brittany reinforcement of 1595. The rest were levies and conscripts of the English shires.

The second category was four strong companies, in all about 500 men, that had landed in Waterford in March. These had come from Picardy, where they had seen service in the war which Henry IV of France waged against the Spanish forces, that, until the Peace of Vervins, resisted him in Calais, Amiens and other towns. The third and largest part of the army was made up of raw recruits, the 1,500 men who had landed late in July and about 350 more who had followed them to Dublin at the beginning of August. The July contingent was almost unmanageable. They resisted efforts to train them, could not 'be kept from brabling one with another', sold their clothes and arms and deserted freely. A thousand of them had to be sent off immediately after their arrival to Kells; to have left them in Dublin would have been dangerous. The horse of Bagenal's force were old troops, many of them Irish.

Bagenal's commission, signed by Ormond in June, appointed him chief commander in counties Armagh, Antrim, Down, Louth, Meath, Westmeath, and in Drogheda. It was later noted that he had no command in Tyrone, where the beleaguered fort lay; but since he never got there it made no difference. A general hosting of the Palesmen was ordered for 6 June, but this force, formerly the mainstay of English power in Ireland, had now dwindled to a home guard, and was assigned duty as such. Burgh would not 'pester his expedition' with the Pale muster in 1597. The carriage horses which the Palesmen were bound to contribute did, however, prove useful to Bagenal.

The rendezvous was given for Ardee on 7 August and the army assembled there and marched thence to Newry and on to Armagh. They had four guns with them, the biggest of them a saker, a gun smaller than a six pounder, which was drawn by a train of oxen. They marched through the ruined town of Armagh, with its battered cathedral on the hill and its roofless churches, and encamped a quarter mile beyond it on the right bank of the river Callan.

Next day—it was Monday, 14 August—they beat the Diana, or morning drum, betimes. Leaving their camp to the sutlers, the followers and the camp guard, they drew out their forces with colours flying, and, about eight o'clock, marched for the Blackwater. They were determined, 'maugre the beard' of O'Neill (they were contemporaries of Shakespeare!), to relieve the fort. They had only four or four and a half miles to go. It was a fine day.

The way from Armagh to the Blackwater lay then, as it does now, on the west side of the Callan; it followed the line of the present main road to Dungannon, which, crossing a loop of the stream at Geary's bridge, hugs the left bank. Bagenal knew this country well, and he had good guides. He knew that O'Neill lay between him and the fort; indeed he could see his men 'upon the highway betwixt us and the Blackwater, on the other side of the pass and the river [Callan] which we were to pass the next day'. He did not reckon on getting through without a fight; but he hoped that he might steal a march on the Irish and avoid some of the most dangerous places where they had made 'great plashes' by moving, not on 'the ordinary highway where the rebels lay', but away from it altogether and on the east side of the Callan rather than the west. There, he said, 'we should march all through the hard and open champain, saving the passing through one bog some two or three flight-shot over, where we would maintain skirmish with the rebels till he [Bagenal] had made the bog passable with boughs and sticks for the artillery, horse, and carriages [pack horses]'.

Bagenal marched accordingly. His column extended for, perhaps, a mile from front to rear. The infantry marched in six regiments, each about 500 strong, spaced at the start with intervals of more than a hundred yards between them. The cavalry, the guns with their trains of oxen and horses, and the convoy of pack horses laden with supplies for the fort and no doubt the materials for making the causeway in the bog marched in the intervals. It had been agreed at a council of war held on the previous day that the foot regiments should march thus 'in single bodies' until they were engaged by the enemy, and that then they should join one with another in a fighting formation of vanguard, main battle and rearward 'if they found the ground answerable'. The two regiments of the vanguard were led, the first by Colonel Sir Richard Percy, the Earl of Northumberland's brother, and the second by the Marshal in person. The Marshal thus commanded the van. The first regiment of the battle was led by Captain Cosby as Colonel, the second by Sir Thomas Maria Wingfield, who commanded the battle and was second in command of the whole force. The rear was led by Colonel Cuney. Like Bagenal, Wingfield and some of the other officers, Cuney was, we remember, a veteran of Clontibret. He was the Sergeant-Major, and his immediate command was the van—or first regiment—of the rear; Captain Billings led the rear of the rear. The vanguard of the horse was commanded by Sir Calisthenes Brooke, who was General of the Horse, and the rear by Captain Fleming. The saker was with the main battle.

The regiments evidently marched not company by company in column of fives, but formed in as much readiness to fight as possible, with their pikes all together in the centre and their shot in sleeves or wings on the flanks. No doubt it was partly to have room for this that Bagenal and his council of war elected to move over the open ground rather than by the narrow road. Away out in front, forming the advance guard, were the two wings of shot of the forlorn hope, detached from Percy's regiment, one of them led by Captain Lee, the other by Captain Turner; these two officers and almost all their men were very soon to be killed.

The country beyond Armagh is a place of little hills, a terrain that falls away not very noticeably towards the wide Blackwater in the north and through which the Callan meanders. In the sixteenth century it was wooded, mostly with a shrubby brush-wood of alder, willow and holly, with here and there stretches of ash and oak, and it was in places very boggy. There was at least one clear place which was part of the battlefield and which Lord Deputy Mountjoy later called a 'fair meadow'. Bagenal's army marched, says one of his officers, over 'hard and hilly ground, within caliver shot of wood and bog on both sides'. Among the hills, behind the trees, in the bogs O'Neill, O'Donnell and Maguire had more than 5,000 men.

The battle began about half past eight o'clock when Bagenal's vanguard was attacked from both sides half a mile beyond the camp by O'Neill's nephew Brian MacArt and then, as they marched forward, by Randal MacSorley MacDonald of Antrim.

The tactics of the Irish were the tactics of Clontibret used over again, but this time used to perfection. The fact that Bagenal marched through the country rather than by the road seems to have made no difference to them; they plagued his men as roundly on the right bank of the Callan as they would, presumably, have done on the left. Shifting their places in concealment behind the trees, or skipping at will out of range in the bogs, O'Neill's musketeers and calivermen subjected the column—and particu-larly the many raw men in the column—to the old ordeal of attack on the march. The nature of the ground kept the English cavalry from riding down their attackers; they had no option but to keep on and to suffer like the men on foot. As the advance continued, Bagenal's whole force, from the forlorn hope to Billings's men in the rear, came under fire.

In the absence of a better plan—and there does not seem to have been one—instinct urged the English forward. They were, as at Clontibret, running the gauntlet, yet this time they had not so far to go, and the faster they went the briefer—they hoped—would be their trial. But the difficulties of the ground and the conflict between forcing their way through and throwing out skirmishers to defend themselves from attack interrupted the regularity of their pace. The inevitable happened. The intervals between the regiments widened and grew wider. The little hills and the tops of the browning trees rose up between van, battle and rear and each marched in its own wilderness. Soon Bagenal had lost control of what was, in any event, a scratch army that had never acted together before, and, in effect, three conflicts were being waged instead of one. Ormond, wise before and after the event, claimed later that this was a danger 'whereof I often warned the Marshal to take special care before he went hence'.

In all Percy, who led the first regiment of the vanguard, marched about three miles towards the fort, the remainder of the column somewhat less. They went first over the 'hard and hilly ground' above the Callan; then apparently they crossed the Callan and went over a hill (we may call it the first hill) to boggy ground where there was the ford whence the battle takes its name; then uphill again (the second hill); then down to a field of still green corn surrounded by more bog—seemingly the bog 'two or three flight shot over' where Bagenal anticipated a skirmish; and finally up once more to higher ground on which stood a sconce or breastwork (the third hill).

In general the march can still be traced on the ground, but not with certainty of detail. No 'Yellow Ford' is now known, and no contemporary map or narrative gives exact information of its whereabouts. It may have been a ford of the Callan, but this is unlikely. The narrative seems to require a site further on, in the townland of Tulligoonigan; the Irish historian O'Sullivan speaks of the ford not as a river crossing, but as a place where 'oozed the discoloured water flowing from the bogs', whence, he says, it possibly derived its name.

The dangerous places were this ford, which was between the first and second hills, and the cornfield and bogs, which were between the second and third. O'Neill had plenty of time to prepare the ground. He plashed the shrubbery and dug pits to impede cavalry action in various places, but his main obstacle was a long and deep trench, or series of trenches, extending for, as an English account says, a mile—O'Sullivan claims only half that length—between two 'bogs or rotten plashy ground on either side' and cutting across the cornfield. This trench, which was 'full of water and thorns' and which had a bank surmounted by 'a thorny hedge' behind it, was a formidable barrier.

No matter how far north of Armagh Bagenal marched in his effort to outflank O'Neill, he would eventually, if he was to reach Williams, have to cross the Callan and turn westward towards the Blackwater. This explains why, despite his efforts to march round O'Neill, he still fell foul of the trench or trenches which O'Neill had dug to stop him. Bagenal was prepared for a bog which he knew would be difficult to cross; the trench made it more difficult still, and it was so sited that, linking the bogs as it did, it must impede any advance from Armagh, whether that advance was made by the road or east of the Callan. If Bagenal knew the ground O'Neill knew it better.

Percy was compelled on his way forward to halt many times to keep contact with the Marshal's regiment which came behind; but he pushed on and eventually reached the second hill. Here, while he waited for Bagenal, Percy was assailed by O'Neill's skirmishers, who swarmed in the woods that clothed the western slope of the hill. Captains Lee and Turner with the forlorn hope were down among the trees trying to force a way through for Percy's 'gross' or main body. Partly to assist them and partly to get away from a place where he was losing men in the open to an enemy 'in covert', Percy soon followed. He burst through the wood, crossed the bog and cornfield, forced his way over the trench, and then, 'after our men were put in order, being scattered by the depth of the bogs, the height of the trench and straitness of the pass', marched to the top of the third hill and 'maintained skirmish' there. Captain Lee and an unknown number of the men were killed in this advance. Percy was now far ahead of the remainder of the column. He could see in the distance, their colours defiant, Williams's ragged garrison marching out from the fort to meet him, men who, when they 'had descried the English colours threw up their caps for joy, hoping to have a better supper than the dinner they had that day'. But O'Neill lay in between, and although Percy counted about him only 500 of his foes he was in fact surrounded by greatly superior numbers and was in danger.

Bagenal, at a long interval, followed Percy with the rear of the van and the leading squadron of the horse. Harried like the rest of the column almost since they left the camp, these men came under still heavier fire at the second hill. Behind them again, and hidden from them by the configuration of the ground, Cosby moved up with the first regiment of the main battle. Further back, and at an ever widening interval, was Wingfield. Wingfield had the saker. It kept sinking in the boggy ground and had to be pulled out many times, the men straining with the oxen to get it clear. For all the good it did it would have been better to have left it behind. It stuck at the ford, and for a while it seemed that nothing would move it.

Wingfield grew anxious. He heard heavy fire behind him and knew that the rear must be stopped and closely engaged. In front he saw only the Irish. Leaving his regiment to hold the ford and to protect the saker, he spurred forward, passed Cosby and sought the Marshal. He realised that the head of the column was moving away from the tail, and he proposed that Bagenal should stop the vanguard and bring it back to hold the ford while he himself went back with the battle 'to fetch off the rear'.

But Bagenal, before he agreed, wanted to see things for himself. Conscious at least of the necessity of stopping Percy, he sent him orders to retire to the second hill and to join forces with his own regiment there. He then went back with Wingfield to the ford, where the soldiers of the battle, making a tremendous effort, pulled the saker clear. There was still no sign of the rear, and the Marshal and his second-in-command now rode forward again to the second hill to see if Percy had obeyed orders and come back.

They shuttled about in vain. Things had gone beyond the point where any orders of theirs, even if they could be obeyed, could control the issue. O'Neill and the terrain had taken over. Half the column, from Wingfield's regiment backwards, was now pinned down; by the time it managed to wrench itself free and could struggle on the whole vanguard was shattered. Percy had not come back, whereupon Wingfield reminded Bagenal 'what danger might happen to the army by this disorder of the vanguard, and that he much doubted the rear had been cut off, desiring that he would send again to the vanguard and that he would take his own regiment to fetch off the rear, which the Marshal allowed of'. So, said Wingfield later, 'they parted', parted, as it happened, for the last time. Wingfield returned to his own men and soon 'saw the rear coming up, for whom he made a stand with his regiment at the bog ford'.

Meanwhile Percy was in difficulties. Bagenal's order to retire had been brought to him by Captain Malbie and he had made desperate efforts to disengage and to draw back. 'Our retreat', he said, 'was more in disorder than our going on, because our loose wings, having spent their powder coming in, gave way to the enemy, being both horse and foot, to charge us in the rear, which our new men quitted, and threw away their arms.' Seeing their advantage, O'Neill's horsemen charged home, and they were followed by a swarm of targetiers, or sword and buckler men, who, with no shot to withstand them, burst in among the pikes. Soon Percy's men were fighting for their lives.

And then in the mêlée, as they were borne back fighting and dying towards the trench, they heard their own horsemen calling to them from beyond that barrier that the Marshal was dead. Percy 'commanded the soldiers to turn faces about, with which, and the report that the Marshal was slain, our men were so dismayed that from retiring they began to fall into rout'. Redoubling their efforts, the Irish 'came on amain with a full cry after their manner'. The regiment broke and was 'driven in great disorder over the trenches', in which some were 'stifled, tumbling one over another'. Percy, struck by a gunshot on the breastplate, was stunned and thrown down 'into the mud', to be pulled out and led to safety by his Irish horseboy. But the majority perished. Evan Owen, Percy's Welsh ensign, 'being a resolute man' and seeing that all was lost, broke the flag pole which he carried and wrapped himself in the colours, which were 'heavy and new, full of half moons'—that is, they displayed the silver crescent which was the badge of the Percys. Owen was cut to pieces, 'for he would not part with his colours till he was slain'.

So the forlorn hope and the first regiment of the vanguard were, as fighting formations, eliminated. The few survivors joined what was left of Bagenal's regiment. Earlier this regiment led by the Marshal—who was now determined to push on since Percy had not come back—had shaken itself free from its assailants on the second hill and had pressed down the slope towards the trench. But Bagenal, raising the visor of his helmet to look about him, was struck in the face by a gunshot and killed in this moment of his advance.

Wingfield assumed command on Bagenal's death, and he and Cuney, the Sergeant-Major, who was next in rank, decided to return to Armagh. The army was 'even then in defeating'; the foot was beginning to break up at the head of the column and the horse could find 'no going where the rebels stood, by reason of a main bog'. It was a matter of saving what could be saved. To add to the difficulties that beset them, the saker stuck again, and finally; this time a carriage wheel was broken and all the oxen were killed. And their powder—already scarce—blew up. In the careless manner of the time, a soldier went to replenish his flask from an open barrel, touched it with his lighted match and exploded not only the contents, but a second barrel as well which stood close by. He 'spoiled many men and disordered the battle', and the black cloud of smoke that hung long in the air seemed an omen of destruction to the rest.

At this stage Wingfield's regiment was either on the second hill or still at the ford, and Cuney's and Billings's had passed the ford and were close to the second hill. The rear, led by Cuney, had shortly before this come down to the ford in one body and had then passed over with Cuney's regiment in front; after that they had pressed forward up the slope. Billings says that his men were held up here by overwhelming numbers and 'could not gain a butt's length [about 200 yards] in three-quarters of an hour'. Cuney had to help them. Their ammunition failed and their wings of shot were beaten back on their pikemen and they had to clear their front with pike charges. O'Neill and his allies, moving as the column moved but always seeking to clog its movement, were now close up to the English with all their forces and the crisis of the battle had been reached.

Following the decision to retire, Cuney went to prepare his own men and Billings's and Wingfield rode forward to tell Cosby and to order him to 'maintain the rear' in the march back to Armagh. After Bagenal's death his regiment, led now by Captain Evans, had gone on and had crossed the trench, but they were soon beaten back. They were so hotly engaged that they could do nothing to help Percy, and when Percy's fugitives, aided by Sir Calisthenes Brooke's horse, reached them they were between the trench and the foot of the second hill, fighting desperately and with their powder almost exhausted. Presently they were forced back on Cosby, who had come as far as the top of the hill, whence, as he held back his own assailants, he looked down on the slaughter below. It was at this moment that Wingfield reached Cosby, gave him his orders, and then went back towards the ford.

Cosby's regiment and the fugitives from the van were now the rearward, and Cosby should have turned and headed for Armagh. These were his orders, founded in a regard for the safety of the whole force. But in these moments of confusion and disaster safety may have lain in different directions for different men. One may have thought of falling back, another of still pushing on—after all, the fort was much nearer than Armagh. Whether their view of safety was thus different from Wingfield's and they were willing to disobey orders to achieve it, or whether, as was said, they saw some of the fugitives from the vanguard still in distress and tried to save them, Cosby and Evans, after Wingfield had left them, moved not back but forward. Percy says that while he tried to gather his survivors these two officers 'drew down' with their regiments and forced some of Percy's men, although they were without ammunition, to go on with them towards the trench. This, he says, 'was the hazard of the whole army'. It was at any rate, as a forward move, abortive. Unsettled by those among them who had already suffered one repulse and assailed with fury by the Irish, Cosby's men broke. Evans was killed and Cosby himself was taken prisoner.

It was now the early afternoon and the battle had been in progress for about four hours. Wingfield had started Cuney and Billings on their return journey. Cuney's men, unaware before this of what was happening in front, were amazed to see the fugitives from the van come running back and to hear of Bagenal's death. The rear squadron of horse helped the two regiments to disengage and they marched, guarding the dead body of the Marshal and carrying large numbers of wounded, towards the ford. As they came down towards it, they 'saw the enemy, both horse and foot, with the colours flying which was taken from the vanguard of all, minding to make good the ford before us', but Billings got there first and held it.

There was one further struggle in the rear. Wingfield, having set his own regiment in motion towards Armagh, was told of Cosby's disobedience of orders and that his men and the remains of the vanguard were caught and were in trouble. He sent on to stop Cuney, and then returned at once, together with the leading squadron of horse, now—Brooke being wounded—under Captain Montague. When they reached Cosby's men they charged, horse and foot, and 'saved five hundred men's lives, besides divers colours, which were then utterly broken'. Gathering the survivors, they brought them back to Cuney, whose regiment now became the battle and was sent on. Wingfield, as the new rearward, followed close behind him with Montague's horse on his flank. The saker and large quantities of supplies, arms and equipment were abandoned. When they reached the ford Billings's regiment was sent on as a vanguard to clear the way to Armagh, in which direction O'Neill's horsemen had now begun to show themselves. Billings scattered these enemies with the fire of 'the biggest of the three pieces of ordnance' which the English had saved, and in the course of the afternoon the whole remaining force, van, battle and rear, reached Armagh and did what they could to fortify themselves in the cathedral and amid the surrounding ruins.

O'Neill had won the greatest victory ever achieved by an Irish force over an English one. The English lost twenty-five officers and over 800 men killed and about 400 wounded. More than 300 of their soldiers deserted to O'Neill, including two of the recently arrived Englishmen. Many fled and were written off as missing. Eleven colours were lost. And Williams had to give up Blackwater fort.

The highest casualties were among the luckless recruits, 'the better half' of whom went down, many 'without making any resistance'. Ormond, whom the Queen chided for not having led the expedition himself, condemned Bagenal and his officers for 'marching so far asunder'. 'Sure the devil bewitched them', he said; and of the recruits he said that they 'came away most cowardly, casting from them their armour and weapons as soon as the rebels charged them'. Even a month later the survivors were 'not yet free from the fear they took in the late disaster'. And yet the English as a whole had fought well. If they had been trapped and if their leadership was faulty, they did their best in a false position, and they stood by one another well. Unfortunately, details of the movements of the victors, who were on their native heath and who were fighting their own kind of battle, are not recorded. We know from the contemporary Irish historians that O'Neill commanded in person on the left of the column and at the trench, that O'Donnell attacked from the other side, and that Maguire led the horse. The rest of what these writers say is made up of grandiose but vague statements, and we can see O'Neill's and O'Donnell's splendid, and splendidly handled, troops only in the glimpses of them afforded us by their enemies. The Irish losses were about 200 killed and 600 wounded.

Over 2,000 of Wingfield's men reached Armagh. Half the cavalry—the ones who had not deserted—burst out and got away to Dublin, with the exception of a Captain Romney, who was dilatory and was killed the next day as he smoked a pipe of tobacco by the roadside. O'Neill and O'Donnell could eventually have slaughtered the surviving foot, and the Irish Council, who sent them a supplicatory letter which the Queen later condemned, feared that they might do so. But they let them go, and Wingfield marched them crestfallen to Newry and out of Ulster.

Neither here nor on other occasions when they had defeated forces at their mercy did the Irish bear out the reputation given them by the anonymous versifier of the sixteenth-century compilation 'A Mirror for Magistrates', who claimed that their 'end of war' was 'to see their enemy dead', and who wrote:

> They know no law of arms nor none will learn:
> They make not war (as others do) a play,
> The lord, the boy, the Galloglas, the kern,
> Yield or not yield, whom so they take they slay.

Those who wondered at the escape of the beaten force were offered two explanations—that O'Neill, since it was costing him £500 a day to keep his army together, was anxious to finish the campaign and was willing to leave things as they were; and that he feared an English landing in Derry—which had been planned but was soon for the time being abandoned—and wanted to be free to resist it. Each suggested an exclusively Ulster viewpoint; there was no question of the continuance of a victorious campaign outside Ulster. Yet Fynes Moryson, speaking later on of the events of this and the following year, of which the battle of the Yellow Ford was certainly the most remarkable, said that they 'became so disastrous to the English and successful in action to the Irish as they shaked the English government in this kingdom till it tottered, and wanted little of fatal ruin'.

Contemporary evidence relative to the battle from the English side is extensive and may principally be found in the reports of several officers and the statements of Ormond and the Irish Council in the Irish State Papers in the Public Record Office, London. (Microfilms are in the National Library of Ireland and the documents are summarized in the *Calendar of State Papers, Ireland, 1598–9*.) See also the documents printed in J. T. Gilbert, *Account of the Facsimiles of the National Manuscripts of Ireland* (1884) and in his *Facsimiles of the National Manuscripts of Ireland* (1882), IV i, where the contemporary picture map of the battlefield (original among the Hardiman collection of maps in Trinity

College, Dublin) is reproduced; note that the terrain between Armagh and the place where Bagenal crossed the river Callan, as it is shown, is telescoped in this map, so that the scale of the central portion is not at all the same as that of the right and left sides. See Plate 13. For further documents see *Journal of the Kilkenny Archaeological Society*, I (1856–7), pp. 256 ff.

Of the many references to the battle made by other contemporary English writers those of Sir J. Perrott, *The Chronicle of Ireland* (ed. H. Wood, 1933), pp. 149 ff and Fynes Moryson, *An Itinerary*, II, pp. 216 f should be seen.

Irish accounts are in the Annals of the Four Masters; Peter Lombard, *De Regno Hibernia sanctorum insula commentarius* (English translation by M. J. Byrne published as *The Irish War of Defence, 1598–1600*); P. O'Sullivan, *Historiae Catholicae Iberniae Compendium* (also translated by M. J. Byrne and published as *Ireland under Elizabeth*); and L. O'Clery, *Beatha Aodha Ruaidh ODomhnaill* (*The Life of Red Hugh O'Donnell*; there are translations and editions by Murphy, Walsh, and O Lochlainn).

Good modern narratives are in C. Falls, *Elizabeth's Irish Wars*, pp. 213 ff and R. Bagwell, *Ireland under the Tudors*, III, pp. 295 ff. For the site see also W. T. Latimer, *The Battles of the Yellow Ford and Benburb* (1919). Note that the map of south-east Ulster made by the cartographer Richard Bartlett at the end of 1602 or the beginning of 1603 (original in Public Record Office, London, MPF 36; reproduced in facsimile with the Ulster Escheated Counties maps of 1609 and published by the Ordnance Survey, Southampton, in 1861) shows the position of O'Neill's trench. Bartlett calls it 'The long trenche of the Ford' and shows it approximately in the townlands of Tulligoonigan and Annahagh, Co. Armagh. He shows also Balle mc Killoura and says 'Here Sr. H. Bagnall the Marshall was slaine'—i.e. about two miles north of Armagh. This is approximately the place marked on the Ordnance Survey 6 inch map as the site of the battlefield. In the account which I have given above I indicate that the Marshal was killed between the Callan and Blackwater, perhaps a mile or a mile and a half from here; all the statements of those who were present at the battle seem to me to bear this out. 'The place where Tyrone gave the defeat to Bagnoll' is mentioned in a 1642 document—see *Ulster Journal of Archaeology*, 3 series, XVII, pp. 47 ff.

For Burgh's campaign in 1597 see *Calendar of State Papers,*

Ireland, 1596–7. Note that the claim that Burgh intended in October 1597 to invade Tyrone (repeated in some modern histories) was not made until *after* his death. For the sites of the three different Blackwater forts see *The Irish Sword,* II, pp. 212 ff.

The account which I have given of O'Neill and O'Donnell's forces is based on my paper 'The Army of Ulster, 1593–1601', which appears also in *The Irish Sword,* in I, pp. 105 ff. For the clandestine sale of English war materials to the Irish see *Calendar of State Papers, Ireland,* 1596–7, p. 323; 1599–1600, pp. 181, 477; 1600–1, pp. 65 f and *Calendar of the Carew Manuscripts,* 1599–1600, p. 492, and compare B. Rich, *A New Description of Ireland,* p. 110 and F. Moryson, *Itinerary,* II, p. 298. For the Blackwater woods see E. McCracken, 'The Woodlands of Ulster in the early seventeenth century' in *Ulster Journal of Archaeology,* 3 series, X, pp. 15 ff. In August 1601, as Fynes Moryson relates, Lord Deputy Mountjoy camped 'near the place where the Marshal Bagnol was slain'. The camp was in a 'fair meadow' on low ground under a hill, and with woods close by 'between the passes and Armagh, a little beyond Armagh towards the north'. The 'passes' in question were the tracks leading towards Dungannon on the north side of the Blackwater. On this occasion Mountjoy 'made that a fair way to Blackwater which the Marshal shunned when he was overthrown'—i.e., he cleared the woods near the highway leading from Armagh. The quotation from *A Mirror for Magistrates* is from L. B. Campbell's edition, pp. 88 f.

Sir Walter Scott refers to the battle of the Yellow Ford in *Rokeby,* Canto Fourth, VI. Of O'Neill he says:

> But chief arose his victor pride,
> When that brave Marshal fought and died,
> And Avon-Duff to ocean bore
> His billows red with Saxon gore.

Avon-Duff is, of course, the river Blackwater and the Marshal is Bagenal.

The saker which the English abandoned at the Yellow Ford was only one of several cannon captured by the Ulstermen during the war. The Blackwater fort guns fell to them. Three falcons (2½ or 3 pounders) belonging to the city of Dublin were captured by Maguire at Enniskillen in 1595 and some guns were taken at Sligo in the same year. Three guns were found by the English hidden away in a crannog in Lough Roughan in Co. Tyrone in

1602. As far as we know, O'Neill made no use of any of these weapons, although they might have served him well more than once, for example, against Docwra in Derry in 1600 or 1601. Why were they not used? Scarcely because the Irish lacked the ability to use them. Possibly because powder was scarce. Much more likely because of the difficulty of dragging them about in Ulster. Field guns were scarcely used at all during the war. The Jacobite Chevalier Johnstone, speaking of warfare in Scotland 150 years later, was to say: 'Artillery, instead of being useful, was, on the contrary, a great embarrassment to us, by continually retarding our marches.' Chinese Gordon said in 1881 that 'artillery is a great encumbrance' in irregular warfare.

Bagenal's phrase 'two or three flight-shot over' must be explained. The allusion is to archery. Flight arrows were the long-ranging ones. The distance would have been more than 600 yards.

Moyry Pass, 1600

Among the results of the battle of the Yellow Ford was the complete expulsion of the English from the lordship of Tyrone. After the battle they held neither the Blackwater fort nor Armagh cathedral, and their most northerly post was in Newry, the frontier town.

The results, of course, were far wider than that. The effects of the greatest defeat suffered by the English in Ireland were felt throughout the island, and they coloured the events of several succeeding years. O'Neill was disclosed as a most formidable opponent of English rule.

In 1599, after a delay that greatly injured the English interest, the Queen filled a post which had been left vacant since Burgh's death by sending a viceroy to Ireland. She sent her favourite, the Earl of Essex. Essex further increased O'Neill's prestige by using—and using up—against Munster rather than Ulster the great military force with which he came provided. In 1600, when Essex's successor Lord Mountjoy arrived, O'Neill was at the height of his power.

Mountjoy was O'Neill's most able opponent, and he was eventually to defeat him; but Mountjoy's early encounters with the Ulstermen were far from being glorious to the English arms. O'Neill in his new strength sought to deny to the English not only the passage of the Blackwater, which was the way to Dungannon and into the heart of Tyrone, and for which he had fought formerly, but also the Moyry pass, forty miles to the south, which was the gateway to Ulster. Moyry or Moyra pass, or Bealach an mhaighre, the celebrated Gap of the North, is the defile in the hills below Slieve Gullion in Co. Armagh through which the old road ran from Dundalk to Newry, and through which the railway now runs from Dublin to Belfast. The road through the pass was in the sixteenth century 'a broken cawsey beset on both sides with bogs, where the Irish might skip but the English could not go'. It was 'naturally one of the most difficult passages of Ireland',

and was the scene of much military activity over the centuries.

Here, in October 1600, O'Neill's stubborn resistance to Mountjoy's efforts to break through provoked 'one of the greatest fights that hath been seen in Ireland'. It was among the more notable of the Earl's efforts to prolong the war until the Queen had had enough of it, or until she died, or until help came to him from Spain.

Mountjoy had gone through the pass without difficulty in the previous May, when he marched north to occupy O'Neill's attention while Sir Henry Docwra's force landed at Derry, an essay in amphibious warfare which fatally weakened the Ulster confederacy and which three years later, following the defeat at Kinsale, ensured its downfall. When on that occasion Mountjoy turned back from Newry to protect a convoy that was following him, he was however given a foretaste of the formidable opposition which he must overcome before he could claim victory over O'Neill.

He had sent Captain Blayney to escort the Earl of Southampton and the convoy which was following the main force through the pass. O'Neill held Blayney up at the Four Mile Water (the stream flowing between the townlands of Foughill Otra and Edenappa, Co. Armagh). Blayney divided his leading battalion into three maniples, right, left and centre, and was about to charge the Irish when the vanguard of the Lord Deputy's army was seen marching down behind O'Neill. They had come back to aid Blayney. The Irish, save for about a hundred men who were left to skirmish, immediately withdrew to the rear of Blayney's column, where Southampton was, and made their attack there. There was a hot fight. Rain fell so heavily that the musketeers and calivermen on both sides were out of action; 'their pieces of neither side could take fire', and they were forced 'to betake themselves unto their swords' and to the throwing of 'staves, darts, and innumerable stones'. In the end the Irish withdrew altogether and the united English force, together with the convoy, marched to Newry.

This was Mountjoy's first experience of an action in the pass. When he returned to the north in September, intending to penetrate to Armagh and to re-establish the garrison there, he was given a far hotter reception.

On this second occasion the English had almost 3,000 foot and 300 horse. They marched on 20 September from Dundalk to the hill of Faughart, the scene of Edward Bruce's defeat and death in

1318, and camped there. The entry to the Moyry was half a mile north of Faughart, and as the English came up O'Neill's forces, which had earlier been visible on the hill, withdrew into the pass.

They did not go far. They skirmished with an English detachment that was sent out to cut wood for fuel and for the building of shelters—the current substitute for tents—in the camp. That night their scouts crept close to Mountjoy's outposts, and, reaching ground that overlooked the camp, shot up the sleeping soldiers. The next day they tried to draw some English horsemen into an ambush.

Thereafter—the Irish weather being no better then than it is now—the skies opened and it rained continuously for four days. On the 25th, when rain gave place to mist, the English moved. They felt their way cautiously forward. Their forlorn hope or advance guard of a hundred picked men and some gentlemen volunteers was led by that old and gallant soldier, Captain Thomas Williams; it was he who had defended Blackwater fort until O'Neill's victory at the Yellow Ford had driven him out of it. Other troops, making up three regiments in all, followed. The way led downhill into the pass where it was 'on all sides naturally fenced with stony cliffs and thick bushes and trees, even to the Three Mile Water or ford' (the stream forming the northern boundary of the townland of Carrickbroad and eventually emptying into Dundalk harbour). Great 'mountains' rose on either hand. Visiblity was bad and Williams and his men, advancing quickly, overran the Irish sentinels. They came to an entrenchment stretching across the path. The defenders retired and they took it. A hundred and forty or so yards further on they took a second trench and 'barricado'. Then they were stopped. The English report says that they were under orders to retire after they had tried the strength of the defences. They turned and fought their way back, being fired on from the trenches, which were quickly reoccupied, and from both flanks. They admitted a loss of seven killed and thirty wounded but claimed that they had inflicted 120 casualties on the Irish.

The report which these men brought back must have made disturbing news on a dispiriting day. They said that there were at least three trenches at the distance of a caliver shot (not much more than a hundred yards), one from another, across the pass. Fynes Moryson, who was Mountjoy's secretary, says that the Irish had 'raised from mountain to mountain, from wood to

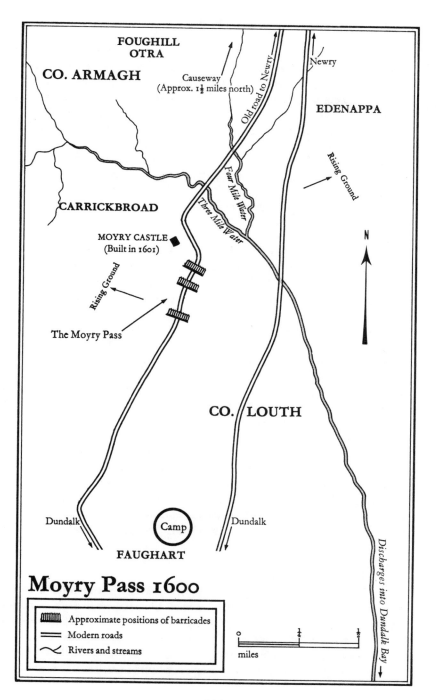

FOUGHILL
OTRA

CO. ARMAGH

Causeway
(Approx. 1½ miles north)

Newry

Old road to Newry

EDENAPPA

Rising Ground

Four Mile Water

CARRICKBROAD

Three Mile Water

MOYRY CASTLE
(Built in 1601)

N

Rising Ground

The Moyry Pass

CO. LOUTH

Dundalk

Camp

Dundalk

FAUGHART

Discharges into Dundalk Bay

Moyry Pass 1600

	Approximate positions of barricades
	Modern roads
	Rivers and streams

0   ¼   ½
miles

wood, and from bog to bog long traverses with huge and high flankers of great stones, mingled with turf and staked on both sides with palisadoes wattled'. Other accounts speak of the 'great hedges' which topped these works, or of 'a kind of rampire raised upon them with earth, stone and thorn'. Where the ground rose above the track the Irish—in their element at this kind of work—had 'plashed' the undergrowth and trees, thus making an almost impenetrable barrier of wattles and intertwined branches on either side of the highway. Their work is reminiscent of that of the Leinster lords of more than 400 years earlier, who had tried to keep the first Norman invaders out of their territories by blocking the paths that led into them. It would not have been easy, said Captain Nicholas Dawtrey, who served in the Moyry pass, 'for swine to pass through, much less men'.

All this was to the south of the Three Mile Water, a stream swollen with the heavy rain; what lay beyond that on the way to the Four Mile Water and the 'broken cawsey' that traversed the bogs south of Newry was unknown to Mountjoy's men but might be equally dangerous. Actually it was discovered later that there were two more barricades, 'which were the strongest of all', south of 'Bollen Clare', or the Four Mile Water. 'These barbarous people', said Mountjoy and the Irish Council in their summary of the actions in the pass, 'had far exceeded their custom and our expectation' in building such defences.

The English marched out again on 26 September, the weather having cleared a little by then, to take 'a better view' of what was before them; but they did not seek to come to close quarters with the defence. From then until 2 October it rained and the wind blew—for it was the stormy time of the autumnal equinox—and both sides lay still. There was a little bickering at the outposts where the Irish reviled the English, calling them cowards for having stolen on them in the mist and inviting them to come on again. On 30 September a force sent to bring a convoy from Carlingford was attacked. But the battle for the pass was not renewed until 2 October.

On that morning, being Thursday, the Irish horse rode up, calling to know when 'the churls' would be finished dinner, and if they would come out to fight them. The worst term of abuse that the aristocratic Irish could throw at an intruder into their proud world was churl. In the afternoon, when the English were drawn out under arms to be mustered, a troop of Irish horse and a force of infantry formed in a battalion of pikes and shot were seen approaching 'in a bravery' from the hills, as if they proposed to attack the camp. Five English regiments were immediately ordered forward, Sir Samuel Bagenal's in the van, St Lawrence's and Morrison's echeloned to the left, and Mountjoy's and Burke's echeloned to the right. Their orders seem to have been to drive the Irish back to their trenches.

Finding O'Neill's men 'ready to entertain skirmish on all sides, and not to give way, as their manner is sometimes to do, to gain more advantage', the English infantry soon had their orders extended and were told to push on and 'to give home to their trenches, and to force them'. There followed 'one of the greatest skirmishes, and best maintained in all places, that hath been in this kingdom'.

Sir Thomas Burke, a son of the Earl of Clanrickard, whose service for the Queen was one of the fruits of the recent settlement in Connacht, had 'the point'; that is, he led the attack. His men endured 'terrible volleys of shot at the barricadoes' and fell on their knees in fear; but Burke called them on, and, seconded by a few of the bravest, rushed to one of the barricades with his company colour in his hand, tossed the colour over, and, leaping in after it, drove out the Ulstermen and held his ground.

The fight continued for some three hours, in which time the attackers penetrated for about a mile into the pass. When they were held up before the third entrenchment, however, Mountjoy realised that he must withdraw. The attack had not sufficient force to overcome the remaining obstacles—the further barricades, the two flooded streams, and the narrow causeway through the bog. To hold what had been gained, exposed as the men were to the fire from the high ground on either side of the path, was as much out of the question as to go on. It was said that the captured entrenchments could not have been held without dividing the army, which would have been dangerous; it is unlikely that, commanded as they were by enemy fire from either side, they could have been held at all. Mountjoy made a virtue of necessity, declared that in any event he had not intended to go forward that day and bid the drums to be beaten and the trumpets sounded for a withdrawal.

The English made 'a gallant and an orderly retreat', or, in other words, they had to fight their way out. The Irish, encouraged by the withdrawal, 'fell on again very hotly', attacking them from both flanks and the rear as they moved back. Bagenal's, St Lawrence's, and Morrison's regiments had the worst of the struggle, and the horse under Godolphin and Davers charged 'in that uneven ground, where never horse served' before, so as to relieve the pressure on the footmen when the fight was at its worst.

By evening the English were out of the pass and had regained their camp. Mountjoy noted afterwards that the Irish 'do call this day's work their great overthrow', and said that 'during their fight the carriages were seen to march away, they were so near to an utter overthrow'. He might say such things, but the fact was that he had exerted his full strength for three hours to break through and had failed to do so. The English admitted as many as 160 casualties after the day's fighting, but claimed that the Irish casualties were twice as great.

Mountjoy made one more attempt to break through, this time by a flank attack. On Sunday afternoon, 5 October, when the storms had abated and the weather for the moment was fine, three regiments of foot and a hundred horse received orders to march. The regiment of Sir Charles Percy, which was the leading one, was sent off to the left to scale the heights above the pass and to move forward until they could enfilade the trenches from above. Sir Oliver St John's regiment followed in support. The third regiment and the horse remained below, probably moving forward along the lower ground in concert with the others. Percy pushed on, skirmishing with the Irish force in front of him as he went, and driving them back a considerable distance. St John was left behind. Noticing that Percy, who had only 230 men in his regiment, had overreached himself and that St John could not hope to come up to help him for some time because of the 'steepness and raggedness' of the ground, the Irish turned and came to close quarters. Contrary, as the English report says, to their custom, they formed up, and, coming on resolutely 'in a gross body' more than 300 strong, tried to envelop Percy's regiment. Percy hit back. He 'charged the rebels on every side' and kept them off until some wings of shot that St John, seeing his plight, had sent forward reached him and made their fire felt on the attackers. Then the Irish 'ran away howling', leaving twelve of their number lying dead within sight.

Yet the English effort on the high ground was no more successful than their previous attempts had been in the pass. Percy and

St John were glad to get back. Although they got down from the heights unpursued, there was more fighting in the pass, where Sir Robert Lovell was shot dead with two bullets as he charged at the head of the squadron of horse. Captains Williams, Rowe and Trevor did well and were mentioned in despatches.

The English gained nothing by Sunday's manœuvre. 'We are now', said Sir Geoffrey Fenton on 9 October, 'but where we were in the beginning.' Mountjoy found it impossible, either by attacking them in front or in the flank, to beat the Irish from the pass. The English casualties of the three days' fighting were said to be fifty killed and 200 wounded, the Irish (according to the English) perhaps twice that number. This would mean a loss to the English in killed alone of about twenty-five on 5 October, including Lovell and Lieutenant Brewerton of St John's regiment.

In the absence of detailed accounts from the Irish side of this or any other part of the fighting of O'Neill's war, we are glad of occasional glimpses behind the scenes vouchsafed to English observers and recorded by them. O'Neill we are told had assigned particular tasks to different units of his forces in the Moyry defence, 'giving unto his especial gentlemen and captains their particular charge and direction where to fight and how to resist us'—although this was not, we might say, a very remarkable matter in a well organised army such as O'Neill's was. Moyry was not the only commitment of the northern allies at this time. Further back, in Breifne and Monaghan, the people were daily employed in digging trenches and building sconces in the passes. O'Neill exhorted them 'with great earnestness to work lustily and patiently', saying that the safeguard of themselves, their wives and children depended on holding back the English, and that if Mountjoy got through then it was 'farewell Ulster and all the north'. This report of a spy sent from Monaghan has the ring of truth.

On the other side of the hill, or in this instance at Faughart church outside the pass, the English had little to cheer them. 'Almost drowned', without dry clothes for twenty days, their horses dying and many of their men sick, they were in poor condition for further service. One officer said that he was hard put to it to keep fires going for his company of raw recruits lately come from England, and that even though he plied them with whiskey and wine eight were down with 'the country disease', which was probably the bloody flux or dysentery. He believed that more men had been killed by the appalling weather than by the enemy. And there were many deserters.

Mountjoy waved the flag again on the 6th, marching out towards the trenches 'to see what stomach the rogues'—meaning the Irish—'had to fight'. But his own rogues had had enough of it. Next day he sent to Dublin for reinforcements. He had already sent to Newry for 300 muskets and calivers, intending to give them to his pikemen to increase his fire power; now he called for 350 picked shot, so many from each garrison company. Yet he did not wait for them to come up. On the 9th he struck camp and retired to Dundalk. He still proclaimed his intention to force the pass; but he said that he needed a breathing space before trying again.

The Moyry pass was not forced. When the campaign was over Mountjoy boasted that he had let the Irish know 'that their fortifications, though very great, were not the hindrance of our passage'; he claimed that he had been held up not by O'Neill but by the bad weather. But he did not move north until O'Neill had got out of his way.

On 10 or 11 October Sir Samuel Bagenal was sent off to Newry with his regiment by way of Carlingford, that is, by the coast road skirting Dundalk Bay and Carlingford Lough. On the 13th O'Neill suddenly moved back from the pass, going himself to his usual haunt in the crannog or island fortress of Lough Lurcan, between Newry and Armagh, and sending his forces towards Armagh. Mountjoy heard of this move on the 14th; on the 17th, accompanied by his whole force, he marched into the empty pass. His captains were under no illusion concerning the strength of O'Neill's abandoned works. One said that if the Irish had continued to defend them they 'could not have been won without the great hazard of the whole army'. Another never saw 'a more villainous piece of work, and an impossible thing for an army to pass without an intolerable loss, especially with carriages'. The English moved back to Dundalk, and then, on the day following, entered the pass again and commenced dismantling the fortifications and cutting back the undergrowth on either side of the track. This done, they moved on to Newry. On 22 October Mountjoy announced from his camp three miles beyond Newry that he had given up for that year his intention of occupying Armagh. He built a fort at Mount Norris, a few miles short of half-way between Newry and Armagh, instead. O'Neill's defence of the Moyry pass had thus postponed the advance to the river Blackwater and Mountjoy's attempt to invade Tyrone.

Why did O'Neill retire from the pass on 13 October? The naïve Four Masters say that Mountjoy 'got an advantage and opportunity of O'Neill's watch on this pass, and proceeded through it . . . without battle or opposition'. They suggest that he slipped through when O'Neill was off his guard. They go on to say that O'Neill later blocked Mountjoy's progress into Tyrone and eventually compelled him to return southward by a route other than that leading through the Moyry pass. It is true that Mountjoy did not reach Armagh and that he had to be content with the establishment of a post at Mount Norris, beyond the pass but far short of the Blackwater; it is also true that, this post established, he marched back to Dundalk not by the pass but by Carlingford; but it is unlikely that he took O'Neill by surprise. Other reasons might be suggested for the Irish withdrawal from the Moyry defences.

Although O'Neill was a great soldier, he was a politician first. A veteran of the Ulster wars, Sir Francis Stafford, wrote privately to the Treasurer at War, Sir George Carey, on 19 October, saying that O'Neill had sought by all possible means, even while the fight in the pass was in progress, to negotiate with Mountjoy. It was quite consistent with his conduct of the war to give the appearance of being determined to fight to a finish and then suddenly to cease fire. Furthermore, Sir Samuel Bagenal's regiment had marched off to Carlingford after Mountjoy had retired to Dundalk. It was possible to go thence by the coast road to Newry, and eventually to work round in O'Neill's rear towards Armagh. Furthermore, Mountjoy had sent for reinforcements. O'Neill may have decided that the time had come for him to take up a new defensive position further back, a position that would cover both approaches to Tyrone, that through the pass and the way by Carlingford and Newry.

Finally, the beginnings of disaster for O'Neill's principal ally O'Donnell had become apparent in Tirconnell. Neill Garbh O'Donnell, Hugh O'Donnell's cousin, had gone over to the enemy. He had ridden in to Derry to Docwra at the beginning of October. Later in the month a spy reported to the English from Fermanagh that Hugh O'Donnell, who was absent in Connacht when the defection took place, had upbraided O'Neill, saying that he had remained too long at the Moyry and that it would have been better if he had let Mountjoy through, had let him plant his garrison at Armagh, and had then caught him and pommelled him on his way back to Dublin. The spy may have imagined or invented a difference of opinion between the Ulster leaders, but, even if he had, the disaster in O'Neill's rear would have been reason enough for the withdrawal.

That Mountjoy, for all his boasting, had had enough of the pass for that year was shown by his returning from Mount Norris by way of Carlingford. The detour did not secure him an uninterrupted passage. O'Neill, who must meanwhile have done what he could in co-operation with O'Donnell to minimise for the moment the effects of Neill Garbh's treachery, was determined to have the last word. The way lay by the sea coast, between wooded and steeply rising ground and the shore of Carlingford Lough. O'Neill moved down in front of the English with a small force. One account says that he had no more than 400 foot, but that they were 'all of his own followers and of his best men'. He may well have discharged most of his costly bonnaghts and those who were with him now may have been his 'regulars'; indeed the expense of keeping his army together may have been an additional reason for his removal from the Moyry pass. He occupied the high ground overlooking the road and dug trenches and raised 'half moons' and 'barricadoes' in terraces, one above the other among the trees. Presently the English came, marching four foot regiments strong, with St Lawrence's regiment in the van and Sir Samuel Bagenal's—in which there were four new and untried companies—in the rear. The Irish opened fire on the head of the column and St Lawrence's men replied 'in that vehemency, as that many times neither could they see us nor we them, by reason of the cloud of smoke between us'.

It was the well tried manœuvre of the ambush, and, as on other occasions, when the English pushed hard enough they got through. Mountjoy's, St Lawrence's and Morrison's regiments moved beyond the danger point, and although O'Neill fell on the rear the march was not long held up. Bagenal's men had to be reinforced by the horse and had to 'charge, colours and all', to keep the Irish off. Mountjoy admitted a loss of some twenty killed and more than sixty wounded. He reached Carlingford on the 13th and, moving on, came to Dundalk and the English Pale on the next day. The whole series of operations, here, at Mount Norris and at the pass, showed that the Ulstermen, after five—some of them after seven—years war, were still full of fight.

The English accounts of the Moyry struggle are in F. Moryson, *Itinerary* (1745 edn), II, p. 137 and in the state papers (printed in abbreviated form in *Calendar of State Papers, Ireland, 1600*, pp. 459–530; and, for the movements in May 1600, pp. 190 and 205). The *Annals of the Four Masters* give no details. The positions taken up by O'Neill's forces in the pass are shown in Richard Bartlett's map of south-east Ulster, 1600 in the British Museum (Cotton MSS, Aug. I ii, 37), which is reproduced in Plate 14.

Kinsale, 1601

It was said of Hugh O'Neill in 1597 that, until the Spaniards came to help him in his struggle against England, 'he will not fight upon the plain, however great advantage he has, but will lay all passes and streights for her Majesty's forces'; he would, in other words, remain on the defensive in Ulster where Queen Elizabeth's superiority of organisation, armament and resources was least noticeable and where his own method of waging war offered the greatest possiblity of success.

The prediction proved true. Until the December morning in 1601* when O'Neill marched towards Lord Deputy Mountjoy's army outside the walls of Kinsale in Co. Cork he avoided committing himself irrevocably to action in the field. Before the battle of Kinsale he attacked only when he knew that he could retain control of his men in the changing situation in which the attack might involve them and could draw them off safely at any moment that he desired. He behaved thus at Clontibret and at the Yellow Ford and the Moyry pass; his victories, and his survival, were consequences of this behaviour. But at Kinsale he exercised no such control. He had no control over the Spaniards who had arrived to help him, but whose freedom of movement had been curtailed by the subsequent arrival of the English; he might certainly count on Spanish assistance as he moved forward, but he could not compel it, and in fact he did not receive it. Nor had he full control over his own men, not at least to the extent of being able to retire at will. The Ulstermen were involved at Kinsale in a battle that was different from anything they had experienced before. Two hundred miles separated them from Dungannon and the rough terrain of their familiar north; despite their best efforts, all their experience as fighters seemed to separate them from the practice in arms that gave their enemies success.

* Dates are given in the old style, which was that used at the time of the battle by the English. The Spaniards, following the Gregorian calendar, introduced in 1582 (but not adopted officially in Ireland until 1782), used the new style.

The purpose of military strategy is to bring about an encounter with the enemy in circumstances in which one possesses every advantage—every advantage of ground, of numbers, of armament, of supplies, and so on—and, having done that, to crush him. If the exercise of caution is necessary to realise that end, then caution is justified, even a caution persisted in through long years and involving withdrawal, retirement, and refusal to accept battle.

O'Neill's caution in the years before 1601 may not have given him many abiding advantages, but without it, since he struggled against an enemy far stronger than he was, he could not have survived. Therefore was it justified. But the question remained whether he had, through these years, retained the power to drop caution and to be aggressive; whether he had his men so well in hand that they could when the occasion arose, as arise it must, pass over to a line of action to which all that they had done up to that had made them unaccustomed. No war was ever won by caution alone, or by a facility in withdrawing from the field at the right moment. History has shown many times—it was shown in South Africa in 1899–1902—that no purely defensive war, not even one in which the defenders have had great initial success, can be won against a stronger power that is determined to go on fighting. The moment would come for O'Neill and his companions—it would come when the Spaniards came—at which they must be prepared to assume the offensive, and to assume it outside Ulster. Their real ability as soldiers would be tested then. And that moment came at Kinsale.

There appear to have been four main reasons for the Irish success in the years before 1601. First there was O'Neill's leadership, which was outstanding and in the Irish context quite unprecedented. O'Neill was the heart and soul of the struggle. He was, we may well say, a man of genius: skilful, patient, infinitely resourceful, a great organiser, a subtle and a crafty negotiator, a great leader as well as a great soldier. 'The reputation he has with the enemy,' said Matthew de Oviedo, Archbishop of Dublin, 'is so great that it alone sustains the war.'

Secondly, the Irish fought for what they believed was a worthy cause. The war was the greatest, as it was the last, effort made to prevent the abolition of the old Irish institutional system by the centralised administration of England. English observers were in little doubt about Irish motives. O'Neill, they said, would not 'be content with less than absolute command like a Prince of Ulster'.

Perhaps indeed he sought more. Hugh O'Donnell, attacking a castle in 1595 and summoning it in the name of 'the Prince of Ireland', drew the response that the defenders knew no other Prince of Ireland than the Queen, whereupon O'Donnell said that those who served the Queen in Ireland were rebels and traitors, and that 'his Prince and the Prince of Ireland' was O'Neill. It was believed in 1600 that this Irish Prince had even higher hopes and that he aimed 'to wear a crown'. In 1601 the object of the Irish, who remembered 'that their ancestors have been monarchs and provincial kings of this land', was said to be 'by strong hand to regain the crown of Ireland to themselves'; in parenthesis, one wonders what regal dignity they were presumed originally to have possessed—the High Kingship? O'Neill encouraged the view that he was fighting to defend Irish institutions. He hoped that 'this island of Ireland shall be at our direction and counsel as Irishmen' and declared that he would do the best that he could for God and his country 'against the enemies and tyrants of the same'. He had, in seeking allies outside Ulster, 'the ancient swelling and desire of liberty in a conquered nation to work upon'. The hope of those who sided with him was to be 'allowed their Macs and Oes', that is, to be allowed to retain their native system of independent lordships each under its own ruling family. They strove 'for the maintenance of their tanist law and old Irish customs', and for 'the gaining of the kingdom to themselves'.

To these motives another was added as the years advanced. Hugh O'Neill soon proclaimed himself the Catholic champion. The European call for a crusade against heresy was heard, and although there had as yet been scarcely any persecution in Ireland for religion's sake, the war became something of a rally of Catholics against Protestants. The Queen's Irish Council summed it all up in 1597 when they said: 'The rebels stand not as heretofore upon terms of oppression and country grievances, but pretend to recover their ancient land and territories out of the Englishmen's hands, and [strive] for the restoring of the Romish religion, and to cast off English laws and government, and to bring the realm to the tanist law, acknowledging Tyrone to be lieutenant to the Pope and King of Spain.' This was a formidable combination of motives. The Irish had here a cause to be defended such as had not called them before. They answered the call by fighting as they had not previously been known to fight.

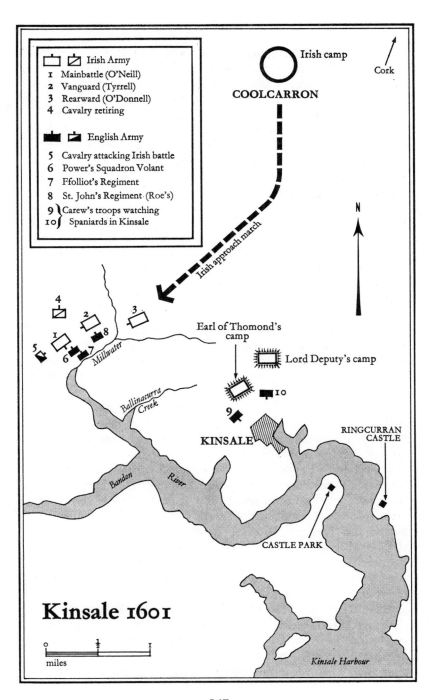

Legend

Irish Army
1. Mainbattle (O'Neill)
2. Vanguard (Tyrrell)
3. Rearward (O'Donnell)
4. Cavalry retiring

English Army
5. Cavalry attacking Irish battle
6. Power's Squadron Volant
7. Ffolliot's Regiment
8. St. John's Regiment (Roe's)
9. ⎫ Carew's troops watching
10. ⎭ Spaniards in Kinsale

Irish camp

Cork

COOLCARRON

Irish approach march

N

4

2

1   8

5   7
6   Millwater

3

Earl of Thomond's camp

Lord Deputy's camp

10

Ballinacurra Creek

9

KINSALE

RINGCURRAN CASTLE

Bandon River

CASTLE PARK

Kinsale 1601

0   ½   1
miles

Kinsale Harbour

Thirdly, the Irish now had an army that had shown itself capable, at least in certain circumstances, of facing the soldiers of the Queen. New military forces that were in effect national militias had arisen in the wake of feudalism and with the passing of the great age of mercenary service all over western Europe. The Queen's army, which was the national militia of England, was the first organised English army in the modern sense. Partly volunteer, partly conscript, equipped for the first time with firearms on the contemporary Continental scale, it was a force which was, in organisation, armament and numbers, infinitely more powerful than any earlier English army. To oppose it Hugh O'Neill, aided by his allies, had created a national militia of his own. He had done this, as has already been said, largely by an extension—it was in fact a transformation—of the Irish scheme of bonnaght, or the service of billeted men. The Ulster army was organised, equipped and trained to a degree hitherto quite unknown in the Gaelic areas.

Fourthly—and this too has been more than once mentioned— the Irish were successful because they had adopted a method of warfare that perfectly suited their traditions as fighters and the terrain over which they fought; a method, moreover, that was in full conformity with the pattern of diplomacy and strategy practised by O'Neill and his allies.

The strategy of the Ulstermen was, up to the date of the battle of Kinsale, purely defensive. At no time had they sought out with intent to attack it a main force of their enemies that was not already seeking them, or carrying out an operation of aggression against them. They had not tried to wrest the initiative from the English. On the contrary, they were content to hold their ground in Ulster; they awaited attack and met it when it came. This generalisation is not disturbed by the fact that the Irish continually raided the English districts, or those of English sympathy. O'Donnell marched more than once into Connacht and O'Neill marched into Munster in 1600. Successful efforts were made to stir up war in the midlands and in the south. But these operations never amounted to an assumption of the offensive.

O'Neill may have hoped, at least in the early stages, that if he prolonged this defensive struggle he might undermine the Queen's resolution to continue the fight, a fight that was becoming increasingly costly for her. If he did, his hope must have receded after 1600 when Mountjoy, who was the best general of the war, entered the lists against him. By then the Queen's ire had been thoroughly aroused. The reality of the Irish war as a desperate struggle with a skilful enemy had been brought home to Englishmen; for the first time they declared their determination to 'wade through seas of Irish blood' to establish their dominion. When Mountjoy deployed in full the resources of England the Irish recipe for victory began to weaken in its effect. Mountjoy was no Burgh and no Essex. He was too wise to let the Irish cajole him back to the 'dallying times of their deluding parlies'— as Barnaby Rich called the early years of the war—too imaginative to permit another Yellow Ford. He profited by the mistakes of his predecessors.

It must have been clear at the beginning of 1601 that, if further help was not forthcoming from Spain and if the Queen lived long enough to see Mountjoy's work carried through, O'Neill and the Ulstermen would be defeated by the overpowering weight of their enemies' resources. O'Neill's survival was at stake; everything depended on his ability to keep his forces in the field until foreign help arrived. And he was successful in doing so. Mountjoy and his lieutenants, Carew in Munster and Docwra in Derry, had reduced him by the summer of 1601 from the height of his power, but they had not driven him to extremities; Kinsale, when it came to be fought, opened more as a battle of desperation for the English than for the Irish.

Hitherto O'Neill and his supporters had won their battles by a brilliant process of luring their unimaginative enemy into positions where they could fight with the odds in their favour. But O'Neill was general enough to know that when the aid arrived which he had been importuning from Spain he must be ready to second it by an aggressive campaign involving at least the risk of a formal encounter with his foe. Clearly he must meanwhile make every effort to organise and train his men, so that, when the testing time arrived, as few as possible of the odds would be against him.

There are many indications of O'Neill's awareness of these matters. We know that he did all that he could to modernise his troops. A Scots observer explained that he 'did train his men and order the war by marshal discipline by reason of his experience and education amongst the English'. He trained pikemen. The pike, which as we know was new then even in the Queen's army, was essentially a close formation weapon, the chief—almost the sole—purpose of which in the sixteenth and seventeenth centuries was the provision of the solidity that was necessary to deliver heavy blows and to resist shock in the pitched battles of formal warfare. When O'Neill was making ready for his march from Ulster to Kinsale to join the Spaniards in the early winter of 1601 it was reported of him that he had 'cast most of his companies into colours and drums [that is, that he had given them company colours and drums] according to the English fashion, and hath created officers of the field, as marshal and provost marshal'. This was an assumption of forms designed not for war as it had been waged in past times by the Irish but for manœuvre and conflict in the open field.

The Irish appeal to Spain was pressed ever more vigorously as time advanced. In June 1600 the Spanish court was told that the Ulstermen were hemmed in between two hostile armies— that is, Mountjoy's and Docwra's—and that they were 'exhausted and impoverished'; if they had the assistance of 6,000 Spaniards, however, and if these forces were equipped with heavy guns, the Irish 'could take any city in Ireland'. By August 'the enemy's strength grows daily and our people are losing courage, seeing succour delayed'. O'Neill believed that he could hold out until September, but no longer. He had carried on the war for six years and had now neither food for his men nor money to pay them. Still, even in October, with 6,000 or 7,000 Spaniards and heavy guns 'we shall be masters of the kingdom'.

The winter of 1600-1 went by, and in the following spring Spain stirred at last. Spanish preparations to invade Ireland were reported with increasing frequency during the summer, and by autumn it appeared certain to the watching English that an attempt to land a force which would assist the Ulstermen would not be much longer delayed. The question was, where such a force should land. Mountjoy moved down from the Ulster border to Trim in Co. Meath at the beginning of September 1601 so as to be ready for all emergencies. The English expected the invasion to come on the south coast, or perhaps in the west. In fact, as recent research has made clear, the Spaniards, after much deliberation and after the failure of a last-minute effort to confirm what they already knew of the wishes of the Ulster leaders, decided to land at Kinsale.

Three alternatives were debated in Spain during the summer. The force which Don Juan del Aguila was appointed to lead and

Don Diego de Brochero to conduct by sea might land in Tir-connell, or it might land on the east Ulster or north Leinster coast, or it might land on the south coast. The objectives of the Spaniards were to help O'Neill and O'Donnell and to advance their own ends by injuring England. The second aim might be furthered by forcing the recall of English troops from the Spanish Netherlands, and it might be accomplished by using a conquered (or a liberated) Ireland as a base for an attack on England. Military requirements in respect of the invasion port were that adequate food supplies should be available there, that the surrounding country should be level and suitable for transport, that it should be accessible to the Ulstermen, and that it should be well placed for seeking out and engaging the English. It was appreciated that a voyage to Ulster would be more difficult for the Spaniards than one to Munster, that operations in Ulster would be difficult for the invaders, and that a Munster landing could be the more readily reinforced. It might on the other hand be hard for O'Neill to cross Ireland from north to south to effect a junction with his allies. Allied action of the Irish and Spaniards which did not require such a junction was apparently not con-templated.

In July a messenger was sent to O'Donnell to seek his and O'Neill's views. At the same time, and despite the difficulties inseparable from such a venture, opinion hardened in Spain in favour of going to Tirconnell. At this juncture Archbishop Matthew de Oviedo, who had been in Ulster in 1600 as a repre-sentative of the Spanish court, came out strongly against an Ulster landing and pressed for a descent on Cork, Limerick, or Waterford. He held that O'Neill's wish was for a Munster land-ing. It was decided that—failing the receipt in time of a reply from O'Neill and O'Donnell—this former opinion of the Ulster leaders as reported by Oviedo should be respected and that the expedition should go to the south coast. Kinsale was eventually selected as the port which promised the greatest possibility of success.

The messenger who had been sent to Ireland arrived back in Corunna on 1 October. He reported that O'Donnell, speaking for O'Neill as well as himself, now advised a landing at Limerick or Galway, or, if neither of these places could be reached, at some convenient place between the Shannon mouth and Lough Foyle. The reason for this change of opinion was said to be that Munster had been overrun by the English since 1600, when the Irish leaders had spoken with Oviedo, that those in the southern province who might have advocated support for the Ulstermen were now in prison, and that the English were building fortifications at Waterford and Cork. In fact no new works appear to have been erected at Waterford or in Waterford harbour at this time, and nothing was done to fortify Cork or the approaches to it from the sea until 1602.

But this news from Ireland came too late. The Spanish expedition had already sailed by 1 October. Whatever effect O'Donnell's statement might have had, if they had known of it in time, on the organisers of the invading force, it was too late to convey any further directive to Aguila. The javelin had been cast.

The Spanish-Irish exchanges of 1600 and 1601—carried on in circumstances of great difficulty and, until the recent publication of Fr John Silke's and Fr Frederick Jones's research, almost entirely unknown to historians—disclose an Irish preference for a Munster landing. The requirement of the Ulstermen, as stated in 1600 and pathetically repeated in 1602 after the débâcle of Kinsale and the death of O'Donnell, was a large Spanish force, to be sent to Munster. If over 6,000 men came, they should land in Waterford or Cork; if between 3,000 and 4,000, in Limerick. The Spaniards should go to Tirconnell only if they were fewer than 2,000 strong. Ulster was not the proper goal of Spanish assistance. It would be hard to feed the Spaniards there and difficult in such country to move their guns about. It was said that once Munster had been gained by O'Neill and his allies Ireland would be won, but, we might add, a joint victory of Spaniards and Irish in Ulster—in the unlikely event of the English fighting anywhere in the north save perhaps at Derry—must be indecisive. As the Yellow Ford had shown, the war could not be won in the north.

In view of what happened at Kinsale and in view of modern attempts to show that the Spaniards had landed in the wrong place, we should remember that the arrangements for the invasion always contemplated that the Spaniards and Irish would join forces and strike the English together. The best base of operations would therefore be the best landing place. We should remember too that the Irish had been looking forward for years to a Spanish landing in Munster, and that the English provided against the same eventuality. The English said repeatedly that Munster was the point of danger. The Irish Council forecast in

1596 that the Spaniards would land there and would attempt to seize some town. Government was warned in 1597 that 'the Earl and O'Donnell intend to turn the greatest bulk of the Spaniards into Munster'. Such invaders would not come to a 'desert country' like the north, but to the 'better inhabited parts'. Munster offered the best prospects for the commissariat. The poet Edmund Spenser called it 'a most rich and plentiful country, full of corn and cattle'. Invaders would not starve there. On the other hand, the English 'would wish no greater plague to the Spaniard than to be sent into the north', which could not 'cover the Spaniard with town or castle, nor yield him any property or comfort other than raw beef, which is a nourishment contrary to his humour and complexion'. Munster too was the province 'where the best havens are, and most proper to enter into from Spain'. There was here, of course, much exaggeration, but the English appreciation, which specified the south coast or Limerick or Galway as landing places, was correct.

Even if O'Neill and O'Donnell believed, until news was brought to them of the Spaniards having landed at Kinsale, that their latest message had got to Spain in time, they still had to contemplate action outside Ulster. If the message had got through and if their altered recommendation could have been implemented, a battle of Limerick or a battle of Galway might have been substituted for the battle of Kinsale. There are no indications that the English would have faced such encounters with worse chances of success or the Irish with better.

When O'Neill wrote to Aguila after the Spanish landing had taken place he appears to have suggested that the Spaniards should put to sea again and should come to Sligo or Killybegs, where the Ulstermen would meet them. The operations of Docwra and Neill Garbh O'Donnell had by that time become ominous; the latter had seized Donegal at the beginning of August and had proved impossible to eject. The threat which these activities constituted must by October have made an added reason for trying to attract the Spaniards towards the north. Besides, Aguila's force—although we have no way of knowing if O'Neill knew this—was far smaller than the 6,000 men which had been the Irish requirement for operations in Munster.

The Spaniards, who were less than 3,500 strong, landed at Kinsale, thirteen miles south of Cork, on 21 September. Mountjoy, who was then in Kilkenny and who knew of the landing by the

23rd, reacted at once. He realised that it was no longer a question of 'the war of Ireland', but of 'the war of England made in Ireland'. The decision of that war was to be sought at Kinsale and 'all providence bestowed on any other place is vain'. Speed in commencing operations against the Spaniards was to him essential. The reaction of O'Neill and his allies appears to have been somewhat slower.

Mountjoy was in Clonmel by the 25th and in Cork by the 27th. He had already issued orders for a general concentration of troops against the invaders. He hoped, he said, to beat 'their great breeches' as well as ever he had beaten 'the Irish trews'. The Waterford garrison was to stand fast, but every other soldier in Munster and all who could be spared from other areas— including some 1,400 men from the forts on the Tyrone border— were to march to Cork. Captain Williams who had already hung on at the Blackwater in the months before the battle of the Yellow Ford was left with one company to hang on there again. The rest marched south. There were 1,200 men in Cork on 21 September, 3,000 on the 24th, and 6,900 by 14 October. Munster was not to see such marching again until, almost 200 years later, the French were in Bantry Bay. Mountjoy's greatest fear was for his supplies, without which he could not keep his men together. 'The state of the kingdom', he wrote to England, 'depends on our ability to keep the field. If we break for want of victuals the country will revolt and then the Spaniards will take the towns.' He demanded, and was given, supplies from England.

Everything now, of course, turned on O'Neill's response to the challenge presented by the arrival of his allies. He received letters from the Spaniards within a few days of their landing. Mountjoy's reaction to the altered situation was made clear to him by the withdrawal of most of the English forces from Blackwater fort, Mount Norris, Armagh and Newry.

O'Neill's first task was, in these altered circumstances, to win back those of his former adherents who had previously been led to make their peace with the Queen. Then he took up the old game of raiding the English Pale, where the haggards were full and the utmost damage might be done at this season. By the second week of October his men were spoiling without resistance in Louth and some of them had gone as far south as Slane and Duleek. Captain Richard Tyrrell led a detached force of Ulster bonnaghts who raided and plundered from Athlone to Tipperary.

The Irish continued these operations until November, by which time twenty-two villages had been burnt in Meath alone, but—if that was their purpose—what they did had little effect on Mountjoy. The Deputy refused to split his forces to protect the Pale. Nothing could turn him away from the Spaniards.

It was said that O'Neill took a long time to make up his mind about going to Munster. He 'better trusts himself', remarked one of many speculators concerning his intentions, 'with twenty kern naked in a wood than with five hundred Spaniards in a town'. Even as late as the third week of November spies were saying that he would never go south. The Earl probably promoted doubts to increase security; it was good to keep the enemy guessing. He seems to have taken in hand at once the organisation of a field force and the making of arrangements for the defence of the north in his absence. Both Chichester at Carrickfergus and Docwra at Derry had strong forces and they were both reinforced after the date of the Spanish landing. Mountjoy commanded them to 'be stirring lustily'. It was a risk to leave them behind; O'Neill had to provide as well as he could to hold them off from Tyrone and from the territories of his adherents.

O'Neill's place of assembly was at Lough Ramor in Cavan, where he set up a camp in October. He had 1,500 foot and 200 horse there before the end of the month and, it was said, more than twice that number a week later. He moved about constantly, his last reported journey being towards Coleraine to O'Cahan, to whom with his own brother Cormack he gave joint command of the force watching Docwra. Then, on 9 November, he left Dungannon, took command of his army, and, accompanied by Maguire, O'Reilly, the MacMahons and others, marched south.

He was no hustler, however, and he was still near Kells in Co. Meath—no more than fifteen miles from Lough Ramor—on the 18th. He was 'close in his resolutions' and the English spies could make little of him. They said that his arrangements were for night marches, each man carrying his own provisions of meal (requisitioned in the Pale?) and butter and—if he had a firearm—his own powder and shot. Every horseman was to take spare shoes for his horse and every footman an extra pair of brogues.

Meanwhile O'Donnell also had moved. He too had had, in turning his back on his lordship, a momentous decision to make. The defection to the enemy of his cousin and rival Neill Garbh

O'Donnell, which as we have seen had taken place in October 1600, had torn Tirconnell in two. Neill had helped Docwra to take Lifford and had himself taken Donegal Abbey in August 1601. When the Spaniards landed O'Donnell was blockading Neill in this last place. When the Tirconnell men marched to Munster they had to leave this vigorous and so far victorious rebel in their rear; for O'Donnell certainly Kinsale must be decisive.

As with O'Neill, the government spies doubted that O'Donnell would leave Ulster. He seemed to have much too much on hand there to withdraw. But he mustered his men at Ballymote in Co. Sligo and on 2 November, with what immediate hopes and fears we know not, but certainly with extraordinary courage, he marched south. He was in motion towards the Spaniards a week before O'Neill. With him went the three MacSwineys, the traditional leaders of the Tirconnell galloglas, O'Rourke, Mac-Dermot and many north Connacht men. They gathered strength as they went on. Their way led through Roscommon and Galway to the Shannon near Shannon Harbour, where they crossed. They moved between the Devilsbit and Slieve Bloom mountains to a place five miles south of Roscrea. Here, near the headwaters of the river Suir, they camped and awaited O'Neill's coming. It was said that O'Donnell, who 'chafes mightily' at the delay, had a thousand foot and 200 horse, O'Rourke 500 foot and forty horse. Tyrrell, who was reported to have joined them, was credited with 400 foot and forty horse.

O'Neill did not come—he was still in the midlands—but Carew, the President of Munster, did. Learning that O'Donnell was moving towards him, Mountjoy bowed to the wishes of a majority of his captains and detached Carew with about 2,500 men to engage him, or at least to prevent his closer approach. Carew left the camp which had been established to blockade the Spaniards at Kinsale on 7 November and came up by Cashel, blocking O'Donnell's way south along the valley of the Suir. But O'Donnell outwitted him. At a time of 'extraordinary ice' and 'heavy slippery snow' the Donegal and Connacht men decided to wait no longer for O'Neill. They moved rapidly westward, over the Slievefelim mountains, across Limerick and eventually into Cork. Carew was unable to keep up with men who could cover forty miles in one march—he had never heard of such a thing before—and he returned to the Lord Deputy.

O'Neill's progress was less speedy. He came through Westmeath, Offaly, Leix and Tipperary, crossed the Suir and eventually joined O'Donnell westward of Bandon. He had about 3,000 foot and 400 horse, so that the combined Irish strength may have been greater than 5,000. Tyrrell, earlier reported with O'Donnell in Tipperary, was, according to Mountjoy, the last of the Irish leaders to come up.

We should pause to pay tribute to those who had accomplished this remarkable feat. When news of the Spanish landing reached the continent the Venetian Ambassador in Paris reported the French belief that Spain had thrown her troops away. Aguila's men would not, said French opinion, be able to join O'Neill. They and the Irish were at opposite ends of the island and the English held the country between them. But now the Irish had come to join Aguila. In order that they might do so they had turned their backs on a homeland that was in danger. Docwra and Chichester, already threatening, must in the absence of so many fighting men from Ulster become a menace indeed. And yet the Ulster army had marched away. There was no precedent for this in Irish history, and there are few examples of such happenings in the histories of other countries; Washington could count on few soldiers, of all the thousands who served him, who would leave their homes to fight in other parts of America. We might be inclined to blame the Ulstermen for their delay. They were warned in advance of the landing and might have begun their preparations to co-operate with the Spaniards earlier than they seem to have done. In fact, however, we know very little about them. We must suspend judgment for lack of evidence. But we must not omit to commend them for what they did. Their march across Ireland was heroic.

The position at Kinsale in the first week of December when O'Neill moved the combined Ulster forces down the Bandon river valley towards the town was not unfavourable for the Irish and their Spanish allies. Aguila had, since the date of his landing, conducted himself well. Although he had lost his outlying positions at Ringcurran (the present Charles Fort, commanding the river mouth) and Castle Park (on the site of which James's Fort was built in 1604), he still held on to the town and he had shown that his men were full of fight. They sallied out on 10 November and again, in greater strength, on 2 December. They were a trained army of an effective strength of over 3,000 men. Not as powerful as their opponents, they must still, even if they had had to continue fighting alone, be regarded as a formidable force.

The English too were combative. Mountjoy's effective strength after Carew had rejoined him was perhaps 7,500; his total force, swelled by reinforcement from England, was larger, but increasing numbers of his men fell sick. He had come in close on the north and west sides of the town and he dug trenches and worked his batteries with vigour. On 1 December he tried unsuccessfully to storm a breach. Carew's force (reinforced and transferred to the command of the Earl of Thomond) was encamped westward of Kinsale, where it completed the ring of the investment and interposed its strength between the town and the newly arrived Irish. After five weeks fighting the English had made good their original boast that the Spaniards 'dare not look out of Kinsale after all their brags'. But they themselves could still not look in. The failure of their efforts to storm the breach, the vigorous sorties of the defenders, the arrival of the Irish and the news of the arrival of more Spaniards in Castlehaven—thirty miles to the west along the coast—all served to mark a period in their operations. After the first week of December the investment of Kinsale became a blockade. Mountjoy ceased to push his attack; he entrenched his camps and prepared to hold on. Sickness increased in his ranks. After the Irish moved in he was completely cut off from Cork and from the supplies that were consigned to him by land and his men suffered short commons. The forage for his horses gave out. His effective strength must have dropped beneath the numbers of his enemies.

It was in these circumstances that the battle of Kinsale was fought—an engagement that lasted no more than three hours, a struggle in which a large force was overthrown by a smaller one, a catastrophe that decided the fate of Ireland.

The Irish, coming down the valley from Innishannon, encamped on 21 December at Coolcarron to the northward of Kinsale and between it and Cork. They had been reinforced by 500 or 600 Munstermen and by 120 to 200 Spaniards from Castlehaven, where Pedro de Zubiaur had arrived on 1 December with six ships earlier detached from the invasion fleet. O'Neill had in all perhaps 6,500 men, many of whom must have been veterans of several years' experience.

Very early on the morning of 24 December—Christmas eve according to the Old Style calendar which the English were still using—the whole Irish force marched towards Kinsale. They were arranged in infantry columns which could be deployed in the three traditional fighting divisions of van, main battle, and rear. The horse were, as was usual, in a separate formation, and apparently all together. The night was stormy and vivid lightning flashed continually.

O'Neill, according to his apologists, marched unwillingly. The Four Masters tell of a council meeting held in the Irish camp at which O'Neill advised caution but O'Donnell said that he would be ashamed not to help the Spaniards, 'even if his death or destruction, or the loss of his people should result from it'. O'Neill we are told noted the difficulties of Mountjoy's position, caught as he was between the Irish on the one hand and the active Spaniards on the other, and said that he should be blockaded rather than attacked. Now that their supplies had been cut off the English were in difficulties, although we may doubt if things were quite as bad as Lughaidh O'Clery, O'Donnell's biographer, says: 'the entrails of the horses and the corpses of the dead men lay among the living throughout the tents, so that there arose an intolerable stench in consequence of the great blasts of air mounting up from the filth and the dirt of the lower part [of the camp]. It was the idea and the opinion of many of themselves that the greater number of them would die if they were let alone without being attacked, owing to the contagion and sickness.' Yet many men and horses certainly had died, and the shortage of forage was so great that, unrelieved, Mountjoy would have had to order his cavalry in a few days' time to break through to Cork in search of it. According to Carew, and as the battle was to prove, the cavalry was Mountjoy's mainstay.

In these circumstances, O'Neill is reported as having said, the Irish had only to hold their ground and their enemies would soon be in dire straits. There was no reason to change their tactics; they had always tried to starve rather than to overrun entrenched enemies; they should try to do so now. Soon after his death—and perhaps during his lifetime as well—O'Neill was being spoken of as another Prosper Colonna, a new Fabius Cunctator—a 'delayer', or a cautious general. His whole career shows that this reputation was deserved. It is possible—we may even say it is likely—that he acted up to it at Kinsale. O'Donnell however was precipitate. According to report, it was he who had persuaded O'Neill 'to try an assault' on Blackwater fort in October 1597, and he was called 'the firebrand of all the rebels'. He too may well have behaved characteristically at Kinsale. On the other hand, the story of a difference of opinion between the Irish leaders as to whether they should advance or postpone action may be no more than an effort to explain away defeat. It seems unlikely that O'Neill would, at this vital moment, act against his judgment. Even if O'Donnell had said wild things about death and destruction and 'the loss of his people' O'Neill must have kept his head.

Of the three Irish divisions, Tyrrell commanded the van, which consisted of Meath and other Leinster men, Munstermen and the small force of Zubiaur's Spaniards led by Alonzo del Campo. O'Neill himself led the main battle, which was the strongest formation and was made up of Ulstermen—according to the English they were 'all Tyrone men'. O'Donnell commanded the rear, which was composed of Tirconnell and Connacht men. There were in all perhaps 5,000 Irishmen and Spaniards.

What was their objective as they advanced? Did they intend to make a general attack on Mountjoy? Clearly their intention was aggressive and they anticipated action. Their movement was not just another feint in the Ulster manner, for the terrain, as they knew, was not suited to that. They knew the ground well. When O'Neill was encamped with O'Donnell two miles east of Kinsale in March 1600 he 'had taken a full view of the harbours of Cork and Kinsale'. He must have been well aware in 1601 that any movement of his forces over this ground, particularly in the presence of an enemy who was strong in cavalry, involved the distinct possibility not only of collision but of a formal battle.

What kind of engagement the Irish expected is, however, uncertain. According to the evidence, their intention was to move up at dawn, or just before it, and to place part of their army under the walls of the town, where they could collaborate with Aguila's force. Mountjoy says that the Irish vanguard was to have joined Aguila's men on the west side of the town and that their combined force was to have attacked the Earl of Thomond's camp; at the same time O'Neill and O'Donnell, leading the main battle and rearward, proposed to attack Mountjoy's own camp, which stood about half a mile north of the town. The Four Masters also speak of this intention to attack the two camps. All the accounts say that the Spaniards in the town, as well as the Irish, were to advance. Their collaboration is spoken of as a simple matter of an Irish attack on the English assisted by a Spanish sortie; the Spaniards were either to unite with the Irish or else to attack the

English on one side while the Irish attacked them on the other.
Most of the contemporary writers indicate that it was Aguila who
proposed the joint movement, that he was importunate in his
demand for it, and that O'Neill agreed to his proposal unwillingly.
An English statement current in Paris a few weeks after the battle
and relayed by the Venetian ambassador in that city to his
superiors in Venice speaks of an Irish intention of reinforcing
Aguila in the town with a thousand Irishmen and 500 of Zubiaur's
Spaniards (more than were present on the field) and implies that
the joint attack on the English was intended not to overwhelm
Mountjoy but to cover this movement. A report compiled in
Spain by Fr Mansoni, S.J. in March 1602 says that O'Neill was
to advance to an agreed position and that Aguila was, when he saw
him there, to sally out, join him and bring him in to the town.
Most of these statements are vague and none of them is detailed.
We grope for information.

For the three nights previous to this fatal day the English, in a
difficult position and expecting attack, had held their squadron
volant, or flying squadron, ready for all emergencies. This was Sir
Henry Power's regiment of picked men, who were relieved of
all other duties so as to be available in an emergency. There is no
doubt that Mountjoy expected to be attacked. We are told that he
had direct information of his enemies' intentions, gleaned according to the statements of some of our informants from intercepted
letters. Philip O'Sullivan, whose history was published in 1621,
says that these were letters from Aguila to O'Neill; the Venetian
report which we have just mentioned calls them letters from
O'Neill to Aguila; another English account says that the English,
to suit their purpose of provoking an engagement, intercepted and
then released a despatch in which Aguila called on O'Neill to
attack; Moryson, Mountjoy's secretary, contents himself with a
general statement that 'many intelligences confirmed that Tyrone
on the one side and the Spaniards on the other had a purpose to
force our camp'. The Four Masters, backed up by one of the
English accounts, allege treachery. They say that Mountjoy was
forewarned of what was to occur by 'a certain Irishman'. An
English account names the traitor—Brian MacHugh Óg Mac-
Mahon. The evidence for a leakage of information by which
Mountjoy profited seems either contradictory or too profuse to
be altogether reliable. Carew too claims credit for penetrating the
minds of the Irish leaders. He says that some of his spies brought

him the news from the Irish camp. There is ground for a strong presumption that the English were directly forewarned—they were certainly aware of a general intention on O'Neill's part to come on; but it is questionable if any attempt to surprise the English that O'Neill and his allies might have made on any night about the time of the battle could have been succeessful—or that O'Neill might have hoped that it would. Mountjoy did not need intercepted letters, or the word of an informer, or the gleanings of spies to warn him of the danger in which he stood. He was in too tight a corner not to watch anxiously at night—every night; defeat for him could mean annihilation.

On the morning of the 24th Sir Henry Power's squadron volant was in its place, standing to. In advance of it were the scouts, under Sir Richard Graeme. Mountjoy and Carew were sitting up in the former's quarters awaiting developments.

The Irish appear to have bungled their approach march. They had only a distance of five or six miles to cover from their camp to the town, and the whole night in which to cover it, yet they allowed themselves to be caught soon after dawn by the watchful English before they had brought their full force up and before they had fully deployed. They marched first southward, and then, swinging to the west towards Millwater, they moved towards positions whence they could approach the town from the north-west. The Irish authorities say that they lost their way for a while in the darkness. They say too that O'Neill and O'Donnell had disagreed, and that each strove to have the place of honour in front of the other. (Oh, the humiliation of defeat that such stories should have been told to explain it!) Whatever happened during the march it seems clear that when day dawned on Christmas eve some of the Irish had fallen behind in their time schedule; yet it is possible also that the foremost units found themselves further advanced than they expected when, in the bleak morning light, they recognised their surroundings.

The foremost Irish and the English scouts seem to have seen one another about the same time, about half an hour before dawn. There is some evidence to show that O'Neill should have been in position to attack then, or perhaps we should say in position to join the Spaniards. His rearward, under O'Donnell, had not come up, however, and he had not deployed. His force, which, when the English scouts saw it first, had been marching towards the town in good order of battle, was soon halted. The Irish musketeers and calivermen began to light their matches. The English saw this; soon the English matches, in turn, betrayed to the Irish the presence of the defending force.

The rest was swift—very swift—to follow. Mountjoy had begun to think that nothing would happen that night when the alarm reached him. He at once ordered a general stand-to and went forward with Sir Richard Wingfield, the Marshal, towards the scouts. We are told that he selected a position in which to fight if the Irish advanced further; perhaps we should say that he confirmed an earlier selection of it. Each of his units had specific duties allotted it: five regiments of infantry were to remain in the main camp, which was his own, and four in the Earl of Thomond's smaller camp. Three troops of horse were later added to these defensive forces. Thus the greater part of the English army, under Carew, watched the Spaniards and acted as a general reserve. The remainder, led by Mountjoy himself and consisting of three regiments of infantry—Power's, Ffolliot's and St John's —and most of the cavalry was to confront the Irish. Carew disposed of almost 5,000 men, Mountjoy of no more than 2,000. With Mountjoy were from 400 to 500 horse. Very many of these English troops were men of Irish birth, and there had been some hope among the Irish that they would desert to O'Neill; there is no evidence that more than perhaps a handful of them did.

At daybreak the Marshal with about 400 horse and the squadron volant faced the halted Irish about a mile or a mile and a half west of Kinsale, rising ground intervening between them. This must have been in the neighbourhood of Ballinacurra creek.

Why had the Irish stopped? They may have done so because they saw the English in front of them, or because they were waiting for O'Donnell, who had not yet come up, or because they were uncertain of what lay ahead of them and wanted time to reconnoitre. They can scarcely have been waiting for Aguila to come out, for, as far as we know, they would have had to penetrate further eastward, between the Earl of Thomond's camp and the river, before they could expect to make contact with him. O'Sullivan tells us that O'Neill, while his forces were thus halted, went to the top of a hill whence he could see the English camp and that what he saw of English preparations and Spanish inactivity decided him in his subsequent course of action.

Whatever the reason or reasons for the Irish delay or hesitancy, it lost them the initiative. From this on it was Mountjoy who called the tune. He ordered the Sergeant-Major, Sir John Berkeely, to bring up Ffolliot's and St John's regiments, and when the Irish, in order as their apologists say 'that they might regain their ranks and good order', withdrew a little, he followed them. The Irish crossed a stream. This was probably the Millwater creek, and they were now moving away from Kinsale. Marshal Wingfield sent some horse and some of Power's companies after O'Neill and ordered Ffolliot to follow Power. Firing commenced. The Irish skirmished as they fell back, but made no serious effort to deny the passage of the stream to the Marshal.

Still retiring, the Irish moved quickly across boggy ground to firm land beyond. They were now about two miles from the town. Their resistance stiffening, they formed their van and main battle on the firm ground. O'Donnell, leading the rearward, had come up close enough to have contact by this time, but whether the rearward was formed at the same time as the other divisions is unknown.

Each of these divisions was a huge mass of infantry, the model for which was the celebrated Spanish *tercio*, the most widely respected battle formation of the age. The Spanish *tercio* was made up of 3,000 or so heavy infantrymen, partly armed with the pike, partly with the musket or arquebus (that is, the caliver). The pikemen formed a great mass or square at the four corners of which stood—like bastions—small squares of arquebusiers; further men with firearms formed borders or fringes along the sides of the square. Combining the defensive strength of massed pikes with the missile power of firearms, the *tercio* had proved itself the dominant force on European battlefields of the past half century. But it was not without defects. It was unwieldy, it made manœuvre difficult, and it was better adapted to defence than to attack. It was soon to be superseded by smaller formations, by such formations indeed as Mountjoy used. *Tercio* formation would however have appeared as the ideal arrangement to O'Neill and his advisers, with their Spanish associations. It was the formation with which the Irish soldiers serving Spain in Flanders—some of whom were with O'Neill—were familiar. Kinsale, O'Neill's only formal battle, was the only occasion on which the Irish tried to use this—for them—complicated pattern in drawing up their troops. Its use was to prove disastrous. In O'Neill's hands the great masses proved brittle as well as unwieldy. Co-operation between them proved impossible. The formation was probably the worst that troops with the background of performance of the Ulstermen could have attempted; yet, granted O'Neill's purpose of making formal soldiers out of his men, it was inevitable that they should have tried to form in this way.

As the Irish were forming they left their loose shot to skirmish at the boggy ground in front of them and to contest English attempts to cross it. The Marshal sent a hundred horse and a hundred shot to drive these in; but the Irish for a while prevailed and the English shot were forced back on their own horsemen. A reinforcement was sent in and the Irish skirmishers in turn fell back.

Meanwhile the Marshal, with some of Power's men, had found a passage across the boggy ground, and he soon brought over some of the horse to the 'plain', or firm, open ground where the Irish masses stood. The Irish main battle, O'Neill's own division, was closest to him, and this Wingfield attempted to charge; but his cavalry, behaving as cavalry very often did when sent against formed infantry in that age, wheeled off to a flank rather than charge home. The Irish greeted their apparent discomfiture with a loud shout.

Up to this, there was no question of O'Neill's being in difficulties. His attempt to surprise the English had certainly failed, and he had been made to give ground rather than push on to the rendezvous with the Spaniards; but his skirmishers had behaved with their usual skill, he was deployed in a position in which the English, if they attacked him, would have boggy ground in their rear, and he had a local superiority in numbers. His three battles, as was to appear presently, were too widely separated, and if he was to fight here he would have to do so without hope of immediate Spanish assistance, yet it cannot be said that his position was bad.

But then began the deluge. The remainder of the English horse, Mountjoy's best troops in such an open field as this, came up, that is, all Mountjoy's own and Carew's horse under Sir Henry Danvers and the Earl of Clanrickard's, Graeme's, Fleming's and Taaffe's horse under the Marshal—every cavalryman that the English had save the three troops retained in front of the town under Carew. The Irish horse, as strong numerically perhaps as the English but, for all O'Neill's training, of a poorer quality than their opponents, began to show fright. O'Neill had tried to make his horsemen fight in the accepted manner of the time, and, as he had given drums to the foot, had provided them with cavalry trumpets, but they still remained light horsemen. They could manœuvre to perfection and harass their foes effectively, but they could not withstand the shock of a charge. There is no record of these horsemen having contributed anything of consequence to the battle up to this; and, save for O'Sullivan, no writer says anything of them unless that they helped to bring up the rear when the Irish drew back. O'Sullivan seems quite mistaken in saying that O'Donnell led the Irish cavalry in an attack on the Marshal's men at the stream; everybody else who mentions him says that O'Donnell was with the rearward. The Irish cavalry was not conspicuous until it is recorded that, in the face of their opposite numbers in Mountjoy's force, they turned tail and left the field. If they had simply ridden off, it would have been bad enough—it would have been bad enough to have left the English cavalry in undisputed mastery of every part of the field not covered by the infantry; but the retiring Irish cavaliers fell in on their own main battle on their way off and disordered its ranks.

The Marshal, concentrating his attention on this main battle, attacked it from the rear with his reinforced cavalry—who were now able to ride where they wished—and apparently in front with the foot. As the Four Masters say, he 'proceeded to kill, slaughter, subdue and thin' O'Neill's shot and pikemen. Already disordered by their own horse, whose flight must further have disheartened them, and disturbed by the accidental explosion of a bag of gunpowder, the formation of the battle was soon broken in upon. The solidity of the great mass, where, in the closely packed ranks, there were so many men who were unable to defend themselves and where all were novices at the kind of work required, was an obstacle rather than an advantage. There followed, once the crust of their defence was broken, a short, sharp fight and then, when the rear of the mass gave way, a sudden streaming off of fugitives with the English horse hacking at them and goading them as they went.

It was the beginning of the end. The day, within what must have been a very short space of time, was lost. Fortune, that had hitherto smiled uniformly on O'Neill and O'Donnell, now deserted them utterly.

Tyrrell, with the Irish vanguard, was formed at some distance to the left of the main battle. The main battle, which was now broken, had formed the right wing of the Irish line, the van was the centre, and the rear, which was further off, was the left wing. This alignment is in itself evidence that the swift advance of the English had taken O'Neill unawares, for the more usual—although not invariable—battle order would have placed his division in the centre and Tyrrell and O'Donnell to right and left of him.

The rear, O'Donnell's division, which was the last to come up and which was at this time probably still in motion, was not confronted by any English force. The van was, however, while Power's and Ffolliot's regiments were advancing to attack the main battle, St John's regiment, which formed the English rear, was posted opposite Tyrrell and within caliver shot of him, that is, within about eighty yards. Roe, who commanded the regiment in St John's absence, had instructions to stand firm and to await further orders.

Tyrrell did not move until the Irish main battle was broken. All the indications are that the main battle stood for only a very short time. When it began to stream away to the rear Tyrrell put the vanguard in motion to his right and moved to interpose between the pursuers of the main battle and the remainder of the English. Mountjoy at once ordered Roe to charge, and St John's regiment, moving forward, fell on Tyrrell in flank as he passed across its front. Tyrrell's men, although they were disordered, do not appear to have been very roughly handled—they were, for one thing, far more numerous than their attackers—yet they too drew off. They marched to the top of a hill whence the greater part of them soon decamped. Alonzo del Campo's Spaniards, who were with them, made a stand, but they were caught by the pursuing horse and suffered considerable loss before they surrendered.

Thus were two of the three Irish divisions dispersed. O'Donnell's rearward was only very slightly engaged, and seemingly not at all by the English foot. O'Donnell himself is described as having vainly exhorted such fugitives as came his way to face about and to reform. 'Rage and anger had seized on his soul', and he inveighed against O'Neill's men because they were the first to give up. But his own men were no better. The sight of more than two-thirds of their army in retreat and of the English troopers cutting down the fugitives at will all over the field was too much for the Donegal and Connacht men. They too marched off. The battle was over.

The English cavalry did not continue the pursuit much beyond the battlefield. Their horses were exhausted. The Irish loss was, according to the English, considerable; they claimed that 1,200 men, Irish and Spanish, were killed on the field. The Irish say that 'the number slain was not very great on account of the fewness of the pursuers in comparison with those flying before them'. The English won their remarkable victory at a cost to themselves of very few casualties.

And the Spaniards, what had they done? Fr James Archer, an Irish Jesuit who was in Kinsale while the engagement was being fought, said of Juan del Aguila a few days later: 'If, even when the battle was on, he had done nothing more than display his troops before the enemy, victory would certainly have been ours'. The Irish, said Fr Archer (although when he made the statement he was in touch with none of the defeated force), when they saw that Aguila did not make the expected sortie, 'lost heart and are convinced that they were betrayed'. The debate has been continued since the date of the battle: was Aguila blameworthy? —could he, if he had behaved differently, have brought about a different result?

When the victory was won Mountjoy's three regiments and the horse marched back to the English camp, reaching it about noon. Overjoyed at a success so much greater than they could have hoped for, the English fired a feu-de-joie. To the waiting Spaniards in the town this discharge of guns or musketry had a different meaning. All the evidence (save that presented by bitterly disappointed and scarcely objective witnesses) indicates that the Spaniards knew nothing of the battle until it was over. It seems too much to say that they had not heard the firing, but it was distant firing, and it was moving away from them. O'Neill had not come to the appointed place—there seems no doubt of that; therefore Aguila had made no move. But Mountjoy's volley, fired closer to the town than the battlefield, was almost certainly interpreted by Aguila as an indication—at last—of the Irish advance. He marched out and approached the English. What he saw showed him very clearly what had happened. Mountjoy's men waved in triumph the Spanish colours—the white flags, each with its red saltire—which they had seized from the vanquished. Aguila returned to the town. Nine days later he surrendered on terms.

It is highly questionable if, contained as they were by Carew,

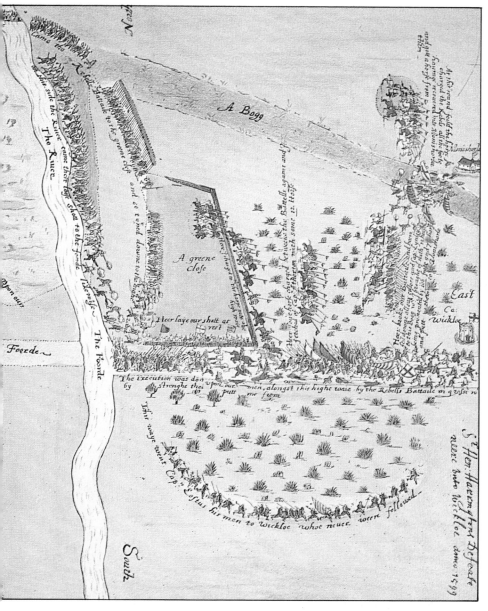

9. Irish warfare at the time of Hugh O'Neill. In this picture map an English column is ambushed by Irish rebels in Co Wicklow.

10. A galloglach soldier. A long-hafted axe and mail shirt were standard
equipment for these sixteenth-century mercenaries of Scottish descent.

11. Two kern, or lightly-armed Irish infantry, are depicted in this
sixteenth-century drawing by Lucas de Heere. The sword shown is of
the typical ring-hilted Irish type.

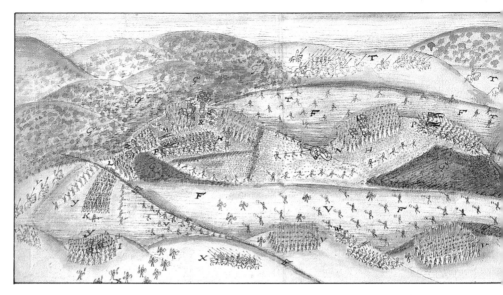

12. The battle of the Yellow Ford, 1598. This contemporary drawing, probably by an English survivor, shows Bagenall's army under attack from the forces of O'Donnell and O'Neill.

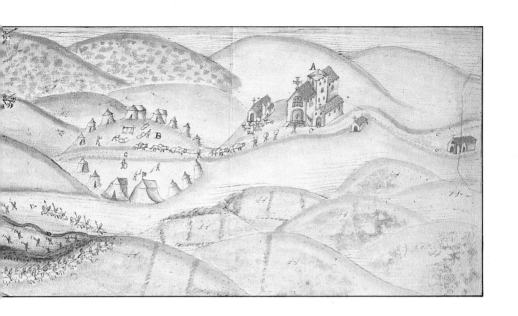

13. Detail from a picture map of the battle of Kinsale, 1601.

Tyron and O'Donnell with
the Rebells Horse vnder
vmber a welve

he Rebells battell over
thrown by owre Horse
he Squadron together

The vauntgarde of y Rebells
runne away with out any
stroke stricking

14. An Irish nobleman of the sixteenth century. He is armed for war in
a suit of plate armour, as was the custom for both English and Irish
officers during the period of Hugh O'Neill's wars. In contrast, common
soldiers on both sides wore little or no armour.

the Spaniards could have done anything in time to save O'Neill. Although it may be said that they were unimaginative, over-cautious, even unco-operative in failing—suppose they had heard the firing during the battle—to make an attempt to create a diversion, none of these things can give ground for a condemnation of them; none certainly is evidence either of treachery or of incompetence on Aguila's part. The Jesuits Frs Archer and Mansoni blame Aguila. Archbishop Mathew de Oviedo, who was with Fr Archer in Kinsale, says that Aguila failed to sally out as he had agreed to do. But these were ecclesiastics whose zeal, as their statements show, exceeded their military knowledge.

Considered objectively, the Irish movements in the battle were at best unfortunate and at worst clumsy. Aside from the fault in disposition that placed their three divisions too widely apart—and whatever difficulties they had during the approach march coupled with the confusion of the morning's withdrawal may account for some, at least, of this—the horse made no serious effort to play their part. They made no attempt to take on the English horse. The formed bodies of foot did not charge, perhaps because the enemy's horse had been allowed to establish superiority at the outset—a matter which was certainly ironical, for if the fight had been postponed for a few days Mountjoy would meanwhile have had to send off his horse to Cork for want of forage. The vanguard moved in to second the main battle too late, and by a risky flank movement that met with its inevitable punishment. The three bodies allowed themselves to be dispersed piecemeal; just as no effective attempt was made by one to support another at an early stage, no effort seems to have been made by one to retire on another when they recoiled under attack.

The efforts of the Irish apologists to account for the Irish defeat have done little to help. O'Donnell who, it is suggested, brought on the fight commanded the division least engaged. His delay fits in so badly with his impetuosity that it has to be accounted for by the story of the dispute with O'Neill about precedence, and, lest that should not be enough, by the statement that O'Donnell missed his way in the darkness. Although the weather was wretched and the way probably difficult the distance to be covered was short; there can scarcely have been a great error of direction or timing. It is inconceivable that O'Neill was unprepared for combat. Apart from the fact that he could not hope to co-operate with the Spaniards without fighting, he had his whole force with him and was manœuvring close up to the English at a time when they, as their only hope of extricating themselves from a daily worsening position—when their ammunition and supplies were giving out and their sick list was mounting —would jump at any chance of engaging him. O'Neill had no secure line of retreat—and no bogs or hills close by—such as he invariably had when his intention was merely to 'feel' the enemy. If he did not intend to fight he was running such a risk as he had never before contemplated.

The reason for the defeat of the Irish appears to be that they had assumed the trappings of a contemporary campaigning force, but that the practice was not theirs. Hitherto when they had retired they had gone to a place where they could not be pursued, and whence they could strike again. When their enemy had got in their rear and on their flank at Kinsale, as they themselves had so often surrounded the marching armies of the Queen, not all the training that O'Neill had given them nor all the enthusiasm that he had breathed into them could save them. The rule of the *tercios* was to stand firm, to be surrounded, to be fired into, to be shot down—but to fill up the gaps, and always to stand. The discipline and training of the Irish were not yet such that they could obey that rule. For all his greatness, O'Neill was not capable, at the moment when all Ireland stood watching him, and when his Ireland was fighting for its life, of ensuring that an outmoded caution was put aside and the last blow struck. It was a hard fate that the Irish memory of former success and of the methods by which it had been gained should ensure for the English victory in the one battle of the war that counted. 'So was it seen that when Tyrone was assailed in Ulster for the most part he prevailed, but when he came out of these confines from his friends and fastnesses he usually received the foil.' Thus Sir James Perrot. And no less a personage than Frederick the Great was to say: 'If I were mindful only of my own glory, I would choose always to make war in my own country.'

A great deal has been written about Kinsale, and very naturally so since it was of all Irish battles that which produced the most dire consequences. The contemporary accounts from the Irish side appear in the *Annals of the Four Masters*, O'Clery's *Beatha Aodha Ruaidh O Domhnaill*, and P. O'Sullivan's *Historiae Catholicae Iberniae Compendium* (translated in M. J. Byrne, *Ireland under Elizabeth*, pp. 146 f). See also C. P. Meehan, *The Fate and Fortunes of O'Neill and O'Donel*, pp. 530 ff. English accounts and references are in *Calendar of State Papers, Ireland*, 1601-3, pp. 240 ff; *Calendar of the Carew Manuscripts*, III, pp. 191 ff; *Pacata Hibernia*; F. Moryson, *Itinerary*; *Trevelyan Papers*, II, pp. 104 ff (Mountjoy's report).

For an assessment of O'Neill see C. Falls, 'Hugh O'Neill the Great' in *The Irish Sword*, VI, pp. 94 ff. For O'Neill's motives and those of his adherents see: *Calendar of State Papers, Ireland*, 1592-6, pp. 422 f; 1596-7, pp. 117 f, 140, 436; 1599-1600, pp. 8, 209. *Calendar of the Carew Manuscripts*, IV, p. 168. Moryson's work already mentioned, II, p. 275. Sir G. Carey's 'Discourse of Ireland' (1601), printed in *Desiderata Curiosa Hibernica*, I, pp. 5 ff. Captain Thomas Lee's 'A Brief Declaration of the government of Ireland' (written before 1594) in the same, I, pp. 89 ff. Peter Lombard, *De Regno Hiberniae sanctorum insula commentarius* (translated M. J. Byrne), pp. 360 ff. The Scot who spoke of O'Neill was Denis Campbell, Dean of Limerick, whose 'Observations' are published in *The Miscellany of the Maitland Club* (1847), IV i, pp. 41 ff. O'Neill and O'Donnell's visit to Kinsale in 1600 is recorded in *Calendar of State Papers, Ireland*, 1600, pp. 20, 70. Perrot's comment on O'Neill is in his *Chronicle of Ireland* (ed. H. Wood) p. 176.

English statements on places of possible Spanish landings are made in *Calendar of State Papers, Ireland*, 1596-7, pp. 124, 153, 155, 234, 244, 258, 450 and in many places in the *Calendars* for subsequent years. The Spanish evidence appears in Rev. John J. Silke, 'Why Aguila landed at Kinsale' in *Irish Historical Studies*, XIII, pp. 236 ff (and the same writer's 'Where was "Obemdub"?' in *The Irish Sword*, VI, pp. 276 ff—where O'Neill's letter written to Aguila after the latter's arrival is mentioned). See also Rev. F. M. Jones in *The Irish Sword*, II, pp. 29 ff. For Aguila see H. Mangan, 'Del Aguila's defence of Kinsale (1601-2)' also in *The Irish Sword*, I, pp. 218 ff. (In this the late Mr Henry Mangan, who devoted a good part of his long life to the study of 'what happened at Kinsale', also discusses the matter of treachery in the Irish camp); an indictment of Aguila by Rev. F. M. Jones in the same journal, II, pp. 217 ff followed (pp. 220 ff) by comments by H. Mangan on what Fr Jones has to say; and 'A Vindication of Don Juan del Aguila', also by H. Mangan and in the same journal, II, pp. 343 ff. See F. M. Jones, 'Correspondence of Fr. Ludovico Mansoni, S. J.' in *Archivium Hibernicum*, XVII, pp. 9 ff and 36 ff and Professor P. McBride, 'Some unpublished letters of Mateo de Oviedo, Archbishop of Dublin' in *Reportorium Novum*, I, pp. 91 ff.

The siege of Kinsale is well treated in F. M. Jones, 'The Spaniards and Kinsale, 1601' in *Journal of the Galway Archaeological and Historical Society*, XXI, pp. 1 ff, in M. Mulcahy, *A Short History of Kinsale* (1966. This includes a map of the Kinsale area), and in articles by S. O'Grady in *The All Ireland Review*, I, No. 34 (25 August 1900) and subsequent numbers. On the general background of Spanish assistance for Ireland see Rev. John J. Silke, 'Spain and the invasion of Ireland, 1601–2' in *Irish Historical Studies*, XIV, pp. 295 ff. The flags captured from the Irish are shown in the large pictorial map of the battle which hangs in the Library of Trinity College, Dublin. Not all of these flags were Spanish ones, although only Spanish flags—which display the red ragged cross of Burgundy on a white field—are shown in the map. O'Neill displayed also what Scott quaintly calls (*Rokeby* 4 canto, vi. 5, 6) 'the banners of his Tanistry'. Of the captured colours Moryson (*Itinerary*, II, p. 52) says 'among the rest especially the Spanish colours, for such most of them were, the rebels in woods not using that martial bravery'; and an anonymous 'soldier of good place in Ireland' in a letter published in 1602 (quoted in C. Maxwell, *Irish History from contemporary sources*, p. 196) says: 'The enemy lost two thousand arms brought to reckoning, besides great numbers embezzled, all their powder and drums, and eleven ensigns, whereof six Spanish'. Spanish colours are mentioned in a letter written to the Lord Deputy on 27 May 1596: 'Certain Spanish leaders have come with colours to train the Irish to the war for a time' (*Calendar of State Papers, Ireland, 1592–96*, p. 531).

Note that St John's regiment, as the English rearward, was as much out of place on the English side as Tyrrell's division was on the Irish side. Strictly speaking, the rearward should have been on the left, whereas St John's formed the right of Mountjoy's force. All this is evidence for the speed of Mountjoy's attack; he went in headlong, not giving the Irish time to finish forming.

Note too that the map of the action in *Pacata Hibernia* (Plate 15) confuses the Irish vanguard and rearward; it mistakenly places Alonzo del Campo's Spaniards with the rearward. The Spanish *tercios* are described in O. L. Spaulding and J. W. Wright, 'Warfare in Modern Times' in *Warfare* (1924), pp. 452 ff.

Benburb, 1646

The Irish lost the battle of Kinsale in 1601 because of their failure to withstand an English attack in the open field. Forty-five years later another army of Irishmen, an army which must have included many of the sons of those who were vanquished at Kinsale, was completely successful in a formal engagement fought in the open at Benburb, Co. Tyrone. If there was a stigma attached to Kinsale, Benburb removed it; yet Benburb decided nothing, whereas Kinsale had decided practically everything.

The victor of Benburb was Owen Roe O'Neill, who was the son of Art MacBaron, the great Hugh O'Neill's brother. Owen Roe was able to do what had proved impossible for his uncle because he was a professional soldier with a lifetime's experience of battles and of the handling of armed men; he was indeed one of the greatest of Irish soldiers. His own failure—his failure to profit by his victory at Benburb—was part of the outcome of his uncle's defeat. The problems that beset Ireland in the middle of the seventeenth century were greater than those of its beginning. They had been added to by the consequences of Kinsale and by the beginnings of a revolution in England. Besides, Benburb was peripheral to an even greater extent than the Yellow Ford; it had few consequences outside Ulster. Owen Roe would have had to fight another battle if he was to make anything of his success. When, in the tortuous development of the Irish affairs of that time, the opportunity to fight such a battle arose, the victor of Benburb was dead.

Owen Roe, who was born perhaps as early as 1580, went to the Low Countries shortly after the turn of the century. He was commissioned Captain in the Irish infantry regiment of Henry, the son of the great Hugh O'Neill, in 1606. Although Irish soldiers had been serving Spain in the Low Countries since 1587, Henry O'Neill's—or, as it came to be called, the Earl of Tyrone's —was the first Irish regiment to be raised there for the Spanish service, or more correctly for the service of the Archduke Albert and his wife the Infanta Isabella. The regiment saw plenty of service. The Archduke continued the war against the United Provinces, which had earlier revolted from Spain, until 1609. Owen Roe fought at the siege of Rheinberg and elsewhere. His company was disbanded when the war ended and he went to Spain, but he soon returned to Flanders. Henry O'Neill died in 1610 and the regiment passed to his brother John, who was then a child; Owen Roe, who had been promoted Major, commanded the regiment in John's name from 1614. He saw further service when the war with the Dutch was resumed in 1621, and he had built up a sufficient reputation by 1634 to be given a regiment of his own, a regiment that was recruited largely in Ireland.

The outbreak in the following year of war between Spain and France gave O'Neill his last opportunity of military service on the continent. During the next few years, when he was, as he said himself, a veteran of thirty-five years' service who had played his part in every campaign that had been undertaken in that time, he served with even greater distinction than before. He was military governor of the frontier town of Arras when it was besieged by the French in 1640, and although he was eventually forced to surrender the town to superior numbers he did not give up without heavy fighting; his men, as their enemy noted, marched out of Arras with the honours of war, '*bale en bouche, tambour batant, mesche allumée et enseigne déployée, comme ils ont accoustumé de marcher à la guerre*'.

Taken up as he must have been with the concerns of an active military life, and that at a time when such soldiers as the great Maurice of Nassau, his brother Frederick Henry, Prince of Orange, the Marquis of Spinola and the youthful Condé were transforming the art of war—and were doing so on the ground over which he himself had to fight—Owen Roe O'Neill still found time to keep in touch with Ireland. He never forgot his origin, never gave up hope of being able to bring about an improvement in the affairs of the Irish Catholics, and never withdrew his opposition to the new order that had been established in Ireland after his uncle's defeat and flight to the continent. He was irreconcilable. He was one of the first of a long line of Irish exiles who lived two lives—a lifetime of service to a new country and a lifetime of opposition to those whom they believed to have injured the old.

In 1627, when the difficulties of the new king, Charles I, were added to by the outbreak of war between England and France,

O'Neill encouraged the Spanish court to intervene once more in Ireland. It was suggested that, failing direct Spanish intervention, Irish troops might be sent from the Low Countries to aid an attempt to set up an Irish republic, a scheme that was no doubt inspired by the English support of the republican Dutch. In 1640, when the English government permitted further recruiting in Ireland for the Spanish service, it was particularly requested by the English that the recruits should not be placed under the command either of the titular Earls of Tyrone and Tirconnell or of Owen Roe O'Neill, because these men were known to be badly affected to King Charles. In 1641, when the Irish revolt broke out, O'Neill was, as a matter of course, involved.

O'Neill was then at Douai and Lens beyond the French border and later in the frontier province of Hainault, fighting the French. He said that the Irish should, as their last chance, defend themselves and their religion, and it was said of him that he had promised to bring assistance to Ireland 'within fifteen days after the people were up'.

The Irish insurrection of 1641 was the outcome of misgovernment. It was also another round in the struggle of Gaelic Ireland against the unpalatable changes that were being forced upon it by a victorious England. 'The old leaven still fermented inwardly', as the Earl of Castlehaven said soon afterwards. The Old Irish believed 'that the English conquest was but mere usurpation without any just title, and that the right both to the supreme sovereignty and proprietorship too of all the lands of Ireland still remained according to the ancient Brehon laws in the surviving heirs of the more ancient natives, the Milesians'.

The efforts of the king's representatives to rule the country as a whole and as the one administrative unit which it became after 1603—never having been an effective political unit before—had, by 1641, produced both uncertainty and discontent. The Irish landholders, in particular, feared for the future. The struggle between the king and his parliament was coming rapidly to a head in England, and it appeared that Charles was anxious to us Ireland to strengthen his own position. Irish land titles had already been questioned in recent years, and since a revolution in landholding had taken place within the previous half century there was much about them to question. And there was much to apprehend. Landholders feared victimisation; threats of forfeiture could be used to force them to provide some of the money

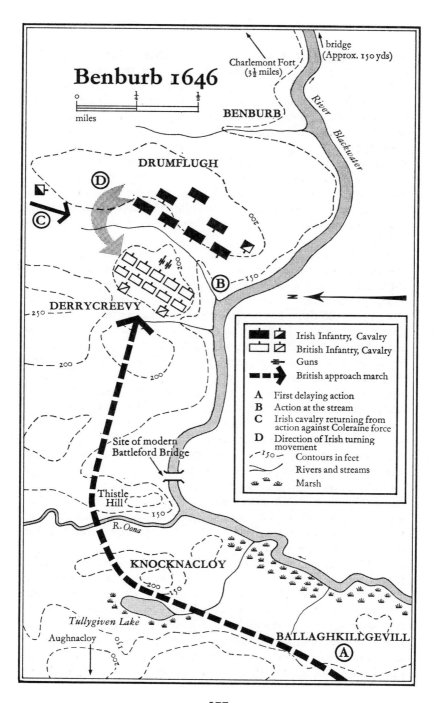

Benburb 1646

miles

0   ¼   ½

bridge
(Approx. 150 yds)

Charlemont Fort
(3½ miles)

BENBURB

River Blackwater

DRUMFLUGH

200

150

200

200

C

D

DERRYCREEVY

250

200

200

B

N

Legend:

■	▨	Irish Infantry, Cavalry
□	▨	British Infantry, Cavalry
╪		Guns
➔		British approach march

A   First delaying action
B   Action at the stream
C   Irish cavalry returning from action against Coleraine force
D   Direction of Irish turning movement

150   Contours in feet

    Rivers and streams

Marsh

Site of modern
Battleford Bridge

Thistle
Hill

150

R. Oona

KNOCKNACLOY

200

150

Tullygiven Lake

Aughnacloy

150

200

BALLAGHKILLGEVILL

A

177

which the crown so desperately needed. And if the money were to be so extorted, what security would the extortion earn them?

More ominous still was the religious position. The vast majority of the Irish, both those of Gaelic blood and the Anglo-Irish, were Catholics, whereas the government was Protestant. The hope of a religious toleration founded on a better security than the personal approval of a harassed king had receded as the years went by, and the Catholics, to whom most of the country's wealth still belonged, were now faced with the necessity—unless they could take steps to change matters—of continuing to exist as inferior citizens in their own country. Worse indeed might befall them if the Puritans, who were bound to oppress them, should prove victorious in England.

The Irish Catholics had reason to feel discontented, and the example set by their neighbours in Scotland was not lost on them. If the Scots could fight for their religion so might they.

The Ulstermen had even greater incentives than their fellow-countrymen in the other provinces to seek safety in action. Their defeat in 1603 and the 'flight of the Earls' in 1607 had resulted in a colony of English and Scots settlers being planted in their midst. When Mountjoy, Docwra and Chichester had burst into Tyrone they had dragooned the inhabitants of this territory of their enemies and had slaughtered numbers of them. The planters had dispossessed most of those who remained. The survivors of this treatment and the new generation of the descendants of the survivors cherished a notable grievance.

In this state of general discontent Old Irish and Old English were drawn together in a new political alliance. They were all Catholics. Although their backgrounds were quite different, both elements felt that they were being subjected to tyranny. Neither was willing to submit without a struggle, particularly at a moment when events both in England and Scotland plainly suggested that those who struggled might win.

In October 1641 the Gaelic Irish, or Old Irish or original inhabitants of Ulster, rose in arms against the planters who had dispossessed them. They swept down the valley of the river Blackwater and took Armagh and Dungannon, the ecclesiastical and civic centres of the old order which the planters had made towns of the new, and Charlemont fort, Mountjoy's strongpoint of 1602. They pushed the planters eastward, over the Bann and into Down and Antrim. In the other direction, after much bloodshed, they sent them flying for refuge to Enniskillen and Derry. Soon, many of the Old English of the Pale and the descendants of the Norman invaders in other parts of Ireland joined them. Depending on the common ground of their Catholicism, their sense of grievance and the loyalty which, as they said, they all owed to the king, the Irish Catholics organised themselves in the body known to history as the Confederation of Kilkenny. They claimed to be 'the sole subjects in Europe incapable of serving their sovereign in places of honour, profit and trust'— this because of the discrimination practised against them as Catholics—and they said that they had taken up arms for the liberty of their country, believing that they could enjoy that liberty while continuing to 'live happily under the crown [but not under the parliament!] of England'.

In 1642 Owen Roe O'Neill, who had been 'eating his heart out' in Flanders since the previous year, was at last released from military duty there and succeeded in getting away from Ostend, bound for Ireland. He had with him some 150 or 200 veterans of the Spanish-Irish regiments, some of them officers, and he brought warlike supplies which included a few petronels, or short firearms for mounted men, carbines or light muskets, and gunpowder. A priest who was active in the plot to send aid to Ireland described him as 'of great prudence and conduct, very adroit and crafty in the handling of great matters'; he was a much better soldier than the other Spanish-Irish Colonel, Thomas Preston, who also came to Ireland to assist the Catholics at this time. Preston was 'very brave'. but was 'not a man of much prudence', although he was more popular than Owen Roe.

O'Neill reached Doe Castle in Co. Donegal in September 1642 and proceeded to Charlemont to join Sir Felim O'Neill, the leader of the northern revolt. Ulster proved a bitter disappointment for him, nor was he the last to find the realities of oppression at home even less attractive than the plotting and the vacuity of exile. The nostalgia of the Flanders years under the influence of which he had been wont to speak of 'our afflicted country' gave place to another feeling. After more than forty years' absence—and a year of war—he found that Ulster 'not only looks like a desert, but like hell, if there could be a hell upon earth'. It was a place of broken buildings, destruction and sterility. In it both sides burnt and robbed with cold-blooded cruelty. The Catholic soldiers wanted arms, powder and discipline. The people were 'so rough and barbarous and miserable that many of them were little better in their ways than the most remote Indians'. Although O'Neill could claim that his return had kindled hope, the Ulstermen had 'only javelins, skeans and five hundred muskets', if as many, with which to make head against their enemies. 'I am', he wrote, 'killing myself bringing them to some order and discipline, so as to be able to withstand the enemy.' He demanded guns and ammunition from the continental friends of Ireland and declared that he would throw up his work in Ulster and return to Flanders if help was not sent to him, 'for it is not right that I should seek to ruin myself, and the reputation I have won by the services I have rendered during my whole life'.

He got little help, either from the continent or from the representatives of Catholic Ireland at Kilkenny, until 1646. Yet he did not carry out his threat to return to Flanders; instead of doing so he held on as best he could in south Ulster and north Leinster, where he reversed the strategy of his uncle by defending that area against attack, not—as in Hugh's time—from the south, but from the north. Hugh's retreat, when he was pressed, was northward; Owen Roe's was to the south, into the country of the little lakes in Cavan, Westmeath, Longford and Leitrim, one of the most remote areas in Ireland until modern times.

O'Neill's greatest opponent was the Scotsman Robert Monroe 'General-Major' of 'the army of the united British Protestant forces' in Ulster, who, following an arrangement between the Scots and English parliaments, brought a first instalment of 2,500 Scots soldiers to Carrickfergus in April 1642 to help the planters— an army later to be increased to 10,000. Like O'Neill, Monroe was a veteran of the continental warfare who had returned to serve his own country. While O'Neill was still fighting in the Netherlands Monroe soldiered with Gustavus Adolphus and the Swedes in Germany. He held the rank of Colonel in the Scots army with which Alexander Leslie confronted King Charles near Berwick in 1639 and he made a bad name for himself in the following year when he used the ruthless methods of the Thirty Years War against those who opposed the National Covenant in Aberdeenshire. The men whom Monroe led to Ireland were some of the famous Lowland Scots blue bonnets who had 'appealed from tyranny to God' and who had sworn 'to adhere to and defend the true religion', the men who had invaded England and advanced to Newcastle in 1640. They were organised in the six regiments of the Earls of Argyll, Eglinton and Glencairn, Lords Lindsay and Sinclair and Colonel Hume.

On his arrival in Ireland Monroe began a co-operation of several years with the forces which had been raised by the Ulster planters, a service which involved him in much marching and occasional fighting in Down, Antrim, Armagh, Monaghan, Cavan and Tyrone. His superior of the Scots army, Alexander Leslie, who was created Earl of Leven in 1641 and who followed him to Ireland with reinforcements, gave him good advice. Leslie, 'that old, little, crooked soldier', was a celebrated man. He had fought for the Dutch against O'Neill's Spaniards and after that had served Gustavus Adolphus. He was the successful defender of Stralsund against Wallenstein in 1628. Leslie knew O'Neill, or at least knew of his reputation. He asked why O'Neill, a renowned soldier, had come to Ireland to lead rebels, and O'Neill threw back the taunt; he had, he said, a better right to defend his own country than Leslie had to take arms against his king and to invade England. Before he returned to Scotland Leslie warned Monroe that if O'Neill succeeded in raising an army he would defeat him.

O'Neill was soon appointed provincial general in Ulster by the Supreme Council of the Confederate Catholics, but in his championship of the dispossessed in their struggle against the planters he represented an issue too dangerous for the Confederation fully to subscribe to it. He was the representative of the Old Irish in an alliance in which the Old English were predominant. Furthermore, his command ordinarily confined him to operations at a distance from the centre of influence at Kilkenny and the strategic centre at Dublin. Consequently he was kept short of supplies. For almost four years from the time of his arrival he was hampered by lack of arms, ammunition and money. He could hope to do no more than contain the British forces of Monroe and the planters, the most consistently powerful army of the enemies of the Confederation, and protect the midlands, and ultimately Kilkenny, from their attack.

O'Neill confronted Monroe at Anaghsawry, near Charlemont fort, in April 1643, but without coming to an engagement. In June he was caught by a force of the planters at Clones and defeated. In September he rebuffed troops from Drogheda and Dublin at Portlester in Co. Meath. In 1644, following a truce with the viceroy Ormond, the Earl of Castlehaven was appointed by the Supreme Council of the Catholics to lead an army into Ulster and to co-operate with Owen Roe against Monroe's forces. Monroe and the planters had refused to accept the truce. Castlehaven, who, as he himself put it, 'did not desire fighting', sheltered for a time at Charlemont fort and then marched round Monroe and got away to the south, boasting that he had kept the rest of Ireland 'from being troubled either with Scots or Ulster people that year'.

In 1645 the Irish scene was for the moment transformed by the arrival of a most forceful individual, John Baptist Rinuccini, Archbishop of Fermo, the papal nuncio. Rinuccini brought with him 2,000 muskets and cartridge boxes (or perhaps bandoliers), 400 pairs of pistols, 4,000 swords, 2,000 pikeheads and gunpowder and match. He also brought money. The share of these armaments and this money which he allotted to Ulster and the influence which for a time he exercised in favour of the Old Irish in Kilkenny gave Owen Roe his first opportunity of warring in Ireland in the continental style. The nuncio's supplies made possible the battle of Benburb, just as O'Neill's successful retention of Charlemont fort through his lean years set its pattern.

Owen Roe, backed by Rinuccini, organised an army of about 5,000 men in the spring of 1646. He raised or made up to strength seven regiments of foot and as many troops of horse in a camp on the hill of Gallanagh near Lough Sheelin on the Cavan-Westmeath border. The best of these men were the veterans who had already completed more than three years' service in his own forces, and many of whom may have been trained before that in the army which Sir Thomas Wentworth, later Earl of Strafford, had raised when he was Lord Deputy. The others were recruits, who, now that pay was forthcoming at the rate of three shillings and sixpence a week—the Leinster soldiers of the Confederation got only two and sixpence a week each in 1644, with six shillings for the troopers—must have been easily attracted from a population unsettled by war. Owen Roe was a strict disciplinarian who subjected his men to rigorous training; although his army was composed of the same kind of material as that which Hugh O'Neill had had at his disposal fifty years earlier, Owen, unlike Hugh, was able to fashion his men into a powerful military instrument, capable of being used successfully in formal warfare.

Weapon types had not changed greatly in the half century that had elapsed between Hugh's time and Owen's. The matchlock musket, with an effective range of about a hundred yards (the caliver had largely disappeared by the sixteen-forties), and the pike were still the weapons of the infantry. The matchlock, which was the original type of firearm mechanism, was fired by bringing a fuse or lighted cord of tow called a match into contact with gunpowder which had been placed in a pan or small open container on the outside of the breech end of the barrel of a firearm; the resulting flash entered the touch hole, exploded the main charge of powder in the breech, and fired off the ball or bullet. Practically all the firearms of Benburb were of this kind.

In addition to the matchlock two other types of mechanism had made their appearance by this date, the wheel-lock and the flintlock, and it is probable that both were used by Owen Roe's men, as they were almost certainly used by Monroe's. The wheel-lock, which in the seventeenth century was the ordinary pistol mechanism, needed to be spanned, or wound up like a piece of clockwork; it effected ignition of the priming powder in the pan by sparks which resulted from the friction of a piece of pyrites or flint in contact with a revolving wheel. The flintlock was fired by causing a piece of flint to strike a small plate of steel, which latter was so placed that the resulting sparks fell among the powder and fired it; it was the most recently developed of the gunlocks and was destined, on further development, to supersede the other two and to become the form generally used in Europe until it, in turn, was superseded in the nineteenth century by the percussion lock. Flintlocks were unusual weapons in 1646. In some of the English regiments and in some regiments in Ormond, the Lord Lieutenant's, army weapons called firelocks, which were most likely flintlocks rather than wheel-locks, were the sole missile weapons of one company, the other companies being armed with matchlocks and pikes; but these new types of firearms were ordinarily issued in the Irish war only to special independent companies or to troops who were 'commanded' or detached for special duties. It is most unlikely that O'Neill's army had many of them. European cavalry of the first half of the seventeenth century was ordinarily armed with pistols or carbines, usually wheel-lock weapons, but including an increasing proportion of snaphaunces or early flintlocks; but in Ireland, and more particularly in Ulster, the lance or horseman's staff (presumably couched, and not—as formerly—used overarm) was the more usual arm of the mounted forces. Both Monroe and O'Neill had lancers.

O'Neill's men were almost certainly still clad in the distinctive

Irish dress of shirt and jacket, trews and mantle, although the coat, breeches and hose of those parts of Ireland that were more open to anglicisation must even then have been widely worn in Ulster. There is more than one reference to the Ulstermen, like the Highland Scots, 'casting off their clothes except their shirts' when preparing to fight. The pikemen and to a lesser degree the musketeers of the age ordinarily wore helmets and back and breast plates, but armour was scarce among the Ulstermen, and indeed among the Irish as a whole. In Monroe's regiments there were twice as many musketeers as pikemen; in O'Neill's the proportion was about half and half. The musketeers had bandoliers from which were suspended twelve or more charges of powder made up in containers. Priming powder was carried separately in a flask and bullets in a bag, and a coil or link of match depended from the bandolier.

If, despite the development of new types of firearms, weapons and equipment saw little alteration in the period between the battles of Kinsale and Benburb, methods of fighting underwent a major change. We have seen that at the time of the earlier battle the mass formations of infantry that were characteristic of the European warfare of the sixteenth century were already giving place to smaller and more manageable formations. This process, which was in reality the result of constant experimentation in how best to combine firearms with the older weapons, was continued in the seventeenth century. Owing principally to the outstanding contributions to military science made by Maurice of Nassau and continued during the Thirty Years War in Germany by the great Swedish soldier Gustavus Adolphus, the system of relatively small tactical units had, by 1646, completely replaced larger formations. Infantry battalions, each about 500 strong, were now arranged for battle in double or sometimes in triple lines in which the firepower of musketeers was co-ordinated with the shock strength of pikemen. Overcrowding was as far as possible avoided, every man had a combative part to play, and the battalions not immediately engaged had the equally important function of serving as supports and reserves. The period was still one of transition towards the classic linear formation of the eighteenth and the first half of the nineteenth century, but it was also one in which fighting was a much more rationalised affair than formerly, and in which drill and training had become essential for successful soldiering.

Both Monroe and O'Neill were early in the field in 1646. Monroe began moving westward from his winter quarters in Antrim and Down at the end of May and reached Poyntz Pass north of Newry on 4 June. He had over 6,000 men, made up of his own six Scottish regiments, four English or Anglo-Irish regiments and eleven or twelve troops, or about 600, horse. The troopers were all Protestant Ulstermen, although some of the troops had been raised by the Scots. Monroe also had six field pieces which, since the Irish horses were too small for use as draught animals, were drawn by oxen. And he had a full supply train, carried on pack horses. He proposed to form a junction at Glaslough, west of Armagh, with a second British force of about a hundred horse and 240 musketeers with which his son-in-law, Colonel George Monroe, was marching southward from Coleraine to meet him. A third force, called by contemporaries the Lagan army and consisting of some 2,000 planters of that area under Sir Robert Stewart, was moving in Monroe's direction from the Foyle valley and had come by 4 June to the neighbourhood of Clogher, Co. Tyrone. This was part of a force of three regiments, five troops and some independent companies which the refugees from the planted areas who had fled westward had earlier raised.

It was proposed that Monroe and the Coleraine men should, on meeting, turn into the midlands, that is, into the territory of the Confederation, and should carry the war perhaps even as far southward as Kilkenny. The Foyle valley force, acting in concert with Monroe and perhaps making a detachment to reinforce him, was to enter Connacht, to which province they had already sent 1,500 foot and four troops of horse. Sir Charles Coote had captured Sligo for the Parliamentarians in the previous year and had pushed on to oppose the supporters of the Confederation in Galway; Coote had not yet been checked, as he later was, by Preston.

In these circumstances it remained for Owen Roe O'Neill to operate against Monroe. O'Neill marched from the hill of Gallanagh about 31 May. He had his own regiment and that of Alexander Mac Donnell, the son of the Earl of Antrim—each of fifteen companies and nominally 1,500 strong—and the smaller ten-company regiments of Colonels Richard Farrell (the Longford regiment), Sir Felim O'Neill, Mac Neny, O'Donnell and Maguire. He may have had nine rather than seven troops of horse by this date, but, although he had them on earlier occasions, he seems now to have had no guns. Later on, even though he had captured Monroe's guns at Benburb, his first request to the Supreme Council of the Confederates, on sending them news of his victory, was for two cannon. Advised of the movements of his opponents by messages from Charlemont and from the crannoges in Lough Oughter, at Crom, Ballydonnelly, Co. Tyrone and elsewhere, in which he had tiny garrisons, O'Neill traversed Cavan and Monaghan and reached Glaslough on 3 June. Moving again on the morning of the 4th, he descended the valley of the river Blackwater and encamped that evening with his whole army at Benburb on the north bank. Meanwhile the British forces continued to converge on Glaslough.

By marching thus to Benburb O'Neill had placed himself midway between the three forces of his enemies, who were advancing as from the three points of a triangle towards the rendezvous whence they were to move south. Even if they were all to avoid contact with him for the moment, they could not leave him in their rear and pursue their purpose, for there would then be nothing to prevent O'Neill from raiding the hitherto untouched areas of Down and Antrim in the absence of such a great part of their defenders. O'Neill must have known however that, believing him to have walked into a trap, his enemies would hasten to engage him and that their anxiety to catch him before he followed the policy of former years and bolted for Charlemont, or else withdrew into the difficult country of the Slieve Beagh mountains south of Clogher, would bring on Monroe at least, who had the greatest force, at redoubled speed. Further, O'Neill must have realised how difficult a change in the direction of Monroe's march would make it for the other British columns to effect a junction with him, or even to keep contact with him. Finally, he was aware that, occupying as he did a central position in regard to the converging columns, and above all since he had placed the river between himself and Monroe, he might defeat the Coleraine force before Monroe could reach it, or could deploy against him. Using the river as a shield, O'Neill might hope to cause Monroe to attack him precipitately and at a disadvantage. His central position was worth much to him, and with Charlemont behind him he had a fortress into which—suppose all went wrong—he could at any time retire. This was manœuvring for position of a kind that had not previously been seen in the Irish wars. It may not seem inappropriate to call it a small foretaste of

Robert E. Lee who was to say over 200 years later, 'there is no better way of defending a long line than by moving into the enemy's country', or of Lee's Lieutenant, Longstreet, who 'believed the receipt for victory to be to manœuvre an army into a position such that the enemy would be compelled to attack at a disadvantage, and there await the blow'.

While marching towards Poyntz Pass on 4 June Monroe had sent forward a detachment of seventy-two horse under a namesake of his own and the Lieutenant of his own troop, Daniel Monroe. The Lieutenant was ordered to cross the Blackwater at Benburb, to advance northward into Tyrone until he met the Coleraine column, and to 'certify' Colonel Monroe of the rendezvous at Glaslough on the day following. On his way through Armagh, however, Daniel Monroe met what was believed to be a 'fore troop' of O'Neill's army and was stopped. He took a prisoner and sent him back to General Monroe, to whom the prisoner was willing to talk. The General, who had halted and encamped by that time, was told that his opponent had about 6,000 men and a fortnight's supplies and that he was marching that day from Glaslough to Benburb and Charlemont.

If Owen Roe had purposely sent this information he could not have hoped for a better result. Monroe, who had believed up to this that the Irish 'had no considerable army on foot', was electrified. He must have thought that O'Neill was still passing across his front and that the occasion demanded instant activity for he broke up his camp and ordered his infantry to march ten miles more to Hamilton's Bawn and his cavalry more than fifteen miles to Armagh. He roused the infantry again at four o'clock on the following morning and, Lieutenant Monroe having been ordered back during the night, concentrated his whole force at Armagh. Unfortunately, he met no further Irish troops in that neighbourhood. He had hoped to catch at least O'Neill's rear guard, but O'Neill had almost certainly reached Benburb by the left and not by the right bank of the river; his whole army was already safely encamped beyond the Blackwater; and the horsemen whom Lieutenant Monroe had met at Armagh were not part of O'Neill's moving column but scouts whom he had sent there from Benburb.

Monroe rose betimes on Friday, 5 June. He was aware by then that O'Neill had got ahead of him. Leaving his army in Armagh, he made a personal reconnaissance towards the river at Benburb, where there was a ford and a bridge. He found the Irish strongly posted along the high ground by the ruins of the old O'Neill castle on the northern bank, overlooking and completely blocking the passage. We can imagine how they looked at each other across the wooded ravine, O'Neill no doubt using the 'prospective glass' which he had had at Portlester in 1643 when he levelled the gun that 'most strangely killed the Lord Moore'; on the one side the buff-coated Scotsmen and the ejected planters, standing at the beginning of their centuries of distrust; on the other the dispossessed gentlemen of Ulster, Rory Maguire, Philip MacHugh O'Reilly, Henry O'Neill, Owen O'Doherty and the rest—'old beaten soldiers', beaten, that is, into adamant, who 'had learnt the art military in the Vulcanian academy of Flanders'.

Whatever the feelings evoked by the occasion, it was clear that Monroe could not attempt to cross the Blackwater at Benburb with any hope of success. Nor could he cross at Blackwatertown— the site of the historic Portmore that had provoked the battle of the Yellow Ford and that was now held by O'Neill's men—or Charlemont, or anywhere else downstream. Yet if he was to come to grips with O'Neill he must get to the other side. There remained only the upstream crossing places, the nearest of which was the ford near Caledon beyond the great bend of the Blackwater, more than five miles in a direct line from Benburb. Monroe, following a consultation with his officers, decided to cross at Caledon. He explained this decision by saying that his advance in this way was calculated to 'draw the enemy from his advantage', that is, that it would prevent O'Neill from attempting to fall on the advancing Coleraine men—that it would, in fact, place him directly between the converging forces of the two Monroes— and that it would result in the turning of the strong position held by the Irish at Benburb. General Monroe claimed further that his movement would cut O'Neill off from 'his victuals', that is, that it would interpose Monroe's army between O'Neill and his supposed base in the Lough Sheelin area, Monroe's baggage, which he proposed to keep with him, being secured in his own rear. In fact, however, the lines of communication were of immediate importance to neither side. Monroe, as more than one contemporary noted, expected O'Neill to run rather than fight, and he believed that the only hope of preventing his doing so lay in crossing where he did.

Monroe sent orders to Armagh for the resumption of the

march, turned his back on his opponents and made for Kinard, where, within five miles of the prospective rendezvous of Glaslough, the track entered the ford and led up again on the far side to Caledon. The army was across by about three o'clock. The train which may have come along later and which contained, as an Irish account specified, the camp equipment and six weeks' supplies of biscuits, flour, meal, beer, wine, whiskey and sugar, was brought over the river and left under guard on the left bank. The troops turned downstream and, with their cavalry in front, continued their march northward. Although they were now moving away from the rendezvous and from the Lagan force, they were closer to Stewart's men than they had been up to this. A junction was still possible. We are not told if any contact was made.

Owen Roe was kept well informed of these movements. Monroe's march from Armagh indicated either an intention of crossing the Blackwater further upstream or of seeking a junction with the Lagan men. Whatever his opponent's purpose might be, sufficient time must elapse before the British, now that they had turned away, could make head against him for O'Neill to deal with the Coleraine column. He detached Lieut.-Colonel Brien Roe O'Neill with the greater part of his cavalry and a small party of foot, instructing them to move towards Dungannon and to intercept George Monroe.

When General Monroe again turned towards him after crossing at Caledon Owen Roe knew that the battle was impending. Monroe's scouts came as far north as the hill of Knocknacloy, where the Blackwater bends eastward towards Benburb and the Oona stream joins it. They were soon forced back by the Irish. During the afternoon Owen Roe marched out of his camp and took position on the hill of Drumflugh, which is a mile west of Benburb. He also sent what remained of his cavalry and a substantial force of infantry—one account says that it was his own regiment—across the Oona and towards Monroe. These men, before whom Monroe's scouts fell back, took position where the track from Caledon ran between boggy ground on the one hand and rising ground on the other and where a stream ran across the path, at Ballaghkillgevill south of Knocknacloy, and prepared to dispute Monroe's passage. This was at that time a wooded area and the site of a bealach—a way or pass—such as had so often made possible the delaying actions of Owen Roe's uncle Hugh.

The Irish intention was again to cause delay, a delay in which Brien O'Neill might make certain of eliminating George Monroe.

Viscount Montgomery of Ards, Monroe's son-in-law, who acted as commander of the horse in George Monroe's absence and who led the forlorn hope, or most advanced body, of General Monroe's army, was stopped for a time at Ballaghkillgevill, where the opposing forces 'saluted one another very roughly'. The whole column was held up, although the footsoldiers, who must by then have grown weary of the march, were doubtless glad of the opportunity to rest by the wayside. Their muskets were heavy and their pikes, which were carried slung in pairs in the baldrics of the pikemen, were heavier still. Montgomery eventually forced his way through, the Irish retiring before him into places where his horse could not follow them and giving fire from their rear. The column pushed on between Tullygiven Lake and Knocknacloy, turned to the right to conform to the bend of the Blackwater, and came to the Oona. It was then perhaps six o'clock. O'Neill had sent forward 500 more infantry to strengthen his skirmishers and a fire fight again developed, perhaps at the passage of the Oona. Monroe used his field guns and 500 'commanded' or detached musketeers under Lieut.-Colonel Cunningham to clear the way, and the Irish, their delaying mission accomplished, continued their retirement. According to one account they were led by Colonel Richard Farrell, an experienced soldier who had been Major of a regiment in Germany.

Monroe pushed on. His men were moving slowly now. They had covered fifteen miles from Armagh; one contemporary writer tells us that they marched fifteen miles on the day of the battle in an effort to catch O'Neill before he escaped them; another says that they covered thirteen or fourteen miles before they came within sight of the Irish. Many of them must have been close to exhaustion before the battle began.

They ascended the rising ground at Derrycreevy and there at last—in front of them at Drumflugh—they saw the men whom they had believed not to have hearts to face them. At times during their tremendous march, as Monroe admits, O'Neill's enemies had hoped that the impossible would happen and that the Irish might, in some foolish burst of confidence, quit Benburb and advance to meet them. Each time they were held up it must have seemed that they might after all, have to march no further. But the main body of the Irish had moved no more than a mile; and those who had come further towards them had gone skipping away again in front of them like the cowards they had always known them to be.

Knowing of Monroe's advance, Owen Roe O'Neill had had three alternatives. He might, as Monroe expected, have retired to Charlemont. He might have crossed the Blackwater at Benburb and moved in safety and in the certainty of plunder towards the south-east. He might have chosen his ground on the north bank and prepared to fight. Clearly this 'man of few words, cautious and phlegmatic in his operations', this 'great adept in concealing his feelings', as Rinuccini described him—this Stonewall Jackson, this Parnell—had made his choice at an early stage. Monroe had been led on, and the rate of his progress had been regulated. ·

The Irish were formed in two lines, each made up in the contemporary manner of brigades or battalions (both names were used) of foot. Each brigade consisted apparently of an administrative regiment formed for battle with its pikes in the centre and its musketeers on either flank. The men stood in line and were arranged in files six to nine deep. There were four brigades in the front line and three in the second, and they were drawn up chequer-wise, the brigades of the second line standing behind the openings between the brigades of the first. Musketeers who were surplus to the linear formation of each brigade were drawn up in its rear and were available for 'command', or detached duty. It is not possible to say where the different Irish regiments stood, but Farrell seems to have been on the right and Rory Maguire's regiment, which was in the centre of the second line, seems to have been placed further back than the others and to have formed a reserve. The available cavalry, in squadrons three or four deep, was on the wings,

As Monroe came up his battle formation was quickly assumed from column by the formal drill movement of squads or groups of files. The complete—and time-consuming—mathematical reconstruction required by the larger formations and more numerous weapon categories of earlier days was no longer necessary. His advancing column had the cavalry in front, followed by the field guns, and the infantry in the rear. He deployed facing O'Neill in two lines with the Blackwater on his right and 'a marrish [or moorish, or like a moor] bog' on his left, and he placed his six guns 'upon the declining of an easy hill' in front. His infantry was arranged, like O'Neill's, in brigades, five in either line; but the ground on which he was constrained to form was too narrow for his numbers, and there was not sufficient space between his front line brigades to receive those of the second line 'in case there should be use of their assistance in the front', nor could the front line have fallen back into the intervals of the second without causing disorder. Monroe's cavalry was drawn up behind him ready to charge 'through the intervals betwixt the brigades of foot'.

The fields which were to form the battleground 'were in most parts level', but there were 'scrogs and bushes' in front of the Irish line; O'Neill, says one account, was drawn up 'on a scrog-gred high hill' below which, 'down next the river', there were 'scroggie woods'. The ground, across which the modern road from Benburb to Aughnacloy winds its way, is not now wooded. Thistle hill, which stands above the confluence of the Oona and Blackwater and in the vicinity of which the last of the delaying actions took place, is visible from the Irish position at Drumflugh, but the ground beyond Derrycreevy, over which the British approached, is concealed by Derrycreevy ridge. A small stream, draining the 'marrish bog' on Monroe's left, ran between the two armies and discharged into the Blackwater below Monroe's right.

The action began with a cannonade from the British guns, and for a while Monroe was the aggressor. His intention appears to have been to turn the Irish left, to force O'Neill away from the river and from Charlemont, and to drive him back on the Coler-aine column—which was still, as far as Monroe knew, advancing from Dungannon. To this end Lord Montgomery 'aimed at a ford that was near [at] hand and between himself and the Irish [and] thought to lead his horse that way and beat General O'Neill's army in the flank'. The ford was on the stream in Monroe's right front. A force of commanded men went with Montgomery, and 'the Scotch musketeers from thence began the fight'. O'Neill's skirmishers accepted the challenge and the struggle was, says Monroe, 'begun hot on both sides'. 'At length [this from one of the Irish descriptions] the Irish horse from the left wing charging them home, drove them with loss and pursued them beyond the brook, which when they had done they returned to their former post.' The first round had gone to O'Neill.

After this Monroe's men were on the defensive. They must

indeed have been worn out, and the vigorous action of a charge was probably beyond them. The cannon twice brought down two files of the Irish, but the gunners were firing at men who were on a slope above them and their service was even less effectual than was usual in that age.

For a time the Irish too stood waiting, although the soldiers, to whom the fire was galling, more than once cried out to be led forward. Then horsemen were seen advancing over the rolling ground to the north, riders who came 'in great haste in a gallop, all in a sweat both horse and men'. Both sides saw them, and Monroe thought for a while that they were the Coleraine men come to join him at a moment most opportune. They were the cavalry of Brien Roe O'Neill's detachment. Brien Roe had come upon the Coleraine column 'in a straight' near Dungannon, where he was 'scarce seen until [he was] among them'; George Monroe's men mistook their attackers for Owen Roe's whole force and promptly fled. Brien Roe pursued for four miles and was then recalled by an express from his general. Drawn on as he came by the sound of the guns at Benburb, he rode as fast as he could go for the battlefield. His troops now came into place to complete Owen Roe's line. The Irish, whose timing throughout was excellent, had disposed of one column of their enemies; they had concentrated on their own ground and were now ready to engage Monroe. It was perhaps eight o'clock. The setting sun shone in their faces. The wind, which had been blowing strongly from the south-west during the day, had begun to fall.

We are told that the Definator of the Franciscans, Fr Boetius Mac Egan, who was Rinuccini's representative and chaplain-general of the army, gave general absolution. Owen Roe O'Neill harangued those of his men who could hear him. He reminded them that their opponents were the men who had persecuted them for their religion and had banished them from the homes of their fathers, that they themselves were 'gentlemen as good as they were'—a nice touch, for his listeners were the proud remnants of an aristocracy that had been evicted by mere tillers of the soil— and that they had arms in their hands as good as their opponents' arms. 'Let your manhood be seen by your push of pike', he cried. 'Your word is *Sancta Maria*, and so in the Name of the Father, Son and Holy Ghost advance!—and give not fire till you are within pike-length!'

The Irish advance appears to have been a gradual and strongly resisted movement, the weight of which was finally transferred from the centre to the British left wing. O'Neill's men, 'maugre all resistance, were masters of the field pieces' and Lord Blayney, who was 'Captain of the artillery', was killed. Monroe's horse, charging forward through the intervals in his first line, tried to break up the Irish brigades, but their animals must have been almost foundered by fatigue; the riders were unequal to the task and soon turned tail. The Irish foot came on, led as the rule was in that stern age by their officers, each of whom bore a pike. The wind was still in the faces of the musketeers, a thing to be avoided if possible, for not only was the thick smoke of their own and their enemies' discharges blown back to blind them (as it was to blind the Highlanders at Culloden) but a high wind could blow the priming powder out of pans unsheltered by musketeers' bodies and could make it impossible to fire at all. Five of the contemporary writers note, as contemporaries would do, being susceptible to what was involved, that at the outset the wind and sun favoured the British, and some of the unmilitary ones say that Monroe's long march was undertaken in order to make sure that this would be so. But fifteen miles' march was too dear a price to pay for such an advantage, even if it could have ensured it. At the time of the battle the wind, we are told, was dying, and during the last moments—if it had not set by then—the sun was at O'Neill's back rather then Monroe's.

The Scots and Anglo-Irish officers 'stood it manfully' as their enemies came on and 'left not their ground till they were beaten down by push of pike'. It was said that the Irish pikes were longer and their pike heads 'four square and small' and 'far better to pierce' than the short-shafted and broad-headed pikes of their opponents, and that these things gave the Irish side an advantage. 'There was the best pikemen in the world on both sides, breast to breast, pointing at each other; the shortest [pike] before he [that is, its bearer] came home fell from his master's hands, the carrier being dead.' Pikemen were certainly tempted to lessen the great weight of their weapons by cutting off a foot or two from the shafts and thus reducing their extreme length of sixteen feet, but there is no real reason to believe that such short-sightedness was confined to the British soldiers.

As the Irish, after as it seems an hour or so of dour fighting, 'broke upon the enemy unto the very battalion', Monroe tried to draw his first line into his second, but he was too tightly packed and his stricken brigades became piled together in confusion. The Irish must already have advanced their second line units into the intervals in their first line. Monroe sent forward his cavalry again, but once more fruitlessly. Cavalry could seldom, at that time, upset good and unbroken pikemen, and when the pikemen had musketeers to aid them mounted troops had even less chance of success. Owen Roe ordered Colonel Richard Farrell to move in closer on his right wing 'and give the onset on the enemy flank, by whose approach the enemy did stagger and brought the odds on his own side'. The fighting had by this time become desperate. 'Whole regiments fell dead to the ground from the enemy, their second or relief advancing as far as the former were tumbled upon the senseless corpses of their comrades'—flowery language, but of an unmistakable implication; none but the fiercest fighting could be so described. Monroe's left was turned, his whole line was slewed round and was forced back towards the river. In the simple statement of the time, O'Neill 'used his very best endeavours to have the wind and sun in his back, which by his dexterity was brought to pass, being an extraordinary advantage in such an occasion'. Monroe fought no longer 'either to lose or win all' but with fading hope of preventing himself from being overrun.

In the end that was his fate. His cavalry rode off, leaving their less mobile comrades on foot to be cut to pieces. He himself escaped with difficulty and, says the record, without his periwig and cassock. Only Sir James Montgomery's regiment, which was on the right beside the river, got off in a body. O'Neill's brigades seem to have worked round to overlap what remained of Monroe's left and, in part at least, to face south, or even southeast. Over and above those who fell at Derrycreevy and between that place and the present Battleford bridge, Monroe's casualties were suffered between the battlefield and Caledon—some of them at Tullygiven Lake—and between the Blackwater and Armagh; some of the fugitives went back by the way they had come, others managed to cross the river and tried to run south. Many were drowned. Some collapsed from exhaustion and were found dead but unwounded. Monroe's total casualties are variously given; they seem to have been between 2,000 and 3,000—or perhaps the Irish authorities are right and they were higher. Viscount Ards and others were taken prisoner. The British lost all their baggage, and O'Neill gained the spoil of a rout—colours, cannon, drums, hundreds of muskets, pikes, the sergeants' halberds, pieces of armour, a mass of equipment. The Irish loss was small. Three hundred is the greatest figure given for those who were killed and wounded on O'Neill's side. Farrell suffered from a shoulder injury—but recovered to lead the last remnants of the Catholic army of Ulster in 1652 as a Lieut.-General. Colonel Manus MacNeill, Manus, the son of Neill Garbh O'Donnell, and others were killed.

The contemporary comments on the battle are interesting. Monroe was chastened: 'The Lord of Hosts had a controversy with us to rub shame on our faces till once we shall be humbled, for a greater confidence did I never see in any army than was amongst us'. The old Ulster soldier of Clotworthy's regiment who wrote such a valuable account of the war agreed: 'Too much confidence makes security, and security makes carelessness: and so it happened that day.' Rinuccini exulted at the victory and noted the opinion of the historically minded: 'The annals of the history of this island show that at no period has a greater defeat and loss of life been sustained by any enemy and that, four hundred years ago, only one equally crushing had been sustained by the Scots.' His reference was to Falkirk, where Edward I overwhelmed William Wallace in 1298. The Supreme Council of the Catholic Confederation told the Pope that 'there has probably not of late years been in northern Europe a battle fought with more determination throughout so many hours, and with such carnage'. They were guilty of exaggeration. The casualties, whatever about the determination, were greater at Marston Moor and Naseby, and far greater at Rocroy.

The Council's secretary was among the first to ask the inevitable question: 'Who could have imagined that this so entire and so celebrated victory would not have conduced very much to the asserting of those interests for which that nation fought?'— in other words, if Benburb was such a famous victory why did it not change the course of Irish history?

On the second day after the battle Owen Roe marched towards Clones and chased Stewart and the Lagan men back to Derry and Enniskillen. His was the only army in the field in Ulster. He hoped by August to have 10,000 men under arms—a big army for that age and place—and to be able to root out 'all the round heads' of the province. Unlike the other O'Neills however— certainly unlike Shane the Proud—Owen Roe's horizon was wider than the tops of the Ulster hills. He listened to the nuncio's plea, 'quitted the opportunity of conquest in Ulster' and marched south. He helped to strengthen the nuncio's intransigence and to upset the arrangements which had been proceeding for a peace between the Catholic Confederation and Ormond, the king's representative. But he did not release the Catholics from their dilemma of at once supporting and opposing the king.

Owen Roe O'Neill was a great soldier, but he was not a Cromwell. He could win a pitched battle, but he could not overcome the Irish hydra, as Oliver—being Hercules—overcame the English one. The Gaelic majority whence Owen Roe was sprung were the only real revolutionaries; they were the counterparts in Ireland of the English republicans. But Owen Roe could not—and probably with his visions of Irish unity had no wish to—supply the political leadership which they lacked. Their hope of a radical modification of the conquest was indeed foredoomed to failure because it could be achieved only at the expense of their Anglo-Irish comrades in arms—men who waged war but sought a compromise that must fall far short of Gaelic aspirations—and in despite of the king, the parliament and the ambition of England. This was a combination which had crushed the original inhabitants of Ireland before and could crush them again. The Catholics, whose motto was union—*Pro Deo, Rege et Patria Hibernia unanimis*—were fundamentally divided; and they were opposed by the parliamentarians and Ulster Scots and alternately cajoled and cuffed by Ormond. This was the Irish hydra, before which a textbook victory like Benburb, the only Irish battle of annihilation, was thrown away.

The fullest contemporary accounts of the battle of Benburb are in: J. T. Gilbert (ed.), *History of the Irish Confederation and the War in Ireland* (the account by R. Bellings, Secretary of the Confederate Catholics). The same editor's *A Contemporary History of affairs in Ireland, from 1641 to 1652* (this contains Monroe's report, the statement on the battle in 'The Aphorismical Discovery of Treasonable Faction', Henry O'Neill's 'Impartiall Relation', and other contemporary descriptions). E. Hogan (ed.), *The History of the Warr of Ireland from 1641 to 1653 by a British Officer*, of the

Regiment of Sir John Clottworthy (1873). T. ODonnchadha (ed.), *Cínn Lae Ó Mealláin* (the best edition of O'Mellan's diary, in *Analecta Hibernica*, III, published by the Irish Manuscripts Commission in 1931). G. Aiazza and A. Hutton (ed.), *The Embassy in Ireland of Monsignor G. B. Rinuccini* (Rinuccini's report. See also Fr Stanislaus Kavanagh's *Commentarius Rinuccinianus*, II—Irish Manuscripts Commission). As well as these see the account in T. Carte, *The Life of James, Duke of Ormond* (1851) and Massari's statement in 'My Irish Campaign' (*Catholic Bulletin*, 1917).

The best of the more modern accounts are: H. Tohall (An Ulster Archaeologist), 'The Battle of Benburb' in *Transactions of the Ossory Archaeological Society*, I (1874–9), pp. 307 ff (amplified by the same writer in 1910 in *Ulster Journal of Archaeology*, 2nd series, XVI, pp. 78 ff, 140 ff). W. J. Latimer, *The Battles of the Yellow Ford and Benburb* (published as a pamphlet in Dungannon in 1919. This gives Latimer's considered view. He had already published in 1896 'The Battle of Benburb' in *Journal of the Royal Society of Antiquaries of Ireland*, XXVI, pp. 29 ff and in 1911 a paper of the same name in the *Ulster Journal of Archaelogy*, 2nd series, XVII). These papers of Tohall and Latimer are largely concerned with the dispute regarding the site of the battlefield which was occasioned by statements made by Thomas Davis in his *National and Historical Ballads* in 1846. Davis and Tohall held that the battle was fought at or near Knocknacloy; Latimer believed that the battlefield was at Drumflugh—Derrycreevy. Colonel J. J. O'Connell (author of *The Irish Wars*) and such modern writers as Mathew O'Conor (*The Irish Brigades*, 1855, p. 448), C. P. Meehan, Canon O'Rourke, E. A. D'Alton, D. Coffey, J. F. Taylor and others have followed Davis and Tohall. I follow Latimer. (My reasons for doing so are given in my paper 'O'Mellan's account of the Battle of Benburb, 1646' in S. Pender (ed.), *Essays and Studies presented to Professor Tadhg Ua Donnchadha*, pp. 141 ff. See also my note on the site of Ballaghkillgevill in *The Irish Sword*, I. p. 153). The local historian J. J. Marshall (*Benburb: its battlefields and history*, Dungannon, 1924, pp. 13 ff) also accepts Drumflugh as the battlefield.

For the Catholic Confederation see J. C. Beckett, 'The Confederation of Kilkenny reviewed' in *Historical Studies*, II (edited by M. Roberts, 1959), pp. 29 ff. C. P. Meehan's *The Confederation of Kilkenny* (2nd edn, 1882), though superseded by modern research, is a readable narrative. *The Earl of Castlehaven's Review or his Memoirs of . . . The Irish Wars* (1684) gives interesting military information.

Owen Roe O'Neill's career in the Low Countries may be followed in Dr Brendan Jennings (ed.), *Wild Geese in Spanish Flanders, 1582–1700*, published in 1964 by the Irish Manuscripts Commission. See also J. F. Taylor, *Owen Roe O'Neill* (1896) which gives a picturesque account of the siege of Arras, and E. O'Neill, *Owen Roe O'Neill* (1937).

For the tactical and organisational changes of the half century before the battle see Michael Roberts, *The Military Revolution, 1560–1660* (Belfast, 1956). For the weapons see my 'Limerick, 1651: the weapons of the siege' in *Commemorative Booklet of Tercentenary of the Siege of Limerick* (1951) and 'The Weapons of Benburb' in *An Cosantóir* (Dublin, June 1945) and for the pikemen as the first tactically self-sufficient infantry with real offensive power see O. L. S. Spaulding and J. W. Wright, 'Warfare in Modern Times' in *Warfare* (1924), pp. 398 ff. The R. E. Lee and Longstreet references are quoted in Sir F. Maurice, *Robert E. Lee the Soldier*, pp. 141, 203.

Rathmines, 1649

Warfare in Ireland from the commencement of the rebellion in 1641 to the time of the surrender of the scattered remnants of the Catholic and royalist forces to Cromwell's Parliamentary government in 1652 was bloody and confused. Historical writers have, on the whole, made heavy weather of it in their attempts to describe it. The civil wars of the same period in Britain, which were likewise characterised by the effusion of blood and the confusion of loyalties, are seen in retrospect as the opening passages of a revolution which led our neighbours to world power; but neither the course nor the issue of the war in Ireland was heroic, or can be made to appear so.

The Catholic Confederation, which claimed to represent the majority of Irishmen, was not an inspired body. It reflected but did not reconcile the diverse and often conflicting aims of the different elements which composed it, the 'Old Irish' and 'Old English' elements, the different 'septs or families' that were the relics of earlier localism, the townsmen and countrymen that were the survivors of two civilisations, the urban civilisation of the invasion and the rural civilisation of the invaded. When the Confederates spoke of the 'native Irish' they excluded those whose nationality was a mere matter of 500 years, that is, they very largely excluded themselves, for the 'Old English' element was predominant among them. The Confederates were royalists, but they could not help the Marquis of Ormond, the leader of the Irish royalists and the official governor of the country, who sought in his turn to help the king. They were rebels, but they could not strike out for themselves, get rid of Ormond and attempt a revolution. The Marquis of Clanrickard had noted in 1642 that they seemed 'in outward appearance and according to outward rules' to be 'in opposition to His Majesty and his government', whereas 'by profession and protestation' they were 'directed to his service'. They could neither join Ormond against the Parliamentarians and Scots nor oppose all three in the name of Ireland. They did nothing whole-heartedly, whether negotiation or fighting. They had no centralised control of their own forces and no way of curbing the personal antagonisms of their provincial commanders. The spleen that upset the relations between Owen Roe O'Neill of Ulster and Preston of Leinster was never resolved. Since the Confederate Catholics never had a policy that progressed beyond opportunism, they never had a military objective or a military plan. They went down in the end in frustration and confusion, and when they were gone the decisiveness which they had so conspicuously lacked—decisiveness as much as might—triumphed and Cromwell was able to implement England's wishes for Ireland.

Ultimate victory depended, in this as in all the Irish wars, on possession of Dublin. The rebellion had commenced in 1641 with an abortive plan for the seizure of Dublin Castle. If this could have been made good, or if the combined armies of Ulster and Leinster under O'Neill and Preston could have taken Dublin after the victory of Benburb, the fighting might perhaps have had a different result. But Dublin was held for England throughout, and it fell ultimately to the English Parliament. Ormond held Dublin until June 1647 when, discouraged by his failure to make peace with the Confederates and by the eclipse of royalist hopes in England—the defeated king had just then been transferred as a prisoner from the Commissioners of Parliament to an increasingly mutinous Parliamentary army—he handed it over to the 'new English' Parliamentarians and eventually left Ireland. If he had handed it to O'Neill or to Preston there might have been some hope of an Irish solution for Irish problems, but Ormond—to use his own phrase, and one that history has never forgotten for him—preferred English rebels to Irish ones.

Less than two months later, on 8 August, Colonel Michael Jones, the new Parliamentary commander in Dublin, shattered Preston at Dungan's Hill, near Trim, Co. Meath.

Preston was described in his own time as a man 'wavering in his resolutions, imperious in his commands and fiery in his deportment'. These faults may have resulted from the fact that he was also 'delicate in his diet'. He was perhaps a martyr to indigestion. He had moved about ineffectually in the approaches to Dublin while Ormond decided its future. He laid siege to Trim at the end of July. Ormond's surrender included Drogheda, Dundalk, Naas and Trim—where there was a substantial garrison of troops well affected to the Parliament—as well as

Dublin, and Jones set out on 1 August to oppose Preston and to raise the siege. Jones had about 800 horse, 4,000 foot and seven guns and he was joined at Skreen near the hill of Tara and ten miles east of Trim on 4 August by forces from Drogheda, Dundalk and east Ulster. These amounted to 700 horse, 1,200 foot and two guns. Thus reinforced, Jones approached Trim. Preston, who had an army of about 1,000 horse, 7,000 foot and four 12-pounder demi-culverins, decamped as Jones came up, crossed the Boyne and made for Portlester, the 'old lurking, place' so frequently occupied by Owen Roe O'Neill in earlier years. Hoping to draw Preston out of this fastness, Jones moved through Trim and attacked Tremblestown castle, where there was a Catholic garrison. Preston came out, but his subsequent movements were unexpected. With the apparent intention of stealing a march on the Parliamentarians, he recrossed the Boyne and moved towards Dublin. Unfortunately—if we measure him against the speed of Monroe or O'Neill—he was dilatory. He marched no more than ten miles and encamped for the night 'in a very commodious and safe place from incursions of all enemy as long as he pleased' at Agher on the road to Maynooth. He was still closer to Dublin than his opponents, but he was no Owen Roe and on the following morning it was he, and not Jones, who was caught at a disadvantage.

Jones, aware of the Irish withdrawal and fearing that they might attempt to beat him in a race for Dublin, had sent 500 horse to watch them. He followed them with his whole army early on the morning of the 8th. He was much stronger in cavalry than Preston and there is little doubt that he could have stopped the Irish if they had continued their advance towards the capital. The Irish may have realised this. At any rate they did not continue. Quitting their 'safe place' at Agher, they moved about two miles to their left towards Dungan's Hill, which is in the townland of Drumlargan, south-east of Summerhill (the Lynch's Knock of the seventeenth century) and there attempted to form for battle in, as an unsympathetic commentator records, 'the very untowardest place that nature could devise'.

Jones soon caught up with them, perhaps indeed before they were ready to receive him. He reached Lynch's Knock about ten o'clock and advanced rapidly towards Dungan's Hill, below which, and under fire from Preston's guns, he deployed. Preston's infantry were drawn up in 'a brave field of wheat', where, says

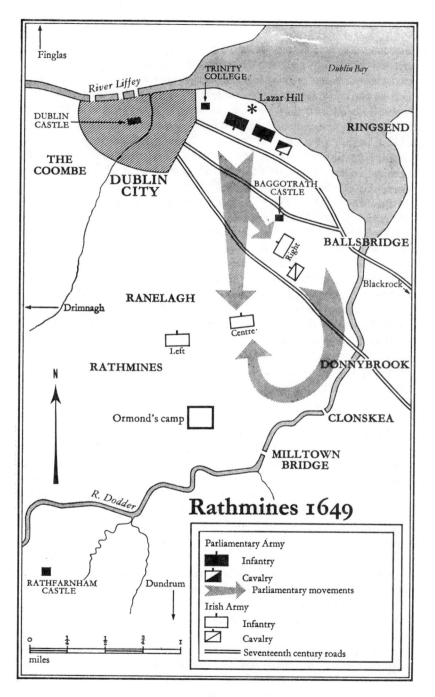

Finglas

River Liffey

TRINITY
COLLEGE

Dublin Bay

Lazar Hill

✳

RINGSEND

DUBLIN
CASTLE

THE
COOMBE

**DUBLIN
CITY**

BAGGOTRATH
CASTLE

BALLSBRIDGE

Right

Blackrock

Drimnagh

RANELAGH

Centre

Left

DONNYBROOK

RATHMINES

N

Ormond's camp

CLONSKEA

**MILLTOWN
BRIDGE**

R. Dodder

Rathmines 1649

RATHFARNHAM
CASTLE

Dundrum

Parliamentary Army	
■	Infantry
◩	Cavalry
➤	Parliamentary movements
Irish Army	
▢	Infantry
◨	Cavalry
═══	Seventeenth century roads

0   ¼   ½   ¾   1

miles

one account, the ridges were 'so tough and high and the corn so extraordinary high grown' that the men could not see about them and neither horse nor foot could serve. (An interesting reference this to the old practice of planting corn in ridges.) Four troops of horse—about 180 men—stood in what is described as a narrow laneway on the right of the infantry, and on the right of that again, beside a bog and beyond 'a goodly plain made fallow and already harrowed', stood 800 fighters of a kind more usual in Ireland in the sixteenth than in the seventeenth century. These were Antrim Scots. Catholics and men born either in Antrim or in the Highlands or Western Isles, they were quite distinct from Monroe's Scots, who were mostly Lowlanders and all Covenanters, or Protestant extremists. The Antrim Scots, led principally by the famous Alasdair Mac Colla Chiotaigh Mac Donald, had taken sides with Sir Felim O'Neill's Ulstermen in 1642. Alasdair had led Montrose's Irish auxiliaries in Scotland in 1644 and 1645. Returning to Ireland in 1647, he was soon to fight and die at Knocknanoss, near Mallow, Co. Cork, the second great Confederate defeat of the year. Preston's Scots were the comrades of Alasdair's men. Like their forefathers of Hugh O'Neill's time, they were called redshanks by the contemporary writers. They were equipped principally with swords and targets, or circular shields, in the Highland manner, and were most courageous fighters.

There were additional troops of horse on Preston's left wing, and a large force of horse was posted behind the infantry in reserve. Although it is said that the ditches, or road or field boundaries, obstructed the lateral passage of their forces and were a great disadvantage to the Irish, the Parliamentarians did not think so; to them the enemy 'stood possessed of great ditches within which he was as in so many strong works entrenched'.

Jones attacked the Irish right. Part of his infantry fell on the redshanks, who stood up to them manfully and—like good Highlanders—charged three times 'unto the very body of their army', but who were eventually overthrown with heavy loss. His left wing cavalry caught the horsemen in the laneway. Preston's troopers could neither get out nor be relieved, and most of them were killed. The Parliamentarian superiority in the mounted arm gave Jones a tremendous advantage, which was increased at an early stage of the struggle when the troopers on Preston's left together with his whole cavalry reserve abandoned the infantry and fled. About 3,000 of the latter, 'seeing now all turned to naught', withdrew into a bog, but Jones's horse and foot 'did leaguer [that is, beleaguer, beseige] the said bog' and eventually, after the battle had been in progress for about two hours, no more (says Jones's apologist) than about 500 of them escaped.

Preston's total casualties are given as between 2,000 and 5,000; battle casualties in this war of prejudice and passion were higher than ever before in Irish history. He lost his guns and his valuable draught oxen. 'This field lost by Preston, except Benburb, was the richest camp that was yet won in Ireland.' The long list of Preston's officers who were given quarter—even though his men may have been refused it—and were made prisoner shows a representative collection of the names of the Palesmen and the 'native Irish' of Leinster, together with a few Highlanders or Antrim Scots. The Parliamentarians said: 'This was the most signal victory with greatest loss to the rebels that ever was gained in Ireland since the first conquest thereof by the English. For which', they added, 'the Lord make us truly thankful.'

Dungan's Hill, the ideological opposite (if one may so put it) of Benburb, was all but decisive. It was a death blow to the Confederate Catholics in Leinster and it strengthened Jones's hold on what from that time forward (although contemporaries might not have looked upon the matter in that way) was quite clearly the bridgehead from which England would re-conquer Ireland.

The Marquis of Ormond returned to Ireland in September 1648. King Charles was executed in the following January, and in due course Ormond was continued as Lord Lieutenant by the dead king's son. The battle of Rathmines, fought on 2 August 1649, was a fantastic conclusion of Ormond's last effort, in a war of many lost opportunities, to undo the harm that he had done when he surrendered Dublin to the late king's enemies.

The two defeats of Dungan's Hill and Knocknanoss shook the Confederation to pieces, and the king's fall and ultimate execution led to a further shuffle of loyalties. When Ormond advanced towards Dublin in June 1649 in the hope of recovering the city from Michael Jones he had with him his former enemy and the victor of Knocknanoss, Murrough O'Brien, Earl of Inchiquin, who had abandoned the Parliament and brought his Protestant troops over to the Royalists in the previous year. He had also the Confederate generals, Preston and Castlehaven. The remnant of the Confederates had belatedly declared their resolution to make a stern struggle for the monarchy and had made a truce with Inchiquin and—twelve days before the king's death—a final peace with Ormond. The only force missing from the Irish alliance in 1649 was Owen Roe O'Neill's Ulster army.

In view of what was so soon to happen and in view of the fact that O'Neill, before his death, was to be allied with Ormond, it is difficult to resist the conclusion that the best soldier of them all had chosen the wrong moment to stand aloof. Rinuccini had resisted with all his might the efforts of the Supreme Council to negotiate with Inchiquin and Ormond, and O'Neill had backed the nuncio, even to the point of incurring denunciation as a rebel and a traitor. He was still intransigent. And of course Preston and Castlehaven were in no mood to co-operate with him. It was ironical that Pope Innocent X had chosen this time of dissension and conflicting loyalties, and this time of Owen Roe's eclipse, to send him the sword of his great predecessor Hugh O'Neill, which up to that had been preserved by the Franciscans. It was fatal to whatever slender hope might still have remained for the Irishmen that Owen Roe's splendid army was missing from their forces.

Ormond's army reached a final strength of 11,000 men, the greatest force that the king's representative had yet commanded in this war. Moving leisurely, he encamped at Finglas, north of Phoenix Park, on 19 June with 1,500 cavalry and 5,000 infantry. By July the Parliamentary garrisons in Drogheda, Dundalk, Newry and Trim had surrendered to Inchiquin, who joined Ormond with about 4,000 men. Believing that the combined force was still not capable of taking Dublin by assault, Ormond proposed to blockade Jones and to starve him out. He left 2,500 men under Lord Dillon on the north side of the river Liffey and moved his main camp to Rathmines on the south side, pitching his tents, as Ball, the historian of Co. Dublin, tells us, on and about the ground where Palmerston Park now extends.

This part of Dublin does not impress one nowadays as standing much higher than its surroundings. The quiet, tree-shaded neighbourhood seems secluded. But before all those streets were laid out and all those houses built, before the railway line was laid down and taken up again, when there was open ground broken only by the boundaries of the fields as far as St Stephen's Green and beyond, and as far along the river Dodder as Ringsend—in those days Rathmines commanded a fine prospect. The city was two miles distant. To the right of the city, looking northward, was the rivermouth and further to the right again the open sea. The whole extent of Jones's authority was on view, stretching from the Coombe by what is now the top of Grafton Street to Trinity College. There were few houses between Ormond's camp and the Coombe. It was in this area, on the left bank of the Dodder, in Ranelagh and Donnybrook and Ballsbridge, that the last battle to be fought in Dublin until 1916 took its surprising course.

Whatever slight hope Ormond had of taking Dublin vanished on 26 July, when Jones was heavily reinforced. Ormond, we are told, was about to construct a battery at Ringsend in the hope of preventing the entry of ships to Dublin when Colonels Reynolds (the Commissary-General) and Venables, who had been sent from Chester by the English Parliament, arrived in the Liffey with 2,000 foot and 600 horse. When this first instalment of Oliver Cromwell's army had landed Jones was almost as strong numerically as Ormond; as he was soon to demonstrate, he was in the quality of his troops far stronger. Cromwell himself was at Bristol, whence—as Jones bade rumour whisper to Ormond— he intended crossing to Munster. Ormond and his numerous generals were thoroughly upset, both at the arrival of the reinforcement and the disturbing reports of Cromwell's intentions. They thought that if they should take Dublin—'which was very doubtful'—and lose Munster—which, if Cromwell should land there, was certain—'it would prove but an ill exchange'. On the other hand, if Cromwell took Munster and they failed to take Dublin all would be lost. They tried to provide against some of these gloomy eventualities by sending Inchiquin off with the better part of three regiments of horse to organise the defence of Munster. They themselves continued their improvisation.

Ormond, who seems to have distrusted his heterogeneous army —Preston's men had suffered defeat at his hands at Ross in 1642 and Inchiquin's men had opposed all the others as recently as May 1648—had difficulty in keeping up the blockade. Some of his advisers proposed that they should retire to Drogheda and their other garrisons and watch events. Others, afraid that Jones might by a sudden move cut them off from their troops on the north side of the Liffey, wanted to remove from Rathmines to 'a securer quarter' at Drimnagh. It was eventually decided to assault Rathfarnham castle, which lay close behind them and which was held by a small force of Parliamentarians.

Rathfarnham was taken by storm on 28 July. Emboldened by this success, a council of war decided on 1 August to attempt what might have been done earlier. It was resolved to work down between the Dodder and the city and to cut Jones off from the meadows beside the Donnybrook road (Leeson Street) and the Blackrock road (Baggot Street), where the Parliamentarians had been grazing their horses. If Jones was denied this pasturage it was believed that all his horses would be starved within five days. When Ormond's troops had first come to Rathmines they had crossed these meadows and had surprised two forts which Jones was building 'at Lowsey Hill', or Lazar (a leper) Hill in the present Townsend Street area. They had also 'beaten the rebels [for so they regarded the Parliamentarians] out of the College'—Trinity College, which then stood outside the little city. They had failed to hold what they had won, however, and Jones still had access to all the ground lying between the eastern extent of his fortifications and Ballsbridge. Ormond had another reason for the operations which were decided upon on 1 August. If he succeeded in working down towards Ringsend he might establish himself there, however belatedly, and he might cut the entry to the city by water.

The key to these positions was Baggotrath Castle, which stood near the present Baggot Street bridge. Jones, fully aware of its potential danger, had partly demolished this place, but Ormond, having sent Preston, Castlehaven and others to view it, believed that he could seize it by night and make it defensible. Once established there, he proposed to dig 'a running trench' towards the Liffey, to build a fort which would mount six guns at the river end of the trench, and thus to 'disturb all future landing'.

On 2 August, after midnight, Ormond sent Major-General Purcell—an old soldier of the Confederation, who had served with Preston and Castlehaven since 1642 and had commanded the cavalry at Knocknanoss—to occupy Baggotrath. Purcell had 1,500 foot and he was accompanied by 800 pioneers. But Purcell—most strangely—took several hours to cover the short distance between the camp and the ruined castle; according to Jones, the ruin was less than a mile from the camp.

Ormond remained awake, on the alert for a move from Jones. Sir William Vaughan joined Purcell with a party of horse in the early hours of the morning. Castlehaven and Lord Taaffe (he whom Inchiquin had defeated at Knocknanoss) had been ordered to support Purcell with 2,000 horse and Lieut.-Colonel Gerard's company of fusiliers, or special service troops armed with flint-lock fusees, but it is uncertain when they arrived on the scene. At daybreak Ormond rode down to Baggotrath and was sur-prised to find that Purcell had arrived only shortly before that and that most of his work still remained to be done. He found too that he had failed to surprise Jones. The Parliamentarians were arrayed outside Dublin, partly concealed behind burnt houses at Lowsey Hill and in a hollow between Baggotrath and the bank of the Liffey. Advised during the night of enemy activity beyond the meadows, and seeing Purcell's men and correctly interpreting their intention, Jones, as he was to report later, 'found a necessity for removing them, and that speedily'.

Thus had arisen one of those tantalising situations—one of those terrifying situations—which test the qualities of military commanders. Should Ormond hold on or draw off? He soon realised that, under the eyes of Jones, he could do neither without bringing up his whole army to support Purcell. As many another commander had done, and was subsequently to do, Ormond surrendered to circumstance. If a stand-to was necessary in any event, it might be as well to go on with the work of making Baggotrath defensible as to retire. He called Vaughan and Purcell, commanding the horse and foot respectively, told them that he believed Jones would hazard all to prevent their holding Baggotrath, since their doing so would be so dangerous to him, and gave them instructions where to place their men. He then left them, returned to his tent and lay down. He believed that an action was impending, but he was exhausted and felt that he would have time for a nap before it began. There is no record of the orders which he issued to the remainder of his forces, but he did instruct the whole army to stand to arms. The full deploy-ment which would have resulted, had there been more time for it, would have made a right wing of Vaughan's and Purcell's men, a centre of Inchiquin's infantry, and a left wing of the remainder of the forces, who never, as it happened, got far outside the camp. Ormond's unwonted confidence in his men and his optimistic appraisal of the situation must strike us as quite absurd.

Jones did not sleep. Advancing rapidly across the meadows—up, as it were, from Merrion Square to the canal—he attacked

Baggotrath with his whole force of 1,200 horse and a considerable part of his 4,000 infantry. His strength and his determination were overwhelming. Vaughan's men and that part of Castlehaven's and Taaffe's horse which had joined them were routed in the first charge. Vaughan was killed. The survivors, who must have been very numerous, rode hard for Donnybrook and Ballsbridge, intent on putting the Dodder, which was fordable along the greater part of its course, between them and the ironsides. They kept on through Dundrum until they reached the mountains. Purcell's foot and Gerard's fusiliers, who were part of Ormond's Life Guard, held out for a short time at Baggotrath, where there was a 'strong dispute'; but they were soon forced back and eventually overrun. Gerard was taken prisoner. Most of the men were either killed or taken. This part of Dublin was not to see such mortality again until 1916, when, close by, the Sherwood Foresters were to suffer so heavily at Mount Street bridge.

With Baggotrath and the works that had been scarcely begun by Purcell's pioneers in his hands, Jones felt that he might perhaps improve on an unexpectedly good situation. It was then ten o'clock. The Irish right wing was no more. Jones regrouped and, advancing through the fields on a wide front, moved up to his right towards Ranelagh. He sent some of his troopers along by the Dodder in an effort to gain the Irish rear.

Ormond was awakened by the noise of volley firing. He rode back by the way that he had come an hour previously and witnessed part of the onslaught on his right wing. He saw Jones's cavalry coming 'through gaps and in files' into enclosures where some of his own horse were still drawn up. He came back again as the enemy continued to advance and joined his centre or main battle, which consisted of Inchiquin's men under Colonel Gifford and which stood perhaps in Ranelagh. This seems to have been the force that was said to have been drawn up in 'a large ploughed field looking towards the Castle of Dublin'. He stationed his brother Colonel Richard Butler and Colonel Miles O'Reilly with two regiments close to the main battle, and apparently on the right of it, and gave them the instruction that, given during an engagement, has so often had fatal consequences—that they were to await further orders.

There were some guns commanding a laneway in the line of Jones's advance, but he, 'gaining field after field', came up to them and captured them and pushed on. Meanwhile his troopers, having made their way perhaps along the river valley by Clonskea, had reached Milltown. Turning northward by another laneway, they appeared suddenly behind Ormond and Gifford. They were, said Ormond, enabled to do this because his brother's and O'Reilly's men, who would otherwise have blocked their advance or driven them off in confusion, had quit their post. 'How they were forced thence, or upon what occasion they charged', he wrote afterwards, 'I know not.' He allowed for the fact that they might, in the rapidly changing conditions of the battle, and having been given no positive orders, have been induced to move away by seeing an opportunity for service elsewhere. The troopers were held off by Gifford's men, who gave them 'a good fire', but they succeeded in passing on Gifford's flank to rally on their own advancing foot in his front. A further party of Parliamentary horse, together with some infantry, followed up by the laneway and Gifford was soon between two fires. After this his men 'fought no more, but seemed inclinable to accept the quarter which the enemy offered'. They were mostly English troops and, once their lately assumed royalist allegiance had fallen from them, they were in no way different from their opponents; when they had surrendered, they were willing to enter service in the Parliamentary ranks.

Two-thirds of Ormond's army was now gone. He tried to ride to the left or rearward, which was formed somewhere about the present Belgrave Road, hoping to find it still standing firm. But the left, confronted by 'a great reserve' of Jones's infantry, and aware that the right had been beaten and that the centre had surrendered, believed its position to be desperate and had already begun to disintegrate. Its officers did their best, as did Ormond, to remedy matters. (Who were they? Was Preston here, and had he hoped to seek revenge for Dungan's Hill? Where was Castlehaven?) Some of the men rallied and allowed themselves to be led forward, but they soon broke again; they were struck with panic at the sight of their own men running, thinking them to be part of Jones's army rushing down on top of them. Jones, who was a skilful propagandist, had caused the report to be spread that Cromwell—the monster Cromwell—had landed in Dublin with all his forces during the night and that it was he who opposed the royalists. The left ran away without firing a shot. Jones, after two hours' fighting, had won a complete victory on the south side of the Liffey. Lord Dillon, the royalist leader on the north bank, fell back, on hearing the news of Ormond's defeat, into Trim and Drogheda and many of his men perished at Cromwell's hands in the latter place in the following month.

The Irish lost, according to their own admission, about 600 men killed at the battle of Rathmines; Jones claimed as many as 4,000, which was perhaps as many as opposed him. They lost seven guns, all the equipment and stores in their camp and 200 draught oxen. Jones said that he had not at first intended to bring on a general engagement; he believed that the Irish had not expected one, and that they would not willingly have fought, if they could have avoided doing so. Like O'Neill's army at Kinsale, they had been defeated piecemeal by a determined and an aggressive adversary. Ormond had been outgeneralled, outmanoeuvred and outfought by Jones, who, when the fighting was over, cried out: 'Never was any day in Ireland like this, to the confusion of the Irish, and to the raising up [of] the spirits of the poor English and to the restoring of the English interest, which from their first footing in Ireland was never in so low a condition as at that very instant, there not being any one considerable landing place left, but this alone, and this also almost gone.'

Thirteen days after the battle—on 15 August—Oliver Cromwell, general of the Commonwealth army and the new Lord Lieutenant of Ireland, landed at Ringsend, bringing with him, or being followed from Milford Haven by, 12,000 men. To him Rathmines was 'an astonishing mercy, so great and seasonable that we are like them that dreamed'. His bridgehead had been preserved. He used it to reconquer Ireland.

For a good descriptive account of the battle of Rathmines, based on the contemporary information and with topographical details, see F. E. Ball, 'The Battle of Rathmines' in the *Proceedings of the Royal Irish Academy*, XXXII (1902), pp. 246 ff. See also the same writer's *History of Co. Dublin*, Part II, pp. 102, etc. and W. St J. Joyce, *Ireland's Battles and Battlefields* (1892), pp. 47 ff. Jones's report is in *Lieut.-General Jones's Letter to the Council of State* (1649), Ormond's statement in *The Marquesse of Ormond's Letter to His Majestie King Charls II* (1649) and *The Marquis of Ormondes*

Letter to His Majestie concerning the late Fight (also 1649). See also T. Carte, *Life of Ormonde* (1736), II, pp. 72 ff and (edited by the same) *Original Letters and Papers* (1739), II, p. 407.

For further contemporary information see J. T. Gilbert (ed.), *History of the Irish Confederation and the War in Ireland*, VII, pp. 123 ff, Sir Lewis Dyve's *Letter to the Marquis of New-Castle* (1650), *A Bloudy Fight at Dublin between Ormond and Colonel Jones* (1649), and another pamphlet entitled *The present condition of Dublin in Ireland represented in two letters from a Colonell to his brother* (1649).

A survey of the English background appears in S. R. Gardiner, *History of the Commonwealth and Protectorate* (1894), I, and T. Lowe, 'Some aspects of the wars in Ireland, 1641–1649' (*The Irish Sword, IV*, pp. 81 ff) is a good summary of the Irish military background. The battle of Dungan's Hill is described in 'The Aphorismical Discovery of Treasonable Faction' (J. T. Gilbert, *A Contemporary History of affairs in Ireland*, I, pp. 154 ff; in R. Bellings (ed. J. T. Gilbert), *History of the Irish Confederation and the War in Ireland*, VII, pp. 31 f; and in *An exact and full Relation of the great Victory obtained over the Rebels at Dungans Hill* (printed in Appendix to C. P. Meehan, *The Confederation of Kilkenny*, 1882 edition) and there is a modern account by Fr M. Devitt, S. J., 'Summerhill, County Meath, and its neighbourhood', *Journal of the Co. Kildare Archaeological Society*, VI, pp. 440 ff.

For Alasdair MacDonald see G. Hill, *Macdonnells of Antrim*, pp. 61 ff.

The Boyne, 1690

The prize fought for at the Boyne in 1690, as at Rathmines in 1649, was possession of Dublin. By forcing the crossing of the river which was called 'the Rubicon of the Pale', and which 'had, in all former rebellions, been maintained with their blood by those ancient English colonies planted there', King William compelled his Jacobite opponents to give up the capital of Ireland and to retire into the interior of the country. He thus gained the best possible base for his future operations and did all that could be done on land to secure the line of communications with England; communications in which lay, then as in Napoleon's and all other ages, the secret of war.

William's success at the Boyne was, besides, a great victory of prestige. King James had rightly considered the capital of the kingdom worth fighting for. William found it worth winning; for him, as for the Normans and the Cromwellians before him, it proved the key to Ireland.

The battle of the Boyne was thus, despite subsequent propagandist efforts to minimise its effects, a decisive one. The self-styled 'literary agitator'—who was nevertheless a painstaking historian—J. C. O'Callaghan, writing more than a century ago 'in vindication of the national military character from English and Anglo-Irish aggression and calumny', played down the Irish defeat. O'Callaghan referred particularly to 'the excellent retreat of James's army'. He has been followed by many writers. Others, and a great many who chose rather to shout than write, have remembered the Boyne as a 'glorious and immortal' occasion when the Cromwellian settlement—the result of Cromwell's reconquest of Ireland—was preserved. Many times refought, the Boyne is perhaps the best remembered, the best applauded, the best decried battle in Irish history.

The first writer to appreciate the significance of the tactical movements at the Boyne appears to have been Lieut.-General Sir Henry Sheehy Keating, who described them in 1795 when he was still a very young subaltern at the beginning of a warlike and illustrious career. Keating believed that the battle was 'one of the most interesting actions recorded in history' and held that its outcome 'was in a great degree decided by its locality'. James's position at the Boyne was, he said, well chosen, but the king and his advisers were guilty of 'great and glaring misconduct' in not foreseeing the use that might be made of its topographical features. Their omission was punished by their defeat. A re-examination of the evidence regarding the battle seems to bear out Keating's contention.

When William displaced the Catholic King James at the climax of the Glorious Revolution in England, James fled to France. Later, in March 1689, he came to Ireland in the hope of retrieving his position. His supporters were most numerous here and in Scotland, and so Ireland suggested itself as his base and Scotland his stepping stone for a return to the scene of his former dominion in England. But this was not the only reason for the warfare between Williamites and Jacobites in Ireland in 1689–91. Many of the Irish considered the occasion one for the redress of Irish grievances rather than the encouragement of Stuart hopes, grievances arising from religious disabilities, the confiscation of property that had followed Cromwell's victory and the denial of what were claimed to be constitutional rights. James's Irish Parliament, summoned after his arrival, established liberty of conscience, reversed the Cromwellian settlement—thereby re-storing landed property to its condition in 1641—and declared that 'his Majesty's realm of Ireland is and hath been always a distinct kingdom from that of his Majesty's realm of England'. These were more than declarations of allegiance to one king and a denial of support to another. In the English view, they were fighting words that showed not only an unbearable recalcitrance on the part of the Irish but an opportunist determination to seek revenge. D'Avaux, the representative in Ireland of James's supporter, King Louis XIV of France, concluded from his observation of the people that they were irreconcilable enemies of the English and that the real hope of many of them was that King James's arrival among them would 'release them from English servitude'.

King James's Irish army was made up of some old soldiers and many new ones. It had been organised by the Catholic Earl of Tyrconnell, whom James had sent to Ireland in 1685 'to advance Popery'—or so the Protestants said—'and to begin to destroy the Protestant religion'. Tyrconnell had soon become Lieut.-General of the Irish forces, and he was made Lord Deputy in 1687. His formal instructions on assuming the Deputyship went no further than to direct that he should treat Catholics and Protestants alike, for James was genuinely in favour of religious toleration, but Tyrconnell had already begun to purge the army of Protestants, and more particularly of such Cromwellians as remained in it. He had brought in 2,000 Catholic recruits, representing a quarter of the total force, by the summer of 1686, and as his power increased the number of Irish soldiers of the religion of the majority of his countrymen increased with it.

The reorganisation of the Irish forces had, in fact, begun in Charles II's time, when the English standing army also had its real beginnings. There were in Ireland prior to 1684 a troop of Horse Guards, the Regiment of Guards in the Kingdom of Ireland (an infantry regiment which was raised in 1662), 24 troops of cavalry and 75 companies of infantry, all of which units made up an establishment strength of some 1,400 horse and 6,400 foot. The Caroline reorganisation consisted in the grouping of the independent troops and companies of this force into three regiments of cavalry and eight regiments of infantry, the addition of a troop of mounted grenadiers to the Horse Guards and of a grenadier company to the Foot Guards, and an increase in the monetary provision for artillery and dragoons. Tyrconnell's replacements of Protestants by Catholics amounted to some 300 officers and more than 4,000 men. The force which resulted, and which was largely made up of men who had received little training, provided the nucleus of the Jacobite army which opposed King William.

All these Irish regiments save one—Forbes's regiment, a unit that was about a third Protestant, that had earlier been brought over to England, and that was in due course to become the famous 18th Royal Irish Regiment—were disbanded by William on his accession. But their existence continued; most of them remained loyal to James; others split and—allegiance in Ireland being very much a matter of religion—the Protestants and Catholics in their ranks took opposite sides. When James came to Ireland he found three regiments of horse of the old establishment (Tyrconnell's, Russell's and Galmoy's), one regiment of dragoons and five regiments of infantry (the Guards, MacCarthy's, Clancarty's,

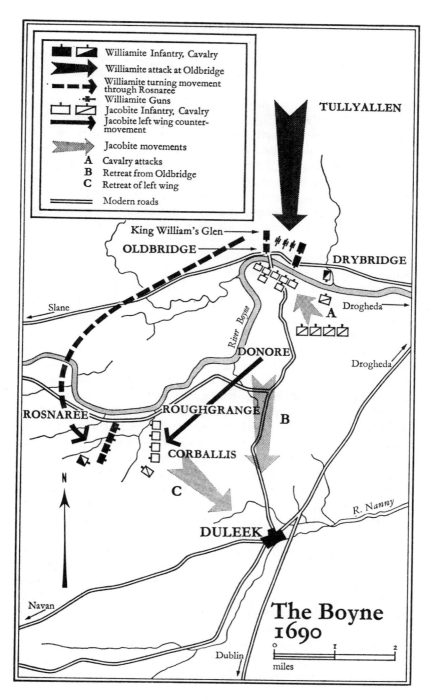

Legend:

Williamite Infantry, Cavalry

Williamite attack at Oldbridge

Williamite turning movement through Rosnaree

Williamite Guns

Jacobite Infantry, Cavalry

Jacobite left wing counter-movement

Jacobite movements

A   Cavalry attacks
B   Retreat from Oldbridge
C   Retreat of left wing

Modern roads

King William's Glen

OLDBRIDGE

DRYBRIDGE

TULLYALLEN

Slane

River Boyne

Drogheda

Drogheda

DONORE

A

ROUGHGRANGE

B

ROSNAREE

CORBALLIS

C

N

R. Nanny

DULEEK

Navan

Dublin

The Boyne 1690

0   1   2

miles

Newcomen's and Mountjoy's) ready to serve him. To these Tyrconnell had already added many newly raised units, and he was soon to add more. The official strength of the Irish army in May 1689, shortly after the arrival of James, was seven regiments of horse, together with the troop of horse grenadiers, seven regiments of dragoons, thirty-five regiments of infantry and the Foot Guards, which last regiment had been increased to two battalions. By November the numbers—again they were paper ones—had risen to eight regiments each of horse and dragoons and forty-four regiments of infantry. There was no lack of men, 'the finest men one could see', said D'Avaux, strong, tall and capable of enduring fatigue; but they were poorly armed— some whom D'Avaux saw carried only staves; their opponents noticed that 'some had scythes instead of pikes'—and they were inadequately trained and most inadequately equipped.

Developments in military organisation and weapons which had taken place since Cromwell's time were reflected in this Jacobite army, a force that shared a common background with William's British regiments, although the French officers who came with James and D'Avaux tried to give it something of the complexion of their own great military machine.

The mounted men included two types that are new to this narrative, dragoons and mounted grenadiers. Dragoons, who had already figured both in the English civil war—when they acted mostly as skirmishers—and in a minor degree in the warfare of the Confederation in Ireland, but who were not numerous before the end of the seventeenth century, were mounted infantry. Montecuculi, the seventeenth-century imperialist general, said that they were 'infantry to whom horses have been given to enable them to move more rapidly'. They were armed with muskets or carbines and pistols, and a few bore halberds. They used their small horses to carry them where their service was needed, but they fought on foot. Mounted grenadiers were quite new, although the weapon from which they and the foot grenadiers took their name was not. In one form or another the 'hand granadoe' was as old as gunpowder. It was a small, hollow cast iron sphere which was filled with gunpowder; the filling hole was stopped by a wooden plug which had an aperture for a length of slow match. Ignited and thrown, the grenade fragmented when the burning match reached and exploded the charge. Horse grenadiers appeared in England in 1683, when a troop was added to each of the existing troops of the Life Guard, and in Ireland in the year following; they were classed with dragoons and were intended, like them, to act as mobile infantry.

The cavalry proper, or horse regiments, continued to be armed with swords, pistols and carbines. They formed for attack in line in three ranks. Cavalry had, in this period, largely given up the movement called the caracole, which consisted of an advance, a discharge of pistols and a wheeling away, and had learnt to charge home with the sword, using the weight of their horses—as the Normans of five centuries before had used it—to increase the shock of their attack. The lancer and the rider who handled his horseman's staff in the sixteenth-century fashion had alike disappeared from the Irish scene.

Infantry regiments were made up usually of thirteen companies each, or of twenty-two companies in the few two-battalion regiments. One company in each regiment was ordinarily—or perhaps it would be more correct to say, was wherever possible—a grenadier company. The foot grenadiers, like their mounted counterparts, were a new type of soldier. John Evelyn the diarist wrote in 1678 of 'a new sort of soldiers called granadeers, who were dextrous in flinging hand granados, every one having a pouch full'. The soldiers of the line companies consisted, in 1690 as fifty years earlier, of musketeers and pikemen, but the pike was falling into disuse and the proportion of pikes to muskets was as low as about one to five. In the Williamite forces it was lower still. Some of the English regiments had no pikes, but Forbes's (later the Earl of Meath's, later the 18th Royal Irish) had fewer than three muskets to each pike; generally there were about six English musketeers to one pikeman. The proportion was about the same in the Dutch regiments, but the Danish infantry had no pikes at all. In battle the musketeers were formed ordinarily in six ranks and the pikemen, unless hostile cavalry was approaching, were drawn up behind them. The first three ranks could, as one body, fire a volley; they discharged their pieces together, the first rank crouching, the second kneeling and the third standing. Fire having been given, these ranks filed off to the rear and reloaded, while the other three ranks stepped forward and gave their fire. But formations were flexible; a different order could, as we shall see in a moment with regard to the Dutch, be adopted to suit particular circumstances. The pikes were in front when it was a matter of resisting cavalry, which was now their main function.

The infantrymen of this period had a new weapon that eventually made a pike of every musket, that solved the old problem of how best to combine the new with the old—firearms with spears, missile arms with arms that merely extended the reach of their holders—and a weapon that has remained part of the armoury of the foot slogger and his successor even to our own day. This weapon was the bayonet, which on its general adoption combined two separate weapon categories and made all footsoldiers of the line alike. Bayonets were introduced into the British army from France, where they seem to have originated much earlier, before the last quarter of the seventeenth century, and their use by 1690 was widespread. The original weapon, or that called nowadays the plug bayonet, was fixed by inserting the haft into the muzzle of the musket, which could not of course be fired while the bayonet was in position. Improved forms of ring and socket bayonet were soon evolved; these, by fitting a sleeve which formed part of the hilt of the bayonet around the barrel of the musket on the outside, permitted the firing of the musket while the bayonet was fixed. These improvements were of very recent introduction in 1690, however, and the bayonets used at the Boyne were no doubt mostly of the plug variety. Some of the Williamite soldiers who fought there are spoken of as 'screwing their swords to the muskets'—hangers or long daggers which could be used as bayonets would have been called swords—to receive a cavalry charge. Bayonets were scarcer in the Jacobite ranks and none seem to have been received from France, but they were by no means unknown.

The standard musket, particularly in the Jacobite army, was still the matchlock. The Williamite English infantry regiments had as many—or perhaps more—of the newer flintlock weapons, called firelocks, fusils or fusees. The French Huguenot infantry regiments were armed entirely with flintlocks, as were most, if not all, of the Danes. The Williamite cavalry carbines were all flintlocks, as were their grenadiers' muskets and of course the weapons of their fusiliers; but one of the Jacobite soldiers, speaking of flintlocks and infantry swords, said 'we had but few of those sorts of arms'.

The Jacobite special service companies were armed altogether with flintlocks, and they had at least two units called fusiliers, part of whose duty was to guard the artillery, for which service, not having matches which might blow up powder supplies, they were particularly suited; but the bulk of their infantry muskets were matchlocks. Most of their arms, of all types, were French. Eight thousand firearms had come from France by the beginning of 1689, when Tyrconnell asked for 6,000 more matchlocks and 5,000 flintlocks. King James asked later for 12,000 or 15,000 muskets, matchlocks or flintlocks, 'the more firelocks the better'; D'Avaux, conveying the request, made it 12,000 *mousquets* and 3,000 *fusils*. Ten thousand grenades with charges and fuses were among the munitions sought.

The clothing of the soldiers in the earlier wars was far from uniform, although red coats, as we have seen, were a mark of English troops by the late sixteenth century. A hundred years later soldiers, as a general rule, all wore uniform. James's troops and William's British troops alike favoured red coats, red being the colour of the livery of the British monarchy. Difficulties of supply, however, made strict uniformity impossible in the Jacobite army and coats of other colours and of white or grey French cloth, and homespun coats which must in colour have been like the American Confederate butternut seem to have been more numerous than red ones. The infantry had broad-brimmed hats, full-skirted coats with wide cuffs, breeches, stockings and shoes; their shirt sleeves, extending to the wrist, were visible below their cuffs. The musketeers wore both waist and shoulder belts, and they carried their ammunition in pouches on the right hip. The bandolier, with its dangling cylinders—never a safe piece of equipment for men with lighted matches—had all but disappeared, the word *bandoulière*, as used in the French documents—*une bandoulière pour soldat, garnie de ses fournimens aussi*—meant seemingly the contemporary shoulder belt and pouch. The dress of the cavalry was like that of the infantry, save that boots were worn when they could be got. Cuirasses had been discarded except by the Life Guard and helmets remained only as iron skull-pieces worn under the hat. The distinctive Irish dress of earlier days had quite disappeared. Later on, it is interesting to note, these Jacobite soldiers were to bring with them into the French army the red coat of the king for whom they had fought. The regiments of the French Irish Brigade wore red coats during the whole century of their existence.

The war fought in Ireland by the supporters of the rival kings began in Ulster, which province was of vital importance to both sides. The Protestant descendants of the Ulster planters, disturbed by the ascendancy of the Catholics under Tyrconnell, took refuge in Derry and Enniskillen, declared for William and prepared to fight. Tyrconnell attempted to coerce them. The road from Dublin to London via Edinburgh ran through Ulster. If King James was to travel by it his northern Irish opponents must first be put down. On the other hand, if King William, whose position was soon established in England, was to win Ireland as well he must first secure Ulster as the obvious point of entry to the island. James held Dublin and the southern and western parts of Ireland. William was supported on religious grounds, because he was *de facto* king of England, and as a matter of policy in relation to property holding only—to any considerable extent—in the north. Ulster must therefore be his bridgehead. As was said on his behalf in March 1689, 'his Majesty's greatest concern hath been for Ireland, and particularly for the province of Ulster'; he proposed to help his Ulster supporters to defend themselves so that, by doing so, he might in due course be able 'to rescue the whole kingdom and resettle the Protestant interest there'. That was why Derry was besieged, and defended.

At the beginning, the pace of operations in a country of tracks rather than roads and at a time when all armies were ponderous and the Irish ones were raw was slow and deliberate. There were bogs everywhere and there was 'no passing but just upon the highways'; the waterlogged country was 'full of bridges', most of which were 'broken down at the ends', so that 'before a man can come at the bridge he must wade at least up to the knee'—so ran an English report.

The English relieved Derry—as they had founded it—by sea, and the siege was raised on 1 August 1689 after the garrison and townspeople had gallantly resisted attack for fifteen weeks. On the day before that the Enniskillen men had defeated a superior Jacobite force at Newtownbutler, Co. Fermanagh. Practically the whole of Ulster was now in Williamite hands and King William's hold on that part of Ireland was strengthened on 13 August when the elderly German soldier of fortune Frederick, Duke of Schomberg—a veteran of the Thirty Years War, and, until the recent expulsion of the Huguenots, a Marshal of France —landed from England with 20,000 men at Bangor, Co. Down. Schomberg advanced to Dundalk, where he was faced, but not engaged, by King James. The armies on both sides were full of raw men, and both sides were cautious. There was some action on the south-western Ulster border. Sarsfield, of whom so much was to be heard later, surprised Sligo and secured Connacht for James. The French general, the Count de Rosen, who had come to Ireland with the king and who had at one time commanded the Jacobites at Derry, threatened Schomberg's communications by attacking Newry on the far side of the Moyry pass. But there was no action at Dundalk; Schomberg did not attempt to push on towards Dublin, James did not try to drive him back. General Keating believed that James 'had Schomberg in a cul-de-sac, his retreat cut off, his army wasting by sickness, shut up in entrenchments, and James himself with a superior army in their front'. He held that Schomberg could have been destroyed if James had had the resolution to attack. It was perhaps not as simple as that. Schomberg's force had certainly deteriorated rapidly, and he suffered from a chronic shortage of supplies; but the Jacobites were little better than amateurs. They needed more time for organisation and training before they were ready to fight, and the delay at Dundalk earned it for them.

Both forces withdrew to winter quarters. Schomberg retired as far as Lisburn, where he could muster of his army of August only 7,000 men. The Jacobites removed to Dublin and other garrisons, congratulating themselves that their enemies had been unable to advance. In the following year both sides were reinforced. The Irish received 7,000 French infantry and a small number of gunners under the Count de Lauzun in March. These were sent in exchange for Justin McCarthy, Lord Mountcashel's brigade of five Irish regiments or 5,387 men, who were reformed as three regiments on their arrival in France and who were the first of the Wild Geese, the forerunners of the famous Irish Brigade. Lauzun's force was made up of veteran French soldiers who might, had they served as they were capable of serving, have been a powerful addition to the Jacobite strength; but they came in Louis XIV's rather than James's interest and their mission was to prolong rather than win the war. The Williamites were also reinforced in March, when a Danish contingent of a thousand horse and 6,000 foot led by the German Duke of Würtemberg-Neustadt and hired from Denmark under a treaty made in the previous September, arrived in Ulster. These were seasoned troops of mixed nationalities; there were Catholics among them, and even some Irishmen. The cavalry, who brought their horses with them to Ireland and who wore cuirasses, were in three regiments and there were eight regiments of infantry who, as we have said, were probably all armed with flintlocks and none of whom were pikemen. They were quartered on arrival in Cos. Antrim and Londonderry. Further reinforcements of English and Dutch regiments came in May, and on 14 June King William arrived at Carrickfergus with more.

William's whole force was soon assembled and he reviewed part of the 36,000 or more men whom he proposed to bring into the field—English, Irish, Dutch, Danish, German and French Huguenot—at Loughbrickland, Co. Down on 22 June. William was anxious to begin the year's campaign as soon as possible and he moved south—towards Dublin—at once. He advanced to Dundalk, partly by Newry and the Moyry pass and partly from Armagh, probably by Newtown Hamilton. The Jacobites had placed a force in the pass 'with the intention of contesting the defiles'. As in 1600, 'a thick mist' reduced visibility among the hills and an advanced party of Williamite foot was ambushed, but the Jacobites soon withdrew and fell back before the oncoming army. They appear to have quitted this position, the strength of which was noted by their enemies and by defending which they could at least have delayed the Williamites, when they discovered that the parallel advance from Armagh by the west side of Slieve Gullion had turned them and that they would be unable to prevent some part at least of their enemy's force from reaching 'the plain south of Dundalk'. They fell back to the Boyne.

To defend the line of the Boyne was the only practicable course open to James if he was to prevent an opponent who had come as far as Dundalk from reaching Dublin. The ground between Dundalk and the capital is in general low lying and easily traversed. The drainage is from west to east, which means that practically all the watercourses must be crossed when moving from north to south, but the Fane, Glyde and Dee, the streams of Co. Louth, were not military obstacles. Neither was the river Nanny in Co. Meath, which at any rate could be by-passed to the west. If James, who had concentrated near Drogheda at the beginning of the campaigning season, were to remove his army altogether and to occupy a position to the westward, on William's flank, he would merely uncover Dublin without threatening William, whose forces might, if required, be supplied by sea and who was under no necessity to protect a line of communication with Ulster. If the Jacobites were out of his way William would certainly move on to occupy Dublin. William's generals had noted as early as March that the defences of Drogheda, the town of the Boyne, were being strengthened and had prepared themselves to fight there.

The Boyne was fordable in many places in 1690; still, William's progress might be contested on its banks. The Jacobite army which occupied the south bank with its centre at Oldbridge, Co. Meath, its right at Drogheda and its left towards Slane was in position to make the attempt. It would have been impossible for William, if the Jacobites were to stand, and he was to retain anything of his reputation, to avoid a battle. Unfortunately, the Jacobite position, although it was the only one that could have been taken up on the river, had two serious defects. The river Boyne, on its eastward course towards the Irish Sea, bends to the north below Rosnaree, flows for over three miles in a northerly direction and then turns east again at Oldbridge. It thus forms a large loop around the ridge of high ground which extends from the south-west to the north-east through Donore. James, who was concentrated in the Donore-Oldbridge area so as to cover the fords at Oldbridge, was within the loop. In other words, when William arrived opposite James across the stream from Oldbridge he found that the bend of the river indented his bank. More than a hundred years later the great military theorist of the nineteenth century, the high priest of the Napoleonic legend, Baron Antoine Henri Jomini, was to remind his many readers that it is well when attempting to force the passage of a river 'to choose a place where the river forms a re-entrant bend or elbow', since such a position permits the attacker to secure a bridgehead by enfilade fire. General Sir Edward Bruce Hamley, the author of *Operations of War*, was to echo Jomini's words; Hamley says that, in such circumstances, an attacking force can by disposing itself around the bend, 'command and enclose the angle of the other bank'. Later still, General Sir Francis Clery was to place it on record in his celebrated book on tactics that 'this configuration of ground is carefully sought for'. This knowledge did not prevent Clery, when he fought in South Africa, from ordering an advance which sent Hildyard's brigade and the Irish Brigade of the time into two loops of the Tugela river at Colenso in 1899, where the Boers, commanding and enclosing the angles—although, unlike the forces of the textbooks, they were the defenders rather than the attackers—completely defeated them. James's position at the Boyne suffered from the same defect as Buller's position at the Tugela. The bend of the river enclosed him to his disadvantage and if William got across behind him at Rosnaree or at Slane his left would be endangered.

The second weakness of terrain as far as James was concerned lay in the fact that an enemy force on the south bank at Rosnaree would be nearer to Duleek than he was at Donore. The only practicable crossing in 1690 of the Nanny, which runs parallel with the Boyne three miles to the south, was at Duleek; over it lay James's line of retreat towards Dublin. If James's enemies could block the passage at Duleek he would be in serious difficulties. In fact, if William could take advantage of his position on the indented bank, and of his superior numbers, to cross behind his opponent and to stop up his line of retreat—meanwhile holding him within the loop—he could annihilate him. The defects of the Boyne as a line of defence were as great as that. James's security depended on his guarding his left.

William's army, having marched by Ardee, Co. Louth, reached the Boyne early on Monday 30 June (Old Style) and encamped near Tullyallen on the left or north bank. They faced the main concentration of James's men, who were encamped on the ridge at Donore. James had a total force of about 25,000, of whom three regiments or about 1,500 men were in Drogheda. That afternoon the Dutch Guards, Dutch William's crack regiment, were ordered down towards the river, where they came under fire from the Jacobite guns, seven of which had opened up after the Williamites' arrival. William himself, viewing his enemies, of whom some were drawn up on the other side of the river, was grazed on the shoulder by a cannon ball. He was heard to say 'No nearer', or words to that effect, when he was struck; he was a brave man, and he continued his inspection.

It must soon have become apparent to him and to his generals of many nationalities that they enjoyed some considerable advantages. Apart from the fact that the river bend suggested the possibility of outflanking their opponents, the bank on which they stood was the higher one, although this was not such a great advantage in the days of short range guns as it would become later. Another feature of the terrain which would aid them if they were to attempt a crossing at Oldbridge was the deep ravine that has since been named King William's glen; this offered a covered approach to the Boyne. But they could see also that the houses at Oldbridge—there are none there now—were occupied by their opponents, and this and the fact that there were many pockets in the gently rising ground on the south bank— pockets in which unknown numbers of troops might be hidden— and that their enemies had a resolute air, suggested that an attempt to cross where they were might be stubbornly contested and that they might suffer heavy losses. The river bank too must have appeared boggy and of uncertain practicability for cavalry. James, whose tents were on the skyline at Donore, might not be altogether within the bend; he might, in fact, enjoy what later writers were to speak of as the advantage of interior lines, or of a central position, if it became a matter of transferring troops to resist a subsidiary attempt to cross further upstream—say at Rosnaree or Slane, places that were nearer to Donore than they were to Tullyallen. The crossing places of the river were well known and William must have had as much information about them as James had.

William made no further move that evening; but he held a council of war. If an attack was to be made on the Jacobites it must be made frontally at Oldbridge, or it might take the form of an attempt to turn their flank or flanks by a crossing upstream or downstream, or in both directions, or it might be a combination of frontal attack and flanking movement. Any attempt on the flanks must cause James to divide his forces, and must therefore weaken him, but it could not be made by the Williamites unless they were prepared to divide their forces too. The prospect of action at any distance downstream was ruled out. There was a bridge at Drogheda, but it was held by James, and the Boyne, which is tidal, was unfordable between Drogheda and a little below Oldbridge. The choice therefore lay between a crossing at Oldbridge and one upstream, or an attempt might be made to combine and co-ordinate the two. There was a bridge—broken by the Jacobites—at Slane, and there were, apparently, several fords between Oldbridge and Slane, the nearest of them being at Rosnaree.

The council must have considered all this. Our information of what was said and what happened tells us that Schomberg, who up to this in the Irish war had shown a caution that we might perhaps have expected in a man of his age—he was seventy-five— proposed the division of the Williamite army into two unequal parts, the smaller of which was to make a frontal attack sufficient to hold the enemy to his original position at Oldbridge, while the larger crossed at a ford or fords upstream and struck James in flank and rear. If such a flanking movement were made during the night and if it should take the Jacobites unawares, it might, as we have seen, result for them in irredeemable disaster. This was what General Keating had in mind when he accused King James and his advisers of 'great and glaring misconduct' in not foreseeing the danger in which they lay and in not 'occupying the pass of Slane with a strong corps of infantry and artillery, covered by works'. Keating seems to have let William and *his* advisers down far too lightly in deeming it merely 'a great neglect' on their part not to have 'intercepted the Irish army at Duleek', since if Duleek had been blocked 'they must have surrendered or been driven into the sea'. Whether Schomberg and those who concurred with him were aware of the full possibilities of the plan which they proposed is uncertain.

Count Solms, the leader of the Dutch, who was later to succeed William as commander-in-chief in Ireland, disagreed with Schomberg. He favoured a single attack of the whole Williamite army at Oldbridge. These two, Schomberg and Solms, ranked above the others, and William, who decided the matter, seems to have combined their recommendations. It was resolved to make both frontal and flank attacks, but more troops than Schomberg had proposed were to be retained at Oldbridge; in the end, two-thirds of the army fought there and only a third made the flank attack, and this detachment was sent off so late that the Jacobites were given plenty of time to make arrangements to meet it.

The detachment did not begin to march until five o'clock, or perhaps a little before that, on the morning of 1 July, the day of the battle. It consisted of the cavalry of William's right wing, two regiments of dragoons and ten battalions of infantry (Trelawney's brigade), or in all about 10,000 men. These troops did not all march together. Schomberg's son, Count Meinhard Schomberg, first led some of the cavalry, some infantry and the dragoons towards Rosnaree; he was followed to that ford or to some of the other fords between Rosnaree and Slane by Lieut.-General James Douglas, who led the remainder of the infantry and a brigade of cavalry. Some of these troops may have gone as far as Slane, but this seems unlikely; it would appear rather that they all crossed downstream from Slane. Douglas, who from his

seniority must eventually have commanded the whole detachment, does not seem to have marched until the younger Schomberg was across. The Jacobite troops, who were by that time
marching themselves to intercept the right wing of their enemies,
saw the Williamites 'marching off from their right . . . the river
being between both for a considerable space.'

Young Schomberg reached the Boyne about six o'clock, or
perhaps half an hour later. He saw on the other side a party of
mounted men of Sir Neill O'Neill's dragoon regiment, to which
King James had entrusted the defence of the Slane-Rosnaree
crossings, and which formed in the early stages of the action the
Jacobite left wing. Schomberg sent some mounted grenadiers
and Dutch dragoons—the special service troops of that time,
successors of the 'commanded men' of fifty years before and forerunners of the pickets of fifty years after—down to the ford.
O'Neill's men opened fire, but Schomberg's got across. O'Neill
had orders 'to defend that pass as long as he could, without
exposing his men to be cut to pieces'. It is to be presumed that he
did so. He himself was mortally wounded; five or six men were
killed and others hurt, but the Jacobites were heavily outnumbered
and were forced back. James and his advisers had by this time
realised that their left was threatened and had begun to detach
troops in that direction. The retiring dragoons were soon
supported, but it was too late to block the fords. Douglas and
the young Schomberg passed all of their 10,000 men across as
the morning advanced.

The Jacobite deficiency on the left was limited to their failure
to deny the passage of the river to their opponents. O'Neill had
done his best, but, although the terrain favoured him—the ground
rises steeply from the south bank at Rosnaree—he was not strong
enough for his task. Very soon the left wing suffered no such lack
of strength. Two regiments of Jacobite cavalry, one of which was
Sarsfield's, came over towards Rosnaree. With them came Lauzun
and the whole French force, six battalions of the best infantry that
James had. These troops were followed by more Irish infantry,
until in the end almost half James's army was on his left; that it
was the stronger half was perhaps shown by the fact that James
himself joined it. This disposition proved quite effective to counter
Douglas's threat. Douglas had moved a little way downstream
from the fords, but he was held up where the Boyne bends
towards the north and the ground begins to rise towards the

Donore ridge. Here, with their right on the river and their backs to Donore and Duleek, probably between Corballis and Rough-grange, stood the French and Irish, blocking his further progress. Douglas drew up facing them, well beyond musket range, and the Irish extended to their left to cover his line. A stream flowed towards the river through boggy ground between the two forces. Two deep and high-banked ditches also ran between them, making cavalry service impossible and a passage on foot difficult. In this place James's left wing and William's right remained facing one another throughout the morning without becoming engaged. The Jacobites had made up for their earlier neglect and had prevented William from turning them. They had secured their line of retreat and had saved themselves from the possibility of disaster. It was, however, unfortunate, in view of what was so soor to happen there, that they had to strip so many men from their centre to do so.

A great deal had indeed been happening at Oldbridge and on the stretch of the river between Oldbridge and Drybridge, or from a mile to two and a half miles west of Drogheda. This was the place in which, had William been a better or a more enter-prising general, the Jacobites might have been squeezed to death in the sack formed by the bend of the Boyne. In it the fighting was soon to be intense.

The morning was at first dull and when the right wing of the Williamites went off it was misty; but the day brightened with the mounting sun and the words of the song that the victors were to sing—'July the first, in a morning clear'—were justified. William, whose guns soon opened fire from the high ground above the ford at Oldbridge and who must have noted with anxiety that his opponents began 'very early' to strike their tents and to move off their baggage from Donore, delayed the attack which he was about to make with his centre and left for two reasons. He was anxious to give Douglas as much time as possible for his manœuvre, for it was still believed that right and left wings, encircling the Jacobites, could meet on the south bank, and he wanted the ebbing tide to have reduced the level of water at the fords before he attempted a crossing. He assembled his columns in the ravine which bears his name and, one supposes, behind the edge of the high ground, between his guns and the camp.

Opposite him the Jacobites were assembling too. They had at

the beginning only two infantry regiments, Antrim's and Clanrickard's, close to the river, but five more battalions, including a battalion of the Guards, were soon ordered down from the camp at Donore to support them. They looked like fighting, although they had done little to make a strongpoint of the village or to erect defences on the river bank. Lord Dungan's dragoons were over to the right, watching the lower ford opposite Drybridge. The Duke of Berwick's troop of the Life Guards and three regiments of horse of the right wing, Tyrconnell's, Parker's and Sutherland's, all under the command of Major-General Dominick Sheldon, were further back, on the rising ground. These troops, amounting, horse, foot and dragoons, to some 6,000 men, made up the whole Jacobite force that was to be in action within the bend of the river. When William developed his strength they would be outnumbered three to one.

The crossing began at Oldbridge about ten o'clock, 'at ebb tide when the water is not so deep'. It developed as time went on into a forward movement on a broad front involving crossings at two other fords further downstream, the one close by and the other at Drybridge.

Count Solms, who had proposed crossing there, was in command at Oldbridge. With him was the commanding general, the elder Schomberg. Solms's troops were all infantry. He had three battalions of Dutch Guards in front and these were followed by the Huguenot regiments of Caillemotte and Cambon and by some English regiments. They marched into the ford eight or ten abreast and their bodies dammed for the moment the flow of the river, so that the water, which when the Jacobites crossed a few days before had not been high enough to stop the drummers beating, now rose to the men's waists. The Dutch grenadiers must have been the first across. They were at once engaged, but their comrades followed quickly and, forming on the bank, tried to push forward. The Huguenots too crossed and deployed.

The Jacobite resistance to this movement brought on the severest infantry fighting of the day. The Irish Guards, led by Major Arthur, and the Jacobite line battalions marched down to charge the Dutchmen and the French Protestants; they 'went on boldly till they came within a pike's length of the enemy, notwithstanding their perpetual fire'. Major Arthur 'ran the officer through the body that commanded the battalion he marched up to'. The Irish Guards lost 150 men killed and perhaps twice as many wounded; of the Dutch Guards 'there fell a hundred and upwards'.

Very soon the Irish cavalry came down to help their comrades on foot. They were led, among others, by Tyrconnell, an unhealthy man of sixty—was he the only Irish viceroy to appear sword in hand in the field?—and by King James's natural son, the Duke of Berwick, later to be a Marshal of France and the victor at Almanza, then a youth of twenty. When these horsemen joined in William's veterans were hard put to it to hold their ground. 'It was Tyrconnell's fortune to charge first the Blue Regiment of Foot Guards to the Prince of Orange [so the Jacobites named William], and he pierced through', an exploit which drew from William, who witnessed it from the further bank, the plaint, 'My poor Guards, my poor Guards, my poor Guards!' The horsemen profited by the situation of the moment which, with the waning of the pike and in the infancy of the bayonet, gave them a temporary superiority over the foot. Horses were fleet, loading slow, the fire of excited men uncertain; the Irish cavalry—probably as much for its horses as its horsemanship, for the light weight native animal of earlier times had given place to a charger of more substance—was already respected by its opponents; after this day's work it was to be feared. Solms's Dutch infantry, who had bayonets, faced the horsemen like the trained soldiers that they were. Their first rank only fired, and then the men fell on their faces and loaded their muskets as they lay—a difficult operation. When 'a choice squadron of the enemy, consisting most of officers' charged them, the first rank rose and fired again; then, when they had 'spent all their front fire' and the horsemen fell upon them, 'the two rear ranks drew up in two platoons and flanked the enemy across', while the rest fixed bayonets and defended themselves. Some infantry regiments that were without pikes carried with them what an eighteenth-century military writer calls 'spars, or long pieces of wood stuck full of sharp spikes of wood or iron'. These were *chevaux-de-frise*, the 'Friesian horse' or 'Swedish feathers' with which, since the time of the Thirty Years War or earlier, foot soldiers had extemporised palisades as a protection against cavalry; they were, in fact, a military precedent of barbed wire. The Huguenots had neither pikes nor *chevaux-de-frise* and when Tyrconnell's and the other troopers fell on them they were unable to resist them. Caillemotte was mortally wounded; many men were killed.

Schomberg, trying to rally among the houses at Oldbridge those with whom he had been exiled from France, was killed by an officer of the Life Guards; he was shot in the back of the neck.

The struggle at Oldbridge continued for more than two hours and was in progress for some time before crossings were made at the other fords. It was, said the Williamites, 'a very sharp fight' for which the Dutch Guards deserved 'immortal honour'; they 'did wonders' and were 'like angels'. But neither the Dutch nor the Huguenots nor the English were able to move far forward from the gardens and enclosures at the village until they were reinforced by additional troops who crossed the river further downstream. The defence, so far, remained unbroken.

 The second Williamite column began crossing a short distance downstream, where the Jacobites did not believe the river fordable, about eleven o'clock. It was led by the Duke of Würtemberg, who had the Danish regiments and Sir John Hanmer's (mostly Dutch) and Le Mellonière's brigades, or about 12,000 men. The crossing was difficult, even though the tide must then have been low. The bottom was boggy. Some of the troops were up to their necks in the water and probably could not have got over at all any earlier. They were resisted at first only by Dungan's dragoons, who attacked the Danish Guards as they came up the bank, but the tiny and hard pressed force of Irish infantry at Oldbridge managed to send a detachment against them, although this movement soon permitted the Dutch Guards to gain ground. With so many men now over the river, the Irish were heavily outnumbered. Yet more Williamites were still to come. Some time after noon King William crossed with the remainder of his cavalry—Dutch, Danish, English and Ulstermen—at the lowest ford, at Drybridge, a passage that was very deep and that involved a difficult crossing of boggy ground on the south side. Again the Jacobite dragoons and cavalry resisted, but the Williamites now had mounted men to take on Sheldon's devoted horsemen. Their cavalry moved upstream. Their whole infantry force within the loop of the river pressed forward. 'Although', says a Danish account, 'the enemy rallied several times and defended himself against our men, he was driven back each time. In the end, as his infantry were more inclined to retreat than to defend themselves [further] he had to quit the field altogether.' These Jacobite infantrymen, most of whom were receiving their baptism of fire that day, were overcome by overwhelming force after a struggle of nearly three hours' duration. Their enemies accused them of having behaved badly, but the record of their almost hopeless resistance scarcely shows it. As they toiled up the hill at Donore and, after a further struggle on the hilltop, marched off through the debris of their camp—the scattered tents, the abandoned baggage—they must have wondered what had become of their French allies and why, with such troops in the field, they had been left to face alone what was so obviously the main attack of their enemies.

But their cavalry, fighting as no cavalry had fought before in Ireland, or has fought since, stood by them to the end. The men who had already distinguished themselves against Schomberg and Solms turned again on the slope of the ridge and bore down on William's masses. With supreme courage—a writer who was present at the battle calls it 'unspeakable bravery'—and with the recklessness that was such a desideratum in so much of the cavalry action of long ago, the Irish horsemen rode out of the dust, cutting and slashing. Berwick was thrown down and trampled, but he fought on until he had only sixteen unwounded men left out of his 200 Life Guards. Colonel Parker's men, who with Tyrconnell's and Sutherland's struck the Williamites again and again, fell about their leader until there were only thirty of them in action out of a full regiment. Lieut.-General Richard Hamilton, the leader of the Jacobite foot, who had been in command at the siege of Derry, was surrounded and captured. Sheldon's losses were tragic, but his men held up the whole Williamite advance for a precious half-hour. The Irish horse, said King James, 'did their duty with great bravery, and though they did not break the enemy's foot, it was more by reason of the ground not being favourable than for want of vigour, for after they had been repulsed by the foot they rallied again and charged the enemy's horse and beat them every charge'.

Yet such valour merely delayed the inevitable. The Irish continued their retirement southward from Donore to Duleek. They were preceded by King James who, escorted by Patrick Sarsfield's regiment of horse and by some of the dragoons, rode to Dublin, where James told the Mayor and Aldermen that although he had justice on his side fate was against him. He was in France within three weeks. He had thought his position at the Boyne 'an indifferent good one' and that 'indeed the country afforded no better', and he had decided to fight there because he was resolved 'not to be walked out of Ireland without having at least one blow for it'; but the blow that was struck by half his force was ineffectual. The remainder, including the French, who lost only six men in the battle, failed to strike any blow at all.

'The failure at the Boyne', said a Jacobite writer, 'sprang from several defects of military management.' There were defects on both sides, but the Williamites, having much the stronger force, could afford to make some mistakes. For the Jacobites, whatever the necessity may have been of guarding themselves against encirclement, the immobilisation of so many men on their left and the making of a detachment that split their army in two were fatal dispositions.

The Jacobites were reunited at Duleek, where both parts of their army—that from Oldbridge and the detachment from the left—came together in retreat. There was some confusion at the narrow passage of the Nanny water, and some of the horse who had done so well at Oldbridge and Donore collided with their own infantry. One Jacobite infantry regiment was overtaken 'in Duleek lane enclosed with high banks' by cavalry, who 'came on so unexpected and with such speed, some firing their pistols' that the infantry thought they were the enemy and broke to let them pass.

There was no pursuit. William's men came no further than Duleek, which, for all the confusion, was successfully negotiated by the Irish and their French allies. The French troops were intact, and a stand made at Duleek by Zurlauben's regiment greatly aided the retreat. The Jacobites saved part of their baggage and—at least for the moment—five of their guns. They lost in killed alone about a thousand men, but the Williamite loss may have been even greater; one of the Williamite writers says that they had 400 killed, another raises it to 500, and the wounded can scarcely have been less than twice as many more.

The Boyne was a significant rather than a great battle. As a result of it William won Dublin and Leinster and more than half Munster—priceless advantages. It was reckoned a great victory by that part of Europe that opposed Louis XIV of France and that regarded William as its leader; but its real significance was, after all, Irish. Although the defeated army continued to fight for more than a year from the date of its discomfiture, it did so with diminishing hope of success. Militarily the Boyne was the decisive battle of the war. Yet the fact that it became the rallying cry of the ascendancy that it served to set up was to suggest that it hadn't really been decisive after all.

The literature of the Boyne is considerable. The most accessible of the contemporary accounts are: G. Story, *Impartial History*, pp. 78 ff; C. O'Kelly, *Macariae Excidium* (ed. J. C. O'Callaghan), pp. 50 ff; J. T. Gilbert, *A Jacobite Narrative of the War in Ireland* (the statement entitled 'A Light to the Blind'), pp. 98 ff; *Memoirs of the Duke of Berwick* (London, 1779), I, pp. 63 ff; Memoirs of King James (in *Life of James II* by J. S. Clarke, 1816, II, pp. 393 ff); J. Stevens, *Journal* (ed. R. H. Murray), pp. 121 f; K. Danaher and J. G. Simms (ed.), *The Danish Force in Ireland, 1690–1*, pp. 42 ff, 62 f; R. Parker, *Memoirs of the Military Transactions in Ireland, 1683–1718*, pp. 19 ff. There is a good bibliography in J. G. Simms, 'Eye-witnesses of the Boyne' in *The Irish Sword*, VI, pp. 16 ff. Modern accounts are in D. C. Boulger, *The Battle of the Boyne* and J. C. O'Callaghan, *The Green Book* (2nd edn, 1844), pp. 106 ff. The general history of the period may be studied in the rather dated book, R. H. Murray, *Revolutionary Ireland and its Settlement* (1911. There is an extensive bibliography). Murray's book will undoubtedly be superseded by J. G. Simms's study, soon to be published, of the Irish struggle against William. For Tyrconnell's purge see P. W. Sergeant, *Little Jennings and Fighting Dick Talbot* (1913).

Keating's book is H. S. Keating, *On the Defence of Ireland* (1795. A second edition, containing many additions and observations dictated by the militaristic nationalism of the time, appeared in 1860). D'Avaux' reports are in J. Hogan (ed.), *Négociations de M. le Comte D'Avaux en Irlande, 1689–90* (Irish Manuscripts Commission, 1934, with Supplementary Volume, 1958). The organisation of the troops is discussed in C. Walton, *History of the British Standing Army, 1660–1700* (1894) and in J. W. Fortescue, *A History of the British Army* (1899), I. For King James's cavalry see D. Murtagh, 'The Jacobite Horse' in *The Irish Sword*, I, pp. 317 ff. For the tactics of river bends see Baron Jomini, *Précis de l'art de la Guerre* (1837—translated by O. F. Winship and E. E. McLean as *Summary of the Art of War*, New York, 1854, where the reference to river crossings is on p. 239), E. B. Hamley, *Operations of*

War (2nd edn, 1869), p. 234 and F. Clery, *Minor Tactics* (8th edn, 1887), p. 237. It is perhaps worthy of note that the famous passage of the Silliaasvogel river (see Sir E. Swinton, *The Defence of Duffer's Drift*, 1904) was in 'a regular horseshoe bend'. For a description and illustration of *chevaux-de-frise* see T. Simes, *A Military Course* (1777), p. 64 and frontispiece, and for the use of bayonets by the English at the Boyne see Davis's diary, *Ulster Journal of Archaeology*, first series, IV, p. 92—Davis speaks of the troops 'screwing their swords to the muskets' and it is he also who tells us of the behaviour of the Dutch at Oldbridge.

On a field where so many uniforms were worn the Williamites were distinguished by sprigs of green in their hats. The Jacobites showed pieces of white paper, white being the French colour. It is interesting that at a later date, in 1798 when green had recently become the Irish national colour, white paper badges were again worn as distinguishing marks, this time by the United Irish insurgents.

Aughrim, 1691

Seen in retrospect, the battle of the Boyne must, as we have said, be regarded as decisive, but it was not the end of the war. The defeated Jacobites were still a fighting force and were still to fight stubbornly before King William could claim victory in Ireland. Although they could not have continued their struggle without the abiding hope of adequate French assistance, the French troops who had been present at the Boyne were soon to leave them. Lauzun's brigade marched to Limerick, and thence to Galway. Recalled by Louis XIV, the French regiments embarked in their transports in Galway Bay in September 1690 and returned rather ingloriously to their own country. Wolfe Tone was to remark, when he himself was a suitor for French help a century later, that Louis, presented with an opportunity of 'separating Ireland from England, contented himself with feeding the war little by little, until the opportunity was lost'. None of the kings, save—irony of ironies—William, comes well out of the Irish war. A contemporary of Tone's said that 'James, with that precipitate despair which marked his character, abandoned his friends in Ireland. The complete reduction of that kingdom was', he added, 'a tedious and difficult work. The obstinate bravery of the Roman Catholic nobility, seconded by the skill of the French officers, protracted the Irish war till the surrender of Limerick on 3rd October, 1691.' Modern opinion finds his summary unexceptionable.

After the Boyne, the Jacobite field force withdrew precipitately behind the line of the river Shannon. Drogheda, Dublin, Kilkenny, Clonmel and Waterford surrendered to William, who sent part of his army under General Douglas to Athlone and marched himself with the main body to Limerick. Douglas failed to secure the river crossing at Athlone and soon rejoined William, who, in the wet August of 1690—we remember Corporal Trim's assurance that 'the whole country was like a puddle'—made a determined effort to take Limerick. But the Jacobite defenders, under the

Frenchman Boisseleau, the Governor of the town, were not to be overcome. They disputed, said King James, 'every inch of ground with all the valour and resolution imaginable', and the English chronicler Story, speaking of the abortive attempt to storm a breach in the wall on the 27th, says that the Irish 'so pestered us upon the counterscarp that, after nigh three hours resisting bullets, stones, broken bottles from the very women, who boldly stood in the breach and were nearer to our men than their own, and whatever ways could be thought on to destroy us, our ammunition being spent, it was judged safest to return to our trenches'. The Williamites had had enough. They raised the siege at the end of August and withdrew their army. In September and October, John Churchill, later to be the great Duke of Marlborough, took Cork and Kinsale for William.

Hostilities were continued during the winter. Encouraged by their success in Munster, the Williamites pushed on into Kerry at the end of the year, but their advance to Ross castle near Killarney was no more than a raid undertaken to hinder the despatch of supplies to the Jacobite forces in Limerick. Kerry, said William's government in Dublin, was 'the granary of Limerick'. Further north, Douglas advanced from Belturbet towards Sligo and Major-General Sir John Lanier moved westward from Mullingar early in the new year. These detachments, neither of which was numerous, can scarcely have been intended to do more than make a reconnaissance in force. If circumstances had proven unexpectedly favourable, they were to have broken into Connacht, but in fact they operated with little effect in the approaches to the Shannon crossings at Jamestown and Lanesborough. They found the Jacobites under Major-General Sarsfield, whose headquarters were at Athlone, watchful and vigorous. Sarsfield went in person to secure Jamestown when Douglas threatened it, but Douglas made only a halfhearted effort to cross the river and soon withdrew. The Williamites encamped and commenced digging a position for a battery at Lanesborough, but they were easily dislodged and their advance party retired in disorder before their supports came up. The Jacobite Colonel Clifford, who operated in Westmeath in February, was routed by Lanier. Lanier had Lieut.-General Ginkel with him. Ginkel had succeeded Count Solms in command in Ireland and had come up from Munster, where he had been supporting the Kerry raiding force and organising operations against scattered Jacobite forces and rapparees in south Limerick and north Cork. Clifford fled to Athlone. The Williamites made no offensive movements after January, and as spring advanced the Jacobites were still drawing supplies from wide areas in Westmeath, Offaly and north Tipperary.

Sarsfield was quite sanguine. In particular, he prided himself on the tenacity with which he had held on to Ballymore in Co. Westmeath. Ballymore, where a peninsula extending into Lough Sewdy terminates in a steep bluff overhanging the water, had been a place of strength for centuries. It was the strongpoint of the Norman Lordship of Lough Sewdy, the western part of the Liberty of Meath—Lacy, and later Verdun, country—and Edward Bruce spent the Christmas of 1315 there. Lying half-way between the two places, it commanded the approach from Williamite headquarters at Mullingar to Athlone. Sarsfield had fortified Ballymore during the winter, and he proposed in February sending 300 men to reinforce the 400 who were already there. He believed that it would be impossible for the Williamites to lay siege to Athlone while Ballymore was held against them; besides, Ballymore protected the district east of the Shannon from which Athlone drew so much of its supplies. Sarsfield's views were not, however, shared by all his colleagues. Clifford, who succeeded to the Athlone command when Sarsfield was ordered to Limerick before the end of February, seems to have doubted the advisability of holding positions east of the Shannon; he abandoned the most remote of them, Dysart castle, eight miles from Ballymore, and—according to Sarsfield—failed either to reinforce or to provision Ballymore.

Since, as we shall see, Ballymore was to prove a Jacobite liability rather than an asset in the campaign of 1691, and since, when all was done, the military part played by Sarsfield in the Irish war was not as considerable as his historic reputation suggests, we might wonder if his name as a national figure is not greater than his capacity was as a soldier. Indeed Sarsfield is enigmatical. Present both at the Boyne and Aughrim, he was actively engaged in neither battle, and the only military service of note which he performed in Ireland was the preservation of Connacht for King James in 1689, the brilliant cavalry raid by which he destroyed part of William's siege train at Ballyneety outside Limerick, and this winter war of reconnaissance and outposts on the Shannon. He was a competent—perhaps one should

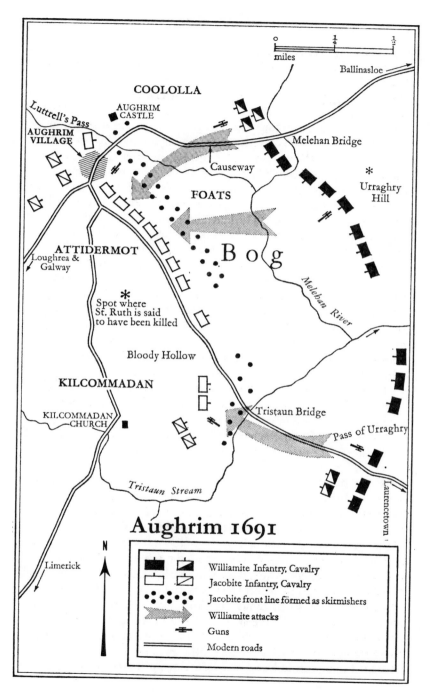

Aughrim 1691

Williamite Infantry, Cavalry
Jacobite Infantry, Cavalry
Jacobite front line formed as skirmishers
Williamite attacks
Guns
Modern roads

say a dashing—rather than an outstanding soldier, with, as far as can be gleaned, a record of early service in the Netherlands in Louis XIV's Dutch war. He seems to have had a lean time in England until James II's accession opened wider prospects for Irish officers such as he who had languished under the cloud of the Test Act in the aftermath of the Popish Plot. He was wounded at Sedgemoor in 1685. Thereafter, when he was in his thirties, his stock rose. He was much in the public eye in England. He succeeded to the family estates of Lucan, served in the Horse Guards, fought in the skirmishes which followed William's landing at Torbay, and fled to France to King James, whom he later accompanied to Ireland. He had the rank of Colonel when he opposed the west Ulster Williamites in 1689. James thought him at this time 'a brave fellow, but very scantily supplied with brains', a sentiment which Tyrconnell—who did not like him—echoed, saying that, although he was very brave, 'he had no head'. The French agent D'Avaux, on the other hand, believed that Sarsfield had 'more to his credit in this kingdom than any man I know' and regarded him as a possible leader of the Irish troops which Justin McCarthy subsequently brought to France. He was a brigadier before the end of 1689 and a Major-General in the following year, when, after the retirement behind the Shannon, he was called 'the darling of the army'. At the beginning of 1691 James made him Earl of Lucan and he was, apparently, advanced to a Lieut.-Generalship.

There are gaps in the record, gaps due to a notable lack of information about one whose place in the Irish pantheon is still secure. Two certainties emerge; the Williamite generals had a far healthier respect for Sarsfield than for any other of his countrymen, and his Irish reputation was made in his own lifetime. It was not for nothing (if we only knew what it *was* for) that a contemporary could speak not only of 'his indomitable courage in the most desperate situations'—everybody admitted that—but of 'the love of the people, who call him the father of his country'.

As it happened, leadership was badly needed by the Irish Jacobites in the spring of 1691. Sarsfield, who had at least one quality of leadership, which is optimism, believed that, given supplies from France, they would have in the coming summer a bigger army and better soldiers than they had had at the Boyne. Sarsfield was one of the twelve officers who acted as a council of war under the Duke of Berwick during Tyrconnell's absence in France, and, during the winter, his was the most effective military control. But there were opinions other than his. There were pessimists in the ranks, or should one perhaps call them realists?

Tyrconnell, who had been created a Duke in 1689, returned from France to Limerick in January. He found two parties among his colleagues, those who favoured the speedy termination of the war by compromise and who countenanced negotiations which were being carried on by individuals with the Williamite government through the winter, and the inflexible ones, who were determined to hold out to the last. These groups, the moderates and extremists of every historic movement, carried forward into a new generation the mixture of compromise and intransigence that had been the bane of the Catholic Confederation of half a century earlier. Although the distinction between Old Irish and Anglo-Irish had become less noticeable, there were still, following the century's vast changes in the ownership of Irish land, great prospective differences in the upper stratum of those who supported King James. Although, on the material plane, all were insecure, some felt themselves more likely to benefit by negotiation than others. If William should win, all, or almost all, would share the disadvantage of being Catholics. Their only safety in this regard lay in their numbers, but uniformity of religion did not mean unity. The English writer Cox believed in 1689 that 'no people in the world are more unanimously engaged to King James than the Irish papists'. He thought that the number of Irish Catholics who were fit for war was not less than 120,000 and that 100,000 of these, who held property worth no more than £5 each and had, in effect, nothing to lose, would 'endeavour to prolong the war'. His calculations may have been correct, but, then as always, it was the big men, and not the little men, who counted. The crowning misfortune of the Jacobites was that they were the victims of a clash of personalities. Tyrconnell, who was James's viceroy, and who had done so much to build up resistance to William, disliked Sarsfield—and Sarsfield disliked Tyrconnell. It was an unpromising situation for the commencement of a campaign.

It seems to have been accepted by both sides since the beginning of the year that the Williamites, failing an earlier termination of the struggle, would open their campaign by an attack on Athlone. As dictated by circumstance, Ginkel's strategy was simple. He must force his way into Connacht and win Galway and Limerick, the last Jacobite links with France. He still held the initiative, and Tyrconnell and his military colleagues were still, as they had always been, on the defensive.

The Jacobites got little from France before the reopening of general hostilities. Tyrconnell brought nothing save money, and not a great deal of that. The French government was certainly impressed by the obvious determination of the Irish to continue the struggle, and a French fleet which came to Limerick early in May brought arms, ammunition, clothing for the troops and some provisions—all items of which the Jacobites were badly in need. The fleet brought too a new commander, Lieut.-General the Marquis de St Ruth, who replaced Berwick—who had left for France in February—and was given a military authority independent of Tyrconnell's. With St Ruth came two French Maréchaux-de-Camp (they probably held the acting rank of Lieut.-General), d'Usson and de Tesse, and a few more officers. But there were no French troops. As far as troops were concerned, the Irish were left to fend for themselves.

Ginkel was ready by the end of May. He assembled eight regiments of infantry, six of horse and one of dragoons, together with his artillery, which consisted of over thirty siege guns, six mortars and twelve field guns, at Mullingar. The troops whose winter quarters were in Ulster and who made up eight further infantry regiments, two regiments of dragoons and one of horse, were ordered to assemble at Belturbet and to move southward to join him. The Duke of Würtemberg's troops, consisting of most of the Danish, Dutch, French Huguenot and three English battalions and about 2,000 horse and dragoons who had wintered in the south, mustered at Cashel on the 25th, reached Birr on the 30th, and moved on towards Athlone. When his whole field army was assembled at the Shannon, Ginkel expected to have over thirty battalions of infantry and over forty squadrons of cavalry and dragoons, or some 25,000 men. On the other side of the Shannon, St Ruth's army assembled to meet this formidable opposition. Many of the Jacobite troops had been dispersed during the winter to live off the country and to act as rapparees, or men engaged in guerrilla warfare, in the regions nominally occupied by the Williamites. These were now recalled to the ranks and every effort was made, consistent with the limited resources available, to build up the field force. All available troops were moved up, from Limerick and elsewhere, and encamped at a strength of from 15,000 to 20,000 men at Ballinasloe in Co. Galway.

The first of the fighting occurred, as Sarsfield had expected it would, at Ballymore. Sarsfield's appreciation of the possible consequences was scarcely correct. Ginkel, who, having marched from Mullingar, had shortly before been joined by the troops from Ulster, came to the fieldworks which defended the causeway leading in to the Ballymore position at noon on 7 June. He opened fire with his field guns, and, when this proved ineffective, dug positions for some of his siege pieces and mortars. This work was completed by nightfall and the batteries commenced firing at dawn on the 8th. Fire was continued for most of the day. The garrison, which had been strengthened by the despatch of troops under Lieut.-Colonel Ulick Burke from Athlone, replied as well as it could with musketry and the fire of two small field pieces mounted on cart wheels, but was forced to surrender at seven o'clock in the evening. Ginkel was at that time preparing to mount a further attack by boat from the rear. Ballymore delayed Ginkel's progress for two days, a length of time which, despite J. C. O'Callaghan's assertion to the contrary, could have made little difference to St Ruth's preparations to defend Athlone. As a result of the action at Ballymore, Ginkel came to the Shannon as a victor. The better part of a thousand Jacobite soldiers—most of them good men whom St Ruth could ill afford to lose, and some of them fusiliers armed with flintlocks—were thrown away. Ginkel repaired the works at Ballymore, left a small force there to protect his line of communications, and moved on. He was joined by Würtemberg's troops from Munster a few miles outside Athlone.

Ginkel found the English town of Athlone, or that part on the east bank of the Shannon—the only part which Douglas had been able to take in the previous year—defended against him. He attacked it on 20 June and, by nightfall, had forced the small body of Irish troops who sought most gallantly to defend it across the bridge into the Irish town on the Connacht bank. The retiring Jacobites rendered the bridge impassable by breaking down two of its nine arches. (This was the bridge which had been erected in 1567 and which was replaced by the present structure in 1844.) Encouraged by success, Ginkel positioned his batteries and cannonaded the Irish town at short range from the 22nd to the

28th. He attempted at the same time to force a passage across the broken bridge; he had so far succeeded in this by the morning of the 28th that only the chasm where the arches were broken lay between his men and the defenders, and beams and planks had been thrown across that in preparation for what it was expected would be the final charge. Fighting had been intense and casualties heavy on both sides. It was at this well remembered moment that the finest action of the war, and perhaps the finest military action in Irish history, took place. Volunteers were called for to throw down the planks. A sergeant of Maxwell's Ulster regiment of dragoons—we must thank King James for remembering that his name was Custume—leaped down from the breastwork and, accompanied by ten of his comrades, commenced to pitch the planks into the river. They came under a storm of shot and were all killed. A Lieutenant and twenty men replaced them, of whom but two survived. But the last plank was thrown down and the efforts of the Williamites to work their way over the bridge were, almost at the moment of accomplishment, frustrated.

This heroic action and the fierce resistance which had, up to this, denied a passage to Ginkel's greatly superior force deserved a better sequel. In the end, Athlone was won easily. Its defence, like the struggle on the ridge of Inkerman, was a soldiers' battle; Tyrconnell, St Ruth, d'Usson, who commanded in the town, Sarsfield, who was apparently near by, Major-General Maxwell, whose troops manned the river defences—none of the Jacobite leaders deserves much credit for the attempt to stop Ginkel. They allowed themselves to be surprised, and if their inadequacy in this regard was the result of the jealousies that characterised their dealings with one another, so much the worse for their reputations.

Ginkel made another attempt to force the bridge on the 29th, but the fascines and a covered gallery which were pushed forward as a protection against the Jacobite grenades and musketry were set on fire and the attackers were again forced back. They decided to renew their efforts on the day following, this time at the unexpected hour of six in the evening when their guards were due to be relieved.

The Jacobite force in Athlone castle and the Irish town was not great, but it had shown itself to be adequate to hold the bridge. St Ruth's error lay in his failure to reinforce the troops in the town to the strength necessary to resist a more extended attack. He had brought up 1,500 men from his camp at Ballinasloe when

Ginkel took the English town. The remainder of his army followed and was encamped by the 27th, or perhaps before that, within two miles of Athlone. The Danes believed that St Ruth had 30,000 men, made up of thirty-three regiments of infantry and eighteen of horse and dragoons, but this estimate is undoubtedly much too high; he appears to have had much less than 20,000—a force that seems to have been adequate however, if it had been properly handled, for a far greater resistance than he was to make at the Shannon. St Ruth had drawn up his army behind the Irish town during Ginkel's attack on the 29th, but he had retired to his camp when the fighting died down. He had given belated orders— which were not carried out—to have part of the town defences on the unthreatened west side thrown down so as to provide for the speedy entry of reinforcements. In fact, he was over-confident; he took it for granted that Ginkel had been repulsed by 30 June and that he would soon withdraw.

Athlone was taken 'by as perfect a surprise as ever was'—the words are those of Felix O'Neill, a Jacobite officer who was to be killed at Aughrim shortly after they were written. Hazarding almost all on what would probably have been, for that season at least, a last throw at Athlone, Ginkel attacked suddenly on the evening of the 30th. Major-General Hugh Mackay, the famous Williamite supporter who had been defeated at Killiecrankie in 1689, and who had recently arrived in Ginkel's camp, led a storming party of picked troops on the bridge, while the German officer in Danish service, Major-General Tettau, a skilled engineer, led another waist deep across the river, which at that time had 'never been known so shallow in the memory of man'. Tettau's troops, who crossed, grenadiers in front, a little below the bridge, stormed over a breach which had been made in the fortifications beside the castle and burst into the town. Soon the whole attacking force of 2,000 men, the best soldiers in Ginkel's army—English, Danish, Dutch and Huguenot—was across the Shannon. All was over in half an hour. The battered town was cleared. The castle surrendered on the following day. Ginkel's way seemed clear for an advance into Connacht.

Three courses of action were now open to the Jacobites. They could attempt to blockade Ginkel in Athlone, or at least to interrupt his movements when he sought to debouch from it, although they were scarcely equipped for such an effort, nor did the terrain favour it. They could retire at once to Galway or Limerick, or, by dividing their forces, to both. They could choose their ground and accept the risk of battle. We are told that St Ruth's inclination was to fight, that he regretted what had happened at Athlone, and that he sought an opportunity for revenge. Tyrconnell and Sarsfield—in agreement for once—held that the infantry should retire to Limerick, where the former had gone, and where he was so soon to die, but that the cavalry should be sent into Leinster, where they might upset Ginkel's whole programme by falling on his line of communications with Mullingar and Dublin. This was an ambitious scheme, and we can see Sarsfield, if he was really a forerunner of J. E. B. Stuart—and if St Ruth was a Lee, and if the Irish cavalry was as good as the Williamites thought it was—carrying it out with perhaps dramatic results; if we knew more about Sarsfield we might have grounds for connecting this proposal with his earlier efforts to hold on to Ballymore, since retention of Ballymore—if it had been possible—would greatly have facilitated it. But the wishes of St Ruth, who at least was no Lauzan (was it because there were now no French troops involved?), prevailed. The Irish retired to Ballinasloe and chose Aughrim as their battlefield.

They were shaken by the abrupt decision at Athlone, but since few regiments had been engaged there their casualties had not been excessive. John Stevens of the Grand Prior's (later Brigadier Talbot's) Regiment says that the march to Ballinsasloe was performed 'with great confusion and disorder, such a panic fear having seized our men that the very noise of ten horsemen would have dispersed as many of our battalions'. Half of his own regiment had melted away, and, as another writer records, the Connacht regiments, which were on, or near, their home ground, 'grew very thin'. Many, as was to happen after Bull Run, and as has happened on occasions innumerable, 'walked quietly off' But this was no more than the inevitable straggling. When the River Suck was reached the army pulled itself together. The detachments from the Shannon fords, which were now outflanked, joined the main body. Continuous cavalry contact was kept up with Ginkel's forces. Ginkel, on the other hand, was unaware what the Irish would do, and for some time even where they had gone. He marched from Athlone on 7 July and reached the Suck on the 11th, his baggage following. He was near Ballinasloe before he discovered that St Ruth was still close in front of him. Encamping for the night on the east bank of the

15. William of Orange, victor of the battle of the Boyne, 1690 (Jan Wyck).

16. The battle of the Boyne, 1690. A contemporary painting by Jan Wyck.

17. Dutch infantry of the late seventeenth century. Dutch regiments
fought in the Williamite armies at both the battle of the Boyne, 1690,
and the battle of Aughrim, 1691.

18. Patrick Sarsfield, Earl of Lucan. At the battle of Aughrim, 1691, the Jacobite commander probably led the large cavalry force on the right wing of St Ruth's army.

19. The military forces available to the government at the time of the
Wexford rebellion were composed largely of locally-recruited part-time
militia and yeoman regiments, similar in type to these Dublin
volunteers, painted in 1779 by the English artist, Francis Wheatley.

20. English dragoons of around 1800. A small force of these regular
cavalrymen were attached to Needham's command at the battle of
Arklow, 1778.

river, he sent scouts forward to the rising ground on the Co. Galway side; these eventually reached Garbally, whence they made out the main Jacobite force in the distance.

Meanwhile, St Ruth had had plenty of time to view the country and to choose the ground upon which he proposed to fight. It was decided not to try to contest the crossing of the Suck, but to retire to Aughrim, five miles to the west, and to fight there.

The position chosen was the long ridge—Kilcommadan or Aughrim hill—which stretches south-eastward from the ruined castle and village of Aughrim and which forms the western skyline for the traveller who, with Ballinasloe and Garbally behind him, moves on towards Loughrea and Galway. St Ruth occupied the eastern slope of this ridge. His left rested on the castle, a ruin even then, his right on Tristaun stream. His front, which faced Ballinasloe and, thirteen miles to the north-east of it, Athlone, was almost a mile and a half long. Across this front, from the castle almost to the present Tristaun bridge, stretched a bog, and beyond St Ruth's left, towards Cololla lake, was still another bog. The ground is drained eastward by streams flowing towards the Suck; one stream flows beside the castle, and, joining another that issues from Cololla bog, continues south-eastward parallel with the ridge until it meets the Tristaun stream; the confluent waters become the Ballinure, and eventually the Cloonascragh, river. The Irish position was, on its flanks and along its whole length, protected by these bogs and streams, and although the streams have in modern times been deepened and much of the bog drained, Kilcommadan hill is still clearly a natural defensive position. It must in 1691 have stood up like a bulwark above a waterlogged countryside.

At that date there were only two approaches to it from the east. The greater part of the bog in front was impassable, but a narrow causeway—now crowned by the Loughrea road—led on the Irish left towards the castle, and a broken esker, or low, irregular gravel ridge, gave access to the Irish right at the present Tristaun bridge. These were the two 'passes' mentioned by contemporary writers, the 'old broken causeway, only large enough for two horses to pass it at a time', and, at Tristaun bridge, the so-called pass of Urraghry.

The Jacobite order of battle provided for two lines of infantry with cavalry on either wing. The first line was commanded by William Dorrington, Colonel of the Foot Guards and Governor of Limerick during the winter, who had been promoted Major-General at the beginning of the year; Major-General John Hamilton commanded the second line. There were about thirty-five infantry battalions, amounting to perhaps 14,000 men, on the battlefield, and there were, in addition, some 2,500 horse and 3,500 dragoons, that is, a total of about 20,000 men. The William-ite writers make the total greater, the Jacobites less, but this figure seems to represent what is for us the closest possible approach to accuracy. All the Irish horse regiments that existed at that date, and, as far as we know, all the dragoons, were at Aughrim, and the only infantry units not present were the seven or eight battalions which formed the garrisons of Limerick and Galway—that is, not counting Balldearg O'Donnell's raw force in north Connacht, and the scattered rapparees. The Jacobites had thus mustered what they could, but their regiments were not nearly at full strength.

Major-General Dominick Sheldon, who had behaved so well at the Boyne and with whom was Brigadier Henry Luttrell, commanded the four regiments of horse and four regiments of dragoons which made up the cavalry of the left wing. The cavalry of the right wing, a troop of the Life Guard, three regiments of horse and more dragoons, was apparently commanded by Sarsfield. Sarsfield's position is curiously uncertain. One con-temporary writer says that he was on the left, another that he was in the rear. The widely accepted statement that he commanded a reserve of cavalry is almost certainly inaccurate, since there was no reserve save Galmoy's Regiment of horse, which was in the left rear. St Ruth's second in command was de Tessé, who had direct command on the left side of the field, St Ruth himself assuming responsibility for the right.

Although his order of battle followed the accepted pattern of the time, St Ruth's disposal of his forces for action scarcely did so. His encampment extended across the flat top of the ridge and perhaps along its western slope, where a by-road runs now from Aughrim village through the townlands of Attidermot and Kil-commadan. Looking eastward from the camp site, the ground is seen to fall away in a decided, regular slope towards the bog. The road from the village to Tristaun bridge, which existed—although probably more as a track than a road—in 1691, runs across this sloping ground, which is still firm, although con-tinuously falling to the bog, beyond it. The ridge falls off towards the left, in the direction of the ruined castle; the slope is gentle and the ground firm in this area, down almost to the stream, but there are undulations and concealed pockets between the road and the bog. Towards the right, in the direction of Tristaun, the road dips into what is called the Bloody Hollow, and between that place and Tristaun bridge the surface is broken and undulating. The stream at Tristaun bridge flows in a narrow bottom; beyond the stream, the ground rises in a bluff to the end of the broken ridge of the esker, which curves away eastward in the direction of Laurencetown.

In 1691, as we know from the descriptions of the fighting and from a map prepared for Story's work, the lower slope of the ridge, extending downwards from the road, was broken up by hedges and ditches which served as field boundaries. Part of the Jacobite infantry—almost certainly the whole of the left centre of the front line—was, during the battle, in position in this area. Advantage was taken of the nature of the ground to place the relatively inexperienced troops in sheltered positions behind the low field boundaries, where they were likely to do better than in the open, and the lines of the hedges and ditches were adapted to suit the tactics which St Ruth, who showed himself to be a most resourceful leader, proposed to adopt. Such a disposition of force and such a preparation of the ground were unusual in that formal age. St Ruth, says Story, 'showed a great deal of dexterity in making choice of such a piece of ground as nature itself could not furnish him with a better'. The second line stood in formed battalions, pikes behind the musketeers, and with intervals between the formations, about where the road runs. On the left, the castle, the walls and ditches around it and trenches which had been dug by the troops were occupied by Walter Burke's Regiment. This was the left flank, and it commanded the approach along the causeway. Behind the castle, or to the south of it, two further infantry battalions stood, as one account has it, in a corn-field; another account says that they were in 'a parcel of old garden ditches'. Three of the nine Jacobite field guns were ranged in a battery close to the site of Aughrim church (Church of Ireland). Further back, formed up 'in a hollow' and with a good deal of firm ground suitable for cavalry action stretching between them and the bog, stood Sheldon's horse. Some of Sheldon's dragoons—no doubt dismounted—were further forward, near the castle.

Over on the other wing, St Ruth's right wing at Tristaun bridge or the pass of Urraghry, the rough ground close to the stream was occupied by infantry, who were 'covered by numerous hedges and breastworks'. Behind them, on the ground lying between the stream and the site of Kilcommadan church, was the cavalry of the right wing. In front of them, beyond the stream and thrown well forward among the mounds and hollows of the esker, were dragoons.

Sir Patrick MacDougall, the first and perhaps the most brilliant of the professional soldiers who used the lessons of the Crimean and American civil wars to support their theories, said that 'the army which awaits attack in a chosen and prepared position has a great advantage'. But MacDougall would have distinguished clearly between the natural advantage enjoyed by St Ruth at Aughrim and the danger to which his position exposed him. St Ruth was fighting on the defensive and he was in occupation of a splendid defensive position. If fortune favoured him, he might thwart Ginkel's efforts to dislodge him, but he could scarcely have defeated Ginkel. At best, Ginkel, if he were repulsed, would have been no more than badly shaken. As the Williamites were to find, the approach to the ridge at Aughrim was difficult in the extreme. To mount a counter-attack from it would have been no less difficult. St Ruth's position was a dangerous one because it restricted his ability to manoeuvre. It was a last stand taken up before the end. Perhaps it was this that led the Duke of Berwick to say in his maturity that once Ginkel had succeeded in crossing the bog the battle was lost.

Furthermore, since Limerick was more important to St Ruth than Galway and must be regarded as his base, the Jacobites were drawn up at Aughrim with—in military parlance—their front to a flank. Their line of retreat, the line which what was left of them was eventually to follow, was not covered by their disposition of force on the battlefield; it was rather a prolongation of their right wing. St Ruth's anxiety for the security of his right is evident throughout the battle, and although the struggle was decided by what happened on the Irish left, strategic as well as local considerations in regard to the possibility of a turning movement through the pass of Urraghry powerfully affected it. If the Jacobite field army was cut off from Limerick the war might have been ended at a stroke.

Ginkel crossed the river Suck early on the morning of Sunday

12 July; the infantry marched over the bridge at Ballinasloe—
they must have taken a long time to do so—and the horse and
dragoons crossed at fords above and below it. The morning was
foggy. Up to that the weather had been wet; 8 July was a day of
'violent scorching heat', thunder and heavy rain. The army, which
advanced from the Suck in several columns, was prepared for
battle. Each musketeer carried fifteen charges, each foot regiment
marched with five pioneers in front, and the grenadiers, who
carried 'two shells a piece', marched on the flanks of their regiments. Ginkel had left detachments in Athlone and Ballinasloe, and
his field army cannot have amounted to much more than 20,000
men, that is, the same as his opponent's. He had twelve or thirteen
battalions of English infantry, three Ulster battalions, six Danish,
three Dutch and three French. His mounted force was stronger
than St Ruth's, being made up of thirty-four or thirty-five
squadrons of horse and thirteen or fourteen of dragoons. Four
each of the horse and dragoon squadrons were Enniskilleners, that
is, part of the Ulster Protestant formations which King William
called, when he commissioned them, 'our Inniskilling forces'.

Ginkel's order of battle, which was in general adhered to,
although the nature of the terrain and the exigencies of the
evening's work were to call for adjustments, provided for two
lines of infantry and wings of cavalry and dragoons. The Duke
of Würtemberg, the leader of the Danish mercenary force, was
Ginkel's second in command. Mackay was given command on the
right of the first line of infantry, where there were to be seven
English battalions under Brigadier Bellasis. Tettau was to lead
seven battalions of Huguenots and Danes under Brigadier La
Mellonière on the left. In the second line, which was to be weaker
than the first, Major-General Talmash, who, like Mackay, was a
newcomer to the Irish war, would have about seven more English
and Ulster battalions on the right, while Count Nassau was given
about as many Dutch and Danish battalions on the left. The
mounted force on the right was placed under Lieut.-General
Schravemoer for the first line and the Marquis de Ruvigny for
the second. The original intention was to have twenty-six or
twenty-eight squadrons of horse and dragoons there, with the
dragoons on the extremity of the wing. La Forest-Suzannet and
Holzapfel were the officers assigned to command the smaller
mounted force of about twenty-one squadrons, including the
three Danish regiments, of horse and dragoons on the left.

Again, the dragoons, according to the practice of the time, were to be the flank guard.

The Williamites soon made contact with the Irish. Danish cavalry of Donop's Regiment, riding in advance on the left, met St Ruth's vedettes south of Urraghry hill early in the afternoon. The Danes were reinforced by Cunningham's Enniskillen dragoons, who were switched over from their intended place on the right. These troops drove the Jacobites back on their outposts, and, when Portland's Regiment of horse joined in, the Irish gave ground and retired along the esker towards Tristaun. Ginkel rode forward with his staff when the skirmishers had moved on, and, coming to a height about half a mile east of Tristaun bridge, found that he could look along the slope of the ridge towards Aughrim and that he could make out the greater part of St Ruth's right and centre. He had been given a map of the district, probably by the Trenchs, who were local Protestant landowners, and he was already familiar with the general features of the terrain. He saw that the pass of Urraghry would, if St Ruth continued to hold his position, be difficult to force, but the ground beyond the stream, below the south end of the ridge, towards Kilcommadan church, appeared suitable for the deployment of horse and foot, and the possibility of turning what seemed to be the weaker, and what was tactically the more inviting, of the Irish flanks presented itself.

Meanwhile, Ginkel's army was coming into position behind him and was being drawn up along the high ground of Urraghry from the present Melehan bridge southwards, facing the Jacobites across the bog. Cannonading at long range had commenced. It was perhaps two o'clock and the day had brightened. The skirmishers were still in action near the ford at Tristaun in front of the Irish right wing. Cunningham's dragoons sought to work forward to 'certain ditches nigh the said ford'—or perhaps this refers to their activities when the fight commenced and a ford of the confluent streams where they bend south-eastward is meant—'to keep the enemy from coming over', and to move in, if possible, close to the main Irish position.

Ginkel was not yet certain that the battle would be fought that day. He was still feeling his way. Eppinger's Dutch dragoons had come up. Since skirmishing on the hillocks and broken ground of the esker was dragoon, and not cavalry, work, the earlier absence of Eppinger's men from the place assigned to them in the line of battle may explain the shift of Cunningham's Regiment from the right to the left wing. As at the Boyne, it was the dragoons who began the engagement. Although he was still uncertain of events, Ginkel was determined to win the ford at Tristaun bridge and 'other ways that led to the right of the enemy as the most proper ways to assault them', and Eppinger was thrown in to assist Cunningham and Portland. The two horse regiments of Ruvigny and Lanier were ordered over from the right wing, although not all of Ruvigny's Regiment came. 'Several fresh parties' of the Irish came up to support their skirmishers, Eppinger was foiled in his efforts to get between them and the ford, and the fighting continued as the afternoon waned. 'What was at first only a skirmish had by this time engaged a considerable body on both sides, fresh parties being still sent out,' says Story, 'though after about an hour's dispute the enemy were obliged to retire in some disorder over the brook that flanked the right of their army, no considerable damage being done as yet to either side.'

Ginkel now—it was about four o'clock—consulted his general officers. Some believed that little more could be done that day and the advisability of encamping for the night at Urraghry was discussed, but it was observed that St Ruth was moving troops from left to right—in conformity with Ginkel's movements—and Major-General Mackay, realising that it might now be possible to force a crossing at the more difficult pass at Aughrim castle, came out strongly in favour of an immediate and determined attack on both wings. Contact had been made neither with the Irish centre nor with their left, but it was seen that the Williamite forces had become so closely engaged at the Tristaun stream that it might be difficult to break off the action. There is some evidence too that they had pushed forward in excess of their orders. Ginkel decided to go on.

The battle was thus begun in earnest about five o'clock. The Irish, although they had been under arms all day, were for the greater part rested and in good spirits. Mass had been celebrated in the morning and the troops had been harangued by their preachers, including the redoubtable Dr Alexius Stafford, chaplain of the Foot Guards, and (we are told) by St Ruth. The men had been reminded that they were about to fight for their religion and to fight also to re-establish King James's authority and to secure 'the estates and liberties of an oppressed people'.

St Ruth had been most active; he 'rode constantly from one

side to another, to give the necessary orders, where he saw occasion'. He made some momentous changes in his disposition of force, apparently during the afternoon, while the fighting was heavy on his right wing. He moved both cavalry and infantry from left to right. This rearrangement has been much commented on and is generally accepted as a primary reason for the Irish defeat. But what was involved is not clear. A movement of Irish cavalry had almost certainly been made before Ginkel conferred with his generals and committed himself to a general engagement. Mackay had been led to advise the Williamite right attack by seeing Irish horsemen moving along the ridge. Sir John Dalrymple thought when he wrote his account of the Williamite war in the following century that St Ruth countered Ginkel's early aggression at the pass of Urraghry by detaching 'almost all his cavalry from his left wing to give greater strength to his right', but Dalrymple exaggerated. Sheldon was weakened and Sarsfield— if in fact he commanded the mounted force on the right wing —was strengthened, but there was no wholesale transfer.

The movement of infantry, which seems to have been made later, is the real crux. King James, or whoever composed that part of his memoirs, understood that St Ruth ordered 'the second line of the left to march to the right', but that 'he who was to execute that order [presumably Dorrington or Hamilton, or perhaps Barker, who was General of the Infantry] caused a battalion of the first line to file off with the rest, supposing the bog in the front would prevent the enemy's advancing'. The author of the Jacobite account entitled 'A Light to the Blind' speaks of Dorrington, when hard pressed—but this may have been when he was pressed by the English foot on his left centre later in the evening—ordering over two regiments of infantry that had been placed to guard the pass at the castle. The presumption is that these were the two battalions from the cornfield. Story tells us that 'several bodies of horse and foot' were moved from left to right. We must conclude that St Ruth did make a transfer of troops and that, as the fight developed, it weakened him at a vital point. His right, which he believed to be the weaker and the more important flank, held, but his left did not.

The boggy ground, which was 'to appearance incapable of being passed', proved a serious obstacle to Ginkel and forced him to confine his operations to the two wings. There was a considerable stretch of the front northward of the Bloody Hollow on which no action took place. As the sun declined and the shadows of the summer evening lengthened, the whole Williamite army went in to the attack. Both lines of infantry advanced, and soon 'there was no distance left between the first and second line'; indeed, many of the second line regiments were the first to be engaged, and where the ground suited the battalions were flanked by squadrons of horse.

On the rough stretches by the stream at Tristaun the Irish right wing fell slowly back. The Williamites, who were powerfully aided by their artillery, were fighting here not only in the hope—which they had not yet abandoned—of turning the wing, but also to compel the Irish to move further forces from the vicinity of the castle and thus to lighten the task of their comardes who were trying to win a passage there. The ford was eventually forced, but on the Irish side of the stream were the 'little old ditches', lined by the dragoons and infantry; where the ground was more open further back stood the dread Irish horse, the men who had done so well at the Boyne and who now, according to de Tessé, 'always had the advantage of their opponents'. It was as a protection against these horsemen that the attackers had interposed their own squadrons among their infantry units. 'Here', says Story, 'we fired one upon another for a considerable time and the Irish behaved themselves like men of another nation'. (Which one?—or was it all one to Story provided the very merits of the Irish could be made to look like shortcomings?) They defended the ditches stoutly, 'for they would maintain one side till our men put their pieces over at the other, and then, having lines of communication from one ditch to another, they would presently post themselves again, and flank us'.

Until Mackay's stubbornness and the development of the contest further along the ridge altered the course of the battle, little progress was made at the pass of Urraghry. The Williamite mounted troops were no match for their opponents on this side, nor indeed did the ground permit of much cavalry action. The Danish foot regiments did their best in a place which was 'all cut up by the marsh and by hedges and banks' and 'foot by foot more ground was occupied', but 'the enemy resisted much more vigorously than we had expected'. (Here the Duke of Würtemberg speaks, and he may indeed be speaking of a lateral movement as much as an advance, for the wing extended itself southward.) Although eighteen Williamite guns, 9, 6, and 3 pounders—

Ginkel must have increased his field artillery since he left Mullingar
—were in action on this wing and the Jacobites could muster no
more than three or four guns against them, neither the Danes nor
any other troops succeeded, while the Irish left held, in bursting
through to the level ground south of the ridge. The Huguenot
battalions from the left centre of the front line did best. Led by
their brigadier, La Mellonière, they got as far apparently as the
Bloody Hollow, but they stuck there. They stood behind the
shelter of a barricade of stakes or *chevaux-de-frise* and successfully
defended themselves against the Irish attacks. The name which
the declivity has since borne gives testimony of the fury of a
struggle which it witnessed during the battle and it seems that it
was this struggle of the French.

Further north, the fighting rapidly became even more intense.
A Williamite battery was moved up by the causeway leading to the
castle, the chief of the bog passages 'through which the roads go
to Galway', and fire was exchanged with the Jacobite gunners on
the first slope of the ridge. The whole right wing of foot moved
in, out of range, as yet, of the Irish musketeers. The dispositions
of the order of battle were abandoned and Talmash's battalions
from the second line were soon mixed with those of Bellasis
from the first. It would have been impossible, even if it were
advisable, for this large force to advance on the narrow causeway.
The wide extent of the bog on the right precluded a turning
movement. There was no possibility of progress save by facing
the bog and the stream to the south of the causeway and thus
seeking to widen the front of the attack.

The four English battalions of Earle, Herbert, Creighton and
Brewer advanced into the bog probably due west of Urraghry
House in the townland of Foats or Levallynearl, considerably less
than half a mile south of the Galway road at Melehan bridge. In
front of them, beyond the bog and low against the bright western
sky, was the northern end of the ridge. Between the bog and the
ridge the firm ground rose and then fell again and was cut across
by the hedges. They could see formed troops on the slopes, but
what might lie behind the hedges was unknown. It was about
half past six. The going was very difficult. Most of the Englishmen
were 'up to their middles in mud and water'.

They got across, Earle's battalion in front. They repaired their
formation, under orders to post themselves at the lowest of the
ditches and to hold their ground until the cavalry crossed above

them near the castle and came down to support them. Foulkes's from the first line and Stuart's from the second were coming up behind them on their left. The four battalions were now under fire. The hedges and ditches were quite close to the bog at this point and they were soon seen to be lined thickly with musketeers. Unable to stand for long to be fired on in the open, the English marched forward. Their enemies gave way before them and the first obstructions were cleared. But the Irish retired no further than the breadth of the first small fields. They crouched down again behind the next line of field boundaries and maintained their fire. Earle and his comrades were lured forward from field to field, their opponents retiring from ditch to ditch before them and firing on them from the lateral ditches on either side 'till they were got very nigh the enemy's main battle'. Here they found that openings had been cut in the field boundaries and passages made through which cavalry could ride in among them. Already disordered by the rough handling which they had received on their way up from the bog, fired into by the battalions of the Jacobite second line, and attacked by Sheldon's cavalry, the English infantry broke and retired precipitately. Many were killed and wounded and many, including Earle and Herbert, were taken prisoner. They had had no general officer with them; perhaps this had contributed to their discomfiture.

We pause, as students of military history should, to remark on the tactics of the Irish. We see that the English had been enticed—not for the first time in the Irish wars—into a carefully prepared position. Captain Robert Parker of Meath's Regiment, later the 18th Royal Irish, who fought in the battle and wrote of it afterwards, never realised that the Irish withdrawal, here and on their right wing, was deliberate. He speaks of a retirement after 'one scattering fire' and disparages the Jacobite foot. In the earlier centuries the effort had been to draw English forces into the bogs; now it was to draw them through boggy ground and to use the Irish hedges as fieldworks. As always, advantage was taken of the nature of the terrain to redress the balance as between the better organised and better equipped troops of the enemy and the more nimble, more adaptable products of the Irish countryside. Aughrim, where the Irish army was made up of the same kind of units as its opponents and was, as far as circumstances allowed, trained to fight as they did, and as all armies did at that time, still retained something of the characteristic flavour of the Irish battles; and it was greatly to St Ruth's credit that he appreciated the advisability of letting the Irish infantry fight as they wanted to fight. A century and a half later a romantic Irishman, Charles Beggs, was to extol the system of 'cuts made in hedges by St Ruth at the battle of Aughrim' and to propound a scheme of national resistance of invasion—it was really a blue print for insurrection—based on the successive defence of parallel hedges: 'Every ditch and hill, embankment or undulation, or accident of ground, commanding or bearing upon the approach of the enemy, must be occupied by our gunsmen; and if time permitted, these obstacles to the enemy's progress should be improved by art, with the view of detaining them under our fire and breaking their order of formation. Should the enemy hope to embarrass us by menacing our flanks, we have only to line the lateral ditches with a portion of our men and thus oppose a steady front to his flank attack'. And if we come still closer to our own time and consider how the belligerents of the last world war sought to contain Liddell Hart's 'expanding torrent' we may wonder if the 'men of another nation' were really as primitive as they have seemed to some who have written about them.

But, to return: while the English still sought unsuccessfully to come to grips with the Irish left centre, Mackay was doing his best to get the cavalry across on the right wing. His problem was twofold. He had to organise an approach and a subsequent deployment. Fully aware that the approach must be made over unfavourable ground and that his advance would be contested, he sent infantrymen in first. Kirk's and Gustavus Hamilton's Regiments from the right of the first line, braving the fire of Burke's men, marched against the castle and the trenches. The going was better here and they eventually succeeded in reaching dead ground behind a dry ditch. They could go no further, but they held on. The two battalions of Bellasis and George Hamilton also crossed by 'the defile or dirty lane that leads to Aughrim', or over the ground near it, and, reaching the shelter of a hedge, noted a clearing that had been made for the approach of the Irish cavalry and promptly set about barricading it with turnpikes. These two battalions then formed one body, 'close, without interval', and, crossing a plain field—was it the cornfield?—under heavy fire from the castle and the adjoining works, established themselves in some of the abandoned defences.

How far, one wonders, were these movements favoured by St

Ruth's withdrawal of forces from his left? Modern writers take it for granted that Mackay got in because the Irish had been taken out. Their authority is the memoirs of King James, which, as we remember, recount the removal of one Jacobite battalion from the left of the front line. The memoirs go on to say that 'they who stood in awe of that battalion while it faced them took courage when it was gone'. John Shirley, whose work was published in 1692, takes a different tone. Shirley says that 'the enemy's battalions and squadrons stood firm to the charge' in 'a corn field' after Mackay's troops had got over. We know very little about the disposal, unit by unit, of the Irish troops in any part of the field and although we must allow for the removal as something that weakened the Irish resistance on their left, the details elude us. All that is certain is that, by about eight o'clock, four English battalions had succeeded in making a lodgement on the Irish side of the pass.

Mackay tells us that he caused the stream—that is, either the stream that flows under the bridge beside the ruins of the castle or the Melehan river which drains Coololla bog—to be sounded, so as to measure the possibility of an attack on a wider front than that offered by the causeway. His anxiety mounted as he witnessed the fate of Earle's and the other three battalions. It was further increased by what followed. The two Ulster regiments of Tiffin and St John from the second line, probably Foulks's and Stuart's which had already started, a regiment of Huguenots from the left wing and some more marched into the bog at places to the south of those at which Earle and the others had crossed. The same fate awaited them. The Irish crouched so low behind their ditches that some of the attackers doubted if they were there at all, yet the troops were no sooner over than a furious fire was opened on them at twenty yards' range. They pressed forward and gave fire, 'though they could scarce see one another for smoke'. A vicious fight developed and 'the thing seemed so doubtful for some time that the bystanders would rather have given it on the Irish side'. The 2,000 or so Williamite infantrymen involved were drawn forward and then pressed back as before. The Prince of Hesse, coming over behind them—'I know not', says Mackay, 'on whose order'—with his own battalion from the second line on the left and some of the Dutch infantry, was involved in a mêlée which became 'very sanguinary'. Again the Irish prevailed. The attackers were driven down into the bog, and this time Dorrington's and

John Hamilton's men, 'making use of club musket'—which seems to suggest that they had no bayonets—and fighting until 'the blood flowed into their shoes', pursued them. 'The regiment of Guards [Dorrington's own regiment, veterans of the Boyne] and the whole royal brigade was particularly noted by the field to have performed uncommon execution'. In places, pursued and pursuers crossed the bog together. Gordon O'Neill's Regiment, whose colour was a white flag bearing the red hand of Ulster, reached, and for the moment captured, a Williamite battery—probably one that was placed south-west of Caltragh fort, a half-mile south of Melehan bridge, and one that contained a gun which, as we shall see in a moment, was destined to become historic.

St Ruth was overjoyed at the Irish success. '*Le jour est à nous, mes enfants*', he cried, and he spoke of driving Ginkel back to the gates of Dublin. But he was fighting a defensive battle and the Irish Guards—did they still have the piper who figures in their establishment of 1684?—O'Neill's regiment and the others were soon recalled to their former positions. Major-General Talmash, who commanded the second line of the Williamite right wing, rallied his depleted infantry and, strengthening them with his last remaining fresh men, succeeded in bringing them back over the bog to the Irish lines. The whole force of Ginkel's infantry was now engaged. Up to this, the units had, in very difficult circumstances, gone in piecemeal. They had received little support from actions elsewhere on the field. They had not been under unified control; indeed some of their commanders had exceeded orders. Now things were about to change.

The Williamite right wing cavalry was drawn up on a small patch of firm ground west of the present Melehan bridge, where the batteries were placed that had been firing on the castle and on the Jacobite guns. The guns on the ridge must have been silenced, or at least their effect must have been diminished, by this; otherwise the horsemen could scarcely have remained where they did. There were about fourteen squadrons, or more than a thousand men. Some of the five squadrons of dragoons on this wing, Leveson's and Wynne's Enniskilleners, were no doubt dismounted and were firing on the defenders of the pass. Mackay found that the troopers were most reluctant to face the perils of the causeway, yet there was no other way for them to go forward, since their horses would soon have foundered if they were ridden into the bog. And forward they must go. The Jacobite writer who called

Ginkel's right wing attack 'his last remedium' spoke no more than the truth. Nowhere else, at least for the few hours that remained of that day, was there a hope of success.

Mackay, a courageous man, rode down the causeway to encourage the others, but he was thrown from his horse, and got back only with difficulty. At length, under the Huguenot Marquis de Ruvigny, later to be Earl of Galway, who was apparently the senior cavalry officer present at this moment, the horsemen were led to make the attempt. Scrambling forward two by two and fired on by the Irish infantry and dragoons in the trenches and in the castle, they passed—not without losses—within thirty yards of Burke's men, forded the stream and won over. That part of Ruvigny's Regiment which had remained on the right wing— they were formerly Duke Schomberg's men—and Oxford's Royal Regiment of Horse Guards—later to be the Blues of the Household Cavalry—were in front. Oxford's Regiment, fighting desperately for ground on which to fight, charged forward. They were twice repulsed, but two squadrons of Langston's Regiment, two of Byerley's, Leveson's and Wynne's dragoons, and, seemingly, Wolseley's Enniskillen horse and two squadrons of Villiers's—it was they whom Sarsfield had routed at Ballyneety— came over behind them.

St Ruth was a witness of this operation. What, he asked, could those fellows mean by attempting such a crossing? He said that they were brave men, and he must have realised at once that they were a danger. We Irish—it is perhaps a characteristic of material weakness—are avid seekers and glad acceptors of explanations. Our history is full of disasters simply explained. We account for Mackay's and Ruvigny's success by saying that the defence of Aughrim castle was compromised by a mistaken withdrawal of troops and, to clinch the matter, we say that Colonel Burke was— again by mistake—left short of ammunition. 'A Light to the Blind' says that Burke's Regiment had French muskets, the bore of which was smaller than that of the standard English arms, but that their reserve ammunition contained English musket balls, which were useless to them. Later writers have modified, and amplified, the story. We are told that Burke was given cannon balls instead of musket balls, and that his men were constrained, for want of something better, to fire the buttons from their coats, and chopped rammers. What is the student of history to say? He must remember that the castle continued to hold out after the pass was forced, although this may be because Mackay was content to by-pass it. |Yet he cannot dismiss any part of his evidence. A shortage of ammunition may well have been a contributory factor to the Irish failure on the left wing.

With their cavalry across, the Williamites could develop their attack. Mackay now had a strong force of infantry and cavalry in direct contact with the Irish. The battalions of Kirk, the two Hamiltons and Bellasis, whose progress had hitherto been prevented by the Irish fire and of whom Mackay says that, had they not held firm, 'our right according to all human appearances would have been defeated and the battle lost', could at last move on. So could Talmash's force, weakened though it was by its reverse. Mackay sent the four battalions that were with him and some squadrons of horse against the left of the Irish line in the 'half a score little cabins' that made up the Aughrim village of the time and on the first slope of the ridge behind them. Ruvigny turned south-east with the remainder of the horse; they 'did extraordinary service, bearing down all before them' on the good cavalry ground beyond the ruins of the church, and soon linked up with Talmash. There was for a time 'nothing but a continued fire and a very hot dispute all along the line', the Irish infantry fighting stubbornly to hold their positions and the Williamites fighting just as stubbornly to eject them.

It was the crisis of the battle. If Mackay and Talmash were again forced back into the boggy ground, they must suffer very heavily; if the Irish gave way, St Ruth's whole position would be enfiladed.

The issue was soon decided. Sheldon's cavalry of the Irish left wing, which had not been very heavily engaged during the evening, was still intact. Clearly, Sheldon and his brigadier, Henry Luttrell, should have intervened to the full extent of their ability to hold Mackay back. There is little evidence that they did so. Their numbers had been reduced by the transfer to their right wing; still, even when allowance is made for the probability that their dragoons were fighting with the foot, they can scarcely have been much weaker than their mounted opponents—much weaker, that is, in numbers and material strength; morally, they had already been overcome.

Efforts to reconstruct scenes of passion and violence, conflicts in which the motives and movements of thousands are involved, founder on inability to establish the sequence of events. In particular, it is notoriously difficult to determine a breaking point. When did St Ruth die? Had he died before Luttrell moved off?

There is no evidence that St Ruth was daunted by Mackay's success at the causeway. On the contrary, both Williamite and Jacobite writers tell us that he ordered cavalry—Sheldon's cavalry—to oppose Mackay. Story says that St Ruth ordered a brigade of Irish horse to march up. 'A Light to the Blind' says that he instructed the left wing cavalry 'that had been idle all day' to attack the debouching Williamites. Charles O'Kelly has it that St Ruth resolved 'by advancing with the cavalry to make the victory complete'. King James's memoirs apply the order to 'all the cavalry'. They tell us that St Ruth proposed 'putting himself at the head' of his horsemen, 'which, being extreme good, would soon have dispersed those few squadrons of the enemy who as yet were but a forming', and they credit him at this stage with the admirable outburst: 'They are beaten, let us beat them to the purpose!'

St Ruth was then near the top of the ridge. De Tessé says that he was on the right, which, since—as we have seen—they form-ally shared the battlefield between them, can mean that he was anywhere to the right of the centre. More than one of our authorities says that he was moving over towards his left. Story says that he was moving downhill, and adds that he paused on the way to direct the fire of a battery; we know that there was a battery in the Jacobite centre but have no means of fixing its position on the map. Tradition marks quite emphatically the last point reached by St Ruth, and the Ordnance Survey map shows it more than a thousand yards south of the Church of Ireland rectory. There is no reason to discount this pinpointing. It was a thing to be remembered, and the spot matches the words of Story as being 'just under the enemy's camp' and above the place where Mackay's infantry crossed the bog and 'the main stress of the battle was fought'. Here St Ruth was 'killed with a great shot from one of our batteries'—he was decapitated by a cannon ball. The gun which fired this round was still pointed out to visitors in Dublin Castle up to the end of the eighteenth century, and, as is the way of folklore, tales are still told which credit the marksman-ship to a local renegade. But the shot was almost certainly fired not at a person but a place, the place where the gunner may well have made out the moving figures of the first squadron of the

Life Guard, which accompanied St Ruth. We remember Gordon O'Neill's momentary capture of a Williamite battery on the Urraghry side of the bog. A ball from a gun placed there could, at extreme range, have reached the fatal spot.

The Williamites knew nothing of the momentous casualty until the battle was over. The Irish, on the other hand, learnt of it at once. A cloak was thrown over the body and it was borne away. But the Life Guards had witnessed the disaster, and the news spread. De Tessé soon heard of the 'irreparable loss'. He makes much of the panic that ensued, but shows too that he was unable to control the forces of which he was now in command. Ruvigny's horse, having worked along the undulating ground between the bog and the road, turned upwards and burst into the midst of the infantry. De Tessé charged them with two squadrons (from his left wing?). Struck by three pistol balls and slightly wounded, he was for the moment successful, but his men had already lost heart. Their comrades were everywhere giving way—inconceivably, since they had already for ten hours shown such steadiness—and de Tessé's squadrons soon did the same. We hear no more of them, nor of him.

However, the real deterioration occurred on the left wing, and it is in this regard that we must regret most our inability to establish the sequence of events. Only Charles O'Kelly and the Duke of Würtemberg have stated the time of St Ruth's death; the Duke says that it occurred 'just at the beginning of the action', which must be wrong; O'Kelly's 'about sunset' is vague. The Jacobite writers attribute the moral breakdown to the death of the commander; they say that St Ruth died and the left wing cavalry rode off. We are told that Luttrell was at the pass 'with advanced troops', but that he withdrew from the field after a slight resistance to Mackay, and that Sheldon followed him. We are told further that the Irish infantry broke because their cavalry did not assist them, 'but, instead of that, giving all for lost, thought of nothing but saving themselves and so gave an entire victory to the English'.

Whatever happened happened very quickly. Quite clearly, it was the cavalry that decided the day, the Williamite horsemen by their use of superior numbers at the vital point, by their skill and by their devotion to duty, the Jacobite mounted troops by their faintness of heart. It seems equally clear that Luttrell's and Sheldon's withdrawal was not solely the result of a panic following the death of St Ruth. Rather was it a consequence of deterioration. The Jacobite cavalrymen, who had acquitted themselves so nobly at the Boyne, were now largely of the peace party. They had more to gain by compromise, more to lose by intransigence, than their poorer comrades of the infantry, and if they had any scruples at deserting the ragged foot they overcame them. It was not the first time that the mounted man, the man with the means of doing so, had saved himself and left the man on foot to die. History is full of such treachery, for what was treachery at Crecy where the French knights rode down their own crossbowmen was treachery also at Aughrim, where the upper class deserted the lower.

The Irish army was taken in the flank, the flank that everybody had supposed to be the stronger one, and rolled up from the left. The infantry held out in the centre as best they could after the cavalry had fled, but Ginkel's right wing continued southward, Talmash pressed forward from the bog and the Jacobites were forced quickly backward from ditch to ditch to the top of Kilcommadan hill.

Ginkel's left wing which had been held up for two hours by an unbreakable defence, a defence which had resisted attack and could not be outflanked, now found that it too could move forward. The Jacobite right gave way slowly. The second troop of the Life Guard, charged sword in hand by Ruvigny's Regiment, was almost wiped out; they lost seventy-two men killed and wounded, 'and would have lost more had they not worn cuirasses'. The dragoons and infantry held on for a while with equal tenacity; but the Williamite cavalry—Danish, Dutch, Huguenot and English —forced their way through at last to the open ground at the end of the ridge, where they could act with effect. Half an hour's hot fighting broke up the Irish right.

Night had come on by now and a misty rain was falling. All but the slaughter of the running infantrymen, who were finally scattered on the hilltop, was over. Most of the survivors of the foot regiments fled to the boggy ground to the westward. The cavalry rode towards Loughrea and Limerick. Aughrim castle surrendered. Colonel Burke, who had suffered heavy casualties, marched out with his major, eleven other officers and forty men. The Jacobite defeat was complete. They lost eleven standards of cavalry and dragoons, the colours of thirty-two infantry battalions, nine field guns, all their ammunition, tents and camp equipment, most of their small arms and about 4,000 men killed. The

Williamites too suffered heavily. Their casualties are variously stated; they were probably as many as 2,000.

The debate concerning the effect of St Ruth's death will no doubt be continued indefinitely. His contemporaries on both sides thought him a good soldier, and many of the Jacobites seem to have believed that they owed their defeat to his removal. Charles O'Kelly quotes it as 'the opinion of all' that if St Ruth had lived one hour more he would have won. Nationalist writers of modern times blame St Ruth for having kept his plan of operations to himself and say that his death left his army not only leaderless but ignorant of what should be done next. But this seems unlikely. Ginkel possessed the initiative throughout. St Ruth's total effort must have been to repel Ginkel's attack, which can only mean that he sought to counter each aggressive movement as it was made by his opponent; this was the course which he followed throughout the day, and which his army followed while he remained in command of it. It would be naïve to suppose that he had some masterly counterstroke up his sleeve. In the circumstances of the battle, the best that the Jacobites could have done would have been to destroy for the moment Ginkel's capacity for continued aggression and to have remained unbeaten by nightfall.

The real confusion regarding Aughrim arises from two things: the rush of events after Mackay had forced the pass at the castle and the uncertainty which surrounds Patrick Sarsfield. The battle was over by about nine o'clock. It must have been later than eight o'clock when Mackay and Ruvigny began to debouch from the mouth of the pass. In that short time St Ruth was killed, Luttrell's defection occurred and—to speak with the utmost objectivity— the chances of the attackers steadily improved. Fighting was intense, and events as they occurred must have been infinitely more bewildering for those who were involved than they are for us who try to survey them. But for the Irish infantry the battle was still—indeed it was now more than ever—a matter only of defence.

And Patrick Sarsfield? As we have seen, Sarsfield's position on the field is uncertain, although the happenings of the last phase of the struggle do much to confirm the statement that he commanded the augmented cavalry force on the right wing. These troops had not been heavily engaged during the afternoon or evening. Captain Parker's description of 'the greatest and best part' of the Jacobite cavalry can apply only to them; Parker applies it to Sarsfield's command, but calls the troops to whom he refers 'a reserve body of horse' and says that Sarsfield was posted, not on the right, but in the rear of the centre. Since Parker was one of those who helped to overcome the Irish centre from the north, the Irish right wing would for him, at the end of the battle, have been 'in the rear of their centre'; it would also, since it had not up to that been directly engaged, have been in the position of a reserve. Perhaps this is the explanation of his very positive but perplexing statement.

We are dependent on Parker for much of our information about Sarsfield. It is he who says that St Ruth gave Sarsfield 'positive directions not to stir from thence [that is, from the post in which he was placed] until he received his orders'. This is the nightmare 'order to await orders' which, through history, has broken so many hearts, destroyed so many reputations and lost so many battles. Parker goes on to say that Sarsfield was 'very punctual' in obeying St Ruth, that he had had many opportunities of service but would not stir until he had orders to do so, and that had St Ruth lived 'to order Sarsfield down to sustain his left wing, it would have given affairs a turn on that side'. Later writers have imputed a sinister meaning to these statements, a meaning which they do not necessarily bear. They suggest that St Ruth was jealous of Sarsfield and that he deliberately kept him out of the battle. But is it not just as likely that, fearing for his right, he placed his best man there? Still the enigma.

We are told that Sarsfield's first intimation of disaster was conveyed to him by the fugitives who came streaming down from Kilcommadan hill. There is nothing significant in this. There can have been little time for communication with the right wing. The rout was precipitate and the confusion following St Ruth's death must have been very great; de Tessé, who does not mention Sarsfield, was otherwise engaged. Sarsfield and Galmoy, the leader of the only unit that had been kept in reserve, did what they could to cover the retreat of the survivors. Again, this action of Sarsfield's strengthens the probability that he was on the right.

Save for Sheldon, Luttrell and their men, the Irish fought well. 'Never did the Irish fight so well in their own country as they did this day.' 'Never was an attack made with more bravery and courage, and never was it known that the Irish fought with more resolution.' These are Williamite tributes. The battle in which the Irish lost 'the flower of their army and nation' was, for the more candid of Ginkel's soldiers, an 'unexpectedly successful action'.

Aughrim was the last battle of the war, and the last big battle fought in Ireland. Galway surrendered on 21 July, Limerick on 3 October. A new phase in the history of Ireland was begun.

The documentation on which this account of the battle of Aughrim is based is set out in my article 'The Battle of Aughrim, 1691', which was written in 1942 and is published in the *Journal of the Galway Archaeological and Historical Society*, XX, pp. 1–30. References to King James's memoirs, Charles O'Kelly, 'A Light to the Blind', Parker, Story and other contemporary authorities will be found there. This account has been completely re-written and I have altered some of the statements which I made twenty-five years ago. I was very greatly influenced by the views of my friend Diarmuid Murtagh—since, alas, dead—in changing my earlier statement regarding Patrick Sarsfield's position on the battlefield. Diarmuid Murtagh made a deep study of the Jacobite army, which one hopes will be published some day. He knew more about Aughrim than anybody of my generation, with the possible exception of Martin Joyce, who has lived on the battlefield for years and knows every blade of grass on Kilcommadan hill. In particular, it was Diarmuid Murtagh who first showed me that there was no 'reserve' which Sarsfield could have commanded.

The authorities for the Boyne mentioned on pp. 236 f above are relevant also for Aughrim. There is a good modern account by D. Murtagh in *The Irish at War* (Cork, 1964, edited by me) and his paper on the siege of Athlone, published in the *Journal of the Royal Society of Antiquaries of Ireland*, LXXXIII, pp. 58 ff, should also be seen. For the Athlone bridge of the siege see J. S. Joly, *The Old Bridge of Athlone* (1881). J. C. O'Callaghan's description of Aughrim (*The Green Book*, 2nd edn, 1844, pp. 179 ff) must be read as the work of one deeply committed to make a good case for his countrymen at a time when such advocacy was, on nationalistic grounds, badly needed. We forgive O'Callaghan's exaggeration and lack of objectivity because he was such a patriotic enthusiast, and, asking pardon for our own deficiencies, bow humble heads before his scholarship and his extraordinary industry. His account of Aughrim is the most detailed of all.

In regard to Story's statement 'The place where this battle was fought will make a noise in history for the future' (*A Continuation of the Impartial History of the Wars of Ireland*, p. 136), we might remark that on 12 July 1857, when Sir Henry Havelock was marching on Cawnpore, during the Indian Mutiny, one of his officers reminded him that it was the anniversary of the battle of the Boyne. Havelock corrected him—it was not, he said; it was the anniversary of Aughrim.

T. W. Tone's reference to Louis XIV occurs in his journal under date 21 March 1796 (R. B. O'Brien, *The Autobiography of Theobald Wolfe Tone*, 1893, I, p. 289). The contemporary of Tone whose summary statement is quoted is Thomas Somerville (*The History of Political Transactions and of Parties from the Restoration of King Charles the Second to the death of King William*, 1792, Ch. xii). The quotation from P. L. MacDougall occurs in *Modern Warfare as influenced by Modern Artillery* (1864), p. 169—and see J. Luvaas, *The Education of an Army* (1965), pp. 101 ff for an opinion of MacDougall. Note the wise words of C. F. Clery (*Minor Tactics*, 8th edn, p. 184): 'A defensive attitude should be only assumed with the intention of converting it into an offensive one during the course of the action. To remain permanently on the defensive would at best prevent the enemy from gaining a victory, but would never secure it for the defenders.' The statement of C. Beggs is made in *The Military Resources of Ireland*, 2nd edn. (1857), p. 43 (and see my article 'The defence of Ireland—a century ago' in *An Cosantoir*, October 1948).

A new biography of Patrick Sarsfield is badly needed. J. Todhunter's *Life of Patrick Sarsfield* (1895) is outdated. What has become the popular view of Sarsfield at Aughrim is set out by O'Callaghan (*Green Book*, pp. 198, 215, 218, 222 f), by R. H. Murray (*Revolutionary Ireland and its settlement*, pp. 215, 217 f), by S. Gwynn, (*Studies in Irish History, 1649–1775*, pp. 253 ff and *The Fair Hills of Ireland*—where there are two delightful views of Aughrim by H. Thomson—pp. 260 f) and very many other writers. Mathew O'Conor's judgment of Ballymore, 'vanity induced the defence, and incapacity the surrender' (*The Irish Brigades*, 1855, p. 135), seems unjustified. The best account of Sarsfield's activities during the winter of 1690–1 is given in H. Mangan, 'Sarsfield's defence of the Shannon, 1690–91' (*The Irish Sword*, I, pp. 24 ff).

For the preservation of the gun which was said to have killed

St Ruth see J. Walker, 'Armour and Weapons of Ireland' in *Irish Bards*, II, p. 155. For the stories of the local residents at Aughrim who pointed out St Ruth to the gunner see P. K. Egan, *The Parish of Ballinasloe* (1960), pp. 105 ff. Luttrell's pass, through which the Irish left wing cavalry is said to have ridden off, is marked on the Ordnance Survey 6 inch map, Galway, sheet 87—on which map the course of the battle is best followed. The memorial erected to commemorate the fallen stands where Burke's men strove to defend the causeway. As to the rank of d'Usson and de Tessé, we should note that they are called Lieut.-Generals in the Treaty of Limerick.

Arklow, 1798

The reader can scarcely have failed to note the Williamite view
that Irish soldiers had never fought so well *in their own country* as
they did at Aughrim. This sentiment, much more forcefully—
perhaps cynically—expressed by Voltaire, and echoed by a
hundred others, maddened the nationalists of the old school.
Voltaire's assertion that 'the Irish have always fought badly at
home' drove J. C. O'Callaghan to write the essay which forms the
greater part of the famous *Green Book*, an essay in which, by playing up the heroism and skill of Sarsfield and his comrades, the
'literary agitator' strove to refute the man who 'formed the mind
of liberal Europe'.

To fight really well one must not only be *able* to do so, but
must also be equipped for the task. There were many reasons for
the poor equipment of the Irish when they fought at home, the
chief of which—that Ireland is a poor country—we have always
been strangely unwilling to recognise. However this may be, the
two centuries after Aughrim were the great period of Irish
military achievement abroad. The Irish soldier of Voltaire's
century established his reputation principally in the service of
France; in O'Callaghan's, his flags were British, American and
many others, but seldom his own. The Irish people showed their
real spirit in arms in Ireland only once in the eighteenth century.
That was during the insurrection of 1798.

The insurrection was overcome by the government within a
month of its outbreak. It had been anticipated by the authorities
and it was carried on by the insurgents without either a general
plan or effective leadership; but the elements that struggled then
with such bitterness and intensity were irreconcilable. Although
peace was soon imposed, the materials of strife remained. Some
days after hostilities began Lord Camden, the Lord Lieutenant,
predicted that 'the struggle will be violent and bloody, and will
shake the connection between the two countries'. Neither he nor
Wolfe Tone—who wanted to *break* the connection—could have

anticipated that the ordeal of shaking would be prolonged for more than a century. To us, the rebellion of 1798, as well as being the last Irish war until our own day, is the first with a recognisable aim. And perhaps even Voltaire would have admitted that the insurgents, who had scarcely any equipment, fought well.

In Ireland in the eighteenth century the caste of the ascendancy which owed its power ultimately to the British connection and its land to the confiscations and plantations of the past, differed in origin, in outlook and in religion from the remainder of the population. The mass of the people had no power, little wealth and no institutions of their own save their church. In the rebellion of 1798 these two elements were at each other's throats. Fought out in the midst of a great war with revolutionary France, and inspired by French ideas, the rebellion was a double threat to Britain, a threat to the ascendancy on which her Irish power was founded and an invitation to her mortal enemies the French to invade Ireland. If Colonel Blacker dipped his pen in gall, he at least conveyed (for one side) the authentic feeling of the age when he wrote:

> They come, whose deeds incarnadin'd
> 　　the Slaney's silver wave—
> They come, who to the foreign foe the
> 　　hail of welcome gave;
> He comes, the open rebel fierce—he comes,
> 　　the Jesuit sly;
> But put your trust in God, my boys, and
> 　　keep your powder dry.

The physical support of the ascendancy and of the British connection lay in the sabres and bayonets of not much more than 80,000 men. Something less than half of these were soldiers only in name—the District Corps and Volunteers, that is, the yeomanry, which had been formed in 1796, and which was the Home Guard and the political police of the ascendancy. Less than a further quarter—23,000, to be more exact—was made up of the Irish Militia. The militiamen, first raised in 1793, were largely Catholics; although their officers were Protestant and were drawn from the landlord class, the force was considered unreliable. The remainder —cavalry, infantry and artillery—were either weak regular formations or fencibles, that is, men who had been enlisted for service within these islands for the duration of the war. There were some

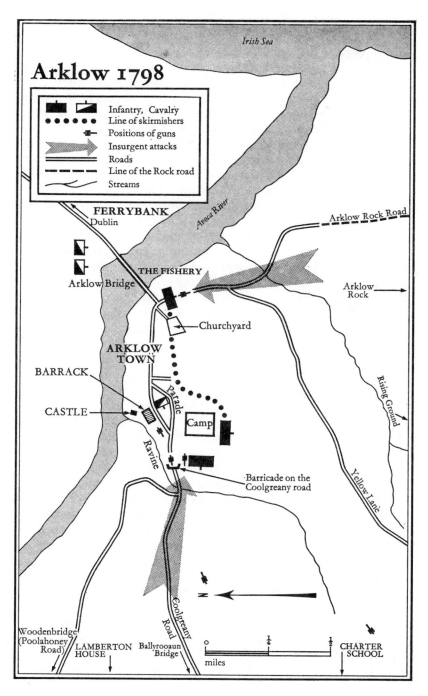

Arklow 1798

Infantry, Cavalry
Line of skirmishers
Positions of guns
Insurgent attacks
Roads
Line of the Rock road
Streams

Irish Sea

FERRYBANK
Dublin

Avoca River

Arklow Rock Road

Arklow Bridge

THE FISHERY

Arklow
Rock

Churchyard

ARKLOW
TOWN

BARRACK

CASTLE

Parade

Camp

Rising Ground

Ravine

Barricade on the
Coolgreany road

Yellow Lane

N

Woodenbridge
(Poolahoney
Road)

LAMBERTON
HOUSE

Coolgreany
Road

Ballyrooaun
Bridge

miles

CHARTER
SCHOOL

8,000 regular and fencible cavalry, 13,000 regular and fencible infantry and 1,500 artillerymen.

This force was not a formidable one. The regulars were seriously under strength. Sir John Moore, who served in Ireland during the rebellion, placed the total strength of the eight regiments of regular infantry at the end of 1797 at 1,803, as against an establishment figure of 5,824. The yeomanrymen were, of course, distributed throughout the country according to their places of ordinary residence, and their service, when embodied, was restricted to their own localities. The troops were widely scattered in small detachments with little or no apparent regard to the dictates of defensive strategy. Discipline was poor. Long continuance on garrison and out-quarter duty and, as far as the officers were concerned, a pleasant, easygoing life in which balls, theatricals and festivities figured prominently, had sapped the morale of the regular cavalry regiments. Most of the officers had leave for the greater part of the year and the men had long furloughs. Only for two months or so during the year were all the troops of a regiment assembled together for exercise and review; men served their full time in the ranks never having left the country and never having heard a shot fired in war. The regular infantry units, which were indeed only cadres, were little better. The fencibles, which were organised both in cavalry and infantry regiments, were quite untried. The fencibles were, says one writer—who is perhaps guilty of a little exaggeration—remarkable for 'the most wretched discipline', and their officers exhibited 'the most dishonourable sentiments and ignorance'. There were on the Irish establishment at the outbreak of the rebellion two Irish and five British regiments of fencible cavalry. The Irish regiments had been raised in 1795 and the British ones had come to Ireland in 1797. There were twenty-five regiments of fencible infantry, all British; eighteen of these had come to Ireland in 1795, two in 1796 and five in 1797.

The militia, which had been continuously embodied, or placed on permanent service, since their first formation in 1793, were all infantry. Their numbers had been made up both by balloting and volunteering, and they were organised in thirty-seven county and city battalions or regiments. Their term of original enlistment had, by the rebellion, just expired, and, although the majority appears to have re-enlisted, there were some raw recruits in their ranks.

The government was, as has been said, worried about the militia. With its formation, and the raising in 1793 of the Connaught Rangers and other regular Irish regiments, arms had been for the first time formally entrusted to Catholics. This was a measure dictated by the necessities of war, since Protestant manpower was not inexhaustible; but was it wise? The militia entered upon the suppression of the rebellion under a cloud. Sir John Moore was very much the regular soldier when he spoke of them. He said that they were 'extremely undisciplined' and, 'except that they are clothed with more uniformity, they are as ignorant and as much a rabble as those who have hitherto opposed us'. Lord Cornwallis, who was both Lord Lieutenant and Commander-in-Chief in the later stages of the rebellion, believed that the militiamen were 'contempible before the enemy when any serious resistance is made to them, but ferocious and cruel in the extreme when any poor wretches with or without arms come within their power'. Although this was not the universal view—Castlereagh, the Irish chief secretary, for example, reflected that 'in no instance has the militia failed to show the most determined spirit'—it was a pretty general one. But events were to show that mistrust of the milita was quite unjustified. In fact, it would not be difficult to make out a case for the militia units as those which put down the revolt. Treated with cold condescension by the military and active mistrust by the civilians, the militia belied the fears of both; the militiamen went on discharging the thankless task of their allegiance even when it meant firing on their fellow-countrymen and co-religionists.

The yeomanry, on the other hand, was the 'sheet anchor' of the administration. The yeomen were the realists. The enemies whom they expected to meet were not the invading French, but the disaffected peasantry; they entered the struggle primarily as the defenders of their own interests, and they were grimly conscious that these interests would be the first to be assailed. The yeomanry was organised under the king's commission in a uniform scheme of small local corps of both cavalry and infantry. The corps were raised and to some extent equipped by the local magnates, but the government provided their arms. They were on permanent service throughout the rebellion, when their numbers, largely because of an addition to existing corps of so-called supplementaries, showed a rapid increase to some 50,000 men. Their purpose was the preservation of the peace, by the fulfilling of which duty it was hoped that the regular and militia army would be released for the defence of the country. In the circumstances of the revolt, however, the yeomanry became a combat force.

If the forces in Ireland were below establishment strength, the number of troops available for action in the field was lower still. Their dispersal for use as police had seen to that. Ten thousand men were required in April 1798 for garrison and non-combatant duties, and the assembly in less than a week of another 10,000 for field service—should the occasion arise—was regarded as a matter of extreme difficulty. Sir Ralph Abercromby, who was then Commander-in-Chief, said that no more than 6,000 could be assembled for action in four or five days if the French should appear either at Bantry bay, where they had come little more than a year before, or the Shannon.

All this was bad enough, but it was not the worst. The civil and military branches of the administration were at loggerheads. Up to December 1797, when Lord Carhampton was succeeded by Abercromby, the office of Commander-in-Chief had been subject to the control of the viceroy. A political rather than a military hand had guided the destinies of the army. The open sore in the Irish body politic which had prevented Catholic emancipation and the reform of parliament and which eventually goaded the people to revolt made the maintenance of an efficient army impossible. A country rapidly becoming lawless suggested a policy of frightfulness, and in carrying out such a policy the troops became demoralised and undisciplined; the worse the troops became, the more lawless grew the country, and the closer Ireland drifted to revolt.

Abercromby, a good general and a humane man, and one who knew Ireland, insisted on having absolute command. He was opposed particularly to the indiscriminate calling out of the troops in aid of the civil power, saying that 'the best regiments in Europe could not long stand such usage'. The culmination of his efforts was the famous general order of February 1798, which pronounced the army to be 'in a state of licentiousness which must render it formidable to everyone but the enemy'. Opposed both in Dublin and London, Abercromby resigned. Years later, he wrote: 'Although the French Revolution and Jacobin principles may be the immediate cause of the events which have lately taken place in Ireland, yet the remote and ultimate cause must be derived from its true origin, the oppression of centuries'. It is interesting that the best two soldiers who served in Ireland during the crisis, Abercromby and Moore, should have shared sentiments so utterly unpopular in their circle. Abercromby was succeeded in an acting capacity by General Lake, who had commanded in Ulster during the provocative disarmament of that province in 1797. It was under Lake that the insurgents were fought; the rebellion was all but crushed when Lake was in turn superseded by Lord Cornwallis.

Many changes had taken place in military organisation and armament in the century which had elapsed since Aughrim. The cavalrymen who fought against the insurgents in 1798 were organised in regiments of eight or nine troops of regulars or six troops of fencibles. The troop was the administrative unit; for tactical purposes, two troops were combined to form a squadron. Troopers carried swords, or, more correctly—since they had but one cutting edge—sabres. They also had pistols and carbines. Yeomanry cavalry may have had only one pistol each and may have used their second pistol holster to carry ammunition and provisions, as their counterparts did in England. Few carbines were carried either by fencibles or yeomen, although the Camolin yeomanry cavalry, which fought at Arklow, had as many carbines as sabres.

Combat formation had been reduced in recent years from three ranks to two, with, in close order, a distance of half a horse's length between ranks and six inches from boot top to boot top—can they ever have maintained such exactitude?—between files. Cavalry was an attacking, not a defensive, force, and with this in mind the troopers were subjected to an elaborate course of training which was designed to secure an exact alignment of their two ranks. Cavalry regulations laid it down as an axiom that the onset of two parallel, even and unbroken lines on an enemy's front 'will always ensure his defeat', and the troopers were trained to trot sword in hand until they were 250 yards from their opponents and then to cover the remaining distance at a gallop— but always in line. To be able to charge in this fashion was all that was required of them. They knew little of dismounted work, skirmishing, patrols or outpost duty. Although they were all classed either as heavy or light dragoons, they resembled the dragoon formations of Aughrim only in name; the old practice of employing dragoons as mounted infantry had died out.

This arrangement had, of course, one supreme advantage.

It ensured, in the onset, a maximum shock. But it had many disadvantages, all of which became apparent in the engagements of the insurrection. The horsemen, on the whole, made a poor showing in 1798. Shock tactics, in the few instances where they could be used, generally failed before the rebels' pike formation, as they had failed centuries before in the classic days of the pikemen, and as Major-General Henry Lloyd—who theorised in 1781 on the results of the Seven Years War, but who knew nothing, of course, of things Irish—suggested they must fail. Furthermore, drill book formation proved largely useless for action in a closed country such as Ireland, where walls, hedges, scattered woodland, patches of bog and broken ground were the ordinary features. Lack of training for dismounted work was shown to be a serious deficiency. It was because of all this that Lake and others requested in June 1798 that reinforcements from England should consist principally of infantry.

The infantry acquitted itself well in Ireland. So did the artillery. Between them, they bore the brunt of the fighting. Infantry was organised in battalions, the regulars and fencibles of ten companies each, the militia of from five to twelve. We may use the words battalion and regiment interchangeably, although regular regiments sometimes had more than one battalion. It will be remembered that the battalions of Aughrim contained each a grenadier company. So did those of 1798, although, the use of grenades having meanwhile almost died out, grenadiers were now the élite of their unit, rather than the bearers of a special weapon. The martial developments of the intervening century included the introduction of a new class of specialised troops, the light infantry, and each battalion now contained a light infantry company as well as a company of grenadiers. Since the duty of protecting the flanks of the battalion was assigned to the specialist troops, the grenadier and light infantry companies were called the flank companies; the remainder were the line or battalion companies. Light infantrymen, who were lightly equipped, and were trained to fight in open or skirmishing order and to act as individuals, were largely a product of the war of the American revolution. They were frequently detached from their battalions and grouped together, as the light companies of the militia were under Moore in his advance into Wexford after the date of the battle of Arklow. Their service foreshadowed the abandonment of linear formation and of the system which compelled men to fight erect and shoulder to shoulder in the open, but this abandonment lay very much in the future.

When light infantrymen were required to form line for combat, they did so in two ranks. Very soon, British infantrymen as a whole were to adopt this formation, which was to be peculiar to them and was to earn their own proud appellation 'the thin red line'. But the infantry line of 1798 was composed of three, not two, ranks. In this order, the front rank frequently fired from a kneeling position and then sprung up to load. The centre rank then fired, the men composing it having stepped a 'moderate pace' to the right to clear their file leaders, or the men in front of them. Next, the centre rank reloaded and resumed its position. Finally, the men in the rear rank stepped a 'full pace' to the right, fired, reloaded and stepped back. Sometimes the rear rank withheld its fire, because, although each motion of making ready, presenting, firing and reloading was carefully regulated by the manual exercise, or book of rules, firing over the combined shoulders of file leaders and centre rank men was a matter of great difficulty; the fact that it was so, and that accidents happened and the all-important alignment was broken, was the reason for the eventual omission of the third rank. Where the nature of the ground forbade linear formation, as in the defence of a built up area, infantry was formed in column and 'street firing' was used: each rank fired and filed off by the flanks to form up in the rear, opening the front for the next rank behind it to fire. Cover was occasionally, but by no means generally, availed of. The battalion was, in effect, a firing machine.

The infantry arm was the musket, supplemented by the bayonet. All firearms were now of the same type. They were all flintlocks, or, as they are frequently called in contemporary contexts, firelocks. The matchlock had disappeared. The musket was the heavy, brass-mounted weapon popularly known as Brown Bess, the second part of which term is merely the German *Büchse*, or gun. Muskets were of a standard bore, about ·753. They had barrels 39 or 42 inches long and steel rammers, and they weighed about ten pounds. Ball ammunition was made up in cylindrical paper cartridges. These were torn open at one end by the teeth, sufficient powder to act as priming was poured into the pan, and the remainder, together with the ball and the paper container, was rammed down the barrel from the muzzle of the gun. The troops, always ready for a joke, called the fifty rounds which each carried on active service 'Lake's pills for a breaking out', in allusion to the general who was most prodigal in the use of musketry as the antidote for insurgency. Really effective musket range was no more than about a hundred yards and the rate of fire of well trained men was about three rounds a minute, aimed fire, or six rounds unaimed.

The bayonet was the same socketed weapon that had completely replaced the original plug and ring bayonets after the date of Aughrim. Its blade was triangular in cross-section and was about sixteen inches long; a slot cut in the socket was engaged by a half turn on the foresight of the musket to hold the fixed bayonet rather shakily in place. Service accoutrements included two whitened leather crossbelts, one to support the bayonet and scabbard, the other the ammunition pouch. Swords were no longer worn in the ranks. Sergeants had lain their halberds aside about 1792 and now carried pikes—like their insurgent opponents! All classes of infantry were armed and equipped alike and all units which fought in the battle of Arklow, to which we must in a moment devote our attention, wore the red coat.

The third arm, artillery, had seen most improvement in the eighteenth century. Although the guns were in type still the same, and remained so until rifling and breech loading were widely introduced sixty or so years later, gun carriages had become lighter and the cannon were in consequence much more mobile. Some of the lighter guns were mounted on 'galloper' carriages, the trails of which were adapted so that they could be used as shafts for horses. The so-called curricle guns seem to have been of this type. Howitzers, or field guns for high angle fire, had been introduced. In order to provide infantry with constant artillery support, the practice of allocating two 6-pounders—the so-called battalion guns—to each infantry battalion had been adopted. These were usually served by gunners of the Royal Irish Artillery, which had been formed in 1756, but it seems that infantrymen sometimes made up part of their crews. The projectiles fired by the field guns were round or common shot—that is, the solid ball—case shot or canister, and grape shot. Each had, of course, a proportion of gunpowder, separately inserted by means of a ladle, or as a cartridge, to make up the charge. Case shot consisted of a number of balls packed together in a cylindrical container; grape, which was designed to provide against the not unlikely eventuality of failure of the cylinder to burst, was made up of balls held together by cord netting. The charges of these two, the forerunners of shrapnel, the explosive projectile of the future, were widely dispersed when fired and were deadly when used at close range against massed attacking forces, as the insurgents learnt to their cost. Napoleon's 'whiff of grapeshot' rattled as destructively at Arklow, New Ross and Antrim as in the streets of Paris. The effective ranges of 6-pounder guns were 600 to 800 yards with roundshot and 300 or more—indeed an effective range of nearly 600 yards was claimed in 1792—with case and grape. Practised gunners could fire even more rapidly than infantry.

The rebellion, as we have said, was anticipated by the government, which was well aware of the intentions of the revolutionary organisation, the Society of United Irishmen, although nobody realised that when the people did rise their effort would be so formidable. Those of us who are willing to believe the worst of England have said sagely that the rebellion was deliberately provoked in order to let blood run and to provide an excuse for the union of the parliaments. Yet, if there was provocation at anything higher than the local level of men constrained by motives of their own to whip their own underdogs it must have been, for the statesmen or the politicians involved, a matter of sheer imbecility. Britain had enough to do to fight France without involving herself in another war in Ireland. And provocation surely implies military preparation, of which there was none. No effort was made, in the months before the outbreak, to build up, or to alert, the forces in Ireland. It seems highly improbable that the rising was 'managed'—mismanaged, yes, both politically and militarily, but not coldly, cynically and criminally brought on.

Fighting occurred in several areas following the outbreak of the revolt on 23 May. The insurgents were in places initially successful and they showed that, where circumstances favoured them, they could for the moment master the tiny government forces by which they were opposed. But the tide soon turned. Meath was quietened. So was Kildare, and within a week the first threat to Dublin had been removed. Meanwhile, however, the people of Co. Wexford, the latest county to suffer the cruelties of military repression, took up arms. By the end of the month a rebel force which increased in numbers as the days went by and the leaders of which declared themselves to be 'associated and united for the purpose of procuring our just rights' had made itself supreme in the southern part of the county. The insurgents scored their initial success when they defeated a detachment of 110 men of the North Cork Militia at Oulart. They then took the towns of Enniscorthy and Wexford. In June, encouraged by their achievements so far and anxious to protect from the inevitable depredations of the yeomanry the districts which they had vacated for their move south, they turned northward and westward. Columns—if one can apply that word to moving masses—were despatched up the Slaney valley, towards Gorey and towards New Ross. These insurgents were defeated at Bunclody, and again outside Gorey, on the first of the month, and their leader Beauchamp Bagenal Harvey—'of all men', says Sir Jonah Barrington, 'probably the most unfit for so desperate an enterprise'—suffered defeat at New Ross on 5 June. A first government attempt to move into Wexford and to confine the most serious part of the rising to that county had led to the occupation of Carnew, Arklow and Bunclody by 1 June. It was intended that the troops from Carnew and Arklow should come together at Gorey, that those who were in Bunclody should join at Ferns, and that the combined force should then attack the insurgents at their main encampment on Vinegar hill outside Enniscorthy and should press forward towards Wexford. The first part of this military movement had been carried out by 3 June.

On the day following, however, the insurgents routed one column of the combined Gorey force at Tubberneering; Lieut.-Colonel Walpole, who commanded the column, was killed. Major-General Loftus, who commanded the second column of 250 men, and who had penetrated south of the insurgents, retired to Carnew and thence into Carlow. Lord Ancram retired similarly with the Bunclody force.

The insurgents gained much by this victory. Because of the direction taken in retreat by Loftus and Ancram, the way northward towards Wicklow and Dublin lay open. The only troops left on the Dublin road south of Wicklow—where there was a small force under Major Joseph Hardy of the Antrim Militia—were seventy-eight men of the same regiment under Captain Rowan in Arklow and Walpole's fugitives. Walpole had had with him at Tubberneering detachments of the Armagh, Antrim (probably the grenadier company) and North Cork Militia, the light companies of the Tyrone Militia and Suffolk Fencibles, the grenadier company of the Londonderry Militia, a few artillerymen and a detachment of the Ancient British Fencible Cavalry. He had had also some yeomanry, and his whole force made up some 600 men. The casualties of the brief encounter amounted perhaps to a hundred. The remainder, completely demoralised, and having lost two 6-pounders and a howitzer to the rebels, fled through Gorey towards Arklow. Later on, the army was to refer to the engagement as the Gorey races.

Sir Watkin Williams Wynne of the Ancient Britons had succeeded Walpole in command and Lieut.-Colonel Cope covered the retreat with some of his Armagh militiamen. But Wynne found it impossible to rally the panic-stricken troops; many threw away their arms and accoutrements and some, fearing ill-treatment if they were captured in uniform, turned their coats inside out.

Nor did the flight end in Arklow. Rowan had thrown up a banquette, or firing platform, against the wall of the barrack yard and had mounted the garrison's one field gun to fire over a part of the wall which—despite many changes—still exists, and to sweep the Gorey road. But Wynne's officers saw no prospect of a successful defence of the town against the Wexford rebels, whose advent was momentarily expected. The wailings of the civilian refugees, who feared massacre, increased the general panic. Wynne himself had been wounded in the hand, and his report suggests that he was agitated. He paused only to requisition cars for his battered and footsore men, some of whom were without shoes, and, taking Rowan's Antrim militiamen and their gun with him, left Arklow at two o'clock on the morning of the 5th. He reached Hardy's position at Wicklow eight hours later. Arklow was abandoned to the rebels—if they chose to occupy it.

News of the disaster at Tubberneering reached Lake in Dublin on the evening of the battle. It was received with consternation. Not even the most sanguine members of the administration could doubt that the rising had by now assumed a serious aspect. Camden, the viceroy, who demanded large and immediate reinforcements from Britain, said that 'the salvation of Ireland, on which Great Britain as an empire eventually depends, requires that this rebellion should be instantly suppressed'. There were 1,500 troops and 4,000 yeomanry in Dublin. If the rebels should continue their advance and if this force had to march out to meet them, the troops would probably find the city in the hands of the United Irishmen on their return. And the prospect darkened as the days passed. When news came that New Ross had been held only with difficulty, chief secretary Castlereagh said that 'there never was in any country so formidable an effort on the part of the people'. It was known late on the 8th, or on the 9th, that the long-feared hostilities had begun in Ulster, where the battle of Antrim was fought on the 7th. An exodus of refugees from Dublin to Wales set in, Camden became worried about Lake's suitability for the supreme command, and the call for help from Britain rose to the crescendo of Rt Hon. John Beresford's 'For God's sake urge them to send at once the strongest force they possibly can'. Britain had been slow to act, but by the 8th 4,000 men—quickly augmented by 5,000 more, including 3,000 of the Guards—were ordered to embark. None of these reinforcements could, however, reach Ireland for several days, and in fact the Wexford rising was to be put down without them.

To assemble a force which might be thrown in the path of the Wexfordmen was, for Camden and Lake, the first necessity. Wynne was superseded on the 5th by General Francis Needham, an old soldier who had seen service in America. Needham reached Wicklow that evening, bringing with him from Loughlinstown camp in south Co. Dublin 360 men of the Cavan Militia under Colonel Maxwell. A small party of the Reay Fencible Infantry came also, then or shortly after. These were all the troops that could be spared from the Dublin area at a time when every man in uniform was reckoned a combatant, bandsmen and even drummer boys carrying arms with the rest. They were rushed to Wicklow in commandeered carriages.

Exclusive of the small Wicklow garrison, to which the Reays were joined, the troops at Needham's disposal amounted to over a thousand. He marched with this force to Arklow on the 6th and entered the town that afternoon. Two small detachments of the 5th and 9th Dragoons—amounting in all to no more than fifty men—came in on the 7th, and Needham began to organise his defences. He reoccupied the barrack, which had accommodation only for two companies, pitched a camp close by and levelled fences to secure a clear field of fire about his position.

Lake soon sent as further reinforcements about 300 Loyal Durham Fencibles under Colonel Skerret and 128 Dumbarton Fencibles. The Durhams had just come to Dublin from Ulster and the Dumbartons were detached from Lake's own bodyguard. Both units were infantry. Again—and the story of the Paris taxicabs at the Marne in September 1914 comes naturally to mind—they were bundled into carriages, jaunting cars and other vehicles for the journey south. The Durhams reached Arklow at one o'clock on the morning of the 9th, the Dumbartons 'about the middle of the day', that is, just as the battle of Arklow was about to commence. They brought Needham's strength to about 1,500, which was made up of some 80 regular cavalry, 100 fencible cavalry and 280 yeomanry cavalry (the North and South Arklow, Camolin, Coolgreany, Castletown and Gorey corps); and, of infantry, parts of the Antrim, Armagh, Cavan, North Cork, Tyrone and Londonderry battalions, the Durham and Dumbarton Fencibles and the light company of the Suffolk Fencibles; together with about eighty dismounted yeomanry and some artillerymen. This little army of untried and demoralised men of fourteen different units, exclusive of the yeomanry, had been brought together only by the unremitting efforts of Lake's staff, efforts which make it quite clear that the vital necessity of stopping the rebel progress at Arklow was fully appreciated.

And yet Arklow had been unoccupied for the better part of two days when Needham arrived there, and more than two further days were to elapse before his strength was built up. If the victors of Tubberneering had been able to continue their advance on the heels of Wynne's broken troops they could almost certainly have been outside Dublin within a few days. What had delayed them?

The Wexford insurgents—men of the fields and of the little towns, farmers, the sons of small landed proprietors, workers—were courageous, determined and capable of great endurance; but it would be absurd to call them soldiers. A handful of them had been yeomen, and there were professional fowlers, seamen and a few ex-soldiers among them, but the great mass was totally unskilled in the use of arms. They had been, by the date of the battle of Arklow, no more than a few days in revolt. They lacked leaders, a plan of operations, money, arms, ammunition, supplies. Few can have had an earlier connection with conspiracy; they were, rather, men driven desperate by the actions of the military and the magistracy. The Society of United Irishmen had certainly been for some time organised on a military basis, but extensive disarmament and the widespread arrest of its leaders had upset its preparations—nor had the Society ever made much progress in Wexford. The fact that there were few troops there before June— no more than 600 men, most of whom were in the fort at Duncannon—suggests that the government had not looked upon

Wexford as an actively disturbed area, and it was said of the yeoman class in that and the neighbouring county of Wicklow that it 'would not disgrace any shire in England'.

This being so, the remarkable feature of the rebellion is not that, the troops being so poor, it did not have more success, but that such poorly led and poorly equipped bodies as the insurgents had any success at all. Their achievements unquestionably establish their courage; 'I never', said a British officer of their behaviour at New Ross, 'saw any troops attack with more enthusiasm and bravery.' But their organisation and their scheme of operations were utterly defective.

The victors of Tubberneering entered Gorey on the heels of their enemies, but they made no effort to maintain contact either with Wynne and the fugitives or with Loftus. In fact, they feared the return of the troops, so that while Wynne and Loftus were marching as hard as they could to get away from Gorey the cautious rebels awaited the attack of one or other of them, or of both. When they learnt on 5 June that Wynne's force had gone to Wicklow and Loftus's to Carnew they rested on their laurels. They reconnoitred and foraged for supplies on the 6th, sending a party towards Shillelagh. On the 7th, they marched to Carnew, which had by then been evacuated by Loftus. They partly burnt the village, the inhabitants of which had earlier made themselves obnoxious to the people of the surrounding countryside, remained in its vicinity for the night and returned to Gorey on the 8th.

All—contemporaries and subsequent writers—have pointed it out as a blunder that the insurgents did not follow Wynne through Arklow to Wicklow. Resolutely faced, Wynne and Hardy could not have been expected to stand, and the next post behind Wicklow was at Bray, twelve miles from Dublin. By wasting their time at Gorey and in their march to Carnew, the insurgents committed, said Rev James Gordon, who witnessed many of the incidents of the rebellion, 'an error of conduct which, providentially for the British empire in general, and the Protestants of Ireland in particular, caused the ruin of their scheme'. In the homely phrase of Luke Cullen, whose researches in the following century disclosed much information on the rising, it was the 'greatest mistake they ever made'.

The insurgents were confused and irresolute. They were uncertain of Loftus's intentions, and in this sense the direction taken by Loftus and Ancram in retreat proved fortunate for the government, since it drew the insurgents' attention away from what an organised force must have recognised as the weak point, the inadequate defences of the southern approach to Dublin. Besides, the insurgents were short of food and of supplies of all kinds. They sent to Wexford for gunpowder, saying that they needed it for an attack on Arklow. The gunpowder, we are told, did not arrive until the 8th, and thus it may well be that lack of ammunition was the greatest contributory factor to the delay. Indeed, there must have been countless organisational difficulties in the way of prompt movement. Routing redcoats was a novelty, and the natural reaction to victory on the part of a disorganised mass of downtrodden men was to pause, if not prematurely to celebrate their liberation. Men who had marched a long way from their homes in south Wexford must have considered their duty done, at least for the moment. Those who had joined them from the northern part of the county were importunate in their demand that the occasion should be improved on by attacking their former oppressors, the nearby loyalists, a demand which led to the destruction in Carnew. There was no single guiding spirit among the insurgents who could see what should be done, and could enforce his will. Hay, a military officer who fought on the rebel side at Tubberneering, is said to have advised an immediate advance to Dublin. On the other hand, Fr John Murphy, the father of the Wexford revolt, opposed any movement which would have taken the Wexfordmen out of their own county. Neither Hay nor Fr John fought at Arklow. A third leader, Fr Philip Roche, left Gorey for New Ross to succeed Bagenal Harvey as General-in-Chief; what effect, if any, his going had on the rebel counsels is unknown.

In all probability, the rebels had too many plans; there was certainly too little authority in choosing which was the best. Just as the insurgent tactics were a matter of charging straight forward or of standing still in position, so also was their strategy simple and guileless. In battle, the movements of their opponents might be seen and countered; in the wider sphere where the enemy's designs were hidden, they groped for familiar landmarks; they were cautious when in doubt, but they were ready to hit out suddenly, as if in relief, when a target presented itself.

The insurgents marched out of Gorey to attack Arklow about ten o'clock on the morning of Saturday 9 June, the day on which Needham was best prepared to receive them. There were more than 20,000 of them, so that the column must have been strung out for over three miles from front to rear along what was then the main road from Gorey to Arklow, the road running through Inch and Coolgreany. They were led by Billy Byrne's Ballymanus corps of Wicklowmen. The head of the column reached Inch about noon and passed through Coolgreany about two o'clock. Luke Cullen says that 'they got drunk in Coolgreany'. Perhaps some of them did; no doubt the available liquor was consumed, but it can have been no more than a drop in the ocean for such a multitude.

They must have presented an extraordinary sight as they pushed on through the blinding dust of that dry, hot summer. The distinct corps formed of the men of the different districts kept together; beyond that, there was no order. About 2,000 of the whole force had firearms, 3,000 or so pikes; the rest had weapons of 'different sorts', that is, they were practically unarmed. Very many were merely camp followers, and there were crowds of women and even children, for the only hope of safety in those killing days lay in keeping up with the fighters; off the beaten path of the revolt the frightened yeomen rode, burning and slaying. Somewhere in the column were either two or three of the captured guns, the howitzer and the 6-pounders, in good condition and with a good supply of ammunition.

The leadership of the rebel army is hard to establish. One leader was Anthony Perry of Inch, a United Irishman and an ex-yeoman. Perry had joined the insurgents six days previously, when they liberated him from prison in Gorey. He had been held as a political suspect by the North Cork Militia, who had treated him barbarously; they had put gunpowder in his hair and fired it with a candle, a torture from the effects of which he had not fully recovered when he was executed six weeks later. Perry had broken down on 26 May and had disclosed to his torturers the names of many of the Wexford United Irish leaders. No doubt he repented of what he had been forced to do: he fought on, with what anguish and bitterness history has not disclosed, to the end of the rebellion. Others of the principal leaders were Billy Byrne, Esmond Kyan, an old gunner who had been released in Gorey with Perry and who commanded the artillery, and Edward Fitzgerald, who led a band of Wexford townsmen armed with muskets and other firearms. Fr Michael Murphy of Ballycanew, one of the most prominent in the battle, did not arrive in Arklow until the fight was almost over. Patrick Redmond, Richard Monaghan or Monk, Murt Mernagh, Nicholas Murphy, Nicholas Dixon, Matthew Doyle and Daniel Kerevan had subsidiary commands. There appears to have been no paramount leader. Of the original leaders of the northern Wexford army—as distinct from those who fought at New Ross—Frs John Murphy, Roche and Kearns were absent.

Attempts had been made up to the eve of the march to prepare the insurgents for the impending struggle, and perhaps this was an additional reason for the delay. The scheme of drill of the military was imitated and some of the leaders taught their men to form line and to break from line to column by platoons and sections. Everywhere that fighting took place during the insurrection we catch glimpses of hasty efforts to piece together the United Irish organisation that had been rudely interrupted by the government disarmament of the people and the arrest of the leaders, and that was at any rate very imperfect in Co. Wexford. There is evidence both in regard to the Arklow force and that which fought at New Ross of a rough arrangement of district companies and of larger groups or corps made up of the united companies of wider areas; for example, the Ballymanus corps of about 1,800 men was made up of separate companies, two of which—the Arklow Northshire and Redcross companies—are named. But there was no time for a proper organisation of masses of men, all of whom were, as one of their number told Luke Cullen, 'novices in the art of war'.

Armament was an abiding problem with the insurgents and the host approaching Arklow was very poorly equipped with weapons. Their most conspicuous arm was the pike, the weapon of eighteenth- and nineteenth-century insurgency everywhere and the weapon that has come traditionally to be associated with rebel Irishmen; pikeman was synonymous with rebel in 1798. Their pikes were of three classes. Most had plain iron or steel spear heads, like cavalry lances, and were in a direct line of descent from the weapons of the classic days of the pikemen, and from the pikes of Benburb. Others were fitted not only with a spear point, but with an edged hook like a sickle springing sideways from the base of the blade; the hook could be used to unseat a cavalryman, or to cut his bridle rein. Pikes of this kind were hybrid weapons in the ancestry of which the medieval bill and the farming implement of the same name, as well as the pike proper, were represented. The third class had an axe blade on the side opposite to the hook; these, which were designed to cut as well as thrust, were halberds rather than pikes and must have been most unwieldy weapons.

The insurgents' pikeheads were hammered out by the local blacksmiths and were mounted on staves which usually ranged from eight to fourteen feet in length. Young ash trees made the best staves. Pikes were admittedly makeshift weapons which were easily and cheaply constructed, but they still had, in 1798, an association with weapons carried by the military. Sergeants bore pikes at that time and fought with them in battle. British officers had done so until 1786, and theorists such as Henry Lloyd, Colonel Francis Maceroni and others could still argue that the pike was a better weapon than the bayonet which had superseded it.

Pikes had figured largely in the preparations for the rebellion. The Society of United Irishmen had, in 1797, ordered all who could not afford firearms to procure pikes. Huge numbers were confiscated by the government—over 70,000, it is said, in the provinces of Leinster and Ulster. Because of this, and because of the spontaneous nature of their rising, many of the Wexford insurgents had turned out with pitchforks, scythes, hay knives, billhooks and other implements of the farmyard and the field. Once the rebellion had begun, however, the manufacture of pikes was recommenced and Wexford town became, under rebel rule, a busy centre of the industry; smiths went openly to work, sawpits were requisitioned, and benches and tables for the carpenters who made and fitted the staves filled the Bull-ring.

In battle, the pike went far to justify the claims of the theorists. Provided the pikemen stood firm, they were as good a buffer against cavalry as the infantry square. No cavalry then in Ireland could break them. Against infantry, if the pikemen succeeded in closing with them, the pike could be more than a match for the bayonet. The difficulty, of course, was to preserve line in attack and to come to close quarters. Where pikemen could be flanked in a mêlée, muskets and bayonets were more manageable and deadlier weapons than pikes; good infantry, because of its fire power and its steadiness in line, could receive and break a pike charge. For pikemen to remain in the open within musketry or artillery range without charging was to invite slaughter. Unsupported pikemen made a poor showing in defence, for troops could move forward and fire into them at close range. Artillery, particularly when firing grape, was the most destructive weapon to which pikemen could be exposed.

Their lack of training served the wielders of the Wexford pikes ill. 'The charge of the pikemen', said Lord Edward Fitzgerald, who, if all had gone well with the plotters, might have led the revolt, 'should be made in a smart trot. On the flank or extremity of every rank there should be intrepid men placed to keep the fronts even, that, at closing, every point should tell together.' But there was no hope whatever, in the circumstances of the revolt, of such expertise.

The insurgents gave the positions of honour, on the march and in battle, not to their pikemen but to those who carried firearms. Men who were lucky enough to capture muskets abandoned their pikes and pitchforks and, whether they knew how to handle guns or not, set themselves up as musketeers; many captured muskets were soon rendered defective by unskilled use, and there appear to have been no gunsmiths outside Wexford town to repair them. Guns of every description and calibre were carried: muskets, fowling pieces—some of which were rifles—and blunderbusses. Sporting guns, in Ireland as elsewhere at that date and for long after, were usually far superior in construction to the military weapons; most of them had longer barrels and were of smaller calibre than the Brown Bess; they consequently had a greater range. But the rebel efforts to close with their opponents and to imitate their volley firing nullified such advantages of range and accuracy as some of their marksmen possessed. Their best guns-men, many of whom were present at Arklow, were the pro-fessional wildfowlers of the Wexford barony of Shelmalier and the fishermen of the Faythe, a suburb of Wexford town.

Ammunition was always scarce. The sources of supply were the small stocks concealed by the United Irishmen or kept by sports-men or found in Wexford and in the houses of the wealthy, cartridges captured in battle, and the contents of the pouches of deserters from the militia. Powder was carried loose in the insurgents' pockets, or in paper parcels; although some of the better equipped musketeers had powder horns and shot bags. Later on, after the date of the battle of Arklow, some of the in-surgents tried to make their own gunpowder, and we read of 'Holt's mixture', so called from the Wicklow leader Joseph Holt, who had it made from sulphur and saltpetre smuggled out to him from the towns and charcoal obtained by burning heath.

The head of the long insurgent column reached the outskirts of Arklow about four o'clock, or a little earlier. The marching men completely blocked the narrow road and their systematic deployment or the alteration of their formation seemed alike impossible. Billy Byrne, who rode with Perry towards the front, made several attempts to improve the order of the Ballymanus corps, but he could not force his way forward to do so, and when he set his horse to jump the roadside fence with the intention of gaining the head of the column through the fields the animal fell and threw him. They were then near Lamberton, about a mile from Arklow, and within a few minutes they were engaged with Needham's outpost at the Charter School, a building which stood at the corner of what was then called the Yellow Lane, a by-road leading—as it still does—from the Coolgreany road to the lower end of the town. Needham was ready. He had mounted patrols on the roads entering Arklow from the south and west; that on the Coolgreany road had come galloping back in the forenoon to announce the insurgent approach.

Although the progressive town of Arklow has greatly changed since 1798, its main features remain much as they were at the time of the battle; of all the Irish battles which were fought in areas subsequently built over, that of Arklow is perhaps the easiest to follow on the actual terrain of the engagement.

The town consisted in 1798 of one main street which ran, as it runs today, parallel with the river Avoca. The barrack, since demolished, stood at the western end of this street. At the eastern end was the bridge, the same structure which still serves to carry the Dublin road to the north or Ferrybank side of the Avoca. The poo er part of the town, called the Fishery, stretched southward from the bridge beside the rivermouth. Two roads approached the town from the south, the Arklow Rock road and the Coolgreany road. The former ran by the seaside from the two pointed hills—Arklow Rock and the Little Rock—which, rising about a mile and a half to the southward, form such notable features of the landscape. It led into the Fishery and is now represented only by a field path across the links. Two lanes connect—and connected in 1798—these two roads: the Yellow Lane already mentioned and a crossroad south of the two pointed hills. The present main road from Gorey, which runs northward to Arklow beside the railway line, had not been constructed in 1798.

The land on which Arklow is built and on which the battle was fought slopes in a north-easterly direction towards the mouth of the Avoca. It appears to have been as much divided in 1798 as it is now by the earth banks and hedgerows which form the field boundaries, and some of which Needham levelled. Of two small streams which flow through the fields outside the town, the first is now partly concealed in a culvert beneath the footpath of the main Gorey road. It enters the river in a deep ravine close to the railway station, and here its course is clearly marked. What is left of Arklow castle, a building in ruins since Cromwell's time, crowns the precipitous side of this ravine. The military barrack, later converted to the uses of the police, stood on the site of that part of the castle which was most shattered by Cromwell's forces. The second stream, rising near the first south-west of the town, flows eastward in a bottom roughly parallel with the main street. It joins the river below the bridge.

There is little to recommend Arklow as a defensive position to be held against a force attacking from the south. It is largely overlooked at short range from high ground to the west and south west. The bridge—the link with Dublin—is in the least defensible position, close to a covered approach provided by a sharp fall where the upland fields to the south of the town give place to broken ground by the seashore. The ravine behind the site of the barrack is too short to protect more than the extreme flank. But, as Needham was well aware, the approaches to the town could be swept by fire.

Needham's disposition of force was designed to protect not only the town but also his camp, which extended on either side of the present Chapel lane towards the railway station. His right, which blocked the entry from the Coolgreany road, rested ultimately on the barrack, although the right flank of his line was placed a short distance west of the barrack yard, probably where the present Martin's lane joins Upper Main street. His centre covered the camp and formed a salient projecting from the back of the town. His left extended through the gardens behind the houses to the vital position at the bridge, which must be preserved since it was his line of retreat; it also secured the entry to the town from the Rock road. The extent of the whole line could not have been much less than 900 yards, at least half of which was in the open, or was protected only by the field boundaries. There must have been many gaps and weak places.

Captain Rowan's detachment of the Antrim Militia, supported by some supplementary yeomen and armed loyalists, was in its old post in the barrack. The entry of the Coolgreany road was blocked by a barricade of cars and boxes and it and the ground immediately to the south of it were held by more Antrim militiamen under their Lieut.-Colonel, Henry O'Hara, a detachment of the Armagh Militia under Lieut.-Colonel Cope, and the newly arrived Dumbarton Fencibles. The fencibles were thrown well forward. Three 6-pounders supported this part of the line, one, or possibly two, of them being Antrim battalion guns. Two were at, or close to, the barricade and the third was probably on the platform in the barrack yard. They were served by Royal Irish Artillerymen under Captain Fleming. Needham's right, where he expected and received the sharpest attack, was thus secured by some 550 men and three of his five guns.

The Durham Fencibles under Colonel Skerret, the second in command of the whole force, prolonged the line south to cover the camp. Their right seems to have been immediately in reverse of the crest of the rising ground between the present Gorey road and the railway cutting. The left of their line was at first drawn back, but it was to be moved forward later, possibly to the crown of the rise. The first of the streams mentioned above flowed parallel with the front of the battalion and something more than a hundred yards distant from it.

The troops to the left of the Durhams appear to have been drawn up facing south to form the head of the salient, and the line soon formed another angle which carried it by the back of the present convent towards the gardens behind the main street and on to the bridge. The second stream flowed in front of this part of the position. The troops holding the line here were the light companies of the Tyrone Militia and Suffolk Fencibles, the Londonderry Militia grenadiers, the handful of the North Cork Militia that was present, the Cavan battalion under Colonel Maxwell, and the remainder of the yeomanry infantry. Some part, or all, of the Cavan appears to have been on the left. The two regiments which were not at Tubberneering and which had not hitherto faced the Wexfordmen, the Cavan and the Durhams, were so placed, at either end of the town, as to strengthen the shaken morale of the remainder.

A second barricade had been built at the corner of the main street where the way led on the one hand to the Fishery and on the other towards the bridge, and the old churchyard close by was occupied and formed another strongpoint in rear of the town. The two remaining guns were placed, as Rev H. L. Bayly, a Protestant clergyman who had taken refuge in the town, tells us, 'on the fields to the left, opposite the Little Rock'. One of them—probably a 6-pounder of the Cavan Militia—seems to have swept the road through the Fishery.

There was no infantry reserve. Every musket—almost half of them carried by Ulstermen—was in the firing line. But the cavalry, under Wynne, was held back. All of the mounted men save one troop of the Ancient Britons and the Arklow Yeomanry were stationed beside the Dublin road beyond the bridge. The detached units were on the parade ground in front of the barrack.

The insurgents paused at Ballyrooaun bridge south of the Charter School. Byrne, who had recovered from his fall, led a body of the Ballymanus corps up the hill towards Needham's outpost. The Wicklowmen halted within pistol shot of the troops. Volleys were exchanged, and when the insurgents threatened to close with their opponents—Ancient Britons, yeomanry or Antrim militiamen under Captain Elliot—the troops abandoned their position and retired to the town. Warned by a galloping trooper, Needham had the drums beaten and the defenders of Arklow stood to arms.

The insurgents came on. Some of them burnt Lamberton, Mr Bayly's residence. Part of the column remained on the road; others entered the fields to left and right and, spreading out, moved down towards the town; still others turned off by the Yellow Lane and crossed towards the Fishery by the back of the town.

These movements took time to perform, and there was much confusion. The guns were dragged up as soon as possible and were in position to fire on the town before the rebels were ready to attack. Either two or all three of the pieces which had been captured at Tubberneering were brought up, and there may have been one or two ship guns from Wexford as well. One gun was taken along the Yellow Lane and was placed somewhere on the high ground where the lane turns north-east, more than a thousand yards from the barrack and too far out to have contributed much to the battle. The positioning of a second gun was more fortunate. It was brought beyond Lamberton, turned off the road by a laneway to the right, and unlimbered in the fields less than

600 yards from the barrack and about 400 yards from Needham's centre, that is, within easy range for roundshot, although still too far away to fire grape or canister with any effect. These two guns appear to have been the captured 6-pounders.

According to the contemporary writer Edward Hay, the insurgent leaders had planned their attack on Arklow during the halt at Coolgreany. Their offensive was designed and subsequently carried out as a simultaneous attack by two main columns, one moving in by the Coolgreany road, the other by the seaside road from the Rocks. Despite the confusion of the approach, the deployment of the huge, headstrong and scarcely dirigible mass of mingled fighters and followers was not ill-managed. It took the greater part of two hours to form the columns of attack, and even then the available force was not arranged so that all could be committed, but the difficulties which confronted the amateur leaders of the revolt were enormous.

Some sections of the marching column turned to the right a mile and a half south of Arklow and went by the crossroad already mentioned to the Rock road. The advance elements of these bodies approached a cavalry post at the Rocks even—as it seems—earlier than the Wicklowmen came to the Charter School. The cavalry decamped and the rebels continued their march. The distance from the Coolgreany road to the Rocks is two miles and from the Rocks to Arklow a mile and a half, so that the men who went that way had further to go than those who remained on the Coolgreany road. They were reinforced for their eventual attack by the great numbers of men who poured along the Yellow Lane after Billy Byrne and his comrades had dislodged the outpost which, on their arrival, had blocked its mouth. The Monaseed corps, to which the celebrated Miles Byrne belonged, was one of those which crossed in this way from left to right behind the town. They went some of the way through the fields, and were fired on from Needham's line. Either they or another body had fired a little earlier on a group of mounted officers who were seen riding over the ground in front of the Durham battalion.

By six o'clock the whole area from the south bank of the Avoca above the town to its mouth beyond the Fishery was occupied by the insurgents, whose crescentic front thus extended for some 2,400 yards. Contemporaries give ample testimony of the 'most awful sight' which they presented; victors are the monopolists of information, and there is far less to tell us what the insurgents thought of the troops. Crouching behind their breastworks or standing in line in the fields, Needham's men saw the same huge semi-circle of their foes that many of them had seen already at Tubberneering. The Wexford and Wicklowmen appeared on the high ground above the hedges and against the skyline. Dust clouds told of their great numbers on the Coolgreany and Rock roads and irregular masses and long straggling lines were seen to cover the sloping fields towards the higher part of the Yellow Lane. Nearest the town were the men with firearms, further back the pikemen, and where the groups were thickest the pikes rose like a forest. Mr Bayly 'saw in a moment thousands appear on the tops of ditches, forming one great and regular circular line from the Gorey [that is, the Coolgreany] road through the fields quite round to the sand banks near the sea, as thick as they could stand'. He says that 'they all put their hats on their pikes, and gave most dreadful yells. I could clearly distinguish their leaders riding through their ranks with flags flying.' Every company appeared with colours and the whole front and the deep masses in rear were flecked with the green and yellow of the banner of the revolt, the national flag of the future, the green flag showing the harp without the crown.

The moment had arrived. Needham, with his back to a river, one narrow bridge as his line of retreat, and nothing behind him but the wilds of Wicklow and the handful of men under Hardy, was about to fight a battle on which the fate of the kingdom might well depend. If his line was pierced and the bridge lost, nothing could save a great part of his men from death.

The rebels moved forward on the Coolgreany road and, musketeers in front, prepared to attack the barricade. At the same time, the defenders of the lower end of the town were engaged by the second column, which moved in by the sea shore and the Fishery.

That part of the Coolgreany road immediately outside the town was formerly known as the Flash. About 300 yards from the site of the barrack it is joined by the Woodenbridge road which, in 1798 as now, turned sharply south to skirt the top of the ravine before it joined it. The point of junction is referred to as the corner of the Poolahoney road in contemporary accounts of the battle. The Coolgreany road was bordered in this area by ditches and, further in, by the thatched cabins on which the right of Needham's line rested. The newly arrived Dumbarton Fencibles, who had 'scarce thrown off their knapsacks' when the alarm drums began to beat, had been ordered out to occupy these ditches and cabins in anticipation of the insurgent approach. They were the first to be engaged. A few volleys were exchanged, and then the High-landers abandoned their positions and went back at the double to the barricade. Raising a wild huzza and led by a mounted man who is said to have called out, 'Blood and wounds, my boys, come on—the town is ours!', the head of the insurgent column rushed forward. They were close to the barricade when the 6-pounders opened on them with grape. Aided by the fire of the infantry, the gunners swept the head of the column and sent the survivors reeling backwards to pile themselves in confusion against the masses which filled the road in their rear. Their leader, whose horse was shot, fell wounded on the road. Presently he raised his head to look about him and was shot dead.

Foiled in their attack on the road, the insurgents soon extended to their right and formed a line through the fields in front of the Durhams. The stream which dropped into the ravine on their left ran between them and their enemies. Needham's line was formed, at least in places, behind the field boundaries, which thus served as breastworks. The insurgents, for their part, lined the hedges and ditches in their front with their musketeers. The intervening space had, however, been cleared by the troops, and to reach the Durhams it was necessary to rush across the open ground which extended on either side of the stream. In these circumstances, a fire fight developed which lasted for two hours and which was interrupted by at least two reckless charges.

In electing, as they did from the beginning, to make a frontal attack on the strongest part of Needham's line, the insurgents had set themselves a most difficult—indeed, for them, an insoluble —problem. They sought to employ methods in the use of which they were most notably amateurs. In the brief, bloody battles of that era the quality of troops was judged by their capacity to receive fire and then, closing their ranks, to press forward. Few but men who were so well disciplined that—even though it meant certain death for many of them—they would automatically advance on being ordered to do so could move on after they had received heavy fire at close range. Yet this was just what these two weeks' soldiers were now called upon to do. G. F. R. Henderson, speaking of course of the days before modern developments, has said that, historically, frontal attacks have failed not because of any defect in principle, but because of imperfect organisation. And the insurgents were defective in organisation as well as training. The simplest tactic of all, the bald-headed charge, was indeed, as they were soon to learn, the hardest to execute.

While the rebel musketeers in the ditches kept up their fire on Needham's line, the leaders, working further back, endeavoured to form the pikemen for attack. But these and the men with other makeshift weapons were the most difficult to manage. Later on, when Billy Byrne, who was among the best of the leaders, was tried for his part in the rising, several witnesses swore that they saw him rally and lead on his men in this part of the field. Byrne, who was of course at this stage struggling against the almost inevitable sentence of death, and who sought to minimise his command, replied that the rebels showed neither regularity nor discipline, that no man thought of remaining with his corps, and that 'the rabble scattered and each man fought for himself'.

The first attack on a broad front appears to have been made soon after the deployment. How many charges, and attempted charges, there were is not clear. Rev James Gordon says three, another account, given in Jones's 'Impartial Narrative' which was published at the time, two; these figures include the first charge along the road. Needham admitted in that part of his report which was not published that 'the perseverance of the enemy was surprising' and said that 'their efforts to possess themselves of the guns on my right were most daring, advancing even to the muzzles, where they fell in great numbers'. One feels that while the battle lasted successive rushes were made, some abortive at an early stage, others deserving the name of a charge.

The brunt of the day's fighting on Needham's side was certainly borne by the Durhams. The pikemen passed through the insurgent musketeers—this alone must have disordered their front —and rushed bravely forward, and when their leaders succeeded in rousing them all at the same time they came on along the whole front. The troops can scarcely have had time as the rebels advanced to fire more than one volley from each of their three ranks, but this fire, supported by grape and canister from the artillery, was always sufficient to break the pikemen. There is no record of the insurgents ever having reached the fencibles. Somewhere in the intervening space, along the line of the present Gorey road, they were met by the storm of lead—the 'sleeping doses' and 'unmannerly grape shot' of the troops—and compelled to 'dance back in quick time'; the phrases are those of a sergeant of the Dumbartons.

It must soon have become apparent to the rebels on the left that the fire of their musketeers alone could have little effect on the troops. As time went by therefore, and as the scanty supply of ammunition ran lower, it became more than ever necessary to find some way of using the pikemen to break the spell of the British volley. As long as the pikemen could be fended off and the troops' ammunition held out, and unless Needham's determination to defend his position was altered by his failure in other parts of his line, victory must rest with the defence.

While this was the state of affairs at the Flash and in the fields to the south of it, the second rebel column had carried the battle into the Fishery. Here the insurgents on the Rock road, who were concealed behind the bluffs which mark the seaward end of the high ground, were out of sight of a picket guard of yeomanry cavalry stationed beyond the Fishery. The men who had come over by the Yellow Lane awaited, on the right of the picket, the arrival of a sufficient number of their comrades who were coming up from the Rocks before they began their attack. The timing of the insurgent movements as a whole was good. The attack on the Fishery began, apparently, at the same moment as the attack at the Flash, but at the Fishery the onset was even speedier. Before the yeomen were aware of what was happening, the insurgents had got in behind them and had set fire to the cabins that were huddled irregularly along the street leading to the bridge. The dry thatch blazed fiercely, and when the head of the column pressed forward from the Rock road the yeomen took fright, wheeled about and galloped madly along the smoke-filled street. Some made for the river and swam their horses across to the Ferrybank side.

Needham had the greater part of his cavalry on this wing, and the advancing insurgents were soon met by a cavalry charge. Wynne, who led it, and who had with him his own men, the regulars and most of the mounted yeomen, came on with spirit, but the rebels, who were by now spread out on the flat ground through which the street ran, met him as boldly. At no time during the rebellion did a cavalry charge hold any terror for the pikemen. The shock of the engagement was most severe along the road and on the sandy ground between it and the river. Knox Grogan, the gouty ex-regular who was the captain of the Castletown Yeomanry, rode on ahead and was killed by a roundshot fired by one of the guns on his own side. His corps was badly cut up. Fighting against them were several men in the Monaseed and Limerick corps of the rebel army—Miles Byrne included—who had joined Grogan's force when it was first formed, but most of whom had left in a body some months before the rising when the test oath, designed to exclude United Irishmen from the yeomanry, was proposed to them.

Wynne's charge failed to stay the progress of the rebels; Needham's statement in his report to Lake that Wynne routed his opponents is quite fanciful. The horsemen soon trotted back and, recrossing the bridge, resumed their station on the Ferrybank side; they were later ordered to shelter from the rebel fire behind the sandhills by the highroad.

But Wynne's failure did not mean that Needham's hold on the lower end of the town was endangered. To fire the cabins and repulse the cavalry were not difficult operations; to storm the position at the end of the main street was. The struggle here, although fewer details of it have survived, was scarcely less furious than that on the rebel left, and it was on a much narrower front. Each attempt which the insurgents made to advance into the town was met by the same devastating fire of the guns and the infantry. The grapeshot 'tumbled them by twenties', yet Bayly tells us that the 'large openings' which were made in the rebel ranks were 'as quickly filled up', and that they 'rushed on like madmen'. Faint-hearted men, of course, hung back, like the follower of the Monaseed corps who was later to inform against Billy Byrne and who admitted that a regard for his own safety constrained him to keep 'along the dyke of a ditch'. But there was no lack of courageous leaders. Perry, who had earlier had his horse killed under him, seems to have fought here. With him were Michael Redmond, ex-yeomen and leader of the Limerick corps, who was killed while leading a charge on the highway, and James Kavanagh of Ballyscarton and Michael Fearet of Tara, both of whom died at the head of their men.

A story told years later by an old soldier of the Cavan Militia who fought at Arklow gives some indication of the fury of the engagement in the Fishery. He said that a bronze 6-pounder of his battalion—a gun which had belonged originally to the Second Newry Volunteer company of 1778, and on which were inscribed the words *Newry Volunteers*—became so hot from the rapidity of its discharge that it was rendered useless and was abandoned in Arklow after the battle.

Needham's guns and the muskets of the troops at the end of the main street and in the houses could sweep the area in front of them with their fire, that is, the confined space between the burning houses and the river bank which the rebels must cross if they were to come to handgrips with their foes. Behind the cabins was a wood and beyond the wood, at the back of the town, an orchard. The fire of the troops on the high ground on which the salient was formed and of those stationed in the ruins of the old Cistercian abbey and in the churchyard adjoining prevented the insurgents in the wood and orchard from working forward to the backs of the houses in the main street, in the line of which there were two gaps, one near the abbey ruins and the other not far from the parade ground. The cabins continued to burn, but the gap at the churchyard prevented the spread of the conflagration into the town. The wind too changed during the battle and this helped to confine the blaze to the Fishery; it was said that the insurgents had started the fire to annoy the defenders, but that 'the wind, at the order of *our God,* turned, drove it from us and confounded them in their own device'. Indeed, no serious attempt was made either to break into the back of the town through the fields or to infiltrate on the north side along the river bank from the mouth of the ravine. After the repulse of Wynne's charge, the insurgents came 'in great force to a passage that led to the centre of the town'—whether on the north side or the south is uncertain—but were repulsed by the fire of a sergeant and twelve men.

The rebel guns kept up 'a brisk fire' in the early stages of the battle. They were served at first by men who had earlier been made prisoners and by some deserters—six Royal Irish Artillerymen and a few Antrim militiamen under a non-commissioned gunner named Shepherd. Shepherd, who had been captured at the rout of the Meath Militia at the Three Rocks in Co. Wexford, served unwillingly and made sure that his practice would not injure his comrades on the other side. When he loaded roundshot he aimed too high and the balls went over the town and fell wide. He was outside the range of grape and wasted many charges. George Taylor tells us that one such charge swept away thirty rebels and that Dick Monaghan, who was watching Shepherd, would have killed him for it, but that Shepherd was saved by Esmond Kyan, who insisted that 'it was the army cannon that had done the execution'. When Kyan and Monaghan became their own artillerists there was an immediate improvement in the fire. Indeed a gun laid by Kyan—most likely the 6-pounder near Lamberton—scored some remarkable hits. One round passed through the ammunition box on the limber of a gun on Needham's right. Another smashed the carriage of one of the Durhams' guns 'to shivers' and killed thirteen of the gun crew and troops who stood by. These men were buried later where they had fallen and their graves were afterwards pointed out to Luke Cullen by the local sergeant of police. A third shot struck the roof of the inn on the reverse slope behind the barrack. (There is still an inn there.) Further shots 'struck several houses and the barrack'.

If this good shooting had been continued it would soon have tipped the balance in favour of the insurgents. Cullen was told that Monaghan wanted Kyan to fire on the barricade on the Coolgreany road. But Fleming, Needham's artillerist, galled by the sudden succes of his opponents' fire, loaded roundshot and began a duel with Kyan. One of the balls struck Kyan on the shoulder and carried away a cork arm which he wore and part of the stump. 'There go my loose timbers', said he, but he was seriously hurt and had to be removed to Wexford for treatment. There was no one to replace him. After that, the rebel guns were not a source of danger for the troops. On the whole, they were kept too far out and their ammunition was soon used up.

Miles Byrne believed that the insurgents would have done better if they had had no artillery. They would then, he says, have made more use of their pikes; as it was, the pikemen remained inactive, admiring the effect of the cannon shots. It is highly probable that the artillery fire and the pike attacks were not co-ordinated, but some of the charges which Needham sustained were desperate enough to have brought victory if the pike alone, as the insurgents handled it, could have achieved it.

A controversy raged for some years after the battle regarding Needham's competence as a leader. Of the contemporary writers, Gordon, Hay and Barrington claimed that the insurgents intimidated him. Gordon says that Needham, losing heart, sent his aide-de-camp Captain Moore to Skerret to ask Skerret's opinion of a suitable place to which the troops might retire. Skerret said: 'We can only hope for victory by preserving our ranks. If we break, all is lost, and after what I have seen of the Durham regiment they shall never retire.' Gordon believed that it was Skerret who had saved Arklow and he accused Needham not alone of faint-heartedness but of the intention, if the retirement had been made, of blaming his second-in-command for it. Miles Byrne went further. He says that a retirement was begun by the Wicklow road and that the Durhams were ordered to cover it. Cullen says that some of the yeomanry cavalry fled over the bridge 'even from the saddle skirts of Sir Watkin Williams Wynne'.

But these things were all hotly denied. Sir Richard Musgrave in particular, the most widely read in his own time of the historians of the rising, defended Needham. In 1802 eleven officers of the Durhams who had fought at Arklow presented an address to Needham in which they expressed their conviction that he had never proposed retreat to Skerret, or to any other officer. Gordon retaliated by reminding them that, after the battle, they had called Needham 'General Needless'—he was called the late General Needham after Vinegar hill, in allusion to his supposed failure to arrive in time in the position assigned to him—and said that they were now concealing the truth to curry favour with the authorities. He claimed that he had a written statement of Skerret's to prove the truth of his assertions. No such statement was, however, made public, and since Skerret had left Ireland by 1802 the matter was soon dropped.

Whether Skerret was the hero of the hour or not, Esmond Kyan's success and the threatening aspect of the insurgents must certainly have disturbed Needham. Who could say what effect a few more shots like that which had shattered the gun carriage might have on the troops who had already run from Tubberneering? And had Needham, in fact, the alternative of retirement? If he had tried to draw back, some of his men could have held out in the barrack, but not all of the remainder could have crossed the bridge. The alternative to fighting it out might rather have been slaughter.

Yet, however deeply Needham may have pondered the chances of a withdrawal, he made—despite the assertions of Byrne and Cullen—no effort to withdraw. He did the opposite. The left of the Durham battalion, which had been enfiladed by Kyan's fire, improved its position by moving twenty paces forward, no doubt to the crest of the rise eastward of the stream; from here, no part of the ground intervening between the troops and the insurgents would have been concealed.

It must have been nearly eight o'clock when the insurgent fire slackened and the final brief and bloody stage of the battle commenced. By this time the supplies of ammunition were running out on both sides and, although neither side knew of the other's deficiency, the issue had resolved itself into a race against time to decide which would be the first to cease fire. It was about then that Fr Michael Murphy of Ballycanew came up. He had been driven to rebellion by the yeomanry, who had burnt his chapel, and he had joined Fr John Murphy, the original leader, at an early stage of the hostilities. Fr Michael, accompanied by an unknown number of fighters, came to Arklow by the Coolgreany road. He met many fugitives retiring and compelled them to turn back with him. Reaching the Flash, he exerted every effort to rally the pikemen and to carry them forward in another charge. Almost certainly, this was after Kyan had been wounded and when the last hope lay in the use of the pike.

Aided by Billy Byrne, who had been indefatigable since the struggle began, Fr Murphy marshalled his men and then, carrying a flag which bore a device of a cross and the inscription *Liberty or Death*, moved forward in the final charge. His advance was along the road, now bloody from the evening's carnage. Beside him were the cabins, blazing fiercely. In front, through the smoke, loomed the mouths of the cannon—there was one less now because of Kyan's work—and the line of bayonets. Byrne, sword in hand, and with the pikemen behind him, faced the Durhams on his right.

At the corner where the Woodenbridge road branches to the left the musketry began to take its toll of the attackers. Many fell here and in the hollow of the stream to the southward. A ball passed through Byrne's high caroline hat. Some men turned tail, but most held on and the charge swept beyond the corner and up the incline towards the barricade, and over the stream and on towards Skerret's line.

Thirty yards separated the waving flag from the barricade when the gunners fired. The flag went down and with it fell Fr Murphy; he was struck in the body by canister and was killed instantly.

The pikemen lost heart soon after the priest's fall and retired out of range behind their own musketeers. Soon these latter, who had held their ground throughout the battle and had at times exchanged volleys with the troops, were seen to move back. Billy Byrne remonstrated with them, asking if they were going to leave the field at the moment of victory. They replied simply that they had fired their last rounds and could do no more. They could not have known that the militiamen and fencibles were counting their last cartridges and looking uneasily behind them to measure again their own chances of retreat. The rebel ammunition had been the first to fail.

In this part of the position, where the fight had been most fierce, a general retirement was begun before half past eight o'clock. The insurgents drew off, as Cullen puts it, 'with a sulky reluctance'. News of the happenings at the Flash was passed from mouth to mouth along the rebel front. As the members of one group saw another retiring, they followed suit, and shortly the whole great force, from one end of the town to the other, had abandoned the attack.

The troops, when the pressure to which they had been subjected was lifted, made but a nominal effort to assume the offensive and at a later stage, when the rebels were clearly in retirement, they made none to pursue.

Miles Byrne and his comrades in the Fishery had fought stubbornly to the last. They must have been within sixty yards of the bridge, but they did not succeed in breaking Needham's defence. When they were seen to be withdrawing, Colonel Maxwell of the Cavan Militia sent a force forward to burn some houses which they had occupied. These houses and the adjacent ditches, probably near the present Hall's lane, had earlier afforded a protection from fire, and the pikemen who held them had constituted a threat to the weakest part of Needham's line. Finally, there was another cavalry charge. The dragoons and yeomanry, crossing from their safe position at Ferrybank, rode after the retreating rebels and spread out to cut down the stragglers. The insurgents withdrew from their right as they had come up, partly by the Yellow Lane and partly southward towards the Rocks.

At half past eight Moore, Needham's aide, wrote a despatch to Lake at the General's direction. He described the battle and said that the rebels had been repulsed at all points with much slaughter, but that they still remained in front of Arklow in great numbers. Further fighting was envisaged. This communication was forwarded from Wicklow at half past ten and received in

Dublin in the early hours of the following morning. When the insurgents had first appeared in Needham's front two files of dragoons had been sent post haste to Wicklow with the news, which had no doubt been relayed at once to Dublin. The chief command must therefore have spent some anxious hours awaiting news of an engagement which they had for so many days, and with so much misgiving, envisaged.

Major Hardy, the Wicklow commandant, addressed Lake from Rathdrum while Moore's despatch was passing through Wicklow. Hardy said that he had been reconnoitring near Croghan, six miles west of Arklow, when he heard the firing at half past six. He had gone up Croghan mountain and had seen that Arklow was being attacked. He had remained there for two hours, during which time the firing was 'formidable and well supported', and he had sent a yeoman to Needham for news. Needham had replied that he was short of ammunition. Hardy had gone then to Rathdrum and, leaving his own men with no more than forty rounds each, had sent the remainder of his ammunition to Arklow. He had called in the Aughrim corps of yeomanry and had then sent a hundred of his own Antrim regiment and fifty of the 7th Dragoons to support Needham. The battle was over when these arrangements were completed, but Hardy feared that 'the rebels are not routed, though held back' and that 'the business may be renewed again in the morning'. The shortage of ammunition was serious; ball cartridge 'is not in Wicklow'. He did not expect much from Bray or Loughlinstown, and urged Lake to send some at once 'in mail coach conveyance or fast carriages or anything most expeditious' from Dublin.

But the rebels had gone by then. Although neither Needham nor Hardy knew it, they were well on their way to Coolgreany with no more definite object in view than reaching that place and encamping there for the rest of the night.

The Arklow force remained under arms, snatching what rest they could at their posts. The cavalry patrolled the front. Moore left the town at half past five on the morning of the 10th, carrying a further despatch for Lake, and the troops began to dig entrenchments at the first light of dawn. The supplementaries and camp followers were ordered to bury the dead; the body of Fr Murphy was recognised and, if the reports are to be credited, subjected to indignities. The casualties of the battle were not, in relation to the numbers engaged and the severity of the contest, very great. The highest figures given for the losses of the troops are eighteen killed and twenty-eight wounded. Making allowance for understatement, we may suppose that one man in every twenty was a casualty on Needham's side. The figure for the insurgents varies from the first estimate of 200 or 300 to later claims of over a thousand. The proportion of casualties must certainly have been greater in the attacking than in the defending force. We do not know how many insurgents were engaged, but if we reckon them at a minimum of 5,000 anything under 500 casualties, killed and wounded—that is, ten per cent—would seem, in proportion to Needham's loss, too small.

The yeomanry were paraded and thanked at ten o'clock and reconnoitring parties were sent cautiously forward. No rebels having been seen, the Antrim detachment and the 7th Dragoons were returned to Rathdrum. A patrol went to Coolgreany on the 11th and saw 'nothing particular'.

The crisis of the revolt was past. Although Camden was to say on the 11th that 'the complexion this rebellion wears is the most serious it is possible to conceive' and Castlereagh admitted on the 13th that he 'had not a conception that insurgents could remain together and act in such numbers', in fact Needham had done what he had been ordered to do, and with their defeat at Arklow the rebels had lost the initiative—and when the initiative is lost no revolution can succeed. The Arklow force was badly shaken. Needham did not advance from the town until 19 June, nor did he come into skirmishing contact again with his late opponents until the 17th, when one of his patrols met a small party near Gorey. But the first of the English reinforcements had arrived by then. Lake was ready to advance into Co. Wexford by the 19th. He closed in on the day following, when Johnson moved from New Ross, Duff from Bunclody, Dundas and Loftus from Carnew and Needham from Gorey, their converging columns reaching a total of 5,500 men, exclusive of yeomanry. The insurgents stood at bay on the slopes of Vinegar hill above Enniscorthy on the morning of the 21st. Tired out from marching and as poorly equipped and badly led as ever, they fought bravely and were defeated by the largest force that had yet concentrated against them. There had been 4,500 men of all arms in New Ross and Duncannon fort on the 15th and a brigade of Guards landed shortly after in Waterford. On the afternoon of the 21st, Sir John Moore, marching through from New Ross, and having won the hardly contested battle of Foulke's Mill on the 20th, entered Wexford town.

There is no military history of the 1798 rising, and some of the general histories are far from objective. The most readily accessible of the latter (a book to which the criticism regarding partiality does not apply) is C. Dickson, *The Wexford Rising in 1798* (1955). W. H. Maxwell, *History of the Irish Rebellion in 1798* (original edition 1845, most recent edition 1903); P. F. Kavanagh, *A Popular History of the Insurrection of 1798* (original edition 1874); H. F. B. Wheeler and A. M. Broadley, *The War in Wexford* (1910— containing the valuable 'Camolin Cavalry Detail Book'); and F. W. Palliser, *The Irish Rebellion of 1798* (1898) are not difficult to get. For the historical background of the rising see J. C. Beckett, *The Making of Modern Ireland* (1966); J. A. Froude, *The English in Ireland in the eighteenth century* (2nd edn, 1881); and W. E. H. Lecky, *History of Ireland in the eighteenth century* (1892). For the Society of United Irishmen see R. R. Madden, *The United Irishmen, their Lives and Times* (2nd edn, 1857–60); F. Plowden, *Historical Review of the state of Ireland* (1803); and R. Jacob, *The Rise of the United Irishmen* (1937). The account of the battle of Arklow given here is based principally on the following contemporary and sub-contemporary material. *Manuscript*: Luke Cullen MSS (Madden Papers, Trinity College, Dublin); Needham's and other military reports (Rebellion Papers, State Paper Office, Dublin—in particular, 620/38/32, 43, 98a, 112, 114, 120, 123a; 620/51/32, 36; 620/56/98). *Printed*: Sir J. Barrington, *Rise and Fall of the Irish Nation* (1833); M. Byrne, *Memoirs* (1907 edn.); J. T. Gilbert (ed.), *Documents relating to Ireland, 1795–1804* (1893); J. Gordon, *History of the Rebellion in Ireland in the year 1798* (2nd edn, 1803); E. Hay, *History of the Irish Insurrection of 1798* (1842); J. Jones, *An impartial narrative of the most important engagements during the Irish Rebellion, 1798* (2nd edn, 1799); Sir J. Moore, *Diary* (ed. J. F. Maurice, 1904); Sir R. Musgrave, *Memoirs of the different rebellions in Ireland* (1801); G. Taylor, *History of the Rebellion in the County of Wexford in the year 1798* (1864); *The tryal of William Byrne of Ballymanus* (1799). There is a good bibliography in C. Dickson's book, mentioned above, which also prints Sergeant Archibald M'Laren's 'A Minute Description of the battle of Gorey, etc.', first published in 1798. M'Laren is the sergeant of the Dumbartons who is mentioned in my account of Arklow. Rev H. L. Bayly's accounts of the battle appear in his letter to his son, written in Arklow on 14 June (Bayly Papers, National Library of Ireland MS 3299, pp. 257 f) and in W. S. Mason, *Statistical Account or Parochial Survey of Ireland* (1816), II, pp. 59 ff.

Maps which should be consulted are: Ordnance Survey 6 inch Wicklow sheets 40 and 45; Allen's map of Co. Wicklow, *c.* 1830 (from Nevill's earlier map of 1760); S. Hall's map of Co. Wicklow, 1822 (in G. N. Wright, *Guide to Wicklow,* 1822). There is a plan of the battlefield in Sir R. Musgrave's book, already mentioned, plate VIII. Additional topographical information appears in my 'The Topography of a Battlefield: Arklow, 1798' (*The Irish Sword,* I, pp. 51 ff, with a map). A graphic picture of the fighting, drawn by Captain John Holmes of the Loyal Durham Fencibles, who was present, was published by W. Allen, Dublin soon after the date of the battle. It is reproduced with a note in *The Irish Sword,* I, facing p.67 and also appears in Plate 24 herewith. It shows a figure which may represent Fr Michael Murphy.

Further information on military formations may be sought in T. Simes's books, *A Military Course* (1777) and *Treatise on the Military Science* (1780) and in *Cavalry Regulations* (1796–9) and F. Grose, *Military Antiquities* (1788). Details of military organisation in Ireland in 1798 appear in the Melville Papers (National Library of Ireland MS 54A, 135) and in the following—J. F. Smet, *Historical Records of the 8th King's Royal Irish Hussars* (1874); R. Miller, 'An Officer's experience in '98' in *Ulster Journal of Archaeology,* 2nd series, IV (1898); J. D. Mercer, *Record of the North Cork Regiment of Militia* (1886); J. Core, *Historical Record of the Royal Tyrone Fusilier Regiment of Militia* (1872); and Sir Henry McAnally, *The Irish Militia, 1793–1816* (1949). The story of the Cavan Militia gun appears in F. C. Crossle, *Volunteers and Yeomanry of the Newry District* (Belfast, 1934), pp. 9, 17. See also my papers 'The Government forces which opposed the Irish insurgents of 1798' (*The Irish Sword,* IV, pp. 16 ff), 'The Insurgent threat to Dublin in 1798' (*An Cosantoir,* July, 1958) and 'The Wexford Yeomanry and Miles Byrne' (*An Cosantoir,* January 1948, which tells of Byrne's connection with the Castletown corps). G. F. R. Henderson's opinion of frontal attacks is given in his *The Battle of Spicheren* (2nd edn, 1909), pp. 271 f. For details of the artillery see A. W. Wilson, *The Story of the Gun* (1944) and A. Manucy, *Artillery through the ages* (Washington, 1962).

More information about the insurgents is given in my 'Insurgent efforts towards military organisation, 1798' (*The Irish Sword*, III, pp. 153 ff) and much may be gleaned from T. Cloney, *A personal narrative of 1798* (1832). T. C. Croker (ed.), *Memoirs of Joseph Holt* (1838) tells of efforts to manufacture gunpowder. For pikes and pikemen see my papers 'The Irish Pike' and 'The Irish Pike: additional notes on its history' (*Journal of the Galway Archaeological and Historical Society*, XX, pp. 99 ff and XXI, pp. 44 ff). Lord Edward Fitzgerald's remarks on the use of the pike are from T. Moore, *Life and Death of Lord Edward Fitzgerald* (1831), II, p. 219. For a contemporary view of the utility of the pike see H. Lloyd, *History of the late war in Germany* (1781), I. p. 36.

Epilogue

For the government, if not for the Anglo-Irish ascendancy as a whole, the most disturbing feature of the rebellion of 1798 was that it was accompanied by a French invasion. The small French force which landed at Killala in Co. Mayo in August of that year, and which was joined by numbers of the inhabitants of the surrounding countryside, routed the troops which were assembled to resist it at Castlebar later in the month. The French invaders considered themselves 'the worthy rivals of the victors of Fleures and Arcola', battles gained from their other enemies the Austrians by the revolutionary armies—Napoleon was the victor of Arcola—in 1794 and 1796. The English looked upon Castlebar as a blow to their insular security; they saw that their fears of centuries had come true, and that they were, at a moment of crisis, struck through Ireland. But the invaders were soon overcome. Unsupported by French reinforcements and inadequately—although gallantly—assisted by the Irish rebels, they were forced to surrender at Ballinamuck, Co. Longford on 8 September.

Ireland was not subsequently invaded. The nineteenth century, the century of the union of parliaments but not of hearts, saw much military activity in Ireland, but it saw no warfare. Revolt was feared and more than once threatened, and the threats did much to shape the Anglo-Irish politics of the century, but no revolt was effected. Shots were exchanged in Dublin in 1803, in Co. Tipperary in 1848, and in Cos. Dublin, Limerick, Cork and elsewhere in 1867, but the occasions of these hostilities cannot be dignified by the name of warfare. Irishmen fought honourably and often gloriously in the world's battles, but there was no fighting at home.

Not until Easter Monday, 1916—in the midst of a world war—did Ireland again seek the arbitrament of battle. The Easter rising and the period of guerrilla fighting which followed in the years 1919–23 have been much publicised, but little has been done to study their military history.* This is a pity. Modern warfare contained, before the epic struggles of the second world war, few instances of conflict in cities. The story of the rising in the streets of Dublin in 1916, where fighting was continuous for six days, more than 12,000 combatants were involved, and there were about 750 military and insurgent casualties, contains much to interest the military student. The ability of the partially trained insurgents to retain possession of the positions which they had occupied, the speedy and effective response of the military to a situation which they had not anticipated and for which their training left them ill prepared, the limitations which were imposed on the artillery by its use in built up areas, the ability to extemporise armoured vehicles—all these things must show that the rising has an interest beyond that which is evoked by the extraordinary effect which it had on the political situation.

And the military interest of the Irish guerrilla war is even greater, for it anticipated many features of the struggles of more recent times—the advantages enjoyed by fighters who can conceal themselves in a sympathetic population; the limitations imposed upon an occupying force by the presence of a population which tries to carry on as usual; the effectiveness of the ambush tactic in circumstances brought about by the use of the petrol engine for military transport. Orde Wingate, as his activities in Palestine in 1937–8 attest, was deeply impressed by the lessons to be learnt from the Irish struggle, and Irish precedents were among the few which the Special Operations Executive of the last war had to guide it.

One may regret that the Anglo-Irish association of so many centuries should have ended on a note of bitterness, but one cannot fail to see a certain appropriateness in the fact that by the twentieth century the wheel had come full circle in Ireland. As Dublin witnessed the first great struggle of the Norman invasion, so did Dublin witness, after seven centuries of strife in other parts of the island, the struggle which was the beginning of the end of English rule over Ireland as a whole; and as the

* The author has attempted preliminary studies of the hostilities of 1916 and 1919-21. See 'A Military History of the 1916 Rising' in K. B. Nowlan (ed.), *Studies in the History of the Easter Rising 1916* (1969) and 'The conduct of the Anglo-Irish war (January 1919 to the truce in July 1921)' in D. Williams (ed.), *The Irish Struggle, 1916-1926* (1966).

warfare of the countryside—the warfare of ambush, obstruction and destruction—was for so long characteristic of early Irish hostilities, so also were guerrilla tactics the outstanding feature of the last warlike contest of Englishmen and Irishmen.

Index

Index

Index

Glendalough, 26
Glenshesk, battle of, 75, 84
Godolphin, Sir William, 138
Gorey, 284 f, 288–90, 294–6, 299, 301, 310, 312
Gormanstown, Viscount, 57, 60, 66
Gormflath, 13 f
Graeme, Sir Richard, 162, 165
Grand Prior's regiment, the, 248
Grenades, grenadiers, 216, 218–21, 229, 231, 246, 253, 280, 284, 296
Guerrilla warfare, vii, 244, 314–16
Guild of St George, the, 58
Gunpowder, ammunition, vii, 8, 64, 79, 93, 97, 102 f, 110 f, 116, 123–5, 131, 155, 166, 170, 172, 179 f, 182–4, 194, 218, 220 f, 263 f, 267, 279, 281 f, 289, 293, 302, 308 f, 313
Guns, gunners, 'shot', 57–9, 64, 66 f, 74, 76–8, 82, 93, 98–100, 102, 106, 110 f, 119, 124 f, 137, 165 f
Gustavus Adolphus, 180 f, 184

Halberds, 94, 196, 218, 282, 292
Hamilton, George, regiment of, 260, 264
Hamilton, Gustavus, regiment of, 260, 264
Hamilton, Major-General John, 250, 256, 262
Hamilton, Lieut.-General Richard, 234
Hamilton's Bawn, 187
Hamley, Sir Edward, 225
Hanmer, Sir John, 233
Hardy, Major Joseph, 284 f, 288, 299, 309
Harold, King, 16, 18
Harold Hardrada, 14
Harvey, Beauchamp Bagenal, 284, 289
Haskulf, 26, 29–33
Hastings, battle of, 12, 16, 27
Havelock, Sir Henry, 271
Hebrides, Western Isles, the, 14, 49, 62, 70, 72, 74, 107, 204
Henderson, G. F. R., 300, 312
Henry II, King, 23, 31
Henry VII, King, 54
Henry IV, King of France, 117
Herbert's regiment, 258 f
Hesse, Prince of, 261
Hicks Pasha, 87 f, 95, 103 f
Highlands of Scotland, Highlanders, the, 14, 48, 50, 70, 72 f, 77, 84, 107, 184, 194, 204 f
Holt, Joseph, 293
Holzapfel, Major-General, 253
Household Cavalry, the, 263
Howth, 17
Hume, Colonel, 181

Inch, 290
Inchiquin, Earl of, 205–7, 209 f

Infanta Isabella, the 175
Inkerman, battle of, 246
Innishannon, 158
Irish Brigade in France, the, 221, 223
Irish Brigade in South Africa, the, 225
Irish Guards, regiment of, 216, 218, 231, 249, 255, 262

Jackson, Lieut.-General T. J. (Stonewall), 191
James (VI of Scotland and) I, King, 8 f, 38, 91, 107
James II, King, 9 f, 214–16, 218, 221–30, 232, 234, 238–40, 242 f, 246, 255 f, 261, 265
Jamestown, 239
Javelins. See Darts
Johnson, Major-General Sir Henry, 310
Jomini, Baron, 225
Jones, Colonel Michael, 201 f, 204–12

Kavanagh, James, 303
Kavanagh, Morgan, 115
Kearns, Fr, 291
Keating, Sir Henry Sheehy, 214 f, 223, 228, 236
Kells, 6, 40, 117, 155
Kenmare, 5
Kerevan, Daniel, 291
Kern, 108, 110, 155
Kerry, Co, 5, 239
Kildare, Co:, and Earldom, 1, 5, 40, 53, 57 f, 62, 283
Kildare, Earls of, 7, 69, 91
Kilkenny, 153, 181 f, 185, 238
Kilkenny, Co., 24
Killala, 314
Killarney, 239
Killeen, Lord of, 60
Killiecrankie, battle of, 247
Killybegs, 153
Kilmainham, 31
Kinard, 189
Kinsale, 239
Kinsale, battle of, 8, 10, 133, 144 ff, 174, 184, 212
Kirk's regiment, 260, 264
Knockdoe, battle of, viii, 7, 48 ff, 77, 82
Knocknacloy, 189 f, 198
Knocknanoss, battle of, 204 f, 208 f
Knox Grogan, Thomas, 302 f
Kyan, Esmond, 290, 304–7

La Forest-Suzannet, Marquis de, 253
Lagan army, the, 185, 189, 196
Lake, General (later Lord) Gerald, 279 f, 282, 285–7, 303, 308–10
La Mellonière, Brigadier, 233, 253, 258
Lances, horsemen's staves, 27, 83, 86, 101, 183, 219
Lanesborough, 239

Index

Index